Internet–Enabled Handheld Devices, Computing, and Programming:
Mobile Commerce and Personal Data Applications

Wen–Chen Hu
University of North Dakota, USA

T0321699

Information Science REFERENCE

INFORMATION SCIENCE REFERENCE

Hershey · New York

Director of Editorial Content:	Kristin Klinger
Director of Production:	Jennifer Neidig
Managing Editor:	Jamie Snavely
Assistant Managing Editor:	Carole Coulson
Typesetter:	Jennifer Neidig
Cover Design:	Lisa Tosheff
Printed at:	Yurchak Printing Inc.

Published in the United States of America by
   Information Science Reference (an imprint of IGI Global)
   701 E. Chocolate Avenue, Suite 200
   Hershey PA 17033
   Tel: 717-533-8845
   Fax: 717-533-8661
   E-mail: cust@igi-global.com
   Web site: http://www.igi-global.com/reference

and in the United Kingdom by
   Information Science Reference (an imprint of IGI Global)
   3 Henrietta Street
   Covent Garden
   London WC2E 8LU
   Tel: 44 20 7240 0856
   Fax: 44 20 7379 0609
   Web site: http://www.eurospanbookstore.com

Library of Congress Cataloging-in-Publication Data

Internet-enabled handheld devices, computing, and programming : mobile commerce and personal data applications / Wen-Chen Hu, editor.

   p. cm.

 Summary: "This book comprehensively reviews the state of handheld computing technology and application development"--Provided by publisher.

 Includes bibliographical references and index.

 ISBN 978-1-59140-769-0 (hardcover) -- ISBN 978-1-59140-628-0 (ebook)

 1. Mobile commerce. 2. Electronic commerce--Technological innovations. 3. Business enterprises--Computer networks. 4. Mobile computing. I. Hu, Wen Chen, 1960-

 HF5548.34.I58 2009

 658.8'72--dc22

             2008019469

British Cataloguing in Publication Data
A Cataloguing in Publication record for this book is available from the British Library.

All work contributed to this manuscript is original material. The views expressed in this manuscript are those of the authors, but not necessarily of the publisher.

Table of Contents

Section III:
Client-Side Mobile Handheld Computing and Programming

Chapter X
Client-Side Handheld Computing and Programming 261

Chapter XI
Java ME (Java Platform, Micro Edition) Programming 286

Chapter XII
Advanced Java ME Programming 306

Preface

With the advent of the World Wide Web, electronic commerce has revolutionized traditional commerce, boosting sales and facilitating exchanges of merchandise and information. The recent emergence of wireless and mobile networks has made possible the introduction of electronic commerce to a new application and research area: mobile commerce. In just a few years, mobile commerce has emerged from nowhere to become the hottest new trend in business transactions. The success of mobile commerce relies on the widespread adoption by consumers of more advanced handheld devices such as smartphones, which include some data-processing capability and thus permit vital activities such as mobile Internet browsing. According to Canalys, a market research company, 118 million smartphones were sold worldwide in 2007 and they accounted for about 11% of the overall cellphone market, an increase from around 53% a year earlier. The market thus appears to be opening up for this new form of commerce, and a book covering mobile commerce programming and its related issues is therefore timely. This book discusses mobile commerce and handheld computing from a technical perspective and consists of three major sections:

1. *Mobile Commerce Systems and handheld Devices,* surveys the software and hardware systems necessary for performing mobile commerce transactions,

2. *Mobile Web Content Design and Implementation,* focuses on handheld computing and programming that require support from server-side programs such as database-driven mobile website construction, and

3. *Client-Side Handheld Computing and Programming,* looks at handheld computing and programming that does not require support from server-side programs, such as stand-alone address book construction.

MOBILE COMMERCE SYSTEMS AND HANDHELD DEVICES

Mobile commerce, which is defined as the exchange or buying and selling of commodities, services, or information on the Internet through the use of mobile handheld devices such as smartphones, is an effective and convenient way for consumers to engage in electronic commerce wherever they happen to be and at times that are convenient for them. Realizing the advantages to be gained from mobile commerce, major corporations have started to offer mobile commerce options to their customers in addition to the electronic commerce services they already provide.

Mobile Commerce Systems

It requires some effort to understand and construct a mobile commerce system because it involves such a wide range of disciplines and technologies. To facilitate this process, in this book mobile commerce systems will be broken down into six components: (i) mobile commerce applications, (ii) mobile handheld devices, (iii) mobile middleware, (iv) wireless networks, (v) wired networks, and (vi) host computers. Since each component is large and complicated enough to be a research area by itself, only elements in components that are specifically related to mobile commerce will be explained in detail. Lists of the technologies used for component construction are given and other important issues, such as mobile security, are also discussed.

Internet-Enabled Mobile Handheld Devices

Internet-enabled mobile handheld devices are a core component of every mobile commerce system, making it possible for mobile users to interact directly with mobile applications. Much of a mobile user's first impression of the application is formed by his or her interaction with the device, so the success of an application is greatly dependent on how friendly and convenient it is to use. This book will first explain the role of handheld devices in a mobile commerce system and then discuss the device components in detail. A mobile handheld device includes six major components: (i) a mobile operating system, (ii) a mobile central processor unit, (iii) a microbrowser, (iv) input and output devices and methods, (v) memory and storage, and (vi) a battery. Each component is described in turn and major products and technologies for the component are given. Several related technologies such as device-to-desktop synchronization are also discussed.

HANDHELD COMPUTING

Handheld computing refers to the use of handheld devices such as smart cellular phones and PDAs (Personal Digital Assistants) to perform wireless, mobile, handheld operations such as personal data management and mobile website construction. It consists of two kinds of computing and programming: client- and server- side handheld computing and programming.

Mobile Web Content Design and Implementation

Here, handheld devices are used to perform wireless, mobile, handheld operations that require the support of a server. Examples of these applications include: (i) instant messages, (ii) database-driven mobile web content searches, (iii) online video games, and (iv) wireless telephony. Server-side handheld computing requires the use of a range of programming and markup languages and tools. Two languages that are widely used will be introduced in this book:

- **WML (Wireless Markup Language):** This is a markup language that formats and styles web pages for display on mobile handheld devices such as smart phones and PDAs. WML is part of the wireless access protocol (WAP) and is based on XML (eXtensible Markup Language).
- **WMLScript:** This is a procedural scripting language and an extended subset of the JavaScript language. It is employed to complement WML, a markup language for mobile handheld devices.

A detailed, step-by-step construction of a database-driven mobile web site will be given.

CLIENT-SIDE HANDHELD COMPUTING AND PROGRAMMING

This refers to the use of handheld devices to perform mobile, handheld operations that require no support from a central server. Examples of these applications include: (i) address books, (ii) video games, (iii) note pads, and (iv) to-do-lists. Various environments/languages are used in handheld computing and programming and are available for client-side handheld application design and implementation. Unlike desktop operating systems, where the market is dominated by Microsoft Windows, it is not yet possible to determine who will be the ultimate winner and become the dominant player in the handheld device market. Android, BREW (Binary Runtime Environment for Wireless), Java ME (Java Platform, Micro Edition), Palm OS,

Symbian, and Microsoft Windows Mobile, which use either C/C++ or Java, will be introduced first, followed by Java ME, which uses Java, and Palm OS, which uses C/C++.

ORGANIZATION OF THE BOOK

Mobile commerce and handheld computing include such a wide variety of subjects and technologies that it is almost impossible for a single book to adequately cover all the subjects involved. This book therefore focuses on introducing the major topics concerning mobile commerce and computing and provides extensive references for readers interested in discovering more information. It is divided into three sections, with a total of fourteen chapters.

Section I. Mobile Commerce Systems and Handheld Devices

Mobile commerce, mobile commerce systems, and mobile handheld devices are fairly new subjects and are complicated. This section, consisting of four chapters, introduces fundamental material related to mobile commerce and handheld computing.

Chapter I. Fundamentals of Mobile Commerce Systems: An overview of electronic and mobile commerce system structures is given in this chapter. An electronic commerce system consists of four components: (i) electronic commerce applications, (ii) desktop or notebook computers, (iii) wired networks, and (iv) host computers. Due to its more complex structure, a mobile commerce system is best divided into six components: (i) mobile commerce applications, (ii) mobile handheld devices, (iii) mobile middleware, (iv) wireless networks, (v) wired networks, and (vi) host computers.

Chapter II. Mobile Commerce Applications: Mobile commerce includes a wide variety of activities, and this chapter surveys some of its major applications, including, among others: (i) mobile advertising, (ii) mobile entertainment, and (iii) travel and weather reports.

Chapter III. Mobile Handheld Devices: Mobile users perform mobile transactions by using their mobile handheld devices. A handheld device includes six major components: (i) a mobile operating system, (ii) mobile central processing units, (iii) a microbrowser, (iv) input and output devices and methods, (v) memory and storage, and (vi) batteries. Other handheld technology such as data synchronization will be discussed too.

Chapter IV. Essential Mobile-Commerce Technology: Mobile networking, security, and payment methods are three important facets of mobile commerce communications. These three themes are fairly complicated and a whole book could be dedicated to any one of them. Therefore, rather than attempt to cover these issues comprehensively, this chapter will provide a brief introduction and discuss related technologies. A case study of handheld security using handheld usage identification will be given at the end of this chapter.

Section II. Mobile Web Content Design and Implementation

Server-side handheld computing uses handheld devices to perform wireless, mobile, handheld operations that require the support of a central server. Examples of these applications include: (i) instant messages, (ii) mobile web content, (iii) online video games, and (iv) wireless telephony. Server-side handheld programming includes the design and development of handheld software such as CGI programs that reside on the servers.

Chapter V. Mobile World Wide Web Content: The first half of this chapter provides the background and discusses system setup for server-side handheld computing and programming. To illustrate the concepts involved, the second half of this chapter examines a case study of adaptive viewing mobile web content using mobile web usage mining.

Chapter VI. WML (Wireless Markup Language): WML is an XML-based language that is used in conjunction with WAP (wireless application protocol) for the formatting of documents. WAP is a suite of network protocols that specify ways of sending data across the airwaves. As with all such protocol suites, they are organized hierarchically. At the bottom there are low-level protocols that are concerned with establishing connections, coding alphanumeric characters, etc., while at the top are the high-level protocols such as WML which perform activities such as passing page information. This chapter introduces fundamental WML elements such as images and tables.

Chapter VII. Advanced WML: Chapter VI covered the use of WML for static web pages, which have fixed content all the time. This chapter extends this to cover dynamic web pages through a discussion of advanced WML, which requires the support of external programs constructed using procedural languages. There are several methods for calling external programs from a WML page. This chapter will introduce one of the methods, CGI, chosen because of its relative simplicity. A case study of a mobile web search engine is given at the end of this chapter to illustrate its use.

Chapter VIII. WMLScript: WML is a markup language that is used for text formatting and display. The functions of a markup language are limited if there is no support from other programming languages. Two kinds of programming languages can be used to extend the functions of WML:

1.   Server-side scripts such as CGI Perl running on servers, and

2.   Client-side scripts such as WMLScript running on handheld devices.

This chapter will introduce WMLScript; CGI was introduced in the previous chapter. WMLScript is a light JavaScript language that must be compiled into byte code on a server before it can run on a handheld device. It is based on ECMAScript but has been modified to better support low bandwidth communication and thin clients. WMLScript can be used together with WML to provide intelligence to the clients but it has also been designed so that it can be used as a standalone tool. This chapter includes a case study that applies WMLScript to permit handheld devices to access searches of web-based genome databases.

Chapter IX. Database-Driven Mobile Web Content Construction: Among the various mobile applications, mobile web content is the most popular. This chapter will be devoted to a detailed consideration of the construction of database-driven mobile web content. Here, handheld programming refers to mobile-commerce programming for Internet-enabled mobile handheld devices and requires the use of various programming and markup languages and utilities. This chapter demonstrates handheld programming by giving a case study, construction of a B2C, mobile, online video-game store. A database-driven mobile web site is often implemented by using a *three-tiered client-server architecture* consisting of three layers: (i) the user interface, (ii) the function module, and (iii) the database management system (DBMS).

Section III. Client-Side Mobile Handheld Computing and Programming

The most popular applications of handheld server-side computing and programming involve database-driven mobile web content, which was described in the previous section. The remainder of this book will be devoted to client-side handheld computing and programming, whose applications do not need support from server-side programs. Client-side handheld applications are varied and numerous and they cover many everyday activities. Popular applications include address books, appointments, and to-do lists.

Chapter X. Client-Side Handheld Computing and Programming: This chapter introduces six popular handheld programming environments/languages: (i) Android, (ii) BREW (Binary Runtime Environment for Wireless), (iii) Java ME (Java Platform, Micro Edition), (iv) Palm OS, (v) Symbian OS, and (vi) Microsoft Windows Mobile. Handheld programming using Java ME and Palm OS will be covered in more detail in the final four chapters.

Chapter XI. Java ME (Java Platform, Micro Edition) Programming: Most client-side handheld programming uses either Java or C/C++. This chapter gives an overview of the basic concepts involved in Java ME (previously known as J2ME), which is a version of Java. To illustrate the use of Java ME, a MIDlet is created that generates a simple greeting on a handheld device.

Chapter XII. Advanced Java ME Programming: This chapter gives an advanced study of Java ME programming based on the introduction to Java ME programming provided in the previous chapter. It focuses on two major topics of particular interest for handheld devices: (i) persistent storage, which is the storage embedded in handheld devices, and (ii) the network connection, which is necessary for many client-side applications such as weather reports and location-based applications that require a network connection.

Chapter XIII. Palm OS Programming: Rather than trying to squeeze all the features and capabilities of a personal computer into a tiny package, Palm OS devices are designed specifically for managing mobile information, communications, and entertainment. This gives Palm OS devices advantages in terms of their flexibility, ease of use, and compatibility. This chapter introduces readers to the basic concepts of Palm OS programming, and includes a detailed explanation of a "Hello, World!" program. Palm OS Resource Editor, which is a visual resource editor that allows users to create and edit XML resource description (XRD) files for Palm OS applications, is also described in outline in this chapter.

Chapter XIV. Advanced Palm OS Programming: Building on the introduction to Palm OS programming given in the previous chapter, this chapter examines one advanced topic of Palm OS programming in more detail, namely the use of forms. Step-by-step procedures are used to guide readers seeking to implement this Palm application. A section on Palm OS references is also provided for readers interested in pursuing this topic in more depth.

ACKNOWLEDGMENT

Handheld devices started to become more popular about ten years ago. Initially, the devices were used for simple personal data management such as calendars and schedules, but handheld technologies are advancing so fast that new applications, techniques, or devices are created almost every day. Mobile users now use their devices to perform complicated tasks such as browsing the mobile Internet, performing mobile-commerce transactions, and checking their emails. Attempts to keep up with the rapidly changing technologies involved have extended this project for several years past what we originally envisaged, and three co-authors had to withdraw from this project. The successful accomplishment of this book is a credit to many people. The reviewers who provided such helpful feedback and detailed comments are particularly appreciated. Special thanks go to the staff at IGI Global, especially to Kristin Roth, Heather Probst, Mehdi Khosrow-Pour, and Jan Travers. Jan Szechi has spent many hours polishing my writing. Finally, the biggest thanks go to my family members for their love and support throughout this project.

Wen-Chen Hu
July 2008

Section I
Mobile Commerce Systems and Handheld Devices

Chapter I
Fundamentals of Mobile Commerce Systems

INTRODUCTION

With the introduction of the World Wide Web, electronic commerce revolutionized traditional commerce, boosting sales and facilitating exchanges of merchandise and information. The emergence of wireless and mobile networks has now made it possible to extend electronic commerce to a new application and research area: *mobile commerce*, defined as the exchange or buying and selling of commodities, services, or information on the Internet through the use of mobile handheld devices. In just a few years, mobile commerce has become the hottest new trend in business transactions. The future of mobile commerce is bright, as shown by the following predictions:

- The dramatic growth in demand for smart mobile devices, specifically handhelds, wireless handhelds, and smart cellular phones, through 2007 is shown in Figure 1.1 (Canalys, 2004a, 2004b, 2004c, 2005a, 2005b, 2005c, 2005d, 2006, & 2008).
- The forecasts of smart mobile device shipments are even more encouraging. Smart cellular phone sales will grow at a rate of more than 30% a year for the

Figure 1.1. Worldwide total smart mobile device shipments in millions from 2003 to 2007

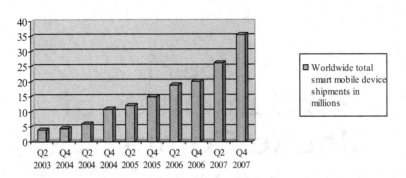

Figure 1.2. Forecasts of worldwide total smart mobile device shipments in millions

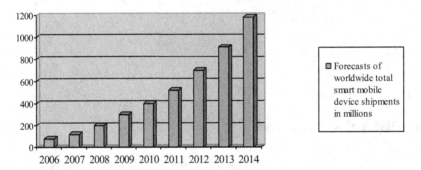

next five years starting from 2008 according to Bill Hughes (2008) at In-Stat. With this rate, the total shipments of smart mobile devices will pass the one billion mark by 2014 as shown in Figure 1.2 (Canalys, 2008; Hughes, 2007; Symbian Limited, 2008).

- Estimated worldwide shipments of the following four types of devices in 2007 were

  o *Cellular phones*: 1.12 billion (Strategy Analytics, 2008),

  o *Laptops*: 110 million laptops shipped in 2007, 33.8% growth from 2006 (IDC, Corp., 2008),

  o *PCs*: 160 million desktop computers shipped in 2007, 4.3% growth from 2006 (IDC, Corp., 2008), and

  o *Smartphones*: 118 million, up 53% from 2006 (Canalys, 2008).

- A report by Juniper Research forecast that the global mobile commerce market would become an $88 billion industry by 2009 (Glenbrook Partners, LLC., 2004), although this is still small compared to the $8.5 trillion of business-to-business electronic commerce recorded in 2005 (Gartner, Inc. 2001).
- In related areas, the market research firm Jupiter Research suggested that ringtone revenues, which have been doubling annually in recent years, will reach $724 million in 2009, while mobile gaming revenues were predicted to reach $430 million the same year. They anticipated that globally m-commerce sales would reach $3.6 billion in 2006 (Brad, 2006).

Mobile commerce is an effective and convenient way of enabling consumers to engage in electronic commerce whenever they wish and from wherever they happen to be. Realizing the advantages to be gained from mobile commerce, many retail companies have begun to offer mobile commerce options for their customers to supplement the electronic commerce service they already provide (Yankee Group, 2002). However, a tremendous effort is required to understand and construct a mobile commerce system because it involves such a wide range of disciplines and technologies. To address these difficulties, this chapter will separate mobile commerce systems into six components: (i) mobile commerce applications, (ii) mobile handheld devices, (iii) mobile middleware, (iv) wireless networks, (v) wired networks, and (vi) host computers. However, since each of these components is sufficiently complex to be a research area in its own right, only the elements specifically related to mobile commerce will be explained in detail. Lists of the technologies used for component construction are given in the first part of this book and other important issues, such as mobile security, are also discussed. Related research on mobile commerce systems can be found in the articles by Varshney, Vetter, & Kalakota (2000), Varshney & Vetter (2002), and Choi, et al. (2005).

System Requirements

A wide variety of technologies are used to build mobile or electronic commerce systems. However, regardless of the kinds of technologies used, the requirements for both mobile and electronic commerce systems include:

- State-of-the-art technology.
- Easy to deploy components that can be readily adapted to suit the needs of content providers, telecommunication companies, and computer/device manufacturers.
- Simple transactions for end users.

- Products that can be personalized or customized upon request. For example, web content can be viewed using either browsers or microbrowsers.
- Maximum interoperability, because so many technologies are now available and new techniques are constantly being invented for mobile or electronic commerce systems.
- Program/data independence, so changing the system components will not affect existing programs/data.
- Rigorous enforcement of end-to-end security and user privacy.

Requirements that apply solely to mobile commerce systems include:

- Enables end users to perform transactions easily, in a timely manner, and ubiquitously.
- Supports a wide variety of mobile commerce applications, such as location finding, for content providers.
- Applications are accessible from a wide range of handheld devices.

SYSTEM STRUCTURES

This section describes the system structures used for both electronic and mobile commerce and explains in detail the procedures that are specific to mobile commerce transactions. A modular approach will be used for this discussion.

An Electronic Commerce System Structure

Electronic commerce describes the manner in which transactions take place over networks, primarily the Internet, and consists of the process of electronically buying and selling goods, services, and information. An electronic commerce system is inherently interdisciplinary and there are many different ways in which it can be implemented. Figure 1.3 shows the structure of a traditional electronic commerce system, along with a typical example. The system structure includes four components, most of which are at least partly shared by mobile commerce systems: (i) electronic commerce applications, (ii) client computers, (iii) wired networks, and (iv) host computers.

Another structure view of an electronic commerce system or a database-driven web site is given in Figure 1.4. It is often implemented using a `three-tiered client-server architecture` consisting, as the name suggests, of three layers: (i) user interface, (ii) function module, and (iii) database management system (DBMS).

Figure 1.3. An electronic commerce system

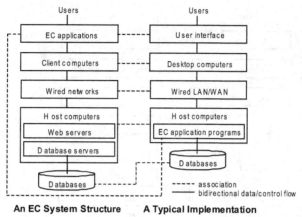

An EC System Structure   A Typical Implementation

Figure 1.4. Three-tiered client-server web system structure

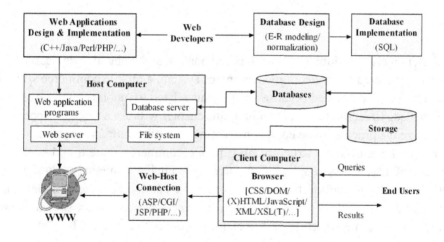

A Mobile Commerce System Structure

Much like the concept of e-commerce, mobile commerce, or m-commerce, refers to a type of business that is conducted 100% electronically through computer networks. The crucial difference is that it is based on buying and selling goods and services via wireless networks with the aid of a mobile device. Mobile payment is a key component of an m-commerce transaction and this can utilize one of several different

Figure 1.5. A mobile commerce system structure

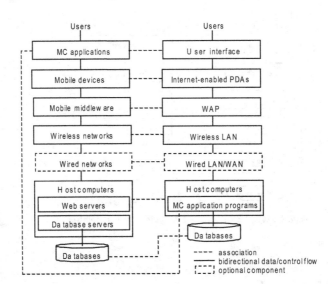

models, namely premium SMS, WAP based portals, and embedded devices/smart clients. Compared to an electronic commerce system, a mobile commerce system is much more complicated because components related to mobile computing must be included. To facilitate understanding, this chapter will use a modular approach to analyze the process involved in constructing a mobile commerce system.

Figure 1.5 shows the structure of a mobile commerce system and gives an example of a typical system based on currently available technology (Hu, Lee, & Yeh, 2004). The network infrastructure for mobile commerce systems consists of both wired and wireless networks. The wired network component shown in the figure has the same structure and implementation as that needed by a standard electronic commerce system, so here we will devote our attention to the wireless network. With the exception of the wired network, the remaining components will be examined in the later sections of this chapter. A mobile commerce system is inherently interdisciplinary and can be implemented in various ways. In Figure 1.5 the system structure includes six types of components: (i) mobile commerce applications, (ii) mobile handheld devices, (iii) mobile middleware, (iv) wireless networks, (v) wired networks, and finally (vi) the host computers, which are similar to those used for electronic commerce.

Mobile Commerce Transaction Processing

To illustrate how the mobile commerce components work together, Figure 1.6 shows a flowchart of how a user request is processed by the components in a mobile commerce system (Leavitt, 2000).

Figure 1.7 shows another flowchart illustrating how a user request is processed by the components in a mobile commerce system, along with brief descriptions of how each component processes the request:

Let us now consider in more detail the components listed in Figure 1.5, and how they relate to the processes shown in the flow charts above:

1. **Mobile commerce applications:** A content provider implements an application by providing two sets of programs: client-side programs, such as the user interfaces that are part of the microbrowsers installed on the users' mobile devices, and server-side programs, such as database access and updating, that reside on the host computers.
2. **Mobile handheld devices:** Handheld devices present user interfaces to the mobile end users, who specify their requests on the interfaces. The devices relay the user requests to the other components and later display the results using the interfaces.
3. **Mobile middleware:** The major purpose of mobile middleware is to seamlessly and transparently map Internet content to mobile stations that support a wide variety of operating systems, markup languages, microbrowsers, and protocols. Most mobile middleware also encrypts the communication in order to provide some level of security for transactions.
4. **Wireless and mobile networks:** Mobile commerce is possible mainly because of the availability of wireless networks. User requests are delivered to either the closest wireless access point (in a wireless local area network environment) or a base station (in a cellular network environment).
5. **Wired networks:** This component is optional for a mobile commerce system. However, host computers (servers) are generally connected to wired networks such as the Internet so user requests are routed to these servers using transport and/or security mechanisms provided by wired networks.

Figure 1.6. A flowchart of a user request processed in a mobile commerce system

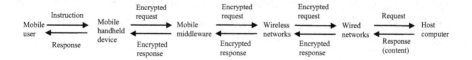

Figure 1.7. Another flowchart of a user request processed in a mobile commerce system

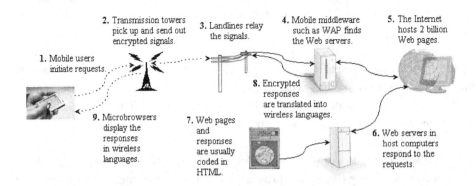

6. **Host computers:** Host computers process and store all the information needed for mobile commerce applications, and most application programs can be found here. They include three major components: Web servers, database servers, and application programs and support software.

ELECTRONIC COMMERCE APPLICATIONS

The emergence of electronic and mobile commerce has led to countless new business opportunities and applications. Electronic commerce, defined as the buying and selling of goods and services and the transfer of funds through digital communications, refers to a wide variety of applications such as auctions, banking, marketplaces and exchanges, recruiting, and retailing, to name but a few. Mobile commerce applications not only include all these existing electronic commerce applications, but also open up new possibilities, for example mobile inventory tracking, which can now be performed at any time and from any location by using mobile computing technology. This section briefly introduces some common electronic commerce applications; a more detailed discussion is provided in Chapter 2, which is dedicated to a comprehensive survey of a wide variety of mobile commerce applications. This sub-section discusses some new business models, which were not previously possible, that have been created by electronic commerce. Other than the "buy-and-sell" model, the following list gives some other common models created by e-commerce (Turban *et al.*, 2004):

- **Affiliate marketing:** Affiliate marketing is a marketing method that allows other Websites to receive a commission by selling products or services offered by others. For example, in Amazon.com's Associates Program the associates drive Internet traffic to Amazon through specially formatted links that allow Amazon to track sales and other activities. The partners can receive up to 10% in referral fees on all qualifying revenue made through their links to Amazon's products and services. Amazon sends monthly payments to these associates.

- **Comparing prices:** This method presents a list of services or products based on a consumer's specifications. For example, mySimon.com is a comparison shopping site for apparel, computers, electronics, jewelry, video games, and other merchandise. It gathers prices on millions of products from thousands of stores, so customers can compare products and find the best price before they purchase an item.

- **Customization and personalization:** Customization or personalization allows the design and creation of content that meets a customer's specific needs. For example, Dell Inc. sells computer systems directly to the public, with each unit tailor-made to the customer's specifications. This direct business model eliminates the time and costs involved in purchasing through traditional bricks-and-mortar retailers.

- **Electronic marketplaces and exchanges:** Electronic marketplaces are Internet websites that act as a meeting point between supply and demand and electronic exchanges serve as central marketplaces with established rules and regulations where buyers and sellers meet to trade futures and options contracts or securities. Electronic marketplaces and exchanges provide benefits to both buyers and sellers because they are more efficient than their traditional counterparts.

- **Electronic tendering systems:** For large purchases of services or goods potential suppliers bid competitively for a contract, quoting a price to the buyer who then selects the most advantageous. Large buyers usually make their purchases through a tendering (bidding) system, which becomes more effective and efficient with the help of electronic commerce.

- **Group purchasing:** Items purchased in bulk benefit from quantity discounts; electronic commerce allows a group of customers or organizations to place their orders together and negotiate a better deal. For example, Amerinet members saved more than $300 million in 2003 through group purchasing health care equipments and products.

- **Naming your prices:** With this model, the product/service prices are set by customers instead of sellers. Priceline.com is the first company applying this method. The following example shows how this works. With Priceline.com's

"Name Your Own Price" hotel reservation service, customers choose the star level of hotel they want, along with the desired neighborhood, dates and price they want to pay. Priceline.com then searches for a hotel room at the customer's desired price. Priceline.com is able to offer this sale as a result of (a) certain hotel suppliers agreeing, for a limited time, to make lower rates available for particular properties through Priceline.com's hotel service and/or (b) the application by Priceline.com of a variable subsidy to certain offers, effectively allowing customers to book a hotel room for a lower price than would have been accepted during the pre-sale period. The site offers no guarantee that any "Name Your Own Price" offer will be accepted, due to the changeability of room availability and pricing, and customers learn the specific hotel name and location only after the purchasing process is complete.

- **Online auctions:** Traditional auctions usually require bidders to attend the auctions in person, and the items offered are limited. Online auctions allow bidders from everywhere to bid products or services provided by various sellers without needing to show up. eBay.com is the world's largest online auction site. It offers an online platform where millions of items are traded each day. Several hundred other companies, including Amazon.com and Yahoo.com, also conduct online auctions.

CLIENT COMPUTERS AND CLIENT-SIDE COMPUTING

Desktop, laptop, and tablet computers make up the client-side of electronic commerce systems, while mobile handheld devices serve the same purpose for mobile commerce systems. An Internet-enabled mobile handheld device is a small, general-purpose, programmable, battery-powered computer that is capable of handling the front end of mobile commerce applications and can be operated comfortably while being held in one hand and enables mobile users to interact directly with mobile commerce applications. The differences between these two types of client machines are listed in Table 1.1.

Client-Side Programming

Electronic and mobile commerce application programming involves a variety of technologies and languages. The issues involved are complex; Parts B and C of this book will be dedicated primarily to a consideration of mobile commerce programming. Electronic and mobile commerce requires two kinds of programming:

Table 1.1. Differences between computers and handheld devices

	Desktop Computers	Laptop and Tablet Computers	Mobile Handheld Devices
Browser	Desktop browsers	Desktop browsers	Microbrowsers
Functions	Full	Full	Limited
Major Input Methods	Keyboards and mice	Keyboard and touchpads/mice	Stylus and soft keyboards
Major Output Methods	Screens and printers	Screens	Screens
Mobility	Low	Intermediate	High
Networking	Wired	Wired/wireless	Wireless and mobile
Transmission Bandwidth	High	High/low	Low
Power Supply	Electrical outlets	Electrical outlets/ batteries	Batteries
Screen	Normal	Intermediate	Small
Size	Desktop	Portable	Handheld
Weight	Heavy	Intermediate	Light

- *Client-side programming* consists of the software that runs on client computers/devices, in particular the web interface. Popular languages for web interfaces include CSS, DOM, (X)HTML, JavaScript, WML, WMLScript, XML, and XSL(T). In addition to the web interface, this can include client-side applications such as address and schedule books. The tools and languages used for client-side application development is based on the client-side operating systems being used, for example Visual Studio for Windows or C/C++ for Palm OS.
- *Server-side programming* refers to the software that runs on servers. This normally deals with requests from browsers and sends the results from databases/files/programs back to the browsers for display. Popular server-side languages include C/C++, Java, Perl, and PHP. Server-side programming also implements numerous applications such as instant messaging and telephony, but as these types of applications are related to standard network programming tasks such as TCP/IP programming they will not be covered in this book.

This sub-section discusses web interface construction; server-side programming will be covered in the section on Host Computers. Web systems can be built using various languages and tools, and several software packages are available that are helpful for web development. Those packages can be divided into three categories: (i) multimedia editors, (ii) HTML editors, and (iii) integrated development environments (IDEs):

- *Multimedia editors* are used to create, edit, and post animation, audio, images, and videos on web pages. Adobe Systems, Inc. provides two popular multimedia editors:
  - o *Adobe Flash* is an authoring environment that can be used to create animation, advertisements and various web-page components, integrate video into web pages and, more recently, develop rich Internet applications. Flash Professional is an IDE, while Flash Player is a virtual machine that is used to run, or parse, the Flash files.
  - o *Adobe Photoshop* consists of image-editing and graphics creation software.
- *HTML editors* are used to create static web pages. Three popular HTML editors are:
  - o *Adobe Dreamweaver*, which offers a WYSIWYG (What You See Is Why You Get) environment that allows web developers to generate HTML and JavaScript source code while simultaneously viewing the results.
  - o *Microsoft Expression Web* is a design tool used to create sophisticated standards-based web sites. It combines both FrontPage and Visual Studio technologies in a new user interface with XHTML, CSS, XML, XSLT, and ASP.NET 2.0. For many applications, the user interface and features of Expression Web and Visual Studio are identical.
  - o *Microsoft SharePoint Designer* enables programmers to develop applications and solutions on top of the SharePoint platform to enhance organizational agility and business process automation, and maximize the value of Microsoft Office applications on the platform.

The category of integrated development environments (IDEs) will be covered towards the end of this chapter in the section on Host Computers.

MOBILE MIDDLEWARE AND WIRELESS NETWORKS

Mobile middleware and wireless networks are needed only for mobile commerce systems. Although mobile middleware is optional, it greatly simplifies the system; mobile commerce is an inherently complex system, and implementing mobile middleware avoids the need to deal with many additional complications.

Mobile Middleware

The term middleware refers to the software layer between the operating system and the distributed applications that interact with it via the network. The primary mission of a middleware layer is to hide the underlying networked environment's complexity by insulating applications from explicit protocols that handle disjoint memories, data replication, network faults, and parallelism (Geihs, 2001). The major task of mobile middleware is to seamlessly and transparently map Internet content to mobile handheld devices that may support a wide variety of operating systems, markup languages, microbrowsers, and protocols. WAP and i-mode are the two major kinds of mobile middleware:

- *WAP (Wireless Application Protocol)* is a secure specification that allows users to access information instantly using mobile handheld devices such as smart phones and PDAs (Open Mobile Alliance, n.d.). WAP supports most wireless networks, including CDPD, CDMA, GSM, PDC, PHS, TDMA, FLEX, ReFLEX, iDEN, TETRA, DECT, DataTAC, and Mobitex. WAP is supported by all operating systems, including those specifically engineered for handheld devices such as Palm OS, EPOC, Windows CE, FLEXOS, OS/9, and Java OS. Although WAP supports HTML and XML, the WML language is specifically designed for small screens and one-handed navigation without a keyboard.
- *i-mode* is a mobile Internet service that has caused a revolution in both business and private lifestyles in Japan (NTT DoCoMo, Inc., 2007). Since its debut in February 1999, 46 million subscribers have been attracted to this service and currently more than 95,000 Internet sites are providing a wide variety of content. The use of packet transmissions offers continuous access, while the use of a subset of HTML makes content creation easy and makes it simple to convert existing websites.

Table 1.2 lists the important characteristics of i-mode and WAP.

Wireless Networks

Wireless communication capability supports mobility for end users in mobile commerce systems. Wireless LAN, MAN, and WAN are the major components used to provide radio communication channels so that mobile service is possible. In the WLAN category, the Wi-Fi standard with 11 Mbps throughput dominates the current market. However, it is expected that standards with much higher transmission speeds, such as IEEE 802.11a and 802.11g, will replace Wi-Fi in the near future. Compared to WLANs, cellular systems can provide longer transmission distances

Table 1.2. A comparison between the two major types of mobile middleware

	WAP	**i-mode**
Developer	Open Mobile Alliance	NTT DoCoMo
Implementation	A protocol	A complete mobile Internet service
Web Language	WML (Wireless Markup Language)	CHTML (Compact HTML)
Major Technology	WAP Gateway	TCP/IP development
Key Features	Widely adopted and flexible	Highest number of users and easy to use

and greater radio coverage, but suffer from the drawback of much lower bandwidth (less than 1 Mbps). A recent trend for cellular systems is for 3G standards supporting wireless multimedia and high-bandwidth services to be deployed. Wireless telephone technology has progressed through several generations:

- *0G (1945-1973)*: mobile radio telephone systems.
- *1G (1980s)*: analog cellphone standards including NMT and AMPS.
- *2G (1990s)*: digital cellphone standards, divided into TDMA-based and CDMA-based standards depending on the type of multiplexing used.
- *2.5G (late 1990s)*: this has a packet switched domain implemented in addition to the circuit switched domain.
- *3G (early 2000s)*: this includes wide-area wireless voice telephony and broadband wireless data, all in a mobile environment.
- *4G (2000s)*: provides end-to-end IP solutions where voice, data and multimedia streaming can function at higher data rates with the benefit of anytime-anywhere operations.

A wide variety of technologies and standards for wireless telephones are available. Some of the most important of these are:

- *CDMA (Code Division Multiple Access)*. This approach is based on a spread spectrum method. The method transmits a signal by "spreading" it over a broad range of frequencies, reducing interference and increasing the number of simultaneous users within a radio frequency band. With CDMA, each conversation is digitized and then tagged with a code.
- *GSM (Global System for Mobile communications)*. This is one of the most popular standards for mobile phones and was specifically developed to provide

system compatibility across country boundaries, especially within Europe. It is based on *TDMA (Time Division Multiple Access)* technology, which works by dividing a radio frequency into time slots and then allocating slots to multiple calls. As a result, GSM allows eight simultaneous calls on the same radio frequency.

* *IEEE 802.11.* This standard includes an encryption method, the Wired Equivalent Privacy algorithm. WLAN (Wireless Local Area Network), which is based on 802.11, allows a mobile user to connect to a local area network (LAN) through a wireless (radio) connection. The wireless data transmission speed of a WLAN is up to 54 Mbps. *Wi-Fi* (Wireless Fidelity) is also based on this standard.

* *IEEE 802.16.* This standard ensures compatibility and interoperability between broadband wireless access equipment. *WiMAX* (Worldwide Interoperability for Microwave Access), which is based on 802.16, provides wireless data over long distances in a variety of different ways, from point to point links to full mobile cellular type access. In practical terms this enables a user, for example, to browse the Internet on a laptop computer without physically connecting the laptop to a wall jack.

Table 1.3 summarizes the major technologies and standards used by the most recent wireless telephone generations.

WIRED NETWORKS

Wired networks are used to transmit data for both electronic and mobile commerce. This component is a requirement for electronic commerce but is not essential for

Table 1.3. The evolution of wireless telephone technology

	2G (10 Kbps – 40 Kbps)	2.5G (20 Kbps – 171 Kbps)	3G (60 Kbps – 54 Mbps)	4G (50 Mbps – 1 Gbps)
CDMA track	IS-95	CDMA 2000	W-CDMA	UMTS Revision 8 (LTE)
GSM track	GSM	GPRS	EDGE	—
IEEE 802.11 track	—	—	Wi-Fi	—
IEEE 802.16 track	—	—	—	WiMAX

mobile commerce, although mobile commerce benefits greatly by incorporating wired networks into its data communication systems because data transmission using wireless networks is more expensive than using wired networks. There are several types of wired networks, the three most important being:

- **Local Area Networks (LANs).** These cover a relatively small area of a few square kilometers or less, such as an individual office building. They generally offer a throughput of between 10 Mbps and 100 Mbps and are usually based on Ethernet technology, which is a network protocol that uses a bus topology and defines a specific implementation of the Physical and Data Link Layers in the OSI model (IEEE 802.3).
- **Metropolitan Area Networks (MANs).** These networks serve a geographical area greater than an LAN but less than a WAN, such as few city blocks or a whole city. MANs typically use wireless infrastructure or optical fiber connections to link sites and may connect multiple LANs together. Their maximum throughput is no less than 44 Mbps and they use a Distributed Queue Dual Bus technology based on the IEEE 802.6 standard.
- **Wide Area Networks (WANs).** These cover a wide geographic area, such as a state or country, and use specialized computers to connect smaller networks, such as LANs. They generally offer a throughput of 1.5 Mbps or more. WANs typically use wide area network services provided by telecommunications carriers, whose technologies include standard phone lines, ISDN (Integrated Services Digital Network), or other high-speed services. Two examples of WAN are the Internet, the largest network in the world, and an airline corporation that uses a WAN to connect its offices around the world.

HOST COMPUTERS AND SERVER-SIDE COMPUTING

This component is similar for both electronic and mobile commerce systems because host computers are usually not aware of differences among the targets, whether browsers or microbrowsers, they serve. The application programs are responsible for communicating with clients and responding to them accordingly. Most electronic/mobile commerce application programs reside in this component, except for client-side programs such as cookies or user interfaces using markup languages. User requests such as checking out or adding items to a shopping cart are actually processed at a host computer, which contains three major kinds of software designed specifically for electronic or mobile commerce transactions: (i) web servers, (ii) databases and database servers, and (iii) application programs and support software. Before examining each of these three kinds of software in more detail, we will first discuss the function of the LAMP stack, which is currently a very popular and widely used web technology.

The LAMP Stack

One technology that is commonly used for web content implementation is the LAMP stack, which is made up of four components (Lawton, 2005):

1. *Linux*, which is a free open-source operating system based on Unix.
2. *Apache web server*, which is an open-source HTTP server for modern operating systems including UNIX and Windows NT.
3. *MySQL*, which is an open source relational database management system (RDBMS) that uses Structured Query Language (SQL), the most popular language for adding, accessing, and processing data in a database.
4. *Script languages*, such as Perl, PHP, and Python:
    *   *Perl (Practical Extraction and Report Language)* is often used for scanning text and printing formatted reports. It provides extensive support for regular expression matching, dynamically scoped variables and functions, extensible run-time libraries, exception handling and packages, and provide/require functions. The use of Perl has grown significantly since its adoption as the language of choice of many World Wide Web developers. CGI interfaces and libraries for Perl have been constructed for several platforms and Perl's speed and flexibility make it particularly well suited for form processing and on-the-fly page creation. Perl5 is a major rewrite and enhancement of Perl version 4 that has added nested data structures and object-oriented features.
    *   *PHP (HyperText Preprocessor)* is a general-purpose server-side scripting language that is especially suited for dynamic and interactive websites. It can be embedded into HTML and offers a widely-used, free, and efficient alternative to competitors such as Microsoft's ASP. The PHP syntax is very similar to Perl and C and is often used in conjunction with MySQL (as the DBMS) and Apache (as the web server). A PHP file may contain text, HTML tags, and scripts. Scripts in a PHP file are executed on the server.
    *   *Python* is a dynamic object-oriented programming language that can be used for many kinds of software development. It offers strong support for integration with other languages and tools, comes with extensive standard libraries, and can be learned in a few days. Python runs on Windows, Linux/Unix, Mac OS X, OS/2, Amiga, Palm Handhelds, and Nokia mobile phones and has also been ported to Java and .NET virtual

machines. Python is distributed under an OSI-approved open source license that makes it free to use, even for commercial products.

LAMP benefits from several key advantages over proprietary software development approaches. The two most important are its low cost, as open source software is either free or inexpensive compared to proprietary software, and its open source coding, which allows anyone to review, modify, and work with it, opening the way for developers to improve the technology and address any issues that arise much more easily.

Web Servers

The first of the components of a typical three-tiered client-server web system such as the one shown in Figure 1.6 is the web server, which is a server-side application program that runs on a host computer and manages the web pages stored in the web site's databases or files. There are several types of web server software, including public domain software from NCSA and Apache, and commercial packages from Microsoft, Netscape, and others. Three popular web servers are:

- *Apache HTTP servers.* These are a collaborative software development effort aimed at creating a freely-available source code implementation of an HTTP (web) server. They are jointly managed by a group of volunteers located around the world. Since April 1996, Apache has been the most popular HTTP server on the Internet. It was developed in early 1995 based on code and ideas found in the most popular HTTP server of the time, NCSA httpd 1.3. It has since evolved to rival almost any other Unix based HTTP server in terms of functionality and speed, featuring highly configurable error messages, DBM-based authentication databases, and content negotiation (Apache Software Foundation, n.d.).
- *Microsoft's Internet Information Services (IIS).* Microsoft provides a web application infrastructure for all versions of Windows Server (Microsoft, Corp., n.d.a) and this is the world's second most popular web server after Apache.
- *Sun Java System Web Servers.* Sun provides organizations with a single deployment platform for web services, JavaServer Pages (JSP), Java Servlet technologies, NSAPI and CGI (Sun Microsystems, Inc., n.d.). It also offers built-in HTTP reverse-proxy capabilities to provide a highly scalable HTTP front-end to application servers or other HTTP origin servers, incorporating a bundled FastCGI interface that provides a stable and scalable platform for third party scripting technologies such as PHP, Ruby On Rails, Perl, Python, and other script languages.

Database Servers

The second component of a three-tiered client-server web system is the database server that manages database access functions, such as locating the actual record being requested or updating the data in databases. Some popular databases include:

- *IBM DB2*: DB2 9 is a hybrid data server that manages both XML and relational data. It includes the following major features:
  - o   XML data store,
  - o   integration with relational data,
  - o   Eclipse-base developer workbench, and
  - o   integration with leading application infrastructures like PHP, Java, and .NET
- *Microsoft*: Microsoft provides two kinds of databases: (i) *Access* for desktop computers and (ii) *SQL Server* for the server engines in client-server solutions:
  - o   *Access*: Microsoft Access is a full-featured multi-user relational database management system that was designed specifically for Microsoft Windows operating systems, making extensive use of drag-and-drop and visual design for queries, forms, and reports. Access comes with an integrated development environment, including incremental compilation, a fully interactive visual debugger, breakpoints, and single step-through, which combine to make Access a powerful platform for developing client-server database solutions.
  - o   *SQL Server*: SQL Server is a comprehensive database software platform that provides enterprise-class data management and integrated business intelligence (BI) tools (Microsoft, Corp., n.d.b). The SQL Server data engine lies at the heart of this enterprise data management solution. In addition to providing support for relational databases or XML, SQL Server provides analysis, reporting, integration, and notification functionality. It is closely integrated with Microsoft Visual Studio, the Microsoft Office System, and a suite of new development tools, including the Business Intelligence Development Studio.
- *MySQL*: MySQL is an open-source, multithreaded, multi-user SQL relational database management system that is used in more than 11 million installations ranging from large corporations to specialized embedded applications. In addition to being a popular open source database, it is a key part of LAMP (Linux, Apache, MySQL, PHP/Perl/Python, described above). More and more companies are using LAMP as an alternative to expensive proprietary software stacks because of its lower cost and freedom from lock-in. MySQL

is flexible and runs on more than 20 platforms including Linux, Windows, OS/X, HP-UX, AIX, and Netware.

- *Oracle databases*, the most recent version being Oracle11g. The migration and evolution of the Oracle database has proceeded as follows (Oracle, n.d.):
  - o *Oracle7 (1992)*, which is a client-server based relational database management system. The query language is based on SQL.
  - o *Oracle8i (1999)*, which is a relational database system with object capabilities included. The *i* in the name stands for Internet. It is a database specifically designed as an Internet development and deployment platform including two major functions:
- *Oracle8i JVM*, a server side Java engine, includes a native compiler, a CORBA 2.0 ORB, an EJB server, an embedded server side JDBC driver, and an SQLJ translator.
- *Oracle8i for Data Warehousing*, a part of the Oracle Internet Platform, supplies a solid foundation for data warehousing.
  - o *Oracle9i (2001)*, which features full XML database functionality and other improvements.
  - o *Oracle10g (2003)*, which is the first database designed for enterprise grid computing. Grid computing provides an environment in which individual users can access computers, databases, and experimental facilities simply and transparently, without having to consider where those facilities are located.
  - o *Oracle11g (2007)*, which is for Linux and Microsoft Windows.

To supplement server-side database servers, a growing trend is to incorporate a client-side mobile database or an embedded database into a handheld device with a wide range of data-processing functionality. Although the functionality is frequently very sophisticated, the flat file system that comes with these devices may not be able to adequately handle and manipulate data. Embedded databases have very small footprints and must be able to run without the services of a database administrator, while at the same time accommodating the low-bandwidth constraints of a wireless-handheld network. Some leading embedded-databases are Progress Software databases, Sybase's Anywhere products, and Ardent Software's DataStage (Ortiz, 2000).

Application Programs and Support Software

The third component of a three-tiered client-server web system consists of the application programs and support software responsible for handling server-side processing. So far, three generations of programming languages and environments have been used for server-side web application development:

1. *1ˢᵗ generation*: Traditionally, conventional programming languages such as C/C++ and Java were used for web development.
2. *2ⁿᵈ generation*: Dynamic programming languages such as Perl and PHP gradually replaced conventional languages, enabling programs to change their code and logical structures at runtime, and to add variable types, module names, classes, and functions as they are running. These languages frequently are interpreted and generally check typing at runtime.
3. *3ʳᵈ generation*: More recently, IDEs (Integrated Development Environments) have begun to be used for web development:
    *   *Adobe ColdFusion*, an application server and software development framework used for the development of computer software in general, and dynamic web sites in particular.
    *   *Microsoft ASP.NET*, part of Microsoft's .NET platform and the successor to ASP technology. ASP.NET is a free technology that allows programmers to create dynamic web applications.
    *   *Microsoft Visual Studio*, Microsoft's flagship software development product for computer programmers. Visual Studio allows programmers to create standalone applications, web sites, web applications, and web services that can run on any platform supported by Microsoft's .NET Framework.
    *   *NetBeans IDE*, an open-source IDE for software developers that is used to create professional cross-platform desktop, enterprise, web, and mobile applications.
    *   *Ruby On Rails (ROR)*, a full-stack framework for developing database-backed web applications based on the Model-View-Control pattern.
    *   *Sun Java Studio IDE*, a development platform with features such as UML modeling, instant collaboration, and application profiling that is used primarily to develop, debug, tune, and deploy enterprise applications, web services, and portal components based on the Java EE platform.
    *   *Zend Core*, a production PHP 5 stack that provides the fully supported, certified, and enhanced capabilities that professionals need for PHP development and production.

SUMMARY

The widespread availability of wireless and mobile networks has extended electronic commerce to another research and application area: mobile commerce. Both mobile and electronic commerce systems involve a range of disciplines and technologies, but this level of complexity makes understanding and constructing such systems an exacting and arduous task. To facilitate this process, this chapter treated mobile and electronic commerce systems as being made up of six components, which can be summarized as follows:

1. **Applications:** Electronic commerce applications are already broad. Mobile commerce applications cover not only these existing applications, but also include new applications that can be performed at any time and from anywhere with the aid of mobile computing technology.

2. **Client computers or devices:** In general, desktop and notebook computers are used for electronic commerce and mobile handheld devices, including smart cellular phones and PDAs, are used to perform mobile transactions. Handheld devices are convenient and have many advantages over desktop computers, but they are limited by their tiny screens, relatively small memory, low processing power, and short battery life, and often suffer from wireless network transmission problems. Numerous mobile devices are available commercially, most of which use one of three major operating systems: Palm OS, Microsoft Windows Mobile, and Symbian OS. At the time of writing, Symbian OS leads the market, although it faces a serious challenge from Windows Mobile.

3. **Mobile middleware (mobile commerce systems only):** Mobile middleware is used to facilitate mobile communication. Although it is not required for mobile commerce systems, it greatly reduces the complications inherent in mobile communication. WAP and i-mode are the two major types of mobile middleware. WAP is widely adopted and flexible, while i-mode has the highest number of users and is easy to use. It is difficult to predict which middleware will be the eventual winner; it is more likely that the two will be blended somehow at some point in the future.

4. **Wireless networks (mobile commerce systems only):** Wireless communication capability supports mobility for end users in mobile commerce systems. Wireless LAN, MAN, and WAN provide radio communication channels so that mobile service is possible. In the WLAN category, the Wi-Fi standard with 11 Mbps throughput dominates the current market, although it is expected that standards with much higher transmission speeds, such as IEEE 802.11a and 802.11g, will replace Wi-Fi in the near future. Compared to WLANs, cellular systems can provide longer transmission distances and greater radio coverage, but suffer from the drawback of much lower bandwidth (less than 1 Mbps). 3G standards supporting wireless multimedia and high-bandwidth services have begun to be deployed for cellular systems, and WCDMA and CDMA2000 are likely to dominate the market in the future.

5. **Wired networks:** This component is a requirement for electronic commerce systems, but is not technically necessary for mobile commerce systems, although mobile commerce systems benefit greatly by incorporating wired networks into their data communication systems because data transmission using wireless networks is more expensive than using wired networks. The three major types of wired networks are (i) LAN (Local Area Network), (ii) MAN (Metropolitan Area Network), and (iii) WAN (Wide Area Network), defined based on the sizes of their areas of coverage.

6. **Host computers:** Host computers process and store all the information needed for both mobile and electronic commerce applications, and most application programs can be found here. They are made up of three major components: (i) web servers, (ii) database servers, and (iii) application programs and support software.

An important issue for both mobile and electronic commerce systems is their application programming. Electronic and mobile commerce programming, which involves a wide variety of technologies and languages, consists of two kinds of programming:

*   *Client-side programming*, which refers to the software that runs on client computers or devices and is mostly related to web interface construction. The most popular languages for web interface construction are CSS, DOM, (X)HTML, JavaScript, WML, WMLScript, XML, and XSL(T).
*   *Server-side programming*, which refers to the software that runs on servers. This software normally receives requests from browsers and sends the results from databases/files/programs back to the browsers for display. The most popular server-side languages are C/C++, Java, Perl, and PHP.

REFERENCES

Apache Software Foundation. (n.d.). *Apache HTTP Server Project*. Retrieved June 21, 2007, from http://httpd.apache.org/

Brad, S. (2006). *Mobile Commerce Hits the Big Time*. Retrieved November 13, 2006, from http://www.wirelessweek.com/article/CA6311136.html?text=qpass

Canalys. (2004a). *A World of Difference*. Retrieved April 14, 2006, from http://www.canalys.com/pr/2004/r2004061.pdf.

Canalys. (2004b). *Global Mobile Device Market Shows Tremendous Growth*. Retrieved March 22, 2006, from http://www.canalys.com/pr/2004/r2004081.pdf

Canalys. (2004c). *Global Smart Phone Shipments Treble in Q3.* Retrieved December 3, 2006, from http://www.canalys.com/pr/2004/r2004102.pdf

Canalys. (2005a). *Global Smart Mobile Device Sales Surge Past 10 Million in Quarter.* Retrieved April 25, 2006, from http://www.canalys.com/pr/2005/r2005041.pdf

Canalys. (2005b). *Smart Phones Up, Handhelds Down Globally in Q2.* Retrieved January 15, 2006, from http://www.canalys.com/pr/2005/r2005071.pdf

Canalys. (2005c). *Global Mobile Device Shipments Hit New Peak in Q4 2004.* Retrieved May 02, 2006, from http://www.canalys.com/pr/2005/r2005012.pdf

Canalys. (2005d). *Worldwide Smart Phone Market Soars in Q3.* Retrieved December 3, 2006, from http://www.canalys.com/pr/2005/r2005102.pdf

Canalys. (2006). *Smart Mobile Device Market Growth Remains Steady at 55%.* Retrieved December 3, 2006, from http://www.canalys.com/pr/2006/r2006071.pdf

Canalys. (2008). *Smart Mobile Device Shipments Hit 118 Million in 2007, up 53% on 2006.* Retrieved February 26, 2008, from http://www.canalys.com/pr/2008/r2008021.pdf

Choi, Y., Yoon, S., Shin, G., & Park, C. (2005). An approach to design of software architecture for mobile-commerce system. In *Proceedings of the 7th International Conference on Advanced Communication Technology (ICACT)*, 2(0), pages 924-926.

Gartner, Inc. (2001). *Worldwide Business-to-Business Internet Commerce to Reach $8.5 Trillion in 2005.* Retrieved February 26, 2006, from http://www.gartner.com/5_about/press_room/pr20010313a.html

Geihs, K. (2001). Middleware challenges ahead. *IEEE computer*, 34(6), 24-31.

Glenbrook Partners, LLC. *(2004). Mobile Commerce Market Forecast.* Retrieved June 2, 2006, from http://www.paymentsnews.com/2004/08/mobile_commerce.html

Hu, W.-C., Lee, C.-w., & Yeh, J.-h. (2004). Mobile commerce systems. In Shi Nansi, editor, *Mobile Commerce Applications*, pages 1-23, Idea Group Publishing.

Hughes, B. (2007). *Size and Growth of Smartphone Market Will Exceed Laptop Market for Next Five Years.* Retrieved March 12, 2008, from http://www.instat.com/press.asp?Sku=IN0703823WH&ID=2148

IDC, Corp. (2008). *PC Market Rebounds with Strong Demand for Portables, Fueling Hopes for Holiday Sales, According to IDC.* Retrieved January 23, 2008, from http://www.idc.com/getdoc.jsp?containerId=prUS20995107

Lawton, G. (2005). LAMP lights enterprise development efforts. *IEEE Computers*, 38(9), 18-20.

Microsoft, Corp. (n.d.a) *Internet Information Services*. Retrieved June 15, 2007, from http://www.microsoft.com/WindowsServer2003/iis/default.mspx

Microsoft, Corp. (n.d.b). *SQL Server 2005*. Retrieved May 6, 2007, from http://www.microsoft.com/sql/default.mspx

NTT DoCoMo, Inc. (2007). *i-mode*. Retrieved June 12, 2007, from http://www.nttdocomo.com/services/imode/index.html

Open Mobile Alliance Ltd. (n.d.). *WAP Forum*. Retrieved from June 13, 2007, from http://www.openmobilealliance.org/tech/affiliates/wap/wapindex.html

Oracle. (n.d.). *Oracle Databases*. Retrieved May 25, 2007, from http://www.oracle.com/database/index.html

Ortiz, S. Jr. (2000). Embedded databases come out of hiding. *IEEE Computer*, 33(3), 16-19.

Strategy Analytics. (2008). *Nokia Reaches 40% Share as 332 Million Cellphones Ship Worldwide in Q4 2007*. Retrieved February 27, 2008, from http://www.strategyanalytics.net/default.aspx?mod=ReportAbstractViewer&a0=3755

Sun Microsystems, Inc. (n.d.). *Sun Java System Web Server*. Retrieved June 19, 2007, from http://www.sun.com/software/products/web_srvr/home_web_srvr.xml

Symbian Limited. (2008). *Symbian Fast Facts Q4 2007*. March 13, 2008, from http://www.symbian.com/about/fastfacts/fastfacts.html

Turban, E., King, D., Lee, J., & Viehland, D. (2004). *Electronic Commerce 2004: A Managerial Perspective*. Prentice Hall.

Varshney, U. & Vetter, R. J. (2002). Mobile commerce: framework, applications and networking support. *Mobile Networks and Applications*, 7(3), 185-198.

Varshney, U., Vetter, R. J., & Kalakota, R. (2000). Mobile commerce: a new frontier. *IEEE Computer*, 33(10), 32-38.

Yankee Group. (2001). *Over 50% of Large U.S. Enterprises Plan to Implement a Wireless/Mobile Solution by 2003*. Retrieved December 10, 2002, from http://www.yankeegroup.com/public/news_releases/news_release_detail.jsp?ID=PressReleases/news_09102002_wmec.htm

Chapter II
Mobile Commerce Applications

INTRODUCTION

Commerce, the exchange or buying and selling of commodities on a large scale involving transportation of goods from place to place, benefits from the convenience and ubiquity conveyed by mobile commerce technology. There are many instances that illustrate how mobile handheld devices help commerce. Important considerations that must be taken into account when trying to categorize applications include the nature of the communicating parties (e.g. people, intelligent agents, databases, sensors), the types of handheld mobile devices involved (e.g., cell phones, smart phones, PDAs, tablets), the nature of the transaction (e.g., push or pull delivery systems), and the actual content of the communication (e.g., a bank transaction, weather alert, or digital image). Not all m-commerce consists of buying and selling; other types of transactions such as banking transactions (e.g. bill paying) or polling (on-line surveys) are also of interest. In fact, "mobile transactions" or "mobile services" are probably more general terms for the concepts that we will discuss here. Obviously, no transaction can take place without some means of communication, whether it be face-to-face speech, so-called "snail" mail, e-mail, telephone, inter-office memos, or other means. Thus, one way in which mobile commerce applications can be dif-

Table 2.1. Taxonomy of transaction characteristics and compatible mobile applications

Characteristics	Types of Mobile Handheld Applications
Voice, human-human, & cell/smartphone/PDA/computer	Talking
Voice, human-agent, & cell/smartphone/PDA/computer	Leaving messages and automated response systems
Voice, agent-agent, & cell/smartphone/PDA/computer	None (agents don't talk, though they can generate speech in order to communicate with humans)
Data, human-human, & cell/smartphone/PDA/computer	Chat rooms
Data, human-agent, & cell/smartphone/PDA/computer	Logging, journaling, editing, e-mail, web browsing, downloading, and on-line games
Data, agent-agent, & cell/smartphone/PDA/computer	Automated fund transfers and automatic toll payment

ferentiated is by their means of communication. For handheld mobile devices this will always involve some form of wireless technology, but the connection could transmit either voices or data.

Another way in which mobile commerce applications can be differentiated is by the nature of the entities originating the communications on either end of the transaction; participants in m-commerce might be humans, or they might be intelligent agents representing humans or business entities, and in either case may be either at a fixed location or mobile. A third way to differentiate mobile handheld applications is by the computing demands they place on the handheld device. Applications which can run on ordinary cell phones are suitable for a mass market, while those that require more powerful clients like laptops are more likely to be aimed at smaller groups of users. Mobile applications that are location-aware will require a client device to have GPS capabilities, so that the user's physical location can be ascertained. Table 2.1 uses these taxonomy features to identify the fundamental nature of applications in each category.

The physical devices that support all of these various applications are evolving rapidly. At present there are a number of differently named devices competing in this application arena, including cell phones, "smart" phones, PDAs, tablet PCs and laptop computers. Future research is likely to focus on designing and producing a single device that will support all of these applications for most users. Although calling such a multi-purpose object a "phone" seems grossly inadequate, it will surely include that communication capability because cell phones are the most popular mobile devices today and are generally regarded as indispensable by their owners. The name that will evolve for this gadget is yet to be imagined.

CATEGORIES OF MOBILE COMMERCE APPLICATIONS

Electronic commerce includes a wide variety of business applications such as tendering and auctions; mobile commerce applications not only cover all the existing electronic commerce applications, but also new applications such as mobile inventory management that are simply not possible for traditional electronic commerce. Mobile commerce applications are involved in almost every aspect of our daily lives, from the way we travel to work to the way we select our meals. Table 2.2 lists some major mobile commerce applications (Gordon & Gebauer, 2001; Sadeh, 2002). More details of some of these applications will be given in the following sections.

Table 2.2. Major mobile commerce applications

Mobile Category	Major Applications	Sponsors	Clients
Advertising	Targeted ads and location-based ads	Business	Travelers
Education	Mobile classrooms and labs	Schools and training centers	Students
Enterprise resource planning	Resource management and managing a mobile workforce	Business	All
Entertainment	Games/images/music/video downloads and on-line gaming	Entertainment industry	All
Health care	Accessing and updating patient records	Hospitals and nursing homes	Patients
Inventory tracking and dispatching	Product tracking and dispatching	Delivery services and transportation	All
Retailing	Paying at vending machines, and checking product prices/information	Retailers	All
Services	Emails, instant messages, searches, etc.	Telecommunication and content providers	All
Traffic	Global positioning, routing services, toll/parking paying, and traffic advisories	Transportation and auto industry	Drivers
Travel and weather	Reservation services	Airlines, hotels, and travel agencies	Travelers

MOBILE ADVERTISING

Income from mobile advertising is a major source of revenue for mobile content providers such as Yahoo! and Google. They use different ways to post advertisements and charge the owners of the advertisements. For example, Google's mobile ads appear on mobile websites or when users search Google from a mobile device. When users click on a mobile ad, Google will send the users to the mobile webpage or offer them the option to connect to the business phone of the ad. Yahoo!'s Mobile Ad Services (Yahoo! Inc., n.d.) offer a wide variety of ad formats, targeting options, and calls-to-action. The services provided could include the following features:

- **Display advertising:** Ads are targeted using the same wide array of options as traditional web banners(e.g. context, demographics, behavioral)—and can take into account the user's location, which is a significant feature when marketing to consumers who are "on the go."
- **Search advertising:** Here leads are generated using sponsored search links that appear at the top of search results in Yahoo! oneSearch.
- **Video advertising:** Video is quickly moving to the "small screen" of the mobile phone, bringing with it new opportunities to engage and entertain consumers through a rich advertising experience.
- **Mobile ad tools:** These offer a way for advertisers to select the call–to–action that works best for their business, for example by allowing customers to click through to a promotional site, find or call a store directly, be sent a coupon, or receive an SMS message.

Figure 2.1 shows screenshots of the type of advertising currently being used by Yahoo! mobile advertisers.

Figure 2.1. Screenshots of Yahoo! mobile advertisements © 2008 Yahoo! Inc.

MOBILE ENTERTAINMENT

Entertainment has always played a crucial role in Internet applications and is probably the most popular application for the younger generation. Mobile commerce makes it possible to download audio/game/image/music/video files at anytime and anywhere, and it also makes on-line games and gambling much easier to access and play. It is projected that the number of mobile gamers will reach a global total averaging 134 million users per month by 2010, with corresponding revenues of $6.1 billion (FierceMarkets, Inc, 2007). The following two sub-sections will discusses two important types of mobile entertainment: mobile TV and music.

Mobile TV

The IDC research firm says that by 2010 about 24 million consumers, representing 9.2% of U.S. cellular subscribers, will watch TV or video on mobile handsets, up from about 7 million this year (Baig, 2006), and revenue will roughly quadruple, to more than $1.5 billion. MobiTV Inc is a global television and digital radio service provider for mobile phone users. It delivers live television, premium and prime-time programming, video-on-demand (VOD), satellite and digital music services from the top broadcast and cable television networks and major music labels to millions of users worldwide. Currently, MobiTV supports more than 160 live and VOD channels such as MSNBC, ABC News Now, CNN, Fox News, Fox Sports, ESPN 3GTV, NBC Mobile, CNBC, CSPAN, The Discovery Channel, and TLC to 200+ devices across multiple networks, serving over 3 million subscribers. Its TV programs can be delivered across any network including 3G, WiFi, WiMAX and DVB-H. Figure 2.2 shows a screen shot of Sprint TV Live powered by MobiTV on a Palm 700p.

Figure 2.2. Sprint TV Live powered by MobiTV shown on Palm 700p © 2008 Sprint

Figure 2.3. Sprint's LG Fusic © 2008 Sprint

Mobile Music

Although many handheld devices include mobile music functionality such as that provided by the iPod, none can achieve the sound quality and convenience of the iPod or other digital music players (German, 2006). Consumers have been slow to embrace music phones for a variety of reasons (Graham, 2006). In addition to the relatively poor sound quality, there are problems with:

- **Ease of transfer:** It is usually difficult to download songs or music from a computer to a handheld device.
- **Price:** The prices of direct-to-phone downloads are usually higher than on-line downloads.

Figure 2.3 shows Sprint's LG Fusic, which features a built-in media player as well as a microSD memory port. This combination makes it possible to store huge amounts of music on the included microSD card and listen to it in stereo with a Bluetooth headset or transmit it to an FM receiver. Features like high-speed EvDO connectivity allow users to watch streaming TV, instantly download songs and play multiplayer games, all at broadband-like speeds.

MOBILE SERVICES

Mobile services cover a wide variety of applications including calendars, email, and news. This section will cover two major mobile services: mobile instant messages and mobile searches.

Figure 2.4. Screenshots of Yahoo!'s mobile instant messaging service, Yahoo! Messenger © 2008 Yahoo! Inc.

Mobile Instant Messages

A natural application for mobile devices is the delivery of messages. For simple handheld devices, this is likely to be a one-directional communication path. Ambient Devices (Ambient Devices, n.d.), for example, markets a number of small messaging devices with attached services. These services can alert subscribers to changes in the weather conditions, financial markets, and the status of on-line auction bids, as well as the arrival of new e-mail. There is a powerful middleware component associated with the Ambient Devices gadgets that aggregates information from on-line sources, condenses and formats this information for its devices, and transmits that information (continuously) to those devices. Any information source can be mapped to any ambient device (e.g. pen, lamp, watch, pinwheel, fob) that has a simple device-specific signaling mechanism to convey information to its owner. Figure 2.4 shows screenshots of Yahoo!'s mobile instant messaging service, Yahoo! Messenger.

Mobile Searches

Mobile search engines such as Google and Yahoo! also provide mobile versions with features not seen on traditional search engines. For example, Yahoo! oneSearch, Yahoo!'s mobile search service, provides the following features:

*Figure 2.5. Screenshots of Yahoo! oneSearch, Yahoo!'s mobile search services ©
2008 Yahoo! Inc.*

- **Adaptive searches:** Users can easily browse the search results, which are shown on one page, grouped into categories. oneSearch is also able to remember the user's location, presenting answers, tailored to where the user is.
- **A wealth of information:** just like a traditional search engine, oneSearch allows users to search anything on the mobile Web, including news, stock reports, and Wikipedia.
- **Local listings:** Location-based applications are popular for mobile commerce. oneSearch provides local listings (arranged by distance and user ratings), addresses, click-to-call numbers, turn-by-turn driving directions and maps.
- **An instant response:** oneSearch can be accessed via microbrowsers or text messages. Mobile users text their questions to 92466 (YAHOO), and they will get the results back in a text message as they use microbrowsers.

Figure 2.5 shows three screenshots of the search results of the query "Orlando, Florida" returned by Yahoo! oneSearch.

MOBILE VIRTUAL COMMUNITIES

The introduction of mobile technologies has had a major impact on *virtual communities* because they allow community members to communicate with each other from anywhere and at anytime. This boosts sharing and exchanges of information, and common interests, ideas, and feelings. Examples of theses influences are given in Table 2.3.

Table 2.3. Examples of virtual communities using mobile technologies

Community Category	Major Events	Members
Commerce	Mobile transactions and payments	General public
Education	Problem solving, information sharing, and mobile learning	Students and educators
Entertainment	Games/images/music/video downloads and information changing, and on-line gaming	General public
Relationships	People matching, love connection, and pen pals	General public
Traffic	Traffic status and advisories and directions	Drivers
Travel	Travel information sharing, and air ticket and hotel discounts	Travelers
Ticketing	Movies, sports, concerts, plays, etc.	General audience

A Case Study: Internet Café

An Internet café is a coffee shop that also offers public access online computers for Web surfing and e-mail transmission and may also serve as an Internet service provider (ISP) or service bureau or offer other services such as online gaming and people matching. It is a perfect place for virtual community members, especially adolescents, to participate in a wide range of activities. This case study first introduces the services provided by an Internet café, and then discusses how virtual-community activities such as online chatting initiated by Internet café customers are affected by mobile technologies.

The services that an Internet café tenders can be divided into two major areas, one service that is tendered in true space, such as serving beverages and pastries, and another that makes available hardware such as computers and joysticks and three major types of software, namely:

1. **Online games:** Distinguished by the style of the online environment, games can be divided into three general types:
    a. **Simple:** As long as the user is connected to a specific Website, the game can be started with ease and is usually not limited by time. This game style inclines toward the multi-user games such as poker.

      b.   **Intranet:** Being limited by equipment, this type of game is usually played at an Internet café or other social venue and the player uses the equipment supplied to navigate around a playing field.

      c.   **Server:** Players must connect to the operators' servers to play, and must buy "tally" in order to keep playing. The plots and characters of the game are all determined by the players, encouraging players to become invested in the game.

2.   **Chat rooms:** These provide network space on operators' Websites for users to talk and invite other users to join in.

3.   **Message boards:** These services include information sharing, article posting, post forwarding, chatting, file downloading, and online gaming.

Customers of an Internet café are able to engage in various virtual community activities such as online chatting by using the facilities provided by the café. In the past, community members on the other end of the communication link were limited to specific physical locations such as their homes or computer labs where they could stay connected and active. However, the latest mobile technologies have almost eliminated this limitation by enabling them to use mobile handheld devices such as smart cellular phones to communicate with other members from anywhere and at anytime. Time-critical activities such as chatting with commuters that were not possible in the past are now feasible because of the new mobile technologies. This therefore boosts sharing and exchanges of information, and common interests, ideas, and feelings.

TRAFFIC

This section discusses how mobile handheld devices affect traffic, especially traffic control. Mobile map services are discussed in this section, although they could also be a part of mobile travel, which is covered in the next section.

Traffic Control

Traffic is the movement of vehicles or pedestrians through an area or along a route. The vehicle occupants and the pedestrians are all mobile objects, and are thus ideal clients of mobile commerce. Also, traffic control is a major headache for many metropolitan areas. Applying the technology originally developed for mobile commerce can improve the flow of traffic in many ways. For example, a mobile handheld device can have the capabilities of a GPS (Global Positioning System), enabling it to be used to determine the driver's exact position, give directions, and advise on the current status of traffic in the area. A traffic control center could use this information to monitor and control traffic flow according to the signals sent from mobile devices in the vehicles. Another example is automated toll-paying systems, which facilitate traffic flow and reduce personnel costs. Two examples of automated toll-paying systems are:

- Automated toll-payment systems such as the Illinois State Toll Highway Authority's I-PASS system (I-PASS, 2004) allow vehicles to pass through toll stations without stopping, and instantaneously transfer the toll payment as the vehicle passes. Users can manage their I-PASS accounts over the internet, U.S. mail, or via phone connections to add value to their accounts and update personal information.
- E-ZPASS, operated by a multi-state consortium consisting of New York, New Jersey, Maryland, Delaware and Pennsylvania, is an electronic toll collection system that takes cash, coins and toll tickets out of the toll collection process. Instead, drivers prepay tolls and attach a small electronic device to their vehicles (E-ZPASS, 2004).

Mobile commerce applications can also be used to address traffic and motorist safety issues. In-vehicle information and emergency-response systems such as General Motors Corporation's On-Star system and Meridian Environmental Technology's local weather information reports fall into this category.

Mobile Map Services

On-line map services such as Google Maps provide great convenience and many features to travelers. Nowadays many also include mobile versions for handheld users, who may not be able to access desktop computers or are away from their offices. Some of the most useful map service functions include:

- *Directions/distances*, usually in the form of driving/walking directions or distance from the starting location to the destination,
- *Maps*, including traditional clear maps with zooming function,
- *Local hangouts and business recommendations*, providing suggestions for where to dine or find a gas station,
- *Satellite imagery*, including near real-time images from satellites, and
- *On-line video*, an advanced feature showing the current activities by the target location.

Several mobile map services are available, with two of the most popular being:

- *Google Maps for Mobile (n.d.)*, a free download that lets users find local hangouts and businesses across town or across the country from their mobile phone, and
- *MapQuest Mobile (n.d.)*, which allows mobile users to choose from a variety of services:
  - *MapQuest Navigator*: This converts a mobile phone into a full GPS navigation system. MapQuest Navigator provides voice-guided, turn-by-turn directions to the desired location, either from a selected starting point or from the user's current location, using GPS technology. Routes can be optimized for speed or distance when driving, or for pedestrian routes.
  - *MapQuest Mobile*: This finds places and provides maps and directions on a cellular phone anywhere, at anytime.
  - *MapQuest Send to Cell*: This allows users to plan a trip by doing research on their computer and then sending the results directly to their mobile phones.
  - *MapQuest for Mobile Web*: This free mobile website allows mobile users to find places, get maps and directions anytime they need them. It provides the same power as MapQuest on desktop computers, but in a smaller version for mobile devices.

MapQuest's main competitor, Google, provides the following functions for mobile users:

- **Detailed directions:** Routes for drivers or pedestrians are displayed on a map with step-by-step directions.
- **Integrated search results:** Local business locations and contact information appear all in one place.
- **Easily movable maps:** Interactive, draggable maps make it easy to zoom in or out and move in all directions, allowing users to orient themselves visually.
- **Satellite imagery:** A bird's eye view is provided for the desired location.

Figure 2.6 shows three screenshots from Google's map services for three user requests:

a. a clear map of the location with the postal code 58202,
b. directions from the postal code 58201 to 58203, and
c. a satellite map of (b) and a menu.

Figure 2.6. Screenshots of Google's map services showing (a) a clear map, (b) directions, and (c) a satellite image of (b) and a menu (© 2008 Google)

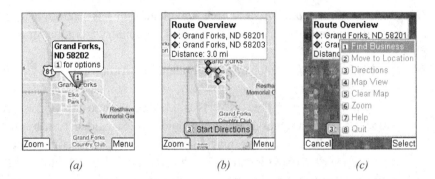

(a)   (b)   (c)

TRAVEL AND WEATHER REPORTS

Travel expenses can be costly for a business or an individual. Mobile commerce can help reduce operating costs by providing mobile travel management services to business travelers. For example, assistance can be provided to customers by using the mobile channels to locate a desired hotel nearby, purchase tickets, make transportation arrangements, and so on. The Travel Section of Yahoo! Mobile includes the following services:

- **Travel guides:** These allow mobile users to research 500,000 places to stay and things to do in over 40,000 cities worldwide, with user reviews, photos, and maps, save favorite places to create a customized trip plan, and take advantage of good travel deals.
- **Trip planner:** This tool enables mobile users to save hotels, attractions, restaurants, maps and more to a customized travel guide. Travel dates, comments, and bookmarks for other sites can be saved and a hard copy printed or the results accessed online it from any computer with Internet access.
- **FareChase:** Yahoo! FareChase is a travel search engine that helps travelers find flights and hotels that meet their budget and travel schedules. Dozens of travel websites are searched and the results displayed. Once the optimum travel plan has been selected, Yahoo! FareChase then links them directly to the travel providers' websites to complete their purchases.
- **Deals:** This service provides a listing of special deals for travelers, ranging from hotels to car rentals.

Figure 2.7. Screenshots of Yahoo! Mobile: Travel © 2008 Yahoo! Inc.

Figure 2.8. Screenshots of Google weather reports (© 2008 Google)

Mobile users can also search for travel-related information on Yahoo! Travel. Figure 2.7 shows screenshots of Yahoo! Mobile: Travel.

Accurate, up-to-date weather reports are also important for travelers, who are likely to pack their bags or plan their trips based on the predicted weather at their destination. Most mobile service providers offer weather reports. For example, Google provides the following local weather information: (i) 3-day weather forecasts, including lowest and highest temperatures, (ii) current temperature, (iii) humidity, (iv) weather conditions with pictures, and (v) wind, including direction and speed. Figure 2.8 shows screenshots of Google weather reports.

OTHER APPLICATIONS

Other mobile-commerce applications, including (i) mobile education, (ii) mobile enterprise resource planning, (iii) mobile health care, (iv) mobile inventory tracking and dispatching, (v) mobile law enforcement, and (vi) retailing will be discussed in this section.

Mobile Education

Many schools and colleges are facing problems due to a shortage of computer lab space, separation of classrooms and labs, and the difficulty of remodeling old classrooms for wired networks. To relieve the pressure on campus resources, wireless LANs are often used to hook PCs or mobile handheld devices to the Internet and other systems. As a result, students are able to access many of the required resources without taking up valuable lab space. Yesterday's educational innovation was the wired laptop university; tomorrow's innovation is the wireless connected university with smaller computing devices and anywhere anytime access to the campus infrastructure. One noteworthy experiment with PDAs in education is the University of South Dakota's move to become the first institution of higher education in the United States to provide Palm handhelds to all its first-year students (University of South Dakota, 2004). The university recently upgraded their PDA platform from the Palm m505, so that the fall 2004 freshman class received the Palm Zire 71 PDA. Faculty upload class materials in the form of web pages and MS Office documents to a server, and students download from that server using cradle/cable connections or infrared ports.

Mobile Enterprise Resource Planning

Enterprise resource planning (ERP) is an industry term for the broad set of activities supported by the type of multi-module application software that assists a manufacturer or other organization to manage important aspects of its business, including product planning, purchasing parts, maintaining inventories, interacting with suppliers, providing customer service, and tracking orders. The ERP issues that are particularly relevant to mobile commerce include tracking the location of goods and services, locating specific items, and transmitting warnings about aging components. Some successful mobile ERP are given as follows:

*   **Pepsi Bottling Group:** The following quote from the Pepsi Bottling Group's 2002 annual report to stockholders (PBG, 2002) reflects that company's confidence in their decision in October 2001 to employ mobile handheld

computing devices in order to boost product sales and aid in the management of inventories.

"The year also marked the rollout of a transformational tool for our U.S. sales teams: the Next Generation Handheld computer, a powerful technology that will provide our sales reps real-time data to make fact-based sales presentations, pre-determine product 'voids' for each account, and help resolve issues such as 'out-of-stocks' and time consuming paperwork."

- **Bayer Yakuhin Corp.:** Bayer has equipped each of its 700 marketing representatives with Toshiba Pocket PCs that provide mobile access to the company's Customer Relationship Management (CRM) database and other systems using Mobile Task Automation software developed by EveryPath, Inc. (Everypath, 2003). Sales representatives can now receive and update information while traveling and synchronize their information with the databases at the company's servers.
- **Hartford Financial Services Group:** The Hartford uses their Claim Expediter system for insurance tracking and communication with field claims personnel via GPRS (Financial Technology Network, 2004). For example, when a customer calls with a claim, the front-end claims handler sends relevant claim details wirelessly to The Hartford's appraisers, who will send the estimation back within minutes to the handler.

Mobile Health Care

Soaring health care costs can be reduced and efficiency enhanced with the help of mobile commerce. By using the technology made possible by mobile commerce, physicians and nurses can remotely access and update patient records immediately, a function which has often incurred a considerable delay in the past. This improves efficiency and productivity, reduces administrative overheads, and enhances overall service quality. For example, physicians at Affinity Health Group in Tifton, GA, have real-time wireless access to the medical records of their patients on Tablet PCs while at their group practice location (Mobile Health Data, 2004) and can also use PDAs to capture charges while practicing at the nearby Tift Regional Medical Center. The group implemented a Cisco Systems Wi-Fi network to access its new electronic medical records system. The Tift Regional Medical Center records system vendor preloaded a charge capture application on the PDAs that can integrate with its records system and the hospital is working on implementing a wireless network of its own. The group practice also has a private web portal connection to the hospital that physicians can access via their Tablet PCs, enabling physicians to obtain radiology images and data from the hospital's clinical information system on their Tablet PCs.

Mobile Inventory Tracking and Dispatching

Just-in-time delivery is critical for the success of today's businesses. Mobile commerce allows a business to keep track of its mobile inventory and make time-definite deliveries, thus improving customer service, reducing inventory, and enhancing the company's competitive edge. Major delivery services such as UPS and FedEx have already applied these technologies to their business operations worldwide with great success. An example of inventory tracking is the launch of Wal-Mart's electronic product code initiative in 2004 (Wal-Mart Stores, Inc., 2004). In its initial phase, cases and pallets of 21 products from eight suppliers shipped to a North Texas Wal-Mart distribution center and then onward to seven local Supercenters had radio frequency identification tags attached, thus allowing more precise inventory visibility from the supplier to the distribution center to the retail store's backroom. The RFID tagging procedure is gradually being expanded to more products, primarily electronic products or other large items such as bicycles or lawnmowers in the first instance, with the tags being applied to the outermost packaging layer.

Mobile Law Enforcement

Most police patrol cars today are equipped with mobile data computers (MDCs), generally rugged laptop or tablet computers (or, for some motorcycle or bicycle officers, iPAQ handheld PCs) with wireless connectivity via public safety frequencies in the 800MHz range to a server at police headquarters. Police officers can run computer checks on license plates, vehicle ID numbers, driver's licenses and other objects such as handguns or bicycles that are registered to particular owners. With appropriate support from the departmental server, the patroller may also be able to download information about arrest warrants, mug shots, street maps, and building layouts, as well as information about legal statutes and department policies. An officer can also use the local processing power of the MDC to write incident reports that can be subsequently uploaded to headquarters, reducing paperwork and saving the officer a trip to headquarters to deliver the report in person. The MDC is not permanently attached to the vehicle, so an officer is able to carry the MDC into the breakroom to write a report or into a victim's home, allowing the victim to review and correct an incident report as it is being written. Earlier wireless devices for police officers, known as MDTs (mobile data terminals), simply provided communication between the officer in the field and a dispatcher in police headquarter.

Services that are now accessed directly by the user of an MDC were previously done for the MDT-equipped officer by the dispatcher and the results were relayed back to the officer by that dispatcher.

Retailing

In Japan, for example, consumers can buy products from vending machines and other compatible devices using one of two e-money platforms that compete for their business. These e-money systems, SUICA and Edy, are both based on SONY wireless smartcard technology (Eurotechnology Japan K. K., 2004). SUICA was developed by the JR-East Railway company and originated as a card for prepaid train tickets and monthly passes. Its initial customer base of train commuters gave SUICA a strong foundation to build on, and it added e-cash functionality in March 2004. Edy is a pure e-cash system that is primarily used as an add-on function of credit cards; partnerships with convenience stores, chains of restaurants and other retailers ensure a basis for the Edy e-cash system. Edy is part of DoCoMo's wallet phone concept, which also strengthens Edy's position in its competition with SUICA. SUICA, Edy, and other similar systems need to be able to provide the option of off-line cash transactions, unlike on-line Internet purchases, because e-cash transactions need to be able to work in any location where actual cash will work, even if the mobile phone has no connection to a telecommunication network. Therefore, using a mobile phone instead of cash requires that electronic money be stored within the mobile phone itself. This is accomplished by storing the balance on an embedded smart card that uses RFID technology to communicate with compatible point-of-sale devices.

Mobile phones can be used not only to pay cash for purchases but also to buy on credit. One way to do this is to store the credit card data inside the mobile phone itself. Nokia has introduced such a system in several parts of the world on a test basis, with the mobile phone communicating with the vendor's system at a point of sale to make a purchase or other transaction. Again, the credit card data is stored inside the mobile phone; the system being tested by Nokia stores only an identification number in the mobile phone rather than the actual credit card number. In Japan, JAVA applications used for credit card transactions communicate with point-of-sales equipment via an infrared link. Other commercial applications allow consumers to pay a parking fee by using their cellular phones, and in many areas mobile phone users can check their bank accounts and perform account balance transfers without needing to go to a bank or access an ATM.

SUMMARY

Various and numerous mobile-commerce applications are available. Mobile handheld devices include high mobility features that desktop or laptop computers do not have. Not only do mobile-commerce applications cover electronic-commerce applications, but they also include new applications not seen before. This chapter introduced the following major mobile-commerce applications: (i) mobile advertising, (ii) mobile entertainment, (iii) mobile services, (iv) mobile virtual communities, (v) traffic, (vi) travel and weather reports, and (vii) other mobile applications. It is important to note, however, that this list is not, and cannot be, comprehensive; several other existing mobile-commerce applications, such as mobile news, were not discussed, and new applications are being invented or developed every day.

REFERENCES

Ambient Devices. (n.d.). *Home Page*. Retrieved July 12, 2006, from http://www.ambientdevices.com

Baig, E. C. (2006). *Will Consumers Tune in to a Tiny TV in Their Hand?* Retrieved August 18, 2006, from http://www.usatoday.com/tech/wireless/2006-08-17-mobile-tv_x.htm

Eurotechnology Japan K. K. (2005). *E-cash and m-cash FAQ*. Retrieved July 25, 2007, from http://www.eurotechnology.com/mcash/index.html

Everypath. (2003). *Life Sciences Discover Mobile Solutions*. Retrieved July 27, 2004, from http://www.everypath.com

E-ZPASS. (2004). *Home Page*. Retrieved July 14, 2004, from http://www.thruway.state.ny.us/ezpass/

FierceMarkets, Inc. (2007). *Mobile Gaming to Top $6B by 2010*. Retrieved March 12, 2008, from http://www.fiercemobilecontent.com/story/forecast-mobile-gaming-to-top-6b-by-2010/2007-01-05

Financial Technology Network. (2004). *The Emerging Wireless World*. Retrieved August 3, 2006, from http://www.financetech.com/showArticle.jhtml?articleID=2 3902279

German, K. (2006). *Samsung Sync (SGH-A707)*. Retrieved November 27, 2006, from http://reviews.cnet.com/Samsung_Sync_SGH_A707/4514-6454_7-32143300.html?tag=tool

Google. (n.d.). *Google Maps for Mobile.* Retrieved May 26, 2007, from http://www.google.com/gmm/index.html?utm_source=us-ha-aws&utm_campaign=gmm&utm_medium=cpc&utm_term=map%20mobile

Gordon, P. & Gebauer, J. (2001). M-commerce: Revolution + inertia = evolution. *Working Paper 01-WP-1038,* University of California, Berkeley, California.

Graham, J. (2006). *Portable Music's Future Could Be in Your Phone.* Retrieved November 16, 2006, from http://www.usatoday.com/tech/wireless/phones/2006-11-07-musicphones_x.htm

I-PASS (2004). *Home Page.* Retrieved July 14, 2006, from http://www.illinoistollway.com

MapQuest, Inc. (n.d.). *MapQuest Mobile.* Retrieved June 21, 2006, from http://www.mapquest.com/mobile/

Mobile Health Data. (2004). *Practice Beats Hospital to Wireless.* Retrieved July 14, 2004, from http://www.mobilehealthdata.com/article.cfm?articleId=938&banner=p4

PBG. (2002). *The Pepsi Bottling Group 2002 Annual Report to Stockholders.* Retrieved July 27, 2004, from http://www.pbg.com/PR/publications.asp

Sadeh, N. (2002). *M-commerce: Technologies, services, and business models,* pages 177-179, New York: John Wiley & Sons.

University of South Dakota. (2004). *PDAs at the U.* Retrieved July 26, 2004, from http://www.usd.edu/pda/

Wal-Mart Stores, Inc. (2004). *Wal-Mart Expands Electronic Product Code Goals.* Retrieved September 14, 2005, from http://www.walmartstores.com/wmstore/wmstores/Mainnews.jsp

Yahoo! Inc. (n.d.). *Yahoo! Mobile Ad Services.* Retrieved July 16, 2007, from http://mobile.yahoo.com/business/advertiser

Chapter III
Mobile Handheld Devices

INTRODUCTION

Mobile users interact with mobile commerce applications by using small wireless Internet-enabled devices, which come with several aliases such as handhelds, palms, PDAs, pocket PCs, and smartphones. To avoid any ambiguity, a general term, mobile handheld devices, is used in this book. A mobile handheld device is small enough to be held in one hand and is a general-purpose, programmable, battery-powered computer, but it is different from a desktop PC or notebook due to the following three special features:

- **Limited network bandwidth:** This limitation prevents the display of most multimedia on a microbrowser. Though the Wi-Fi and 3G networks go some way toward addressing this problem, the wireless bandwidth is always far below the bandwidth of wired networks.
- **Small screen/body size:** This feature restricts most handheld devices to using a stylus for input.
- **Mobility:** The high mobility of handheld devices is an obvious feature that separates handheld devices from PCs. This feature also makes possible many

Figure 3.1. System structure of mobile handheld devices

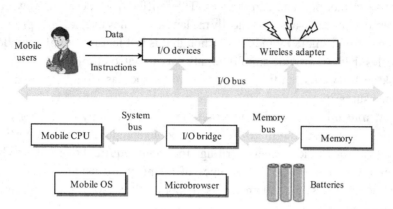

new applications such as mobile recommendations that normally cannot be done by PCs.

Short battery life and limited memory, processing power, and functionality are additional features that impose limitations on handheld devices, but these problems are gradually being solved as the technologies improve and new methods are constantly being introduced. Figure 3.1 shows a typical system structure for handheld devices, which includes six major components: (i) a mobile operating system, (ii) a mobile central processing unit, (iii) a microbrowser, (iv) input and output devices and methods, (v) memory and storage, and (vi) batteries. Brief descriptions of each of these components are given below, followed by a more detailed description in the main body of the chapter.

1. **Mobile operating systems:** These comprise the core software of handheld devices. Mobile operating systems are different from those in desktop computers as they include the following additional features: (i) power management to prolong the battery life, (ii) real-time capability for time-critical operations such as voice communication, and (iii) a wireless infrastructure for wireless communication.
2. **Mobile central processing units:** Mobile CPUs are the core hardware of mobile handheld devices, and the performance and functionality of the devices are heavily dependent on the capabilities of the processors.

3. **Microbrowsers:** Microbrowsers are Internet browsers specifically designed for use in mobile handheld devices. They differ from desktop browsers in several important ways, specifically the languages they use, security protocols, footprint, and smaller windows. Although this last feature, smaller windows, enables them to provide simplified interfaces, it also eliminates much of the desktop browser's multimedia functionality, such as streaming -audio and -video support.

4. **Input and output devices and methods:** There is only one major output device, the screen, but there are several popular input devices, in particular keyboards and touch screens/writing areas, that require the use of a stylus.

5. **Memory and storage:** Three types of memory are usually employed by handheld devices: (i) random access memory, (ii) read-only memory, and (iii) flash memory.

6. **Batteries:** Rechargeable Lithium Ion batteries are most commonly used in handheld devices.

Requirements of a Mobile Handheld Device

It is first necessary to determine which features a handheld device needs in order to conduct effective and efficient mobile commerce transactions and the challenges that must be overcome in the process of developing new mobile handheld devices. The features required of a mobile handheld device include:

- It should be small enough to be held in one hand.
- Input methods must be easy to use and learn.
- The screen must be large enough for mobile users to read the content effortlessly and use the stylus without difficulty.
- Processors should be powerful enough to process users' requests with short latencies, while at the same time consume as little power as possible to extend the battery life.
- The device should be able to run a wide variety of existing software and be simple enough for developers to write software for it or for the various accessories to be used with it.
- The memory and storage must be large enough for most mobile commerce applications.
- Battery life must be sufficient for operations lasting several hours before the batteries need to be recharged.
- Device-to-PC/peripherals synchronization should be convenient and easy.

MAJOR DEVICES

Mobile handheld devices are usually divided into two types: smart cellular phones and personal digital assistants (PDAs). These two kinds of devices started out as very different products, but they have gradually blended into each other and it will soon be difficult to tell the difference between these two types of devices. It is expected that PDAs will be phased out eventually once the functions of smart cellular phones become almost as powerful as those of PDAs. There are numerous handheld devices available in the market today. The following list shows the market shares of the commonly available smartphones and PDAs as of the fourth quarter of 2007 and the first quarter of 2006, respectively:

- *Smartphones*: Nokia (52.9%), RIM (11.4%), Apple(6.5%), Motorola (6.5%), and others (22.7%) (Canalys, 2007).
- *PDAs*: RIM (25.5%), Palm (12.6%), HP (11.5%), Mio Technology (5.9%), Dell (3.9%), and others (40.6%) (PalmInfocenter.com, 2006).

The market for handheld devices is both very competitive and volatile, so these two lists are constantly changing; different market research firms may also give different analyses.

Smart Cellular Phones

Smart cellular phones are voice-centric devices with a data-processing capability. An example is the Palm Treo 700p, shown in Figure 3.2, which is basically a cellular phone with a built-in camera, speakerphone, Bluetooth and IR connectivity,

Figure 3.2. Palm Treo 700p © 2008 Palm, Inc.

Table 3.1. Some specifications of four popular smart cellular phones

	BlackBerry 8700g	Palm Treo 700p/w	Samsung SPH-i550	Sony-Ericsson P910a
Operating System	Blackberry 4.1.0 with Java support	• 770p: Palm OS 5.4.9 and • 700w: Windows Mobile 5.2.2 Pocket PC Phone Edition	Palm OS Garnet (5.4)	Symbian OS v7.0 with UIQ 2.1 User Interface
CPU	Intel PXA901 312 MHz Hermon processor	Intel XScale 312 MHz processor	Motorola MX1	32-bit RISC ARM9 156 MHz
Memory	16 MB RAM and 64 MB flash	128 MB (60 MB user accessable) non-volatile	64 MB ROM and 32 MB RAM	64MB
Input Methods	Touchscreen and QWERTY keyboard	Touchscreen and QWERTY keyboard	Touchscreen	Touchscreen and QWERTY keyboard
Key Features	MMS (Multimedia Messaging Service)	Digital camera and thousands of Palm application software	MP3/ MPEG4 player	MP3 player

wireless e-mail and Internet access, and MP3 audio and MPEG-4 video capability. It can be synchronized with Microsoft Outlook via the included USB docking station. Table 3.1 lists some specifications of four popular smartphones.

Personal Digital Assistants (PDAs)

In contrast to smart cellular phones these are data-centric devices, although they usually also include a voice capability. Advanced *PDAs (Personal Digital Assistants)* provide the functions of telephone/fax, e-mails, PIM (personal information

Figure 3.3. HP iPAQ hx2790 © 2008 Hewlett-Packard Development Company, L.P.

Table 3.2. Specifications of four popular PDAs

	Dell Axim X51v	**Garmin iQue M5**	**HP iPAQ hx2790**	**Palm T|X**
Operating System	Windows Mobile 5.0	Microsoft Windows Mobile 2003	Windows Mobile 2003 for Pocket PC	Palm OS Garnet (5.4)
CPU	Intel XScale PXA270 624 MHz with WMMX	Intel PXA272 Xscale 416 MHz processor and dedicated ARM7 GPS 48 MHz coprocessor	Intel XScale PXA270 624 MHz processor	Intel XScale 312 MHz processor
Memory	64 MB RAM and 256 MB flash ROM (195 MB available)	64 MB RAM and 64 MB ROM (15 MB safe storage available)	128 MB SDRAM and 128 MB Flash ROM	128 MB
Input Methods	Touchscreen	Touchscreen	Touchscreen	Touchscreen
Key Features	Windows Media Player 10	GPS	A biometric fingerprint reader for added security	Built-in Wi-Fi and Bluetooth technology

managers) such as calendars and address books, and networking features. A typical example is the HP iPAQ hx2790, shown in Figure 3.3, which includes features such as built-in Wi-Fi, an integrated keyboard, email and Internet access, a transflective screen, and a 400 MHz processor. Table 3.2 lists the specifications of four popular PDAs.

Tablet/Micro PCs

The newest computer products, known as *tablet PCs* or *micro PCs*, do not belong to either of the smartphone or PDA categories; rather, they are a mini version of PCs. Handheld devices are not PCs, however, because they apply a different technology. For example, Windows OSes are used for PCs or tablet/micro PCs but not for handheld devices, whereas Windows Mobile OSes are suitable for handheld devices but not for PCs or tablet/micro PCs. Figure 3.4 shows the Sony Vaio UX Micro PC, which is a full-functioning PC designed to boost productivity away from the office. It has a 4.5-inch wide SVGA screen, Intel Core Solo Ultra Low Voltage CPU and Microsoft XP Professional operating system, as well as integrated wireless LAN, wireless WAN and Bluetooth technology.

Apple's iPhone

A recent product worth mentioning is Apple's *iPhone*, shown in Figure 3.5. This has proved so popular that up to 700,000 iPhones were sold in just a few days when it first went on sale on June 30, 2007. iPhones introduced a new user interface based on a large multi-touch display and new software that allows users to control everything with just their fingers.

The iPhone, like Apple's other products such as the iPod, is both ingenious and elegantly designed. It combines three products into one device:

Figure 3.4. The Sony Vaio UX Micro PC © 2008 Sony Corporation

Figure 3.5. The iPhone from Apple © 2008 Apple Inc.

- **A mobile phone:** iPhone allows users to make a call by simply touching a name or number in their address books, a favorites list, or a call log. It also automatically synchronizes its contacts with a PC, Mac, or Internet service and allows users to select and listen to voicemail messages in any order.
- **A widescreen iPod with touch controls:** The use of a widescreen with touch controls allows users to enjoy content, including music, audio books, videos, TV shows, and movies, on a 3.5-inch widescreen display and to synchronize content from the iTunes library on their PC or Mac. It can then be accessed with the touch of a finger.
- **An Internet communication device with desktop-class email, web browsing, maps, and searching:** The iPhone features a rich HTML email client and Safari, claimed to be the most advanced web browser ever on a portable device, which automatically synchronizes bookmarks from a user's PC or Mac. Safari also includes built-in Google and Yahoo! search facilities. iPhone is fully multi-tasking, enabling users to read a web page while downloading email in the background over Wi-Fi or EDGE.

Table 3.3 shows the technical specifications of the iPhone. Further details of the specifications are given below:

- **Battery:** The battery life claimed by Apple is longer than for most cell phones. However, it is not easy to replace the iPhone's battery and this cannot be done by the average user.
- **The multi-touch technology:** iPhone's user interface is based on the use of a multi-touch display and innovative new software that allows users to control everything using only their fingers. It is possible to glide through albums with Cover Flow, flip through photos and email them with a touch, or zoom in and out on a section of a web page using iPhone's multi-touch display. iPhone's full QWERTY soft keyboard makes it easy to send and receive SMS messages in multiple sessions and the keyboard is predictive, preventing and correcting

Table 3.3. Technical specifications of iPhone

Battery	Talk time	Up to 8 hours
	Standby	Up to 250 hours
	Internet use	Up to 6 hours
	Video playback	Up to 7 hours
	Audio playback	Up to 24 hours
Camera	2.0 megapixels	
Dimensions	4.5 × 2.4 × 0.46 inches / 115 × 61 × 11.6 mm	
GSM	Quad-band (850, 900, 1800, 1900 MHz)	
Input method	Multi-touch	
Operating system	OS X	
Screen resolution	320 by 480 pixels (160 ppi)	
Screen size	3.5 inches	
Storage	4 GB or 8 GB	
Weight	4.8 ounces / 135 grams	
Wireless data	Wi-Fi (802.11b/g) / EDGE / Bluetooth 2.0+EDR	

mistakes and thus making it easier and more efficient to use than the small plastic keyboards on many smartphones.

- **OS X:** Mac OS X is a development platform that supports multiple development technologies including UNIX, Java, the proprietary Cocoa and Carbon runtime environments, and a host of open source, web, scripting, database, and development technologies. The built-in Xcode Tools combined with friendly user interface make Mac OS X a multifaceted development platform. The current release, Mac OS X v10.4 Tiger, introduces revolutionary new technologies like Spotlight, Dashboard, Automator, Core Data, Core Image, and many others. These powerful additions to the modern, UNIX-based foundation are claimed to make Mac OS X Tiger the most advanced operating system available, giving users access to a wide range of applications and software, including rich HTML email, full-featured web browsing, and applications such as Safari, calendar, text messaging, Address Book, Weather, Stocks, Maps, Notes, and YouTube.

- **Quad-band GSM:** iPhone uses quad-band GSM, the global standard for wireless communications. It also supports AT&T's EDGE network, 802.11b/g Wi-Fi, and Bluetooth 2.0 with EDR, which links to Apple's new compact Bluetooth headset.

MOBILE OPERATING SYSTEMS

Handheld cores are comprised of high-performance, power efficient processors, a robust software infrastructure and comprehensive support network for the rapid development of differentiated 2.5G and 3G mobile devices and other multimedia-enhanced applications. However, adapting desktop operating systems for mobile handheld devices has proved to be a futile endeavor; an example of this effort is Microsoft Windows CE, which was not well received by the mobile industry although it became the foundation of popular Windows Mobile. A mobile operating system needs a new architecture and different features in order to provide adequate services for handheld devices. This section presents a mobile operating system structure and discusses some major systems.

System Structure

Several mobile operating systems are already available, each of which employs a different architecture and implementation. Figure 3.6 shows a generalized mobile operating system structure, which can be visualized as a six-layer stack:

1. **Mobile applications:** This level refers to customer-level applications such as microbrowsers and mobile retailing. Details of various mobile applications will be given in a later section.
2. **Graphical user interface (GUI):** Applications use the API to display information on the GUI, which is more limited in a mobile operating system than the GUI in a desktop OS.
3. **Application programming interface (API) framework:** This level provides the framework between the low-level architecture components and the application layer. By using this framework, application developers do not need to know the details of the underlying low-level components in order to take full advantage of their capabilities.
4. **This level consists of three components:**
   - **Multimedia:** Widely adopting multimedia is one of the reasons for the success of electronic commerce. The same principles can be applied to mobile commerce, particularly as more smart cellular phones are equipped

Figure 3.6.A generalized mobile operating system structure

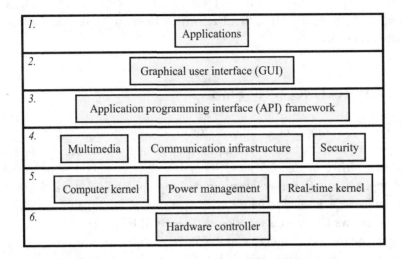

with cameras. This module involves image/video related functionality, audio recording and play back.

- **Communication infrastructure:** Wireless and mobile networks make a crucial difference between mobile commerce and electronic commerce. This module may contain wide-area networking stacks including TCP/IP and WAP, personal area networking stacks including infrared (IrDA), Bluetooth, and USB, abstract API for cellular standards, and GSM and CDMA circuit-switched voice and data and packet-based data.

- **Security:** Security in mobile commerce is especially crucial, as communication through wireless and mobile networks is inherently more vulnerable and open to attack than in the wired networks used for electronic commerce. Mobile commerce security involves a wide variety of technologies, including authentication, cryptography, secure communications, and secure mobile payment methods.

5. **The 5th level also consists of three components:**

- **Computer kernel:** This is the central module of an operating system that provides all the essential services required by the other parts of the operating system and applications. For example, it is responsible for resource allocation, low-level hardware interfaces, and process and task management.

- **Power management:** A problem with all handheld devices is their short battery life. This component manages the power consumption in order to prolong the battery life.
- **Real-time kernel:** This component is not required for desktop PCs because it is usually acceptable for them to take a few seconds, or even minutes, to react. In contrast, mobile handheld devices need real-time responses for time-critical applications such as voice communication.

6. **The bottom level is the hardware controller.** The hardware includes displays and memory. It is expected that hard disks will be added to the list in the near future.

Major Systems

Although a wide range of mobile handheld devices are commercially available, the operating systems, the key components of the devices, are dominated by just a few major organizations. The following two lists show the operating systems used in the top five brands of smart cellular phones and PDAs, in descending order of market share:

- **Smart cellular phones:** Symbian, Linux, Windows Mobile, Research In Motion, and Palm (Symbian Software Ltd., 2007)
- **PDAs:** Windows Mobile, Research In Motion, Palm, Symbian, Linux (cellular-news, 2007)

It is important to remember that these two lists are inherently unreliable because the market share is constantly changing and claims concerning market share vary enormously. It is almost impossible to predict which will be the ultimate winner in the battle of mobile operating systems. The following six sub-sections briefly describe Android, a mobile platform proposed by Open Handset Alliance in 2007, and the above five systems in turn. More details of the six systems, Android, BREW, Java ME, Palm OS, Symbian, and Windows Mobile, will be given in Chapter 10: Client-Side Handheld Computing and Programming.

Android

Android (Open Handset Alliance, n.d.) is a software stack for mobile devices that includes an operating system, middleware and key applications. It includes the following four features:

- **Open:** Android is built on the open Linux Kernel. It allows developers to access core mobile device functionality through standard API calls.
- **All applications are created equal:** Android does not differentiate between the phone's core applications and third-party applications. They can all be built to have equal access to a phone's capabilities, providing users with a broad spectrum of applications and services.
- **Breaking down application boundaries:** Android combines information from the web with data on the phone—such as contacts or geographic location—to create new user experiences.
- **Fast & easy application development:** The Android SDK (Software Development Kit) contains everything developers need to build and run Android applications, including a true device emulator and advanced debugging tools.

Linux

Linux (Linux Online, Inc., 2007) is an open-source operating system, based on the *kernel* developed by Linus Torvalds, a student at the University of Helsinki in Finland, in 1994. The kernel was developed and released under the GNU General Public License and its source code is freely available to everyone. It is this kernel that forms the base around which a Linux operating system is developed. Hundreds of companies/organizations/individuals have now released their own versions of operating systems based on the Linux kernel. Apart from the fact that it is freely distributed, Linux's functionality, adaptability and robustness has made it the main alternative for proprietary Unix and Microsoft operating systems. IBM, Hewlett-Packard and other giants of the computing world have embraced Linux and support its ongoing development. Now well into its second decade of existence, Linux has been adopted worldwide primarily as a server platform. Its use as a home and office desktop operating system is also on the rise. The operating system can be incorporated directly into microchips in a process called "embedding" and is increasingly being used this way in appliances and devices.

Microsoft Windows Mobile

The Smartphone's functions include: voice, SMS, and instant messaging services; email that can be received from sources such as Outlook messaging, collaboration clients, Exchange, IMAP, and POP3 services; and personal information management (PIM) applications such as calendar and contacts (Microsoft Corp., 2003b). The Smartphone 2002 platform is based on the Microsoft Windows CE 3.0 operating system and contains many of the same core applications that are available on Pocket PC-based computing devices, including email, PIM tools, and Pocket

Internet Explorer Web software. The primary Smartphone architecture consists of four layers:

- **Applications/UI:** The top level refers to the Smartphone shell and customer-level applications such as Pocket Internet Explorer, the Inbox, the control panel, and the phone dialer.
- **Logic:** This level contains system application logic that can be used by the application layer. Examples of this include the control of network connections and synchronization capabilities.
- **Core APIs:** This level provides the interfaces between the low-level architecture components (Operating System, Smartphone software, and radio stack) and the application/logic layers.
- **Radio Stack:** The bottom level refers, in general, to the architectural components responsible for voice and data control and data transmission.

In 1996, Microsoft launched **Windows CE**, a version of the Microsoft Windows operating system designed specially for a variety of embedded products, including mobile stations. However, it was not well received primarily because of its battery-hungry hardware and limited functionality, possibly due to the way that Windows CE was adapted for mobile stations from other Microsoft 32-bit desktop operating systems. To compete with Palm OS, Microsoft later introduced Pocket PC (Microsoft Corp., 2003a), which was designed with better service for mobile users in mind and offers far more computing power than Windows CE. Moreover, the latest version has introduced support for Bluetooth, IEEE 802.11b, and mobile phone technologies such as CDPD, CDMA, and GSM, and allows access to corporate information via a number of connectivity options, including VPN, WAN, LAN, and PANs.

ACCESS's Garnet (Palm) OS

Palm OS ran on almost two out of every three PDAs in 2003. Its popularity could be attributed to its many advantages, such as its long battery life, support for a wide variety of wireless standards, and the abundant software available. The plain design of the Palm OS was the reason for its long battery life, approximately twice that of its rivals. It supports many important wireless standards, including Bluetooth and 802.11b local wireless and GSM, Mobitex, and CDMA wide-area wireless networks. The type of software often used on PCs is gradually becoming available for Palm OS, including functions such as spreadsheets, databases, document processors, messaging programs, and multimedia tools. To offset the increasing challenge from Pocket PC 2002, Palm introduced Palm OS 5, which runs an ARM processor, has a high-resolution (320×320) color screen, 16 MB of memory, and built in voice recorder, directional pad, built-in Bluetooth and media playback capability (MP3/OGG/WAV), and is complete with a speaker and headphone jack.

In 2005, ACCESS *acquired PalmSource*. Principal ACCESS technologies now include the Garnet OS, ACCESS Linux Platform, and NetFront browser. Garnet OS (ACCESS Co., Ltd., 2007a) has expanded the solid foundation of Palm OS 5 by incorporating standard support for a broad range of screen resolutions and expanded support for wireless connections including Bluetooth. It also now includes enhanced multimedia capabilities, a suite of robust security options and support for a broad set of languages.

Research In Motion's BlackBerry OS 4.0

RIM has developed a proprietary multi-tasking operating system (OS) for the BlackBerry. The OS now provides support for MIDP 1.0 and WAP 1.2. Previous versions allowed wireless synchronization with Microsoft Exchange Server's e-mail and calendar, as well as with Lotus Domino's e-mail, but the current version OS 4 (Research In Motion, Ltd., 2007) provides a subset of MIDP 2.0, and allows complete wireless activation and synchronization with Exchange's e-mail, calendar, tasks, notes and contacts, as well as support for Novell GroupWise and Lotus Notes. BlackBerry provides a standards-based platform and developer tools, which allow the development and deployment of custom wireless applications. With an HTML web browser, rich Java development tools and seamless integration with existing .NET and Java Platform, Enterprise Edition (Java EE) application servers, the BlackBerry platform can be leveraged by developers, including Independent Software Vendors, third party Systems Integrators and in-house corporate developers.

On the client side, BlackBerry devices are built on a Java-based operating environment, which supports the development of custom Java applications using the industry-standard Java Platform, Micro Edition (Java ME) programming language. BlackBerry devices also include an integrated web browser, which supports access to standard HTML and WML web pages. Because BlackBerry supports standard networking protocols and seamless connectivity to the Internet or a corporate intranet, existing server-side applications can be easily extended to BlackBerry using either a thin-client or thick-client model. These applications can be written in a variety of programming languages, including .NET, Java, web services, C# and .ASP/.JSP.

Symbian OS

Symbian is a software licensing company that develops and licenses Symbian OS, the open operating system for many smartphones. During the fourth quarter of 2007, 22.4 million Symbian smartphones were sold worldwide up 53% from Q4 2006. 77.3 million Symbian smartphones were shipped to consumers worldwide in 2007, up 50% from 2006. To the year of 2007, a total of more than 188 million Symbian smartphones have shipped to customers around the world (Symbian Software, Ltd., 2008). The operating system originally used, EPOC16 from Psion Software was a 16-bit version of an operating system that had been available for several years and was embedded in many mobile stations; this was succeeded by EPOC32, a 32-bit open operating system that supports preemptive multitasking. In the mid-1998, Psion joined forces with Ericsson, Nokia, and Motorola to form a new joint venture called Symbian OS (Dixon, 2003), with the aim of establishing EPOC as the de facto operating system for mobile stations. Unlike Windows CE, it was planned from the beginning to be a full operating system for mobile stations. It includes the following key features: integrated multimode mobile telephony, an open application environment, multi-tasking, multimedia, and data synchronization. Symbian OS v9.5, the latest evolution of Symbian OS, was designed to meet the specific requirements of advanced 2.5G and 3G mobile phones.

MOBILE CENTRAL PROCESSING UNITS

The core hardware in mobile handheld devices is the mobile processor, and the performance and functionality of the devices are largely dependent on the capabilities of their processors. There used to be several brands available, but recently mobile processors designed by ARM Ltd. have begun to dominate the market. ARM is the industry's leading provider of 32-bit embedded RISC microprocessors, with almost 75% of the market. Handheld devices are becoming more sophisticated and efficient every day and mobile users are demanding more functionality from the devices. To achieve this advanced functionality, in addition to the obvious feature, low cost, today's mobile processors must have the following features:

- **High performance:** The clock rate must be higher than the typical 30 MHz for Palm OS PDAs, 80 MHz for cellular phones, and 200 MHz for devices that run Microsoft's Pocket PC.
- **Low power consumption:** This prolongs battery life and prevents heat buildup in handheld devices that lack the space for fans or other cooling mechanisms.

- **Multimedia capability:** Audio/image/video applications are recurring themes in mobile commerce.
- **Real-time capability:** This feature is particularly important for time-critical applications such as voice communication.

A Mobile CPU Architecture

This section provides some general concepts of a CPU and the characteristics of mobile computation as a foundation to understand the requirements of a mobile CPU. The primary emphasis in this section is on the central processing unit (CPU), together with the memory; memory and the CPU are intimately related in the operation of the handheld device. A CPU is the core of a mobile handheld device. A CPU needs components with several different functions in order to implement the necessary computations. A simple block diagram of a CPU with memory is shown in Figure 3.7.

A computer system is made up of a CPU, memory and a bus to interconnect them. The central processing unit (CPU) is made up of three major components, the arithmetic/logic unit (ALU), the control unit (CU), and the input/output (I/O) interface.

ARM Processors

A few mobile processors, such as the Motorola Dragonball and Intel Pentium M, were designed, manufactured, and sold by chip-making companies such as Motorola, Intel, and Texas Instruments. Now, however, the cores and architectures designed by Cambridge-based ARM Holdings Ltd. (n.d.) have begun to dominate

Figure 3.7. A block diagram of CPU and memory

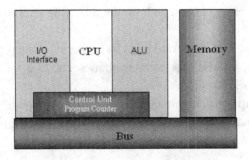

Figure 3.8. A computer system made up of CPU, Memory, and IO

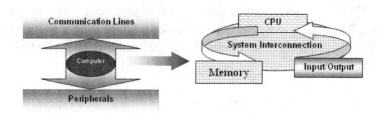

Figure 3.9. A system model of CPU made up of ALU, Registers, and CU

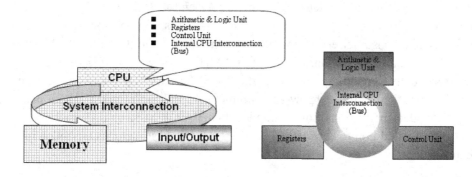

Figure 3.10. A CPU with system bus for control, data, and address

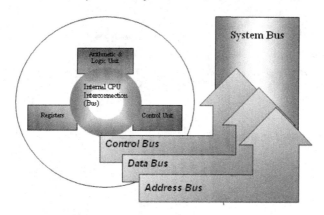

the market. ARM is the industry's leading provider of 16/32-bit embedded RISC microprocessor solutions. The company does not actually produce chips, but instead licenses its RISC processors, peripherals, and system-chip designs to semiconductor companies. ARM's microprocessor cores specifically address the needs of advanced operating systems, real-time, and multimedia applications. The ARM processor range provides solutions for

- open platforms running complex operating systems for wireless, consumer, and imaging applications,
- embedded real-time systems for mass storage, automotive, industrial, and networking applications, and
- secure applications including smart cards and SIMs.

Figure 3.11 shows the ARM11 pipeline structure. This is the first implementation of the ARMv6 instruction set architecture (ISA), and was developed specifically with the needs of next-generation consumer, wireless, networking, automotive products, and consumer-entertainment applications in mind (Cormie, 2003). The ARM11 microarchitecture targets a 330-400 MHz worst case on 0.13µm foundry processes, delivering 400 to 500 Dhrystone MIPS. The ARM11 microarchitecture was designed to meet the low power requirement of battery-powered and high-density embedded applications, consuming less than 0.4mW/MHz on 0.13µm foundry processes. In addition to supporting 32-bit ARMv6 ISA, it includes the following features:

Figure 3.11. ARM11 microarchitecture (© 2003 ARM, Ltd. Reprinted with permission.)

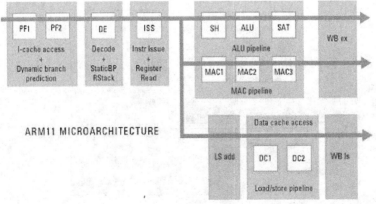

- supporting Thumb 16-bit instruction set,
- ARM DSP extensions,
- SIMD (Single Instruction Multiple Data) media processing extensions deliver up to 2× performance for audio and video processing,
- better power/performance trade-off (0.4mW/MHz in 0.13μm),
- an 8-stage integer pipeline improving performance,
- separate load-store and arithmetic pipelines,
- a 64-bit memory system speeding data access,
- speedy interrupt response and real-time performance, and
- Vector Floating Point coprocessor for automotive controls and 3D graphics acceleration.

In 2005, ARM introduced the ARMv7 revision of its architecture, known as the "Cortex" architecture. Processor designs based on the ARMv7 architecture are targeted at three primary market segments:

- *The Cortex-A (Application) series*, which includes new technologies for next-generation, high performance systems that run open operating systems, such as Symbian, Windows Mobile, and Linux.
- *The Cortex-R (Real-time) series*, which enables higher performance embedded systems to run at lower power and is used in real-time applications such as advanced braking systems in cars.

Figure 3.12. Key technology added to ARM architecture generation © 2003 ARM, Ltd.

V4	V5	V6	V7 A&R	V7 M
			Dynamic Compiler Support	
			VFPv3	
			NEON Adv SIMD	
		Multiprocessor Support	Thumb-2	
		TrustZone		
		SIMD		
	VFPv2			Thumb-2 Only
	Jazelle			
Thumb				

- *The Cortex-M (Microcontroller) series*, which also delivers high performance embedded systems, while at the same time allowing the development of highly cost-sensitive devices, facilitating the migration from the 8 and 16-bit domains.

Figure 3.12 shows the key technology additions introduced in each ARM architecture generation.

MICROBROWSERS

Microbrowsers are miniaturized versions of desktop browsers such as Netscape Navigator and Microsoft Internet Explorer. They provide the graphical user interfaces that enable mobile users to interact with mobile commerce applications.

Features

Due to the limited resources of handheld devices, microbrowsers differ from traditional desktop browsers in the following ways:

- smaller windows,
- smaller footprints, and
- fewer functions and multimedia features.

Several microbrowsers, such as Microsoft Mobile Explorer and Wapaka Java Micro-Browser, are already available. America Online, Inc., the parent company of the Netscape Network, and Nokia are developing and marketing a Netscape-branded version of Nokia's WAP microbrowser with AOL enhanced features for use across a wide variety of mobile handheld devices. Figure 3.13 shows a microbrowser,

Figure 3.13. NetFront Browser v3.4 © 2008 ACCESS Co., Ltd.

Figure 3.14. Four approaches used by microbrowsers to display mobile content

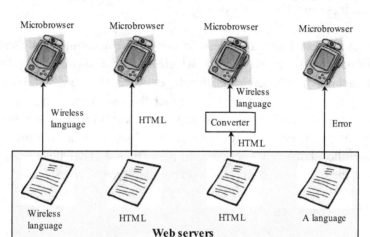

NetFront Browser v3.4 from ACCESS, which supports Visual Bookmarks—a pan & zoom navigation tool for the desktop-like presentation of web pages on mobile devices with limited screen size (ACCESS Co., Ltd., 2006).

Technologies

Several markup languages are used to present mobile content on microbrowsers. These may not be able to handle all the languages currently used, therefore some content will not be displayed by some microbrowsers. Microbrowsers usually take one of the following four approaches, as shown in Figure 3.14, to display mobile content (Lawton, 2001):

1. **Wireless language direct access:** Here, a microbrowser supports some wireless languages, such as WML, CHTML, and XML, and directly displays any content written in a wireless language supported by that microbrowser.
2. **HTML direct access:** This approach displays the HTML contents directly, with no intervention, but may distort the content. For example, large images cannot be displayed on the small screens of microbrowsers.
3. **HTML to wireless language conversion:** Some mobile middleware provides conversion software that converts an HTML script to the script of a wireless language supported by that microbrowser. For example, i-mode includes a Corporate Conversion Server that converts existing HTML files into i-mode-compatible HTML, the CHTML.

4. **Error:** If a microbrowser is not able to handle the content, it displays an error code such as "Invalid WML code."

Some microbrowsers, like most desktop browsers, can automatically send and receive information with the aid of a cache, which is known as Web caching (Davison, 2001). Web caching offers significant advantages, such as reduced bandwidth consumption, server load, and latency. Taken together, these advantages make accessing the Web less expensive and improve performance. These three components unique to mobile handheld devices, namely mobile OSs, mobile CPUs, and microbrowsers, result in a significant difference between the performance of handheld devices and desktop PCs; the remaining components do not play such a crucial role.

Major Microbrowsers

A number of microbrowsers are currently available commercially. Four popular microbrowsers are: (i) Opera 8.65, (ii) Openwave Mobile Browser, Mercury Edition, (iii) Access NetFront Browser 3.5, and (iv) Microsoft Pocket Internet Explorer. Table 3.4 compares these four microbrowsers and detailed descriptions of the microbrowsers are given below. Some companies also provide microbrowser emulators/simulators such as Opera Mini Simulator that enable developers to test their products on desktop computers because small devices are not convenient for

Table 3.4. A comparison of the four leading microbrowsers

	Mobile Browser 8.65	Mobile Browser, Mercury Edition	NetFront Browser 3.5	Internet Explorer 6 for Windows CE
Vendor	Opera	Openwave	Access	Microsoft
Support HTML?	Yes	Yes	Yes	Yes
Support WML?		Yes	Yes	Yes if extra software installed
Major Technologies	Small-Screen Rendering	Progressive rendering of content	Smart-Fit Rendering™	Fit-to-Screen menu
Special Features	Flash	Ajax	Ajax	JScript

mobile application development. Chapter 5 will introduce some of the most popular microbrowser emulators/simulators.

Opera Mobile Browser 8.65

Opera originated as a research project in Norway's largest telecom company, Telenor, in 1994, and branched out into an independent development company named Opera Software ASA in 1995. Opera Software developed the Opera web browser, a multi-platform product for a wide range of platforms, operating systems and embedded Internet products. A mobile device equipped with Opera can surf the same web sites as a personal computer. The Opera 8.65 mobile web browser for Windows Mobile is designed with speed and ease-of-use in mind. It includes the following features (Opera Software ASA, 2007):

* Grab and Scroll (PocketPC only)
* Web search in address bar
* Save image
* Copy text
* Send link as e-mail, SMS, and MMS
* Import IE bookmarks
* Support for Macromedia Flash Player 7 for Pocket PCs
* FlashLite 2.1
* Multiple Windows
* Tabbed browsing (Pocket PC only)
* Zoom
* Download
* Navigation and history
* Bookmarks
* Landscape/Portrait Mode
* Pop-up handler
* Padlock icon on secure sites
* User preferences
* Context menu
* Change encoding
* Desktop mode and Fit to Screen
* Plugin API (Netscape)

Figure 3.15 shows two screenshots of Opera Mobile Browser 8.65.

Figure 3.15. Two screenshots of Opera Mobile Browser 8.65 © 2008 Opera Software ASA

Openwave Mobile Browser, Mercury Edition

Openwave Systems Inc. (http://www.openwave.com/) is an independent provider of open software products and services for the communications industry. Openwave's products include mobile phone software, multimedia messaging software (MMS), email, location and mobile gateways; the company's products enable its customers to deliver differentiated data services. The Openwave Mobile Browser, Mercury Edition, is a redesign of the core Openwave Mobile Browser engine (Openwave Systems Inc., 2006). The Mercury Edition Browser is script-enabled and Ajax capable, enabling broader access to the open mobile internet and compatibility with the newest open web applications. Openwave Mobile Browser, Mercury Edition, also combines improved browser functionality and navigation with its high-speed access to rich content for a superior mobile browsing experience. Key features of the Openwave Mobile Browser, Mercury Edition, include:

- A high performance graphics engine
- Progressive rendering of content
- Optimized table layout
- ECMAScript Mobile Profile (ESMP)
- Multiple screen display modes, with map and zoom capability
- Support for HTML 4.01, WCSS 1.1, WML
- Support for both HTTP and WSP Networking, including Proxyless HTTP
- Full SSL 3.0/TLS 1.0 support, WTLS Class II on WAP Stack

Figure 3.16 shows a screen shot of Openwave Mobile Browser, Mercury Edition.

Figure 3.16. A screenshot of Openwave Mobile Browser, Mercury Edition © 2008 Openwave System Inc.

ACCESS NetFront Browser 3.5

ACCESS Co., Ltd. is a global provider of advanced software technologies for the mobile and beyond-PC markets. Principal ACCESS technologies include the Garnet OS, ACCESS Linux Platform, a software platform that combines the functionality of Garnet OS with a Linux core, NetFront Mobile Client Suite, a client software suite for mobile devices, and NetFront™ an Internet browser. NetFront Browser v3.5 (ACCESS Co., Ltd., 2007b) is the latest version of ACCESS' advanced, versatile, and powerful NetFront Internet browser. Specifically designed and optimized to deliver high performance in resource-constrained environments, NetFront supports almost any OS and CPU and offers low power consumption, easy customization, and a broad range of plug-ins. The NetFront Advantage Optimized for Mobile and Beyond-PC Devices NetFront was designed from the beginning to function as an embedded browser solution rather than as a scaled down version of a desktop browser, but is still able to provide users with a rich and seamless desktop-like mobile Internet browsing experience. NetFront supports a broad feature-set with a compact code size that is ideally suited for the mobile and beyond-PC market. NetFront supports almost any OS and CPU and offers low power consumption, easy customization, and a broad range of plug-ins. Figure 3.17 shows the architecture of the NetFront Browser.

The NetFront Browser includes the following features:

Figure 3.17. The NetFront Browser architecture

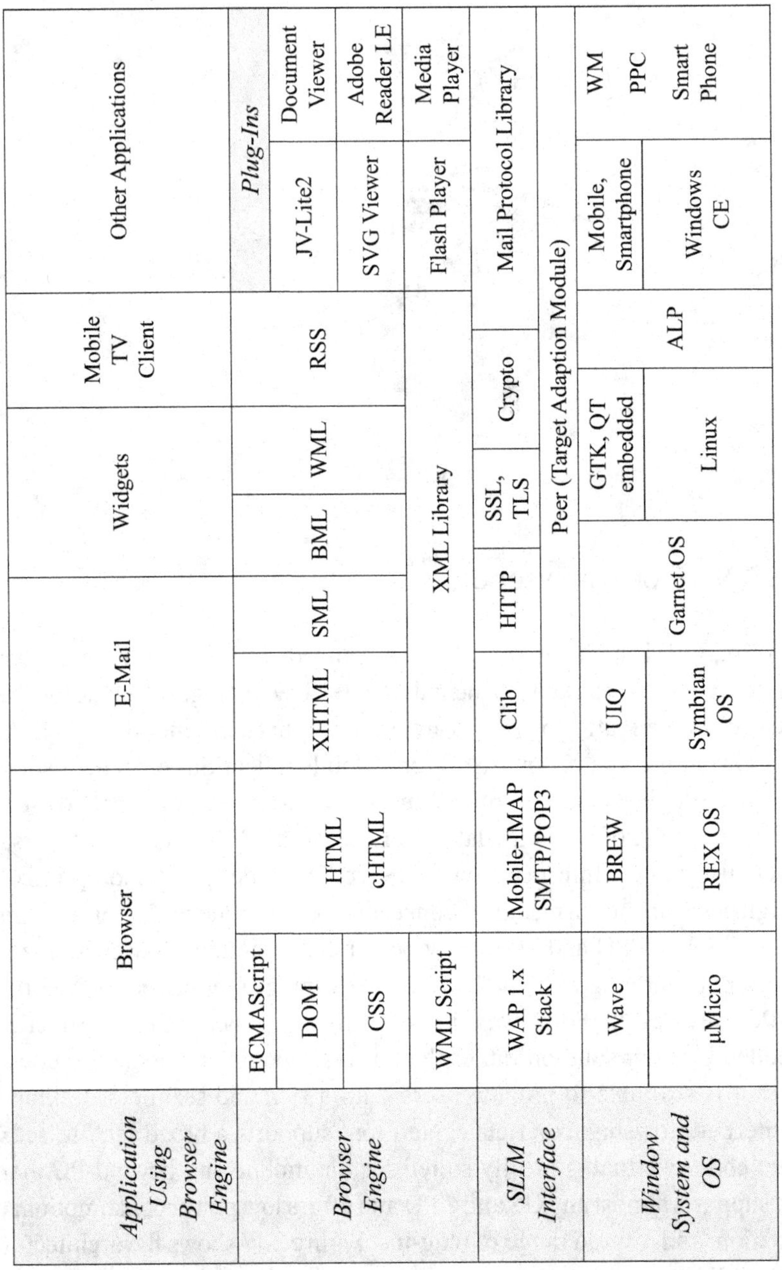

Application Using Browser Engine	Browser	E-Mail	Widgets	Mobile TV Client	Other Applications		*Plug-Ins*
Browser Engine	ECMAScript · DOM · CSS · WML Script	HTML · cHTML	XHTML · SML · BML · WML	RSS		JV-Lite2	Document Viewer
						SVG Viewer	Adobe Reader LE
		XML Library				Flash Player	Media Player
							Mail Protocol Library
SLIM Interface	WAP 1.x Stack	Mobile-IMAP SMTP/POP3	Clib	HTTP	SSL, TLS	Crypto	
Window System and OS	Wave · μMicro	BREW · REX OS	UIQ · Symbian OS	Garnet OS	GTK, QT embedded · Linux	ALP	Mobile, Smartphone · Windows CE	WM PPC	Smart Phone
			Peer (Target Adaption Module)				

- **Adapted for "Web 2.0":** Web 2.0 is the next-generation of the Web and is also widely recognized as a next-generation service framework, based on the view of the Web as a platform.

- **Smart-Fit Rendering:** Browsing web sites developed for desktop PCs on mobile devices can be a difficult and frustrating experience, so NetFront Browser includes Smart-Fit Rendering technology. Smart-Fit Rendering intelligently adapts standard web pages to fit the screen width of any mobile device, enabling an intuitive and rapid vertical scrolling process without degrading the quality or usability of the pages being browsed.

- **Embedded Ajax support:** NetFront Browser provides support for Ajax (Asynchronous JavaScript and XML) an open standard web development technique using XHTML, CSS and JavaScript that enables the creation of highly efficient interactive web applications.

- **RSS support:** RSS is an XML-based format for content distribution that allows service providers to feed news, content, and advertisement directly to the front of the end-user handset, enhancing services personalization and discoverability. NetFront Browser provides a RSS library that enables easier and faster RSS application development within the browser or as stand-alone modules.

- **NetFront Browser Widgets:** NetFront Browser Widgets is a comprehensive web application framework based on NetFront Browser technology that supports the creation and use of dynamic web applications based on open standard web technologies like HTML, CSS and JavaScript.

- **Device interactivity:** NetFront Browser offers device interactivity using a ECMAScript-driven interface "Direct-Connect," which was introduced by NetFront Browser v3.1 in 2004.

- **SVG support:** Scalable Vector Graphics (SVG), a W3C recommendation for a modularized language used to describe two dimensional vector and mixed vector/raster graphics in XML, enhances the wireless experience by enabling rich, interactive multimedia functionality. NetFront Browser features support SVGT 1.2.

- **SMIL support:** The Synchronized Multimedia Integration Language (SMIL) enables simple authoring of interactive audiovisual presentations. SMIL is typically used for rich multimedia presentations that integrate streaming audio and video with images, text or any other media type.

- **User experience evolution:** New libraries and interfaces facilitate the integration of the NetFront Browser engine with any kind of application that needs advanced rendering capabilities. New browser application highlights include support for Visual Bookmark, which is used to manage favorite web pages,

Figure 3.18. The smart slider menu of NetFront Browser © 2008 ACCESS Co., Ltd.

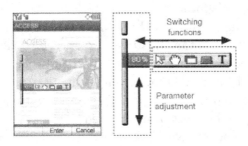

Figure 3.19. The PagePilot mode of NetFront Browser © 2008 ACCESS Co., Ltd.

and PagePilot, a pan & zoom navigation tool for the desktop-like presentation of web pages on mobile devices with a limited screen size.

The following list shows some features of NetFront Browser:

- **Smart Slider Menu:** Smart Slider Menu (Figure 3.18) is a bar displaying short cuts and is designed to enable the user to select functions easily and quickly.
- **PagePilot:** When a user repeatedly pushes the scroll key, NetFront Brower automatically changes its rendering mode to PagePilot mode, as shown in Figure 3.19, enabling pan&zoom navigation.
- **Smart Swing Navi:** When an image is captured by the phone camera, users can scroll or zoom that image by tilting the phone vertically and horizontally, as shown in Figure 3.20.

Figure 3.20. The Smart Swing Navi function of NetFront Browser © 2008 ACCESS Co., Ltd.

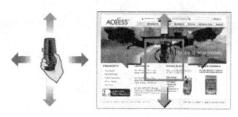

Figure 3.21. The Visual Bookmark function of NetFront Browser © 2008 ACCESS Co., Ltd.

- **Visual Bookmarks:** Visual bookmark helps users to select bookmarks by showing a thumbnail image of each page together with their title and URL (Figure 3.21).

NetFront Document Viewer offers an advanced software solution that enables users to view Microsoft Office documents including Word, Excel, and PowerPoint on their mobile devices. NetFront Document Viewer supports documents created with versions of Microsoft Office 97 and later, and includes user-selectable document zooming and rotation features. NetFront Document Viewer is available as an optional plug-in for NetFront Browser v3.5. Figure 3.22 shows three screenshots of the NetFront Document Viewer:

a. Microsoft Word file at 25%,
b. Microsoft Excel file at 25%, and
c. Microsoft PowerPoint file at 25%.

Figure 3.22. Three screenshots of NetFront Document Viewer © 2008 ACCESS Co., Ltd.

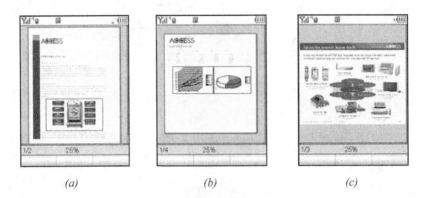

(a)　　　　　　　　　　(b)　　　　　　　　　　(c)

Microsoft Internet Explorer 6 for Windows CE

Microsoft's Internet Explorer 6 Windows CE (Microsoft Corp., n.d.) is the most desktop-compatible browser available for the Windows CE operating system. This browser is preferred for building run-time images that will provide full Internet access, such as an Internet appliance or an interactive television that offers browsing capabilities. Internet Explorer Component Object Model (COM) interfaces can be used to build custom browsers or to add browser controls to an application. Alternatively, it is possible to use the sample Internet Explorer container application source files provided (IESample.*) to create a browser shell and user interface for a specific device. The browser host supports the use of pointing devices and 5-key navigational systems, as well as keyboard and touch screen input. The browser can deal with documents that contain HTML, Dynamic HTML, and CSS data formats and XML support is available if the MSXML parser is included in the OS design. As a scripting host, Internet Explorer supports Microsoft JScript® 5.6 and Microsoft Visual Basic® Scripting Edition, Microsoft VBScript® 5.6, when they are included in an OS design.

Internet Explorer 6 Windows CE offers the following important capabilities for Windows Mobile-based devices:

- A rich web experience without the need to connect through a special content-modifying proxy,
- Implementation of key Internet technology standards, including:

- o Secure Sockets Layer (SSL) to help improve the security of transactions,
- o HTML 4.0,
- o Microsoft JScript for scripting Web page behavior,
- o XHTML,
- o Cascading style sheets (CSS),
- o Frames for basic formatting, and
- o Cookies for storing local data.
- Support for ActiveX® controls, and
- Support for Extensible Markup Language (XML), which enables Web-standard data exchange and the development of rich Web applications for the mobile device.

Internet Explorer 6 for Windows CE delivers the web to small-screen devices in several ways, including:

- A *Fit to Screen* menu option dynamically resizes web pages to optimize the way they are displayed on the smaller, vertically oriented screens of Pocket PC devices, and
- Smart caching determines whether local versions of web pages are available, thus avoiding unnecessary Internet queries, improving download speed, and saving connection charges.

INPUT AND OUTPUT DEVICES AND METHODS

Because of their size, handheld devices necessarily use different input and output devices, methods, and strategies from those used by PCs. This section discusses the various I/O devices and methods used by handheld devices.

Input Devices and Methods

Entering data into handheld devices is never an easy task because the devices are so small. Various input methods for handheld devices have been developed, the most important of which are: (i) keyboards, (ii) navigator, (iii) touch screens, (iv) writing areas on screens, and (v) speech recognition. Another input option that is often used is to receive data and files directly from PCs.

Keyboards

There are four kinds of QWERTY keyboards that are commonly used for handheld devices:

- **Built-in keyboards:** These come with the devices. Unfortunately, the problem with this kind of keyboard is that they are too small for touch-typing. Figure 3.23 shows RIM's BlackBerry 8700c, which contains a built-in keyboard.
- **External keyboards:** This kind of keyboard can be connected to the handheld device via serial cables or wireless technologies such as Bluetooth. They are normally foldable for convenience. Figure 3.24 shows a Bluetooth foldable keyboard for iPAQ from HP.
- **Fabric keyboards:** These can be rolled up or folded around the handheld devices and have been developed to deal with many of the problems inherent in external keyboards. Both wireless and serial cable connections to the

Figure 3.23. The built-in keyboard of BlackBerry 8700c © 2008 Research In Motion Limited

Figure 3.24. A Bluetooth foldable keyboard for iPAQ from HP © 2008 Hewlett-Packard Development Company, L.P.

Figure 3.25. Three pictures of a USB double-sided fabric keyboard © 2008 Peratech Ltd.

Figure 3.26. An on-screen keyboard for a Pocket PC from Microsoft © 2008 Microsoft

handheld device are available for fabric keyboards. Figure 3.25 shows three pictures of a USB double-sided fabric keyboard from Peratech Ltd.

- **Soft keyboards:** These are virtual keyboards that normally appear at the bottom of the screens when selected. A stylus is required to use the soft keyboard. Figure 3.26 shows an on-screen keyboard for a Pocket PC from Microsoft.

Navigators

The navigator, or five-way navigator, consists of the two large, concentric buttons generally located in the center of the lower part of handheld devices. Users press the edges to move up, down, right, or left, and the center button to select items. The navigator works differently in different applications, but is usually an easy

Figure 3.27. A 5-way navigator on a Palm device © 2008 Palm, Inc.

way to operate the device with one hand. Figure 3.27 shows a 5-way navigator on a Palm device.

Touch Screens with Styli

A *touch screen* is a display that is sensitive to human touch, allowing a user to interact with the applications by touching pictures or words on the screen, and a *stylus* is an input device used to write text or draw lines on a surface as input to a handheld device. Figure 3.28 shows a stylus pen with a built in LED tip from Samsung, which helps users click in the right places and facilitates writing by hand at night and in low light environments.

Writing Areas on Screens with Styli

A handheld device equipped with a writing area and a stylus requires a handwriting recognition function, but existing systems have not yet achieved a satisfactory recognition rate. Graffiti, employed by many handheld devices, is the most popular

Figure 3.28. A flash stylus from Samsung © 2008 Samsung

Figure 3.29. A note pad on the Palm screen © 2008 Palm, Inc.

Figure 3.30. A screenshot of the Voice LookUp user interface © 2008 HandHeld Speech

writing software. Figure 3.29 shows a note pad on a Palm screen that allows users to scribble notes directly onto the screen using a special stylus.

Speech Recognition

Some mobile handheld devices can also respond to voice input using voice recognition technology. However, voice recognition technology is still in its infancy and is not yet practical for everyday use. There are currently two kinds of speech recognition programs (Bogue, 2002):

* **Speaker dependent:** Speaker-dependent programs adjust to the way user speaks, which requires a training/learning process. This kind of program tends to be smaller, faster, and more accurate than speaker-independent programs. However, they also require more time to set up because the program must be trained to recognize the voice pattern of each person using it. Figure

Figure 3.31. A screenshot for the Nuance Voice Control user interface © 2008 Nuance Communications, Inc.

3.30 shows a user interface for Voice LookUp, a speaker-dependent program. Voice LookUp (http://www.handheldspeech.com/home.html) works with the address book or contacts list in a PDA. It allows users to find addresses and phone numbers using voice commands, then dial the phone numbers by touching the microphone button. With simple voice commands, users can create email voice-attachments, schedule meetings, and switch from one program to another on their PDA.

- **Speaker independent:** Speaker-independent programs attempt to recognize anyone's speech, without benefit of training. Although they are easier to learn and use than speaker-dependent systems, they tend to be larger and require more power. Figure 3.31 shows a screenshot for Nuance Voice Control (http://www.nuance.com/voicecontrol/), which is a popular speaker–independent system. Nuance Voice Control lets users make phone calls, set appointments, dictate short emails and view web pages on Blackberry, Treo, or Pocket PC using voice commands instead of typing.

Output Devices and Methods

Although several alternative input devices and methods are available for handheld devices, the options for output devices and methods are more limited, with the main output device for a handheld being its screen. Handheld devices normally use synchronization technology to print data and files via PCs; handheld printers are available, but they are not common. Figure 3.32 shows a FUJIFILM's Pivi MP-100 camera-phone *mobile printer* using infrared transmission. It is about the same size as a CD and prints a picture in 21 seconds.

Polymer Vision (n.d.) has developed an innovative *rollable display* module, which can be held in one hand because its screen can be rolled up in a pen-sized case. It includes various functions, e.g., it could be acting as e-books or smart cellular phones using various wired or wireless connections such as Bluetooth and

Figure 3.32. Pivi MP-100 camera-phone mobile printer © 2008 FUJIFILM Corporation

Figure 3.33. A 5-inch, 16-grey-level, rollable screen © 2008 Polymer Vision

USB. For e-books, users are able to read books/articles for 30 hours without battery charge after they are downloaded into internal or external storage up to 8 GB. The 3G HSDPA tri-band phone allows worldwide calls and high speed instant updates from personally selected news sources, special services and email. The 5-inch, 16-grey-level, rollable display, as shown in Figure 3.33, is made of organic thin file transistor backplane with electro-phoretic front plane, making them extremely robust compared to the one made of glass.

MEMORY AND STORAGE

Desktop PCs or notebooks usually have between a few hundred Mbytes and a few Gbytes of memory available for users, whereas handheld devices typically have only few tens or hundreds of Mbytes. PDAs normally have more storage space than smart cellular phones, with the former commonly having 64 Mbytes, and the latter a memory size that may be as low as a few Mbytes. Four types of storage are usu-

Table 3.5. A comparison of the four kinds of storage available for handheld devices

	Capacity	Erasable	Price Per Unit	Speed	Volatile	Writable
Flash Memory	~ 200 MB	Yes	3rd	3rd	No	Yes
Hard Disks	~ 10 GB	Yes	4th	4th	No	Yes
RAM	~ 100 MB	Yes	1st (highest)	2nd	Yes	Yes
ROM	~ 100 MB	No	2nd	1st (fastest)	No	No

ally employed by handheld devices: (i) flash memory, (ii) hard disks, (iii) random access memory (RAM), and (iv) read-only memory (ROM). Table 3.5 compares these four types of storage; a comprehensive survey of storage options can be found in Scheible (2002). Today's wireless devices demand higher memory throughput for more advanced features, such as Internet browsing, e-mail, data streaming, and text messaging. Brief introduction of the four types of storage is given next:

- **Flash memory:** This is a kind of non-volatile storage similar to electrically erasable programmable read-only memory (EEPROM), but updating can only be done either in blocks or for the entire chip, making it easy to update. Flash memory is not as versatile as random access memory because RAM can be addressable down to the byte (rather than the block) level, whereas flash memory allows multiple memory locations to be erased or written in a single programming operation. However, unlike RAM chips, flash memory is a form of rewritable memory chip that is capable of preserving its content without the need for a power supply. Flash memory's price per Mbyte fell 56 percent from 2004 to 2005, followed by another 47 percent drop in 2006 and a further 35 percent in 2007. Figure 3.34 shows a Palm 3234WW flash memory card.
- **Hard disks:** Cornice, Inc. introduced the largest capacity version of its fifth generation hard drive, the ultra-slim Dragon series (Miller, 2006). Available in 8 GB and 12 GB versions, each of which is only 1-inch across, the Dragon series is claimed to be 40 percent smaller than both its predecessors and the drives currently available from its competitors, thus allowing hardware vendors to add larger amounts of storage in smaller devices. Cornice also decreased the power consumption of Dragon by half in the 12 GB model, with the result

Figure 3.34. Palm 3234WW flash memory card © 2008 Palm, Inc.

Figure 3.35. A 1-in 12 GB hard drive © 2008 Cornice Inc.

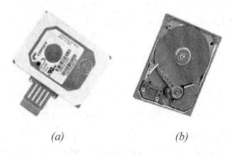

(a)   *(b)*

that it should account for only five percent of the total battery drain within a typical MP3 player system. The new Dragon series drives are protected by Cornice's Crash Guard system, so they are expected to be able to withstand excessive shaking, extreme drops, and other abuse without skipping, stopping, or crashing. Figure 3.35 shows both (a) exterior and (b) interior views of one of the new 1″ 12 GB Dragon hard drives from Cornice Inc.

- **RAM (Random Access Memory):** There are two basic types of RAM, dynamic RAM (DRAM) and static RAM (SRAM). Dynamic RAM, the more common type, needs to be refreshed thousands of times per second in order to hold data, whereas static RAM does not need to be refreshed, making it faster but also more expensive than dynamic RAM. Both types of RAM are volatile; i.e., they do not retain their contents when the power is switched off.
- **ROM (Read-Only Memory):** ROM is manufactured with fixed contents and is usually used to store the programs that boot up the device and perform diagnostics. It is inherently non-volatile storage, in contrast to RAM.

Currently, the cost of NAND flash memory per Mbyte is three times as much as for a minidrive and 100 times as much as for a large capacity drive. Hard drives generally hold up to 400 Gbytes in PCs and up to 120 Gbytes in laptops, while compact-flash-sized minidrives hold up to 6 Gbytes. There are two obstacles preventing flash memory replacing the hard drive:

- Flash memory technology's higher price makes it difficult for the technology to compete with hard drives in larger devices.
- Software applications grow even bigger, thereby requiring more storage capacity.

Flash memory will always be more expensive than hard drives, but in small capacity devices such as digital cameras, cell phones, and embedded controllers, flash memory's benefits are likely to could compensate for its higher costs.

BATTERIES

Replaceable, rechargeable lithium-ion batteries are most commonly used in handheld devices. In smartphones using this kind of battery, the talking time, standby time, and full recharging time currently take a couple of hours, a few hundred hours, and a couple of hours, respectively, and the browsing time will be slightly shorter than the talking time. In the future, it should be possible to use handheld devices without the need to recharge them frequently by replacing the lithium-ion batteries with fuel cells, which although they are not yet practicable are likely to represent the best choice in the long-term. Table 3.6 provides a comparison between lithium-ion batteries and fuel cells, and detailed descriptions are given below.

- **Lithium-Ion Batteries:** Replaceable and rechargeable, lithium-ion batteries are commonly used by handheld devices and their prices have dropped quickly. They generate electricity by chemical reactions and currently provide one of the best energy-per-weight ratios available for rechargeable batteries. However, the life of this kind of battery is short, generally only a few hours of operating time and few hundred hours of standby time. Figure 3.36 shows a BlackBerry C-S2 Lithium-Ion battery, which is used for the BlackBerry 8700 and 7100 series.
- **Fuel cells:** Battery technology will not significantly improve unless and until manufacturers begin to switch to fuel cells, which is unlikely in the near future. A fuel cell operates like a battery, but unlike a battery does not run down or require recharging and will continue to produce energy in the form of electricity and heat as long as fuel is supplied. A fuel cell turns fuel such as hydrogen into electricity using the oxygen in air and a catalyst. The fuel

Table 3.6. A comparison between lithium-ion batteries and fuel cells

	Contents	Output	Type & Method
Lithium-Ion Battery	Lithium ions	Electricity	Rechargeable using a power outlet
Fuel Cell	Natural gas	Electricity and water	Refuelable using fuel such as natural gas

Figure 3.36. A BlackBerry C-S2 Lithium-Ion battery © 2008 Research In Motion Limited

cell harnesses chemical energy trapped in the fuel and converts it into kinetic energy, in this case electricity, without fossil fuels, combustion, or polluting emissions. It offers the prospect of serving as a remarkably efficient and clean source of renewable energy, replacing both batteries and engines in handheld devices. Since the fuel cell relies on chemical energy rather than combustion, its emissions are much lower than emissions from the cleanest existing fuel combustion processes.

DATA SYNCHRONIZATION

Where multiple applications hold the same sets of data, such as addresses, and a change in the state of one of the shared objects is implemented in one application, this change needs to be propagated to the other applications that share that data. The process of sending, receiving, and updating data between multiple systems is called *data synchronization*. One example is when a user keeps a phonebook on both his or her desktop PC and a handheld device. Using data synchronization technology, the user can synchronize the phonebooks on both machines constantly and thus does not need to worry about any inconsistencies between the two phonebooks. Synchronization connects handheld devices to desktop computers, notebooks, and peripherals in order to transfer or synchronize data. Traditional synchronization

Table 3.7. A comparison among the three synchronization methods

	Serial Cables	Infrared Port	Bluetooth Wireless Technology
Price	Low	Medium	High
Transmission Distance	About 1 meter (the cable length)	Up to 1 meter	Less than 100 meters
Transmission Rate	Up to 100 Kbits/s	Up to 16 Mbits/s	Several Mbits/s
Wireless?	No	Yes	Yes

Figure 3.37. A series cable connecting an HP iPAQ and a PC

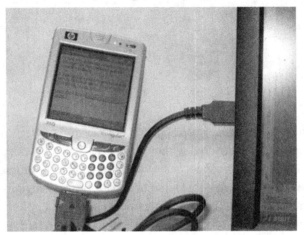

uses serial cables to connect handheld devices and other computing equipment, as shown in Figure 3.38, but nowadays many handheld devices use either an infrared (IR) port or Bluetooth technology to send information to other devices without needing to use cables. Table 3.7 gives a comparison of these three synchronization methods.

Serial Cables

The traditional method of synchronization uses serial cables to connect handheld devices and other computing equipment, as shown in Figure 3.37. For example, cables are generally provided with a digital camera so that the camera can be con-

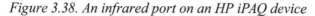

Figure 3.38. An infrared port on an HP iPAQ device

nected to a personal computer and images downloaded onto the computer hard disk. Some cameras also include an audio visual cable to enable images to be displayed on a television. Both utilize Universal Serial Bus (USB) technology, a protocol for transferring data to and from digital devices, and many digital cameras and memory card readers connect directly to the USB port on a computer. USB card readers are typically faster than cameras or readers that connect to the serial port, but slower than those that connect via FireWire. USB is a highly versatile connectivity specification developed by Intel and other technology industry leaders and is arguably the most successful interconnect in computing history. Originally released in 1995 at 12 Mbps, USB today operates at 480 Mbps and can be found in over 2 billion PC, CE, and mobile devices. In addition to high performance and ubiquity, USB enjoys strong consumer brand recognition and a reputation for ease-of-use.

Infrared Port

IrDA Data (Infrared Data Association, 2003), a standard formulated by the Infrared Data Association to ensure the quality and interoperability of infrared hardware, is designed for data transfer over distances of up to one meter, acting as a point-to-point cable replacement. Figure 3.38 shows an infrared port on a Compaq device.

Bluetooth Wireless Technology

Bluetooth wireless technology is a short-range communications technology intended to replace the cables connecting portable and/or fixed devices while maintaining high levels of security. It is designed to simplify communications among handheld devices, printers, computers, and other devices based on short-range radio technology. The Bluetooth specification defines a uniform structure for a wide range of devices to

Figure 3.39. Devices communicating with a notebook using Bluetooth

connect and communicate with each other. It has achieved global acceptance such that any Bluetooth enabled device, almost everywhere in the world, can connect to any other nearby Bluetooth enabled devices. The Bluetooth 2.1 specifications (Bluetooth SIG, Inc., 2004) consist of two documents:

- *the Core*, which provides design specifications, and
- *the Profile*, which provides interoperability guidelines.

Figure 3.39 shows a PDA and a smartphone communicating with a notebook using Bluetooth

Bluetooth enabled electronic devices connect and communicate wirelessly through short-range, ad hoc networks known as piconets. Each device can simultaneously communicate with up to seven other devices within a single piconet and can belong to several piconets simultaneously. Piconets are established dynamically and automatically as Bluetooth enabled devices enter and leave radio proximity. A fundamental Bluetooth wireless technology strength is the ability to simultaneously handle both data and voice transmissions, enabling users to use a hands-free headset for voice calls, print out documents, send faxes, and synchronize their PDA, laptop, and mobile phone applications. It has the following features:

- **Core specification versions:**
  o Version 2.0 + Enhanced Data Rate (EDR), adopted November, 2004
  o Version 1.2, adopted November, 2003
- **Spectrum:** Bluetooth technology operates in the unlicensed industrial, scientific and medical (ISM) band at 2.4 to 2.485 GHz, using a spread spectrum,

frequency hopping, full-duplex signal at a nominal rate of 1600 hops/sec. The 2.4 GHz ISM band is available and unlicensed in most countries.

- **Interference:** Bluetooth technology's adaptive frequency hopping (AFH) capability was designed to reduce interference between wireless technologies sharing the 2.4 GHz spectrum. AFH works within the spectrum to take advantage of the available frequency by detecting other devices operating in the same spectrum and avoiding the frequencies they are using. This adaptive hopping allows for more efficient transmission within the spectrum, providing users with greater performance even if simultaneously using other technologies. The signal hops among 79 frequencies at 1 MHz intervals to give a high degree of interference immunity.
- **Range:** The operating range depends on the device class:
  - o Class 3 radios, which have a range of up to 1 meter or 3 feet
  - o Class 2 radios, which are most commonly found in mobile devices, have a range of 10 meters or 30 feet
  - o Class 1 radios, which are used primarily in industrial environments, have a range of 100 meters or 300 feet
- **Power:** The most commonly used radio is Class 2, which uses 2.5 mW of power. Bluetooth technology is designed to have very low power consumption. This is reinforced in the specification by allowing radios to be powered down when inactive.
- **Data rate:** 1 Mbps for Version 1.2; Up to 3 Mbps supported for Version 2.0 + EDR

SUMMARY

Internet-enabled mobile handheld devices are one of the core components of mobile commerce systems, as they are needed for mobile users to directly interact with mobile commerce applications. Understanding the devices and appreciating their functions and capabilities is vital for the success of mobile commerce applications. A handheld device relies on a wide range of disciplines and technologies for its success. To better illustrate their strengths and limitations, this chapter broke down the functions of a handheld device into six major components, which can be summarized as follows:

1. **Mobile operating systems:** Simply adapting desktop operating systems for handheld devices has proved to be ineffective; a mobile operating system needs a completely new architecture and different features in order to provide adequate services for handheld devices. A generalized mobile operating

system structure can be visualized as a six-layer stack: (i) applications; (ii) GUI; (iii) API framework; (iv) multimedia, communication infrastructure, and security; (v) computer kernel, power management, and real-time kernel; and (vi) hardware controller.

2. **Mobile central processing units:** Handheld devices are becoming more sophisticated and efficient every day and mobile users are demanding ever more functionality from their devices. To achieve this advanced functionality, in addition to the obvious feature, low cost, today's mobile processors must have the following features: (i) high performance, (ii) low power consumption, (iii) multimedia capability, and (iv) real-time capability. The cores and architectures designed by Cambridge-based ARM Holdings Ltd. have begun to dominate the mobile CPU market.

3. **Microbrowsers:** Microbrowsers are miniaturized versions of desktop browsers such as Netscape Navigator and Microsoft Internet Explorer. They provide the graphical user interfaces that allow mobile users to interact with mobile commerce applications. Microbrowsers usually use one of the following four responses to return results to the mobile user: (i) wireless language direct access, (ii) HTML direct access, (iii) HTML to wireless language conversion, and (iv) error messages.

4. **Input and output devices and methods:** Various I/O devices have been adopted by mobile handheld devices. The only major output device is the screen, but there are several popular input devices, among them: (i) keyboards, (ii) navigators, and (iii) touch screens/writing areas that need a stylus, and (iv) speech recognition.

5. **Memory and storage:** Three types of memory are usually employed by handheld devices: (i) RAM, (ii) ROM, and (iii) flash memory. Hard disks, which provide far greater storage capacity, are likely to be adopted for handheld devices in the near future.

6. **Batteries:** At present, rechargeable lithium ion batteries are most commonly used by handheld devices. However, the life of this kind of battery is short and the technology will not significantly improve unless and until manufacturers begin to switch to fuel cells, which is not likely to occur for some years.

Synchronization connects handheld devices to desktop computers, notebooks, or peripherals to transfer or synchronize data. Obviating the need for serial cables, many handheld devices now use either an infrared (IR) port or Bluetooth technology to send information to other devices. The widespread availability of handheld mobile devices and the constantly improving technology that goes into them is opening up new approaches for mobile commerce, which is consequently becoming an increasingly attractive prospect for many businesses.

REFERENCES

ACCESS Co., Ltd. (2006). *NetFront Browser v3.4 Mobile Profile*. Retrieved March 13, 2007, from http://www.access-company.com/PDF/NetFront/NFv3-4_2006.pdf

ACCESS Co., Ltd. (2007a). *Garnet OS*. Retrieved April 13, 2007, from http://www.access-company.com/PDF/garnetos_brochure.pdf

ACCESS Co., Ltd. (2007b). *NetFront Browser v3.5 Mobile Profile*. Retrieved May 10, 2007, from http://www.access-company.com/PDF/NFv35_2007.pdf

Bluetooth SIG, Inc. (2004). *Bluetooth Core Specification v2.0 + EDR*. Retrieved April 12, 2007, from http://www.bluetooth.com/NR/rdonlyres/1F6469BA-6AE7-42B6-B5A1-65148B9DB238/840/Core_v210_EDR.zip

Bogue, R. (2002). Speech recognition for the Pocket PC. *Smartphone & Pocket PC Magazine*, 5(2).

Canalys. (2007). *Smart Mobile Device Shipments Hit 118 Million in 2007, up 53% on 2006*. Retrieved March 5, 2008, from http://www.canalys.com/pr/2008/r2008021.htm

cellular-news. (2007). *Windows Mobile Driving PDA Market Growth*. Retrieved June 21, 2007, from http://www.cellular-news.com/story/23965.php

Cormie, D. (2003). *The ARM11 microarchitecture*. Retrieved July 21, 2004 from http://www.arm.com/support/59XGYS/$File/ARM11+Microarchitecture+White+Paper.pd

Davison, B. D. (2001). A Web caching primer. *IEEE Internet Computing*, 5(4), 38-45.

Dixon, K. (2003). *Symbian OS Version 7.0s—Functional Description*. Retrieved August 13, 2004, from http://www.symbian.com/technology/SymbianOSv7.0s_funcdesc2.1.pdf

Infared Data Association. (2003). *Technical Summary of "IrDA DATA" and "IrDA CONTROL."* Retrieved July 15, 2004, from http://www.irda.org/standards/standards.asp

Lawton, G. (2001). Browsing the mobile Internet. *IEEE Computer*, 35(12), 18-21.

Linux Online, Inc. (2007). *What Is Linux?* Retrieved June 03, 2007, from http://www.linux.org/info/

Microsoft Corp. (2003a). *Pocket PC*. Retrieved June 25, 2004, from http://www.microsoft.com/windowsmobile/products/pocketpc/default.mspx

Microsoft Corp. (2003b). *Smartphone*. Retrieved June 23, 2004, from http://www.microsoft.com/windowsmobile/products/smartphone/default.mspxMicrosoft Corp. (2003a)

Microsoft Corp. (n.d.). *Internet Explorer 6 for Windows CE*. Retrieved September 14, 2006, from http://msdn2.microsoft.com/en-us/library/ms918894.aspx

Miller, J. A. (2006). *Cornice Unveils 1-Inch 12 GB Hard Drive*. Retrieved August 14, 2006, from http://www.palmblvd.com/articles/2006/8/2006-8-12-Cornice-Unveils-1.html

Open Handset Alliance. (n.d.). *Android*. Retrieved from November 23, 2007, from http://www.openhandsetalliance.com/android_overview.html

Openwave Systems Inc. (2006). *Openwave Mobile Browser, Mercury Edition*. Retrieved January 3, 2007, from http://www.openwave.com/docs/products/mobile_widgets/openwave_mobile_widgets_ds.pdf

Opera Software ASA. (2007). *Opera 8.65 for Windows Mobile Beta*. Retrieved May 13, 2007, from http://www.opera.com/products/mobile/products/winmobile/

PalmInfocenter.com. (2006). *Gartner PDA Report for Q1 2006*. Retrieved June 4, 2006, from http://www.palminfocenter.com/news/8564/gartner-pda-report-for-q1-2006/

Polymer Vision. (n.d.). *Technology*. Retrieved May 12, 2007, from http://www.polymervision.com/Technology/Index.html

Research In Motion, Ltd. (2007). *BlackBerry Java Development Environment Version 4.2.1*. Retrieved May 30, 2007, from http://www.blackberry.com/knowledgecenterpublic/livelink.exe/fetch/2000/8067/645045/8655/8656/1313719/Release_Notes_and_Known_Issues_List.pdf?nodeid=1351420&vernum=0

Scheible, J. P. (2002). A survey of storage options. *IEEE Computer*, 35(12), 42-46.Scheible (2002)

Symbian Software, Ltd. (2008). *Fast Facts*. Retrieved February 12, 2008, from http://www.symbian.com/about/fastfacts/fastfacts.html

Chapter IV
Essential
Mobile–Commerce
Technology

INTRODUCTION

Without ways to conduct secure commercial information exchange and safe electronic financial transactions over mobile networks, neither service providers nor potential customers will trust mobile commerce. Various mobile security procedures and payment methods have been proposed and applied to mobile commerce, and this chapter attempts to provide a comprehensive overview of these approaches and the issues involved. A secure mobile commerce system must have the following properties: (i) confidentiality, (ii) authentication, (iii) integrity, (iv) authorization, (v) availability, and (vi) non-repudiation. A discussion of the security issues related to the three network paradigms, wireless local area networks, wireless wide area networks, and WAP, is also included. Among the many themes of mobile commerce security, mobile payment methods are probably the most important. A typical mobile payment process includes: (i) registration, (ii) payment submission, (iii) authentication and authorization by a content provider, and (iv) confirmation. This chapter also describes a set of standards for mobile payments.

WIRELESS NETWORKS

Network infrastructure provides essential voice and data communication capability for consumers and vendors in cyberspace. As part of the evolution from electronic commerce (EC) to mobile commerce (MC), it is necessary for the existing wired network infrastructure, i.e. the Internet, to be augmented by a series of wireless networks that support mobility for end users. Wireless networking technologies are advancing at a tremendous pace and each represents a solution for a certain phase, whether 1G, 2G, and 3G, in a particular geographical area such as the United States, Europe, or Japan. In this section, they will be categorized in terms of their radio coverage as wireless local area networks, wireless metropolitan area networks, or wireless wide area networks.

Mobile Middleware

The term middleware refers to the software layer that lies between the operating system and the distributed applications that interact via the networks. The primary mission of a middleware layer is to hide the underlying networked environment's complexity by insulating applications from explicit protocols designed to handle disjoint memories, data replication, network faults, and parallelism (Geihs, 2001). Mobile middleware translates requests from mobile stations to a host computer and adapts content from the host to the mobile station (Saha, Jamtgaard, & Villasenor, 2001).

WAP and i-mode

According to an article "Frequently asked questions about NTT-DoCoMo's i-mode" (Eurotechnology Japan K.K., n.d.), 60 percent of the world's wireless Internet users use i-mode, 39 percent use WAP, and 1 percent use Palm middleware in 2002. Table 4.1 compares i-mode and WAP, along with details of each.

WAP (Wireless Application Protocol). WAP (2003) is an open, global specification that allows users with mobile stations to easily access and interact with information and services instantly. It is a very flexible standard including most wireless networks, which comprise CDPD, CDMA, GSM, PDC, PHS, TDMA, FLEX, ReFLEX, iDEN, TETRA, DECT, DataTAC, Mobitex, and GRPS. It is supported by most operating systems and was specifically engineered for mobile stations, including PalmOS, EPOC, Windows CE, FLEXOS, OS/9, and JavaOS. The most important technology applied by WAP is probably the WAP Gateway, which translates requests from the WAP protocol stack to the WWW stack so they

Table 4.1. Comparisons of two major kinds of mobile middleware

	WAP	**i-mode**
Developer	WAP Forum	NTT DoCoMo
Function	A protocol	A complete mobile Internet service
Host Language	WML (Wireless Markup Language)	CHTML (Compact HTML)
Major Technology	WAP Gateway	TCP/IP modifications
Key Features	Widely adopted and flexible	Highest number of users and easy to use

can be submitted to Web servers. For example, requests from mobile stations are sent as a URL through the network to the WAP Gateway; responses are sent from the Web server to the WAP Gateway in HTML and are then translated to WML and sent to the mobile stations. Although WAP supports HTML and XML, its host language is WML (Wireless Markup Language), which is a markup language based on XML that is intended for use in specifying content and user interfaces for mobile stations. WAP also supports WMLScript, which is similar to JavaScript but makes minimal demands on memory and CPU power because it does not contain many of the unnecessary functions found in other scripting languages.

i-mode. i-mode (NTT DoCoMO, Inc. n.d.) is the full-color, always-on, and packet-switched Internet service for cellular phones offered by NTT DoCoMo. Introduced in February 1999, it has attracted over 36 million subscribers worldwide. With i-mode, cellular phone users can easily access more than 62,000 Internet sites, as well as specialized services such as e-mail, on-line shopping and banking, ticket reservations, and personalized ringtones that can be downloaded for their phones. The i-mode network structure not only provides access to i-mode and i-mode-compatible contents through the Internet, but also uses a dedicated leased-line circuit for added security. i-mode is the only network in the world that currently allows subscribers continuous access to the Internet via cellular phones. Users are charged based on the volume of data transmitted, rather than the amount of time spent connected. In spring 2001, NTT DoCoMo introduced its next-generation mobile system, based on wideband CDMA (W-CDMA), which can support speeds of 384Kbps or faster, allowing users to download videos and other bandwidth-intensive content with its high-speed packet data communications.

Implementation

Both WAP and i-mode are built on top of existing network protocols such as Internet Protocol (IP) and Transmission Control Protocol (TCP). IP provides a network routing service for upper layer protocols like TCP, which transports data reliably between two end parties of a network connection. This reliable data delivery service is crucial to the success of transactions in mobile commerce systems. In a wireless environment, IP and TCP require significant modification in order to adapt to features like mobility and radio communication.

Mobile IP. Mobile IP (The IETF Working Group, 2003) defines enhancements that permit Internet Protocol (IP) nodes (hosts and routers) using either IPv4 or IPv6 to seamlessly "roam" among IP subnetworks and media types. It supports transparency above the IP layer, including the maintenance of active TCP connections and UDP port bindings. Two types of mobile-IP capable router, home agent (HA) and foreign agent (FA), are defined to assist routing when the mobile node is away from its home network. All datagrams destined for the mobile node are intercepted by HA and tunneled to FA. FA then delivers these packets to the mobile node through a care-of-address established when the mobile node is attached to FA.

TCP for mobile networks. Transmission Control Protocol (TCP) was designed for reliable data transport on wired networks and its parameters have been fine-tuned for such environments. As a result, when it is applied directly to mobile networks, TCP performs poorly due to factors such as the error-prone nature of data transmission on wireless channels, which often suffer from frequent handoffs and disconnections. In order to optimize reliable data transport performance, a number of variants of TCP have been suggested for mobile networks. An idea proposed by Yavatkar and Bhagawat (1994) was to split the path between the mobile node and the fixed node into two separate sub-paths: one of which covers the wireless links and the other the wired links. This approach limits the TCP performance degradation to that incurred in the "short" wireless link connection. The "packet caching" scheme proposed by Balakrishnan *et al.* (1995) tries to reduce the TCP retransmission overhead due to handoff, while the "fast retransmission" scheme suggested by Caceres and Iftode (1996) utilizes the fast retransmission option immediately after handoff is completed to achieve smooth TCP performance during handoff.

Wireless Local Area Networks

Devices used in wireless local area network (*WLAN*) technologies are light-weight, portable, and flexible in network configuration. As a result, WLANs are suitable for office networks, home networks, *personal area networks (PANs)*, and ad hoc networks. In a one-hop WLAN environment, where an access point (AP) acting as

Table 4.2. Major WLAN standards

Standard	Maximum Data Rate	Typical Range (m)	Modulation	Frequency Band
Bluetooth	1 Mbps	5 – 10	GFSK	2.4 GHz
802.11b (Wi-Fi)	11 Mbps	50 – 100	HR-DSSS	2.4 GHz
802.11a	54 Mbps	50 – 100	OFDM	5 GHz
HyperLAN2	54 Mbps	50 – 300	OFDM	5 GHz
802.11g	54 Mbps	50 – 150	OFDM	2.4 GHz

a router or switch is a part of a wired network, mobile devices connect directly to the AP through radio channels and data packets are relayed by the AP to the other end of a network connection. If no APs are available, mobile devices can form a wireless ad hoc network among themselves and exchange data packets or perform business transactions as necessary.

In Table 4.2, major WLAN technologies are compared in terms of their maximum data transfer rate (channel bandwidth), typical transmission range, modulation techniques, and operational frequency bands. The various combinations of modulation schemes and frequency bands make up different standards, resulting in different throughputs and coverage ranges. A detailed coverage of modulation techniques is beyond the scope of this chapter, but interested readers can refer to Chapter 3 of the book by Pahlavan & Krishnamurthy (2002).

In general, Bluetooth technology supports very limited coverage range and throughput and is thus only suitable for applications in personal area networks. In many parts of the world, the IEEE 802.11b (Wi-Fi) system has become the most popular wireless network and is widely used in offices, homes, and public spaces such as airports, shopping malls, and restaurants. However, many experts predict that with their much higher transmission speeds, 802.11a and 802.11g will replace 802.11b in the near future.

Wireless Metropolitan Area Network

The most important technology in this category is the cellular wireless network, with which cellular system users can conduct mobile commerce operations using their cellular phones. Under this scenario, a cellular phone connects directly to the closest base station, where communications are relayed to the service site through a radio access network (RAN) and other fixed networks. Originally designed for voice-only communication, cellular systems are evolving from analog to digital, and from circuit-switched to packet-switched networks, in order to accommodate mobile

Table 4.3. Major cellular wireless networks

Generation	Radio Channels	Switching Technique	Standards (Examples)
1G	Analog voice channels Digital control channels	Circuit-switched	AMPS TACS
2G	Digital channels	Circuit-switched	GSM TDMA
		Packet-switched	CDMA
2.5G	Digital channels	Packet-switched	GPRS EDGE
3G	Digital channels	Packet-switched	CDMA2000 WCDMA
4G	Digital channels	Packet-switched	WiMAX

commerce and other data applications. Table 4.3 lists the classifications of standards in first generation (1G), second generation (2G, 2.5G), and third generation (3G) wireless cellular networks. 1G systems such as the advanced mobile phone system (AMPS) and total access control system (TACS) are becoming obsolete, and thus will not play a significant role in mobile commerce systems. The global system for mobile communications (GSM) and its enhancement *general packet radio service (GPRS)* have primarily been developed and deployed in Europe. GPRS can support data rates of only about 100 kbps, but its upgraded version—enhanced data for global evolution (EDGE)—is capable of supporting 384 kbps. In the United States, wireless operators use *time division multiple access (TDMA)* and code division multiple access (CDMA) technologies in their cellular networks.

Currently, most cellular wireless networks follow 2G or 2.5G standards. However, there is no doubt that in the near future, 3G systems with quality-of-service (QoS) capability will dominate wireless cellular services. The two main standards for 3G are *Wideband CDMA (WCDMA)*, proposed by Ericsson, and CDMA2000, proposed by Qualcomm. Both use direct sequence spread spectrum (DSSS) in a 5-MHz bandwidth. Technical differences between them include their different chip rate, frame time, spectrum used, and time synchronization mechanism. The WCDMA system can inter-network with GSM networks and has been strongly supported by the European Union, which calls it the *Universal Mobile Telecommunications System (UMTS)*. CDMA2000 is backward-compatible with IS-95, which is widely deployed in the United States.

In a wireless cellular system, a wired network known as a radio access network (RAN) is employed to connect radio transceivers with core networks. Two examples

Figure 4.1. UMTS and UTRAN architecture (Vriendt et al., 2002)

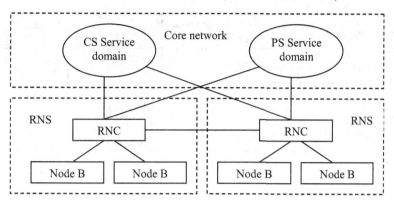

of existing RAN architectures are UTRAN (UTRAN overall description, 1999) and IOS (MSC to BS interface inter-operability specification, 1999). Since UTRAN is the new radio access network designed especially for 3G UMTS, the universal mobile telecommunications system, it deserves further description.

The architecture and components of UMTS and *UMTS Terrestrial Radio Access Network (UTRAN)* are shown in Figure 4.1 (Vriendt *et al.*, 2002). At the highest level, the UMTS network structure consists of the core network and UTRAN. The network subsystem (NSS) of GSM/GPRS is reused as much as possible in the UMTS core network. Two service domains are supported in the core network, circuit switching (CS) and packet switching (PS). By moving the NSS transcoder function from the base station subsystem to the core network, CS provides voice and circuit-switched data services. Evolving from GPRS, the packet-switched service provided by PS optimizes functional relationships between the core network and UTRAN. UTRAN consists of radio network subsystems (RNS), each of which contains one radio network controller (RNC) and at least one Node B (base station). The RNC controls the logical resources for Node Bs in the UTRAN, while the Node Bs in turn manage radio transmission and reception for one or more cells and provide logical resources to the RNC.

Wireless Wide Area Networks

In large geographic areas that lack the infrastructure of wireless cellular networks, satellite systems can be utilized to provide wireless communication services. Communication through satellites is very similar to the scenario in cellular systems, apart

Table 4.4. Major satellite systems

Satellite System	Height of Orbit (km)	Coverage	Latency (ms)
Geosynchronous Earth Orbit (GEO)	35,863	1/3 of earth surface	270
Medium Earth Orbit (MEO)	5,000 – 12,000	A few thousand kilometers	35 – 85
Low Earth Orbit (LEO)	500 – 1,500	Two thousand kilometers	1 – 7

from the differences in transmission distance and coverage range. For example, a user in an airplane can use a satellite communication system to conduct mobile commerce transactions. The messages will first be sent to a base station then forwarded to service provider sites. Satellite systems are generally categorized by the height of the orbit. Table 4.4 summaries their characteristics.

In general, there are three communication configurations in satellite systems: point-to-point links, broadcast links, and VSAT. Point-to-point link configuration means two ground-based antennas establish a point-to-point link through a satellite. Broadcast links are configured so that a single ground-based transmitter can establish a multicast channel with a number of ground-based receivers through the satellite. When subscriber stations are equipped with a low-cost *very small aperture terminal (VSAT)* system, they share satellite transmission capacity for transmission to a hub station and the hub station can exchange and relay messages between subscribers. VSAT can thus provide two-way communication among subscribers.

MOBILE COMMERCE SECURITY

Secure commercial information exchange and safe electronic financial transactions are essential for both service providers and potential customers. Various mobile security procedures have therefore been proposed and applied to mobile commerce. A secure mobile commerce system must have the following properties: (i) confidentiality, (ii) authentication, (iii) integrity, (iv) authorization, (v) availability, and (vi) non-repudiation. This section discusses the security issues related to the following three network paradigms: (i) wireless local area networks, (ii) wireless wide area networks, and (iii) WAP. The future of mobile commerce depends on its ability to securely and safely exchange information between mobile users and content providers. However, applying the security and payment technologies originally designed for electronic commerce to mobile commerce has been less than helpful because electronic commerce and mobile commerce are based on fundamentally different infrastructures (wired versus wireless). A wide variety of security procedures have therefore been developed specifically for mobile commerce. These technologies are extremely diverse and complicated and a comprehensive discussion concerning them is still awaited. Mobile commerce applications are built on top of the existing network infrastructure of wired networks, such as the Internet; wireless networks, such as wide area 3G cellular networks; and Wi-Fi wireless local area networks (WLAN). Therefore, security issues in mobile commerce are tightly coupled with network security.

Properties and Requirements of Mobile Commerce Security

First and foremost, the theme of this section, mobile commerce security, is defined as the technological and managerial procedures applied to mobile commerce transactions to provide the following functions for mobile commerce data and systems:

- **Confidentiality:** The information and systems must not be disclosed to unauthorized persons, processes, or devices.
- **Authentication:** This ensures that parties to a transaction are not impostors and are trustworthy.
- **Integrity:** The information and systems have not been altered or corrupted by outside parties.
- **Authorization:** Procedures must be provided to verify that the user can make the requested purchases.
- **Availability:** An authorized user must have timely, reliable access to information in order to perform mobile commerce transactions.
- **Non-repudiation:** Ensures a user cannot deny they performed a transaction; the user is provided with proof of the transaction and the recipient is assured of the user's identity.

These procedures involve a variety of policies and processes, along with the hardware and software tools necessary to protect the mobile commerce systems and transactions and the information processed, stored, and transmitted by them.

It is first necessary to examine what kind of features mobile commerce security and payment methods are expected to have in order to conduct effective and efficient mobile commerce transactions and what kind of challenges may be faced in the process of developing new mobile commerce security and payment methods. The requirements for mobile commerce security include:

1. Confidentiality, authentication, integrity, authorization, availability, and non-repudiation must be rigorously enforced.
2. They should be interoperable for most systems.
3. They should be acceptable for both current and future systems at minimal cost.
4. They should allow content providers to provide affordable, easy-to-use, efficient and interoperable payment methods to users.
5. No mobile commerce transactions are deferred or deterred because of their deployment.

Security Basics

Without confidence in the security of the underlying networking technologies, mobile commerce will be unimaginable. Network security usually involves communications between two or more participating entities, but the term "security" covers many different aspects. In this section we will focus on those features that are most important to mobile commerce systems.

Security Services

A mobile commerce system needs to provide security services to its participating entities so that business can be conducted successfully in electronic form. These security services include:

- *Authentication.* Before business transactions can be performed, the participating entities (usually the sender and receiver) must confirm each others' identities. This service prevents an unauthorized third-party from masquerading as one of the legitimate parties. Authentication is usually achieved using network-based authentication protocols.
- *Data confidentiality/secrecy.* In an electronic business transaction, it is assumed that only the sender and intended receiver(s) will be able to read the transmitted messages in cleartext. Providing data confidentiality prevents eavesdroppers or interceptors from understanding the secret communication. This is usually accomplished using computer-based cryptographic encryption and decryption computation.
- *Data integrity.* It should not be possible for a transmitted message to be altered, whether accidentally or maliciously, without this being detected at the receiver side of a mobile commerce system. With this security feature, an interceptor is not able to deceive the receiver by modifying the content of a message in transmission. Adding secure electronic signatures to messages provides data integrity.

- *Non-repudiation.* Mobile commerce transactions are official business deals. Neither the sender nor receiver should be able to deny the existence of a legitimate transaction afterwards. That is, the sender must be able to prove that the specified receiver received the message and the receiver must be able to prove that the specified sender did in fact send the message. This is usually done using digital signature techniques.
- *Availability.* The availability of a mobile commerce system ensures that legitimate users can access the business service reliably and securely. The system should be designed to minimize the impact of events such as malicious denial-of-service (DoS) attacks, which can cause mobile commerce services to become unstable or unusable for long periods of time. Deploying network security devices such as firewalls and configuring them along with associated protocols properly is the key to ensuring service availability.

Security Mechanisms

Security services in the modern world must take advantage of the latest advances in computation technology, both hardware and software. To achieve these security goals, digital data are encrypted and decrypted based on cryptographic algorithms. There are two categories of cryptographic algorithms: symmetric key systems and asymmetric key systems.

- *Symmetric key systems.* In this category, the sender and receiver participating in a secure session both own the same digital key. The sender encrypts messages using this key and then sends it to the receiver through the public network. The receiver then decrypts the messages received using the same key. This digital key, however, is never transmitted over the network in cleartext, thus preventing a third-party from obtaining it and thus compromising the secure communication. To agree upon this symmetric key requires both sides to use outside channels, such as a telephone conversation, or a specially designed key distribution center (KDC). The data encryption standard (DES), triple-DES (3DES), and advanced encryption standard (AES) are symmetric key systems.
- *Asymmetric key systems.* These are also called "public key systems." Unlike in symmetric key systems, a participating entity in an asymmetric key system uses two keys–a public key that is accessible to everyone in the world and a private key known only to itself. Applying one or both of these two keys in different orders to data messages provides security services such as authentication and digital signature. The famous RSA algorithm is an example of an asymmetric key system.

Mobile Security

As discussed earlier, mobile security is a crucial issue for mobile commerce. From a technical point of view, mobile commerce over wireless networks is inherently insecure compared to electronic commerce over wired networks. The reasons are as follows:

- **Reliability and integrity:** Interference and fading make the wireless channel inherently error prone. Frequent handoffs and disconnections also degrade the security of wireless services.
- **Confidentiality/Privacy:** The broadcast nature of the radio channel makes it easier for an outsider to tap into. Thus, communication can be intercepted and interpreted without difficulty if security mechanisms such as cryptographic encryption are not employed.
- **Identification and authentication:** The mobility of wireless devices introduces an additional difficulty in identifying and authenticating mobile terminals.
- **Capability:** Wireless devices usually have limited computation capability, memory size, communication bandwidth, and battery power. This makes it difficult to utilize high-level security schemes such as 256-bit encryption.

Security issues span the whole mobile commerce system, from one end to the other, from the top to the bottom network protocol stack, from machines to humans. We will focus only on issues exclusively related to mobile/wireless technologies. Lacking a unified wireless security standard, different wireless technologies support different aspects and levels of security features. We will thus discuss some well-known wireless network standards and their corresponding security issues (Tanenbaum, 2002).

Network Infrastructure and Security

Network infrastructure provides essential voice and data communication capability for consumers and vendors in cyberspace. When progressing from electronic commerce (EC) to mobile commerce (MC), it is necessary for a wired network infrastructure such as the Internet to be augmented by wireless networks that support mobility for end users. Mobile commerce is possible mainly because of the availability of wireless networks. User requests are delivered to either the closest wireless access point (in a wireless local area network environment) or a base station (in a cellular network environment). Although the wired network is not essential in a mobile commerce system, most mobile commerce servers reside on wired networks and user requests are frequently routed to these servers using transport and/or security mechanisms provided by wired networks. However our focus in this section is on the unique aspects of the mobile commerce network infrastructure, which is by definition a wireless mobile network, therefore we have chosen to omit any discussion of wired networks.

Wireless communication capability supports mobility for end users in mobile commerce systems. Wireless LAN and WAN are major components used to provide radio communication channels so that mobile service is possible. In the WLAN category, the Wi-Fi standard with 11 Mbps throughput dominates the current market, although it is expected that standards with much higher transmission speeds, such as IEEE 802.11a and 802.11g, will replace Wi-Fi in the near future. Cellular networking technologies are advancing at a tremendous pace and each represents a solution for a certain phase, such as 1G, 2G, and 3G, in a particular geographical area, such as the United States, Europe, or Japan. Compared to WLANs, cellular systems can provide longer transmission distances and greater radio coverage, but suffer from the drawback of much lower bandwidth (less than 1 Mbps). In the latest trend for cellular systems, 3G standards supporting wireless multimedia and high-bandwidth services are beginning to be deployed. WCDMA and CDMA2000 are likely to dominate the market in the future.

Wireless Local Area Networks and Security

The major WLAN standards were described earlier in the chapter and are shown in Table 4.2. Security issues specific to WLANs can be dealt with in two ways:

Wi-Fi security. The security provisions in the IEEE 802.11 WLAN standard are based on the use of a data link level protocol called Wired Equivalent Privacy (WEP). When it is enabled, each mobile host has a secret key that is shared with the base station. The encryption algorithm used in WEP is a stream cipher based on RC4. The ciphertext is generated by XORing the plaintext with a RC4 generated keystream. However, recently published literature has discovered methods for breaking this approach (Borisov, Goldberg, & Wagner, 2001; Fluhrer, Martin, & Shamir, 2001; Stubblefield, Ioannidis, & Rubin, 2002). The next version, 802.11i, is expected to have better security.

Bluetooth security. Bluetooth provides security by using frequency hopping in the physical layer, sharing secret keys (called passkeys) between the slave and the master, encrypting communication channels, and controlling integrity. Encryption in Bluetooth is a stream cipher called "E_0", while for integrity control a block cipher called "SAFER+" is used. However, "E_0" has potential weaknesses (Jakobsson &

Wetzel, 2001; Biryukov, Shamir, & Wagner, 2000) and "SAFER+" is slower than the other similar symmetric-key block ciphers.

Wireless Wide Area Network and Security

As discussed earlier, the most important technology in this category is the cellular wireless network. GSM and UTMS systems use different approaches to deal with security issues.

GSM security. The Subscriber Identity Module (SIM) in the GSM contains the subscriber's authentication information, such as cryptographic keys, and a unique identifier called international mobile subscriber identity (IMSI). The SIM is usually implemented as a smart card consisting of microprocessors and memory chips. The same authentication key and IMSI are stored on GSM's network side in the authentication center (AuC) and home location register (HLR), respectively. In GSM, short messages are stored in the SIM and calls are directed to the SIM rather than the mobile terminal. This feature allows GSM subscribers to share a terminal with different SIM cards. The security features provided between GSM network and mobile station include IMSI confidentiality and authentication, user data confidentiality, and signaling information element confidentiality. One of the security weaknesses identified in GSM is the one-way authentication utilized, where only the mobile station is authenticated and the network is not. This can pose a security threat, as a compromised base station can launch a "man-in-the-middle" attack without being detected by mobile stations.

UMTS security. UMTS is designed to reuse and evolve from existing core network components of the GSM/GPRS and fix known GSM security weaknesses such as the one-way authentication scheme and optional encryption. Authentication in UMTS is mutual and encryption is mandatory (unless specified otherwise) in order to prevent message replay and modification. In addition, UMTS employs longer cryptographic keys and newer cipher algorithms, which make it inherently more secure than GSM/GPRS.

WAP and Security

Beyond the link-layer communication mechanisms provided by WLANs and cellular networks, the Wireless Application Protocol (WAP) is designed to work with all wireless networks. The most important technology applied by WAP is probably the

WAP Gateway, which translates requests from the WAP protocol stack to the WWW stack so they can be submitted to Web servers. For example, requests from mobile stations are sent as a URL through the network to the WAP Gateway; responses are sent from the Web server to the WAP Gateway in HTML and are then translated to WML and sent to the mobile stations. Although WAP supports HTML and XML, its host language is WML (Wireless Markup Language), which is a markup language based on XML that is intended for use in specifying content and user interfaces for mobile stations. WAP also supports WMLScript, which is similar to JavaScript but makes minimal demands on memory and CPU power because it does not contain many of the unnecessary functions found in other scripting languages.

WAP security is provided through the Wireless Transport Layer Security (WTLS) protocol (in WAP 1.0) and IETF standard Transport Layer Security (TLS) protocol (in WAP 2.0). They provide data integrity, privacy, and authentication. One security problem, known as the "WAP Gap" is caused by the inclusion of the WAP gateway in a security session. That is, encrypted messages sent by end systems might temporarily become clear text on the WAP gateway when messages are processed. One solution is to make the WAP gateway resident within the enterprise (server) network (Ashley, Hinton, & Vandenwauver, 2001), where heavyweight security mechanisms can be enforced.

MOBILE COMMERCE PAYMENT METHODS

Among the many issues that arise with mobile commerce security, mobile payment methods are probably the most crucial. These are the methods used to pay for goods or services with a mobile handheld device. A typical mobile payment scenario is as follows:

1. A user registers for the services via an Internet-enabled mobile handheld device.
2. The user submits his/her payment for the services he/she has received.
3. The service/content provider deals with the request by authenticating and authorizing the user and then contacting a wireless service provider and a financial institution.
4. A confirmation of the completed transaction is delivered to the user.

This section examines the issues involved and describes a set of standards for mobile payments. With the development of commerce, there has been a tremendous evolution in the methods of payment, from the seashell of ancient times to coins and notes, from writing checks to on-line banking. The emergence of e-commerce has revolutionized the traditional methods of payment. With the help of mobile devices, the dream of "transaction without cash on the move" is now possible. Mobile payment enables the transfer of financial value and corresponding services or items between different participators without the need for any actual physical contact between them. The mobile device can be a wireless communication device, such as a mobile phone, a PDA, a wireless tablet, or a mobile computer. Mobile payment can be divided into two categories, generally according to the amount of transaction value. One is micro-payment, which defines a mobile payment of approximately $10 or less, often for mobile content such as video downloads or gaming. The other is macro-payment, which refers to larger value payments.

Mobile Payment Scenarios

The global spread of mobile telecommunications has been so successful that the number of mobile subscribers had risen to one billion worldwide by the end of 2002. In 2003, 60 million users spent more than $50 billion on mobile services. One survey predicted that combined e-commerce and m-commerce volumes would grow from $38 billion in 2002 to $128 billion in 2004. Accompanying this increase in subscriptions has been an evolution in the sophistication level of mobile devices, encouraging the emergence of new applications such as enhanced messaging services (EMS) and multimedia messaging services (MMS). In these applications, consumers are presented with more options, such as the download of images, streaming video, and data files as well as the addition of global positioning systems (GPS) in mobile phones, which will facilitate location-based mobile commerce and make mobile payment methods more feasible.

There are four participants in a mobile payment transaction. The mobile consumer (MC) subscribes to a product or service and pays for it via their mobile device. The content provider/merchant (CP/M) provides the appropriate digital content, physical product, or service product to the consumer. The payment service provider (PSP), which may be a network operator, a financial institution, or an independent payment vendor, controls the payment process. The trusted third party (TTP) administers the authentication of transaction parties and the authorization of the payment settlement. In fact, several of these roles can be merged into one organization, e.g. a network bank, which is capable of acting as CP/M, PSP, and TTP at the same time. In a more general sense, a PSP and TTP can be performed by the same organization.

Content Download

In this scenario, the consumer orders the content he or she wants to download from a content provider. The content provider then initiates the charging session, asking the PSP for authorization. The PSP authorizes the CP/M, and then the download starts. The transaction can be settled by either a metered or pricing model. Metered content includes streaming services, where consumers are charged according to the metered quantity of the provided service, e.g., the interval, the data volume or the number of game sessions. In a pricing model, the consumer is charged according to the items downloaded completely. A content purchase is also available via a PC Internet connection, where the mobile device can be used to authorize the payment transaction and authenticate the content user.

Point of Sale

In this scenario, services or the sale of goods are offered to the mobile user using a point of sale location instead of a virtual site, e.g., a taxi service. The merchant (e.g. the taxi driver) will initiate the payment at the point of sale. The PSP asks the mobile user to directly authorize the transaction via a SMS PIN, or indirectly via the taxi driver through a wireless Bluetooth link. The process is also applicable to purchases from a vending machine.

Content on Device

In this payment scenario, the user has the content preinstalled in his/her mobile device, but he or she must be granted a license to initiate the usage of the content, e.g., the activation of an on-demand game playing service. The license varies with usage, duration, or number of users, and determines the value that the consumer must pay for the desired content.

Mobile Payment Methods

Two common kinds of mobile commerce payment methods are

- **Macropayments:** This kind of payments is commonly used by traditional electronic commerce and involve significant amounts of money, for example more than US $10.00. Payments by credit cards are the most common method for macropayments.
- **Micropayments:** These usually involve small amounts of below about US $10.00, which are too small to be economically processed by credit cards.

Figure 4.2. A typical macropayment scenario

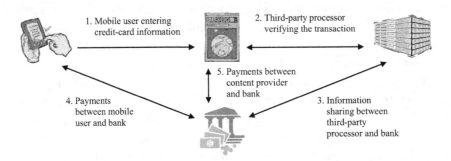

The amounts are usually charged to users' phone bills or accounts.

A typical macropayment/micropayment scenario proceeds as follows, as illustrated in Figures 4.2 and 4.3 for macro and micropayments, respectively, where the number is the order of steps taken:

1. A mobile user submits his/her credit-card or personal information to the mobile content via a handheld device.
2. A third-party processor verifies and authorizes the transaction.
3. The third-party processor routes verification and authorization requests to the card issuing bank or mobile carrier.
4. The user pays his/her monthly credit-card or phone bill.
5. The bank pays the mobile content provider or the mobile carrier pays the mobile content provider directly or through a bank after deducting a transaction fee.

Mobile Payment Operations

In a card transaction, there are usually four stages, including set-up and configuration, the initiation of the payment, authentication of the user, and completion of the payment. In the mobile payment environment, the payment methods can share the same dynamics. Within the four stages, there are certain kinds of operations among the four parties, although not all the operations may be needed, depending on the stages and scenarios.

•   **Registration.** There is a communication between the MC and CP/M that ensures that the content is accessible. During this stage, the MC uses a personal identification number (PIN) for identification and authentication. The

Figure 4.3. A typical micropayment scenario

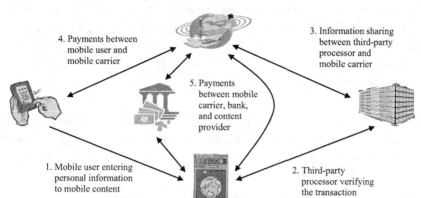

4. Payments between mobile user and mobile carrier

3. Information sharing between third-party processor and mobile carrier

5. Payments between mobile carrier, bank, and content provider

1. Mobile user entering personal information to mobile content

2. Third-party processor verifying the transaction

MC obtains service details such as the category of payment, the characteristic of the content, as well as the confirmation of the payment after the service. During this operation, an identity number is allotted to the consumer, which uniquely defines the identity of the CP/M during each transaction and a service is initiated. In general, this operation ensures the security of the payment.

- **Charging.** Once the registration is completed, the CP/M submits the authentication and authorization requests to the PSP, initiating the charging session. At the end of every service or time interval, the content provider asks for a charging operation. The PSP settles the payment according to the default scheme, notifying both parties. This is usually presented to mobile consumers in the form of a receipt.

- **Request authorization and authentication.** Before the start of a charging session, the mobile consumers must confirm that they are willing to pay for the service. This authorization request is often sent from the PSP in the form of a contract. The contract will describe the conditions and agreements between the MC and the CP/M. The charging session is initiated by the customer's acceptance of the contract. The MC is also requested to authorize the PSP. This can be settled by submitting the PIN from the MC. Authorization and authentication are completed using the same request. Authorization includes the authentication by PIN.

- **User authentication.** The PSP will notify the authentication result of the MC to the CP/M. If the return of authorization request from the MC is positive, the PSP sends the CP/M a session ID, signaling the initiation of a charging session. It is vital to distinguish between micro- and macro-payments, since the security required in the two types is distinctly different. For example, authentication for every macro-payment transaction through a trusted financial entity is extremely important, whereas network authentication, such as SIM, may be sufficient for micro-payments that only use the operator's infrastructure.

Out-of-Band Payment Method

In the "out-of-band" model, content and operation signals are transmitted in separate channels, e.g., a credit card holder may use their mobile device to authenticate and pay for a service they consume on their fixed line Internet or interactive TV. This model usually involves a system controlled by a financial institution, sometimes collaborating with a mobile operator. There are two typical cases:

- **Financial institutions.** Many banks are conducting research designed to turn an individual mobile unit into a disbursing terminal. Payments involved in the financial transaction are usually macro-payments, and various methods can be deployed to ensure the authentication of payment transactions. In credit card payments, a dual slot phone is usually adopted, while other approaches include PIN authentication via a SIM toolkit application or the use of a digital signature based on a public key infrastructure (PKI) mechanism, which requires 2.5G (or higher) technology.
- **Reverse-charge/billed SMS.** In reverse-billed premium rate SMS, the CP/M deliver content to mobile telephone handsets (ICSTIS, n.d.). Customers subscribe to a service and are charged for the messages they receive. This payment model allows consumers to use SMS text messages to pay for access to digital entertainment and content without being identified. In this application, however, it is the SMS message receiver who is charged, instead of the sender of the SMS message. There are a considerable number of vendors who use reverse-charge/billed MSM service payment models.

"Inband" Payment Method

In this method, a single channel is deployed for the transfer of both content and operation signals, for example for a chargeable WAP service over GPRS. Two models of this in-band payment are in common use, namely subscription models and per usage payment models, with the amount of the payment usually being micro-payments. In-band transactions include applications such as video streaming of sports highlights or video messaging.

Proximity

Proximity payments involve the use of wireless technologies to pay for goods and services over short distances. Proximity transactions develop the potential of mobile commerce, e.g., using a mobile device to pay at a point of sale, vending machine, ticket machine, market, or for parking. Through short range messaging protocols such as Bluetooth, infrared, RFID, and contactless chips, the mobile device can be transformed to a sophisticated terminal that is able to process both micro and macro payments (DeClercq, 2002).

Mobile Payment Standardization

Common Issues of Mobile Payment Standards

Mobile payment enables users to globally conduct payment transactions without physical contact. Unfortunately, regional distinctions and market dynamics often impose barriers that impede its development. A set of standards is required that are shared by all four of the parties involved, but dominant corporations are competing for the acceptance of their own standards, which will give them an advantage in their competition with their rivals. Among the different standards that are currently being proposed, the common issues being addressed include:

- **Security.** Fraud deters usage and damages the trust of consumers and merchants in the integrity of the payment network. In addition, it adds considerably to the cost of operation. Therefore, increased security is vital for the development of mobile payment methods to address these issues. The main security elements include:
  - **Authentication:** This allows the payment service provider to determine that the person using the payment product is the authorized user.
  - **Confidentiality:** This ensures that unauthorized parties cannot gain access to sensitive payment data.
  - **Data integrity:** This ensures that payment data is not altered.
  - **Non-repudiation:** This binds the parties to the transaction so that they cannot later deny that they participated in it.
- **Interoperability.** This strengthens any global payment system, ensuring that any participating payment product can be used at any participating merchant location.
- **Usability.** According to studies of consumers' consumption behavior, they do not like to change their established habits and tend to opt for products that are user-friendly. This observation underlies the requirement for usability.

Standardization of the Payment Lifecycle

In support of uniform payment standards, the MPF (Mobile Payment Forum) is working on standardizing the phases in the mobile payment lifecycle, namely device set-up and personalization, payment initiation, authentication and payment completion:

1. **Set-up and configuration.** When a mobile device is used to make a purchase, the owner who wants to get access to the mobile services should be able to set up the payment mechanism in the mobile environment. Set-up and configuration could take place over a mobile network or the Internet, or they could be done physically.
2. **Payment initiation.** In this step, payment information is transmitted to the merchant over a network.
3. **Authentication.** The authentication of the user is essential for any payment transaction. The MPF is considering two-way messaging authentication and SAT (SIM Alliance/Application Toolkit) authentication applications. The SAT authentication standardization includes defining a set of minimum requirements for authenticating, hence the cost of the bandwidth can be considerably reduced.
4. **Payment completion.** This process takes place after the cardholder's details have been authenticated and the transaction is authorized. In a normal physical transaction, this involves the printing of a receipt for the user to confirm that the money has been transferred. In the mobile environment, the MPF is currently studying issues concerning the format and storage of digital receipts, together with the necessary redirection mechanisms.

SET (Secure Electronic Transaction)

Developed by Visa International and MasterCard International, the Secure Electronic Transaction (SET) protocol (SET Secure Electronic Transaction Specification, Version 1.0, 1997) is likely to become the global standard in the domain of electronic commerce over the Internet. This is a technical standard designed to provide security for payment transactions among cardholders, merchants, payment gateways, and certification authorities in wired networks. The SET mechanism is complex, and thus is mostly used in desktop computers and servers.

An SET transaction typically involves a communication between four parties: the customer, the merchant, the customer's bank, and the merchant's bank. Each of these entities needs to know certain information in order to perform its part of the transaction, but none need to know all the details of the transaction. Neither bank, for instance, needs to know what the customer is buying. The merchant doesn't need to know the customer's credit card number. He just needs to know that the customer has enough credit to pay for the order. The customer doesn't need to know who the merchant banks with. Assuming that the customer has an SET-enabled browser and that the transaction provider (bank, store, etc.) has a SET-enabled server, the process works as follows.

The customer opens a Mastercard or Visa account with some issuer (a bank) of credit cards and receives a digital certificate, which represents that customer/card combination in online purchases. The certificate contains both a public key and an expiration date.

1. Merchants also receive certificates from the credit card issuer. These certificates include the merchant's public key and the public key of the merchant's bank.
2. The customer places an order over a web page by computer, phone or PDA.
3. The customer's browser requests and receives the merchant's certificate and confirms that the merchant is valid.
4. The customer's browser sends the order and payment information (as two separate components) in a message that also contains the customer's certificate. The payment information is encrypted with the merchant's bank's public key and can't be read by the merchant. The order information is encrypted with the merchant's public key and can't be read by the bank. Additional information in the message ensures the payment can only be used with this particular order.
5. The merchant verifies the customer by checking the customer's digital certificate. This may be done by referring the certificate to the bank or to a third-party verifier.
6. The merchant sends a message to the merchant's bank which contains the customer's payment information, and the merchant's certificate.
7. The merchant's bank verifies the identity of the merchant and the identity of the customer's bank, which is embedded in the payment information.
8. The merchant's bank requests a payment authorization from the customer's bank. The customer's bank sends this (if the transaction is approved) and the merchant's bank relays this back to the merchant.
9. The merchant completes the transaction with the customer, fills the order, and tells the merchant's bank (who relays this confirmation to the customer's bank) that this order has been completed.
10. The customer's bank generates billing information for the customer and settles accounts with the merchant's bank.

Because SET relies on public key encryption to verify the identities of the customer, merchant and financial institution, as well as the symmetric encryption of an SSL or S-HTTP session, its computational demands are significant.

In a mobile commerce system, a WAP client device normally does not have sufficient processing and memory capability to utilize SET software. A "thin" SET wallet approach (Jin *et al.*, 2002) has thus been proposed to adapt the SET protocol for WAP clients. Under the "thin" SET wallet model, most of the functionality of current "fat" SET wallets is moved to the wallet server. To support a SET payment, a WAP client installed with only a "thin" wallet securely connects with a wallet server, which communicates with other SET entities. When SET purchase requests arrive from the "thin" wallet, the wallet server takes over the responsibility of routing requests and managing digital keys and certificates.

Wireless cellular system operators have an advantage as they become primary mobile payment system providers, because their existing service infrastructures already contain mature subscriber authentication and billing subsystems such as SIM. They can thus act as middlemen, charging an extra service fee, when transactions between merchants and users take place using their network systems. The i-mode model is one of this type.

Another approach is referred to as the "dual-chip" solution. This uses a Wireless Identity Module (WIM) card holding cryptographic keys as a second authentication module for the WAP security service. WIM can be a part of a SIM smart card issued by a cellular system operator or it can be provided by a third party, such as a bank or a financial institution. Motorola's Star Tac Dual Slot handset is capable of reading a third-party WIM card. The mobile payment standardization currently in use was developed by several organizations, as follows:

- **Mobey Forum (n.d.):** Founded by a number of financial institutions and mobile terminal manufacturers, Mobey Forum's mission is to encourage the use of mobile technology in financial services.
- **Mobile Payment Forum (n.d.):** Sponsored by credit card companies, including American Express, MasterCard International and Visa International, the Mobile Payment Forum is dedicated to developing a framework for standardized, secure, and authenticated mobile commerce using payment card accounts.
- **Mobile electronic Transactions (MeT) Ltd. (n.d.):** Sponsored by key handset manufacturers such as Ericsson, NEC, Nokia, Panasonic, Siemens and Sony Ericsson, MeT's objective is to ensure interoperability of mobile transaction solutions. Its work is based on existing specifications and standards, including WAP.

Mobile Security Risk Management

Whenever there are risks or dangers, it is advisable to find ways of dealing with that risk. It is possible, of course, to pretend the risk does not exist and ignore it, but that is not wise when the potential consequences are great. The three main categories into which protective measures can be placed are (i) policies and procedures, (ii) awareness, education and training, and (iii) technology. Risk management also requires an examination of the cost/benefit ratio and a decision to be made as to whether or not the risk justifies the expense. Some protective measures, though desirable, will not be implemented because of the cost or the cost/benefit ratio.

Policies and Procedures

A security policy is a statement of usage rules and principles that specifies which activities are allowed and which are not allowed on that system. Policies will also typically list the rights of the users, and the rights of the employer, legal notices about copyrights and system monitoring, and a statement of management's intent to prosecute misusers. These policies are created and/or approved by high-level management and are intended to be read and adhered to by all users. Procedures are specific processes, approved by management, providing implementations or implementation guidelines that aid in enforcing the policy. By following procedures, users are forced to exercise due diligence, which protects the system from unnecessary risks and careless oversights. However, procedures are followed voluntarily by users, so they will not offer any protection against a malicious user. What happens if a PDA containing important private information is lost or misplaced? A well-established security procedure may be available to ensure an appropriate response. What types of information should have been (or NOT have been) on that PDA? Again, a security procedure could have guide decisions as to what to upload/download between a PC and PDA.

Awareness, Education, and Training

It is not feasible to write policies and procedures that cover all future events. Some are impossible to foresee, others may occur so rarely that they are simply not worth worrying about. Others may just involve the use of common sense, which it is assumed that all users will have. Thus, policies and procedures need to be augmented with some efforts to develop users' knowledge of these procedures, insight and intuition, so that they are more likely to respond correctly. Educating users and raising awareness of security concerns is a responsibility of management.

Technological Tools

Sometimes, a technological solution is available to address a security concern. If so, it may not be necessary to trust users to do the right thing because it will be done automatically by an automated tool. Link-level encryption, for instance, ensures that all transmissions are encrypted and does not rely on users to encrypt their own files before transmitting them, nor does it require the user to safeguard an encryption key. Biometric devices such as fingerprint scanners can be used to implement authentication with a higher level of confidence. Special Publication 800-48, *Wireless Network Security* from the National Institute of Standards and Technology (NIST SP800-48, November 2002) is a useful source of information and guidelines for securing systems with wireless components.

Special Risks Associated with Mobile Security

While most mobile commerce security risks are shared with non-mobile systems, there are a number of risks which are particularly associated with handheld systems and mobile commerce. Special risks that affect mobile handheld systems include:

- Wireless devices broadcast signals may be easily intercepted.
- Broadcast frequencies can be jammed. This is another technique often used in denial of service attacks.
- Handheld devices, with limited processing capability, have modest capabilities for encryption and decryption.
- There is no firewall.
- Mobile handheld devices are easily misplaced or lost. Physical security is therefore more of a problem.
- Limited storage on handheld devices means that some of a customer's private information may be stored at a WAP gateway. This makes the gateway an attractive target for attacks.

Mobile devices, as they become more powerful, will eventually fall prey to all the same types of malware that attack desktop systems and servers. This includes viruses, Trojan horses, worms and denial of service attacks. Some recent examples of such malware are described below:

- **Denial of Service attack:** In the summer of 2000, the SMS Flooder sent a massive amount of spam mail in the form of SMS messages to cell phone targets in Europe. The effect on affected cell phone users was that they were constantly being paged. This large number of SMS messages caused a considerable amount of inconvenience and frustration and effectively became a denial of service attack.

- **Computer Worm:** Cabir, reported in June 2004, is a worm that uses Bluetooth connectivity to infect smart phones running the Symbian OS and Nokia's Seris 60 software. It has been described as a nonmalicious "proof-of-concept virus". Cabir replicates itself across Bluetooth connections and arrives in a smart phone's messaging inbox as a file named caribe.sis. The phone user has to accept the message and then must allow the file (from an unknown source) to install itself before the infection is complete and Cabir can continue to spread itself. The Cabir worm can reach only mobile phones that support Bluetooth, have Bluetooth switched on, and are in discoverable mode.

A CASE STUDY: HANDHELD DATA PROTECTION USING HANDHELD USAGE PATTERN IDENTIFICATION

Mobile handheld devices such as smart cellular phones and PDAs (Personal Digital Assistants) are extremely popular and convenient. People carry them anytime, anywhere and use them to perform daily activities like making phone calls, checking schedules, and browsing the mobile Web. However, they are easily lost or stolen because of their small sizes and high mobility. Personal data such as addresses and messages stored in the devices are revealed when the devices are lost (Ghosh & Swaminatha, 2001). The following two major technologies are commonly applied to handheld data protection:

- **Password/biometric-credentials -based user identification:** Advanced devices use fingerprint, retina, or face recognition to identify the owners (Hazen, Weinstein, & Park, 2003; Weinstein *et al.*, 2002). This approach is not widely adopted because the methods are not yet practical. Most contemporary handheld devices are password protected. However, device users are often reluctant to use this because of the inconvenience of password memorization and entry.
- **Anomaly/behavior -based user identification (Shyu et al., 2005; Stolfo et al., 2006):** This approach to protecting handheld data, discussed in more detail below, detects any unauthorized uses by comparing the current usage patterns to the stored patterns. When the measured activities are outside baseline parameters or clipping levels, a built-in protection mechanism will trigger an action, for example asking for a password, before allowing further operations to proceed.

Several other approaches will be introduced in the next section of this book, Part B: Handheld Security.

The approach to handheld data protection using usage pattern identification can be divided into five steps:

1. *Usage data gathering*, which collects device usage data,
2. *Usage data preparation*, which removes noise from the raw usage data,
3. *Usage pattern discovery*, which finds valuable patterns from the prepared usage data,
4. *Usage pattern analysis and visualization*, which analyzes and displays the discovered patterns to reveal hidden information, and
5. *Usage pattern applications*, which in this case is handheld data protection.

A usage finite automaton can be constructed based on the usage data collected and prepared that is then used to check against any potentially unauthorized use. Preliminary experimental results show this method is effective and convenient for handheld data protection, but the accuracy may need to be improved.

Literature Review

This research is related to three themes: (i) mobile handheld devices, (ii) handheld security, and (iii) handheld usage mining. Related research on these themes will be discussed in this section.

Mobile Handheld Devices

A generic mobile handheld device includes five major components (Hu *et al.*, 2005):

*   **Mobile operating system or environment:** Mobile OSs, unlike desktop OSs, do not have a dominant brand. Popular mobile OSs or environments include: (i) Android, (ii) BREW, (iii) Java ME, (iv) Palm OS, (v) Symbian OS, and (vi) Windows Mobile.
*   **Mobile central processing unit:** ARM-based CPUs are the most popular mobile CPUs. ARM Ltd. does not manufacture CPUs itself. Instead, it supplies mobile CPU designs to other chip makers such as Intel and TI.
*   **Input and output components:** There is only one major output component, the screen, but there are several popular input components, in particular keyboards and touch screens/writing areas that require the use of a stylus.

- **Memory and storage:** Three types of memory are usually employed by handheld devices: (i) random access memory, (ii) read-only memory, and (iii) flash memory. Hard drives are rarely used.
- **Batteries:** Rechargeable Lithium Ion batteries are the most common batteries used by handheld devices. Fuel cells, a promising technology, are still in the early stage of development and will not be widely adopted in the near future.

Handheld Security

Many companies such as the device manufacturer Hewlett-Packard (Hewlett-Packard Development Company, L.P., 2008) and the embedded database vendor Sybase Inc. (2006) have introduced practical handheld security methods where, for example, the owners of lost devices can call the centers to remotely lock down the devices. Those methods are normally workable, but not very innovative. Susilo (2002) looked at the risks and threats of having handheld devices connected to the Internet, and proposed the use of a personal firewall to protect against these threats. Argyroudis *et al.* (2004) presented a performance analysis focused on three of the most commonly used security protocols for networking applications, namely SSL, S/MIME, and IPsec. Their results show that the time taken to perform cryptographic functions is small enough not to significantly impact real-time mobile transactions and that there is no obstacle to the use of quite sophisticated cryptographic protocols on handheld mobile devices. Public keys are used to encrypt confidential information. However, limited computational capabilities and power of handheld devices makes them ill-suited for public key signatures. Ding, Mazzocchi, and Tsudik (2007) explored the practical and conceptual implications of using Server-Aided Signatures (SAS) for handheld devices. SAS is a signature method that relies on partially-trusted servers for generating (normally expensive) public key signatures for regular users. Digital watermarking is particularly valuable in the use and exchange of digital media on handheld devices. However, watermarking is computationally expensive and adds to the energy drain in handheld devices. Kejariwal *et al.* (2006) proposed an approach in which the watermarking embedding and extraction algorithms are partitioned and some tasks are migrated to a proxy server. This leads to a lower energy consumption on the handheld without compromising the security of the watermarking process.

Handheld Usage Mining

Two major methods are commonly used to find usage patterns:

- *Sequential pattern generation* (Agrawal & Srikant, 1995), looks for sequences of maximal length that appear more frequently than a given percentage threshold over a collection of transactions ordered in time.
- *Association rule discovery* (Agrawal & Srikant, 1994), finds unordered correlations between items found in a set of database transactions. In the context of handheld usage mining, association rules refer to sets of applications that are accessed together, with a support value exceeding some specified threshold.

Usage mining can be applied to many areas, especially recommender systems. Two of these systems are explained next:

- Intelligent web recommendations derived from frequent user web-access patterns can help typical mobile users efficiently navigate standard web sites. Zhou *et al.* (2006) proposed an implicit server-side approach using intelligent web recommendations that can significantly enhance the mobile-browsing experience.
- Recommender systems rely on relevance scores for individual content items; in particular, pattern-based recommendation exploits co-occurrences of items in user sessions to ground any guesses about relevancy. To enhance the discovered patterns' quality, Adda *et al.* (2007) suggested using metadata about the content that is assumed to be stored in a domain ontology. Their approach comprises a dedicated pattern space built on top of the ontology, navigation primitives, mining methods, and recommendation techniques.

The Case Study

This following steps can be used to protect sensitive data in a handheld device from unauthorized access (Hu *et al.*, 2005):

1. Usage data gathering,
2. Usage data preparation,
3. Usage pattern discovery,
4. Usage pattern analysis and visualization, and
5. Usage pattern applications for handheld data protection.

Figure 4.4 shows the steps and how the data flows between them. The steps are introduced next, with a more detailed description of Steps 3 and 5 in the next section. If the system detects a different usage pattern from the stored patterns, it will assume the users are unlawful and block their accesses. The users will then need

Figure 4.4. The system structure

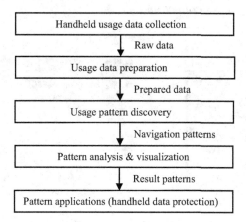

to verify their identities, usually by entering passwords or answering a question, in order to continue their operations. This approach has the advantages of convenience and vigorous protection compared to other approaches like password protection and fingerprint recognition.

Step 1: Usage Data Gathering

This step focuses on collecting data in certain defined categories in order to construct a user usage profile. The data should include the user's unique characteristics of using that handheld device based on the assumption that every user has a set of distinguishable and identifiable usage behaviors that can be used to separate this user from others. This assumption has been verified and applied to other information security applications, including intrusion detection. For example, a cell phone user may follow the patterns below to operate his/her phone the first thing in the morning:

1.   Turn on the cellular phone.
2.   Check phone messages.
3.   Check address book and return/make phone calls.
4.   Check instant messages.
5.   Reply/write messages.
6.   Check schedule book.
7.   Write any notes.
8.   Turn off the cellular phone.

Figure 4.5. (a) The user interface of a Palm© device re-implemented to gather usage data and (b) user entry of data collection time

(a)   *(b)*

The above steps are an example of handheld usage patterns. Other patterns also exist for the user and each user has his/her own unique usage patterns. To collect usage data, users click on the icon "Pattern" on the interface in Figure 4.5.(a) to bring up the interface in Figure 4.5.(b), which asks users to enter a number of days of usage data collection. The collection duration could be a week or a month depending on the use frequencies. The interface, shown in Figure 4.5.(a), is re-implemented so that when an application is clicked, it is recorded and the application is then activated.

Step 2: Usage Data Preparation

The data collected in Step 1 is usually raw and therefore cannot be used effectively. For example, the usage patterns should not include an event such as alarm-clock operation if the user rarely uses the alarm clock. Data preparation may include the following tasks (Mobasher, Cooley, & Srivastava, 2000):

- Delete any events whose frequency is less than a threshold value such as 5. For example, if the usage data is collected for a month, data synchronization can be ignored if it is only performed twice during that period.
- Remove an event if its duration is less than a threshold value such as 10 seconds. An event lasting less than 10 seconds is usually a mistake.
- Repeatedly performing the same action is considered performing the action one time. For example, making three phone calls in a row is treated as making one call.

Figure 4.6. (a) Users deciding whether or not to modify the threshold values and (a) two input fields for threshold values

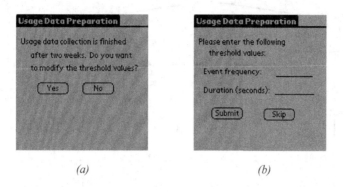

(a)   (b)

The interface in Figure 4.6.(a) allows users to decide whether or not to modify the default threshold values. If the user clicks the button "Yes," the interface in Figure 4.6.(b) allows him/her to enter two new threshold values.

After the raw usage data has been prepared, a usage tree is created. Figure 4.7 shows a sample simplified usage tree where the number and letter inside the parentheses is the number of occurrences and the shorthand of the event for the use of the next section, respectively. For example, (P: 20) means the event "Making phone calls" occurs 20 times. This usage tree is only a simplified example; an actual usage tree is much larger and more complicated. Ideally, a directed graph instead of a tree should be used to describe the usage data, although a directed graph is more complicated and therefore more difficult to process. Using a tree can simplify the processing, but also creates duplicated nodes, e.g., the event "making phone calls" appears four times in the usage tree shown in Figure 4.7.

Step 3: Usage Pattern Discovery

This step focuses on identifying the desired usage patterns. Given the complexity and dynamic nature of user behaviors, identified usage patterns could be fuzzy and not readily apparent. Advanced AI techniques such as machine learning, decision tree and other pattern matching and data mining techniques can be applied in this stage. Many data mining algorithms are applied to usage pattern discovery. Among them, most algorithms use the method of sequential pattern generations (Agrawal & Srikant, 1995), while the remaining methods tend to be rather ad hoc. The problem

Figure 4.7. A sample simplified usage tree

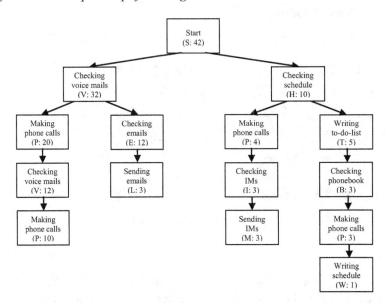

of discovering sequential patterns consists of finding inter-transaction patterns such that the presence of a set of items is followed by another item in the time-stamp ordered transaction set. This research converts the usage tree into a deterministic finite automaton (DFA). Pattern identification is achieved by feeding the automaton with usage sequences. Nothing happens if a sequence ends at an accepting state. Otherwise, a security action will be activated. Details of usage pattern discovery will be given in the next sub-section.

Step 4: Pattern Analysis and Visualization

The major task of this step is to pick useful items from the discovered patterns and display them. If the figure of the usage tree and the usage DFA in the previous section can be displayed on the device screen, this greatly assists mobile users to better manage this. However, creating and displaying complicated figures takes a great deal of computation time and consumes valuable resources such as memory from the device.

Step 5: Pattern Applications for Handheld Data Protection

Usage patterns can be applied to various applications such as recommendation systems (Adda *et al.*, 2007) and web page re-organization (Eirinaki & Vazirgiannis,

2003). Details of pattern applications for handheld data protection will be given in the next two sub-sections.

Usage Finite Automata

Finding a sequence from the usage tree is costly because the running time of the matching operation is at least $O(|V_1\|V_2|)$, where V_1 and V_2 are the node sets of the sequence and tree, respectively. To speed up the searches, the finite-automaton technology suggested by Aho *et al.* (2006) can be applied to usage-pattern matching. A usage finite automaton M is a 5-tuple $(Q, q_0, A, \Sigma, \delta)$ where

- Q, which is a finite set of states,
- $q_0 \in Q$, which is the start state,
- $A \subseteq Q$, which is a distinguished set of accepting states,
- Σ, which is a set of events, and
- δ, which is a function from $Q \times \Sigma$ into Q, called the transition function of M.

For the usage tree shown in Figure 4.7, a usage *DFA (deterministic finite automaton) M* can be constructed by following the steps below:

a. Each path starting at the root and ending at a leaf is a regular expression. For example, the regular expression of the path

```
Checking schedule (H) → Making phone calls (P)
        → Checking IMs (I) → Sending IMs (M)
```

is "HPIM" where the letters represent the events in Figure 4.7.
b. Combine all regular expressions into a regular expression by using the "or" operator '|'. For example, the result regular expression of the usage tree in Figure 4.7 is "VPVP|VEL|VPIM|HTBPW."
c. Convert the regular expression into an *NFA (nondeterministic finite automaton)*.
d. Convert the NFA to a DFA where
   - An edge label is an event such as making phone calls.
   - An accepting state represents a match of a pattern.

To illustrate this, the DFA of the usage tree in Figure 4.7 is shown in Figure 4.8, where the nodes denoted by double circles are the accepting states.

Using a DFA to store usage patterns and search for patterns is an effective and convenient approach, but it also suffers from the following shortcomings:

Figure 4.8. A deterministic finite automaton of the prepared usage tree in Figure 4.7

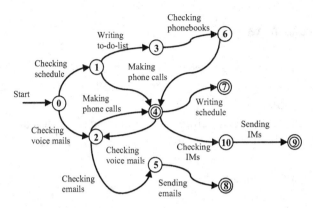

- The DFA may accept more patterns than the usage tree does. For example, the pattern

```
Checking schedule → Making phone calls
    → Checking emails → Sending emails
```

is accepted by the DFA, but does not exist in the tree. However, this feature may not be considered harmful because it may accept more "reasonable" patterns; the above pattern is very legitimate, as users may well use the pattern "checking schedule, making phone calls, checking emails, and sending emails" to operate their devices.
- This approach misses an important piece of information, the event frequency. Step 2, Usage Data Preparation, removes events with frequencies lower than a threshold value. Otherwise, this DFA does not use the frequency information, which is potentially very useful.
- The pattern discovery is virtually not used in this research because the DFA uses all paths from the usage tree. With only minimal use of pattern discovery the usage tree and DFA may grow too large to be stored in the device.

Experimental Results

The DFA can be used to find unlawful uses, which either stop at non-ending states or cannot reach the final states. The finite automaton begins at the state *0* and reads the user actions one at a time. The automaton accepts the user actions if the actions end at any of the accepting states. For example, consider the following sequence of handheld actions:

```
Checking voice mails → Making phone calls
    → Checking voice mails → Making phone calls
    → Checking IMs → Sending IMs
```

Its DFA path is as follows:

```
0 → 2 → 4 → 2 → 4 → 10 → 9
```

which ends at the accepting state 9 and no security action is taken. Another sequence of actions could be as follows:

```
Checking voice mails → Checking emails → Checking schedule
    → Making phone calls → Checking IMs
```

Its DFA path is as follows:

```
0 → 2 → 5 →
```

which stops at the non-accepting state 5, so a security action is taken. A typical action would be to ask the user to enter a password, as shown in Figure 4.9.(a), before he/she is allowed to continue the operations. If the password submitted is incorrect, the interface in Figure 4.9.(a) persists, otherwise the system displays the interface in Figure 4.9.(b), which allows the user to decide whether to continue following the same pattern, as the user may not want to keep being interrupted by the security protocols. The interface in Figure 4.6.(a) is then displayed and the user resumes his/her operations.

This method is both convenient and effective. These searching automata are very efficient: they examine each user action exactly once. The time used—after the automaton is built—is therefore $O(m)$ where m is the number of user actions in the sequence. However, the time used to build the automaton can be large. One major disadvantage of this method is the accuracy problem. For example, often the owner's operations may be interrupted because he/she was trying out new functions or patterns. In other cases presumed unlawful uses may be undetected because the usage DFA includes too many patterns.

Figure 4.9. (a) A security alert after detecting suspicious handheld uses and (b) user entry of whether to continue using this method

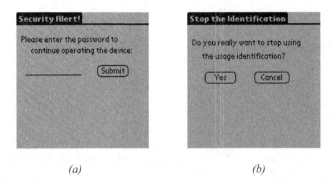

(a)   (b)

Case Study Conclusion

- Handheld devices are easily lost or stolen because of their small size. When people lose their devices, they are worried that the private data such as messages and addresses stored in the devices may be revealed to strangers. This case study describes a way to use handheld usage pattern identification to protect the data stored in handheld devices. Handheld usage data is first collected and usage patterns are discovered and saved. When an unusual usage pattern such as an unlawful user trying to access the handheld data is detected, the device will automatically lock itself down until a further action, such as entering a correct password, is taken. This approach has the following advantages:
  - *Convenience*: It is convenient compared to password-based methods because no user intervention is required after the usage DFA is built unless suspicious actions are detected.
  - *Accuracy*: The accuracy of owner identification should be higher than fingerprint or retina recognition, which is still in an early stage of development, though this claim has not yet been tested experimentally.
  - *Flexibility*: Users can adjust the level of security by trying various durations of data collection or entering different threshold values.
- This approach promises to be an effective and convenient way to protect handheld data, although the accuracy problem must be dealt with before it can be implemented commercially. The following questions must be addressed:
  - *Usage data collection*: How much time should be spent on data collection and how much usage data should be collected?

o   *Data preparation*: What is the optimum frequency threshold value for removing trivial events?

o   *Pattern discovery*: This approach uses a deterministic finite automaton to store usage patterns. Although it is effective, the patterns stored may be too numerous or may not be optimal; it is possible that sequential pattern discovery, the most popular pattern-discovery method, or other pattern-discovery methods may be preferable.

SUMMARY

It is widely acknowledged that mobile commerce is a field with enormous potential. However, it is also commonly admitted that development in this field is constrained and there are still considerable barriers waiting to be overcome. Among these, mobile security and payment methods are probably the biggest obstacles. Without mechanisms for secure commercial information exchange and safe electronic financial transactions over mobile networks, neither service providers nor potential customers will trust mobile commerce. Various mobile security procedures and payment methods have been proposed and applied to mobile commerce, and this chapter has provided a comprehensive overview of them.

A secure mobile commerce system must have the following properties: (i) confidentiality, (ii) authentication, (iii) integrity, (iv) authorization, (v) availability, and (vi) non-repudiation. Mobile commerce security is tightly coupled with network security; however, lacking a unified wireless security standard, different wireless technologies support different aspects and levels of security features. This chapter therefore discussed the security issues related to the following three network paradigms: (i) wireless local area networks, (ii) wireless wide area networks, and (iii) WAP.

Among the many themes of mobile commerce security, mobile payment methods are probably the most important. These consist of the methods used to pay for goods or services with a mobile handheld device, such as a smart cellular phone or an Internet-enabled PDA. A typical mobile payment process includes: (i) registration, (ii) payment submission, (iii) authentication and authorization by a content provider, and (iv) confirmation. This chapter also described a set of standards for mobile payments. Several dominant corporations are competing for the adoption of their own standards, which would give them a significant advantage in their competition with their rivals. Among the different standards, the common issues addressed are: (i) security, (ii) interoperability, and (iii) usability. Mobile payment standardization has been developed by several organizations, including Mobey Forum, Mobile Payment Forum, and Mobile electronic Transactions (MeT) Ltd.

REFERENCES

Adda, M., Valtchev, P., Missaoui, R. & Djeraba, C. (2007). Toward recommendation based on ontology-powered web-usage mining. *IEEE Internet Computing*, 11(4), 45-52.

Agrawal, R. & Srikant, R. (1994). Fast algorithms for mining association rules in large databases. In *Proc. 1994 Int. Conf. Very Large Data Bases (VLDB'94)*, pages 487-499, Santiago, Chile.

Agrawal, R. & Srikant, R. (1995). Mining sequential patterns. In *Proc.1995 Int. Conf. Data Engineering (ICDE'95)*, pages 3-14, Taipei, Taiwan.

Aho, A. V., Lam, M. S., Sethi, R. & Ullman, J. D. (2006). *Compilers—Principles, Techniques, and Tools*, 2nd edition. Addison-Wesley, ch. 3.

Argyroudis, P. G., Verma, R., Tewari, H. & D'Mahony, O. (2004). Performance analysis of cryptographic protocols on handheld devices. In *Proc. 3rd IEEE Int. Symposium on Network Computing and Applications*, pages 169-174, Cambridge, Massachusetts.

Ashley, P., Hinton, H., & Vandenwauver, M. (2001). Wired versus wireless security: The Internet, WAP and iMode for E-Commerce. In *Proceedings of Annual Computer Security Applications Conferences (ACSAC)*.

Balakrishnan, H., Seshan, S., & Katz, R. (1995). Improving reliable transport and handoff performance in cellular wireless networks. *ACM Wireless Networks*, 1(4), 469-481.

Biryukov, A., Shamir, A., & Wagner, D. (2000). Real time cryptanalysis of A5/1 on a PC. In *Proceedings of the 7th International Workshop on Fast Software Encryption*.

Borisov, N., Goldberg, I., & Wagner, D. (2001). Intercepting mobile communications: The insecurity of 802.11. In *Proceedings of the 7th International Conference on Mobile Computing and Networking*.

Caceres, R., & Iftode, L. (1996). Improving the performance of reliable transport protocols in mobile computing environment. In T. Imielinski and H. Korth, (Ed.), *Mobile Computing*, pages 207-228, Kluwer Academic Publishers.

DeClercq, K. (2002). *Banking sector*. Lessius Hogeschool.

Ding, X., Mazzocchi, D., & Tsudik, G. (2007). Equipping smart devices with public key signatures. *ACM Transactions on Internet Technology*, 7(1).

Eirinaki, M. & Vazirgiannis, M. (2003). Web mining for web personalization. *ACM Transactions on Internet Technology*, 3(1), 1-27.

Fluhrer, S., Martin, I., & Shamir, A. (2001). Weakness in the key scheduling algorithm of RC4. In *Proceedings of the 8ᵗʰ Annual Workshop on Selected Areas in Cryptography.*

Eurotechnology Japan K.K. (n.d.). *Frequently Asked Questions about NTT-DoCoMo's i-mode*. Retrieved December 16, 2006, from http://www.eurotechnology.com/imode/faq.html

Geihs, K. (2001). Middleware challenges ahead. *IEEE computer*, 34(6), 24-31.

Ghosh, A. K. & Swaminatha, T. M. (2001). Software security and privacy risks in mobile e-commerce. *Communications of the ACM*, 44(2), 51-57.

Hazen, T. J., Weinstein, E., & Park, A. (2003). Towards robust person recognition on handheld devices using face and speaker identification technologies. In *Proc. 5ᵗʰ Int. Conf. Multimodal Interfaces*, pages 289-292, Vancouver, British Columbia, Canada.

Hewlett-Packard Development Company, L.P. (2005). *Wireless security*. Retrieved January 12, 2008, from http://h20331.www2.hp.com/Hpsub/downloads/Wireless_Security_rev2.pdf

Hu, W.-C., Yeh, J.-h., Chu, H.-J., & Lee, C.-w. (2005). Internet-enabled mobile handheld devices for mobile commerce. *Contemporary Management Research*, 1(1), 13-34.

ICSTIS (The Independent Committee for the Supervision of Standards of Telephone Information Services). (n.d.). *Reverse-billed premium rate SMS*. Retrieved February 17, 2004, from http://www.icstis.org.uk/icstis2002/default.asp?node=6

NTT DoCoMo, Inc. (n.d.). *i-mode*. Retrieved November 28, 2006, from http://www.nttdocomo.com/services/imode/index.html

Jakobsson, M., & Wetzel, S. (2001). Security weaknesses in Bluetooth. *Topics in Cryptography: CT-RSA 2001, Berlin: Springer-Verlag LNCS 2020*, 176-191.

Jin et al. (2002). Research on WAP clients supports SET payment protocol. *IEEE Wireless Communications*, 9(1), 90-95.

Kejariwal, A., Gupta, S., Nicolau, A., Dutt, N. D., & Gupta, R. (2006). Energy efficient watermarking on mobile devices using proxy-based partitioning. *IEEE Transactions on Very Large Scale Integration (VLSI) systems*, 14(6), 625-636.

Mobasher, B., Cooley, R., & Srivastava, J. (2000). Automatic personalization based on web usage mining. *Communications of the ACM*, 43(8), 142-151.

Mobey Forum. (n.d.). *Home pages*. Retrieved October 10, 2006, from http://www.mobeyforum.org/

Mobile electronic Transactions (MeT) Ltd. (n.d.). *Home pages*. Retrieved November 22, 2006, from http://www.mobiletransaction.org/

The IETF Working Group. (2003). *IP Routing for Wireless/Mobile Hosts (MobileIP)*. Retrieved November 6, 2006, from http://www.ietf.org/proceedings/04aug/151.htm

Mobile Payment Forum. (n.d.). *Home pages*. Retrieved October 21, 2006, from http://www.mobilepaymentforum.org/home

MSC to BS interface inter-operability specification (1999). *CDMA Development Group*. CDG-IOS v. 3.1.1.

NIST. (2002). *NIST Wireless Security Guidance SP 800-48*. Retrieved July 13, 2006, from http://csrc.nist.gov/archive/wireless/S05_NIST-tk2.pdf

Pahlavan, K., & Krishnamurthy, P. (2002). *Principles of Wireless Networks: A Unified Approach*. Upper Saddle River, NJ: Prentice Hall PTR.

Shyu, M.-L., Sarinnapakorn, K., Kuruppu-Appuhamilage, I., Chen, S.-C., Chang, L., & Goldring, T. (2005). Handling nominal features in anomaly intrusion detection problems. In *Proc. 15th Int. Workshop on Research Issues in Data Engineering (RIDE 2005)*, pages 55-62, Tokyo, Japan.

Stolfo, S. J., Hershkop, S., Hu, C.-W., Li, W.-J., Nimeskern, O., & Wang, K. (2006). Behavior-based modeling and its application to email analysis. *ACM Transactions on Internet Technology*, 6(2), 187-221.

Stubblefield, A., Ioannidis, J., & Rubin, A.D. (2002). Using the Fluhrer, Martin, and Shamir attack to break WEP. In *Proceedings of the Network and Distributed Systems Security Symposium*.

Susilo, W. (2002). Securing handheld devices. In *Proc. 10th IEEE Int. Conf. Networks*, pages 349-354.

Sybase Inc. (2006). *Afaria—The power to manage and secure data, devices and applications on the front lines of business*. Retrieved February 06, 2008, from http://www.sybase.com/files/Data_Sheets/Afaria_overview_datasheet.pdf

Tanenbaum, A. S. (2002). *Computer Networks* (4th ed.). Upper Saddle River, New Jersey: Prentice Hall PTR.

UTRAN overall description (1999). *3GPP*. TS 25.401 v3.3.0, R-99, RAN WG3.

Vriendt, J. D., Lainé, P., Lerouge, C., & Xu, X. (2002). Mobile network evolution: A revolution on the move. *IEEE Communications Magazine*, 40(4), 104-111.

WAP (Wireless Application Protocol) (2003). *Open Mobile Alliance Ltd.* Retrieved November 21, 2006, from http://www.wapforum.org/

Weinstein, E., Ho, P., Heisele, B., Poggio, T., Steele, K., & Agarwal, A. (2002). Handheld face identification technology in a pervasive computing environment. In *Short Paper Proceedings, Pervasive 2002*, Zurich, Switzerland.

Yavatkar, R. & Bhagawat, N. (1994). Improving end-to-end performance of TCP over mobile internetworks. In *Proceedings of the Workshop on Mobile Computing and Applications*, Santa Cruz, California.

Zhou, B., Hui, S. C., & Chang, K. (2006). Enhancing mobile web access using intelligent recommendations. *IEEE Intelligent Systems and Their Applications*, 21(1), 28-34.

Section II
Mobile Web Content Design
and Implementation

Chapter V
Mobile World Wide Web Content

INTRODUCTION

As handheld computing is a fairly new computing area, there is as yet no generally accepted formal definition. For the purposes of this book, therefore, it will be defined as follows:

Handheld computing is the use of handheld devices such as smart cellular phones and PDAs (Personal Digital Assistants) to perform wireless, mobile, handheld operations such as personal data management and making phone calls.

As explained earlier, handheld computing can take one of two forms: server- and client- side handheld computing, which are defined as follows:

*   **Server-side handheld computing:** Here, handheld devices are used to perform wireless, mobile, handheld operations that require the support of a server. Examples of such applications include: (a) instant messages, (b) mobile web content, (c) online video games, and (d) wireless telephony.
*   **Client-side handheld computing:** This refers to the use of handheld devices to perform handheld operations that do not need the support of a server. Examples of these applications include: (a) address books, (b) standalone video games, (c) note pads, and (d) to-do-lists.

The terms "computing" and "programming" are sometimes confusing and often misused. It is important to remember that *"handheld programming,"* defined as programming for handheld devices, is different from "handheld computing" and is made up of two kinds of programming:

- **Server-side handheld programming:** This includes the design and development of handheld software such as CGI programs that reside on servers.
- **Client-side handheld programming:** This refers to the design and development of handheld software such as Java ME programs that reside on the handheld devices themselves.

Server-side handheld computing and programming usually involve complicated procedures and advanced programming such as TCP/IP network programming. Here we will focus on the most popular server-side handheld application, mobile web content design and development, which can be conveniently considered in terms of three themes:

- WML (Wireless Markup Language), which will be discussed in Chapters VI and VII,
- WMLScript, which will be explained in Chapter VIII, and
- database-driven mobile web content development, which will be covered in Chapter IX.

Other kinds of server-side handheld applications, such as instant messaging, are related to advanced network programming such as TCP/IP and readers may refer to other technical reports or books for more information. The rest of this chapter describes the background and discusses system setup for server-side handheld computing and programming. A case study, adaptive mobile web browsing using web mining technologies, is given at the end of this chapter.

Mobile Web Content

A web site normally displays its content on browsers such as Internet Explorer or Netscape Navigator for PCs by using HTML (HyperText Markup Language) (W3C, 1999). For handheld devices, however, the situation is less clear-cut and there are currently several markup languages available for showing mobile web contents on microbrowsers, with no single language dominating the market. For example, i-mode devices use cHTML (W3C, 1998) and WAP devices use WML (Wireless Application Protocol Forum, Ltd., 2001). Even worse, no one microbrowser dominates the microbrowser market, and a microbrowser may be able to show mobile content using one markup language but not others. For example, Access's NetFront Browser Version 3.4 (Access Co. Ltd., n.d.) can show HTML pages but not cHTML pages, while the WinWAP Mercury Browser can show WML pages but not HTML pages. However, it is likely that very soon all microbrowsers will be able to view HTML pages, rendering the web content into the small screens used by microbrowsers by implementing new technology such as Opera's Small-Screen Rendering software (Opera Software ASA, n.d.c), after which WML and cHTML will be phased out.

DIAL

The incompatibility of mobile markup languages and microbrowsers poses a serious problem impeding the progress of mobile commerce. To address this problem, the World Wide Web Consortium is working on a new technology known as the W3C's *Device Independent Authoring Language (DIAL)* (http://www.w3.org/TR/dial; W3C, 2006). This is a markup language that will be used to make single versions of web sites and applications available to a wide range of cellular phones, PDAs, and other mobile machines. Systems that implement DIAL will be able to recognize devices and adapt their content appropriately to take into account issues such as display size and resolution. DIAL is being developed based on existing and pending standards, and is expected to eliminate the need for authors to create and maintain multiple sites and applications for each type of mobile device. These standards include extensible HTML (XHTML) version 2.0, a proposed standard that combines features of XML and HTML, and cascading style sheets that let content authors and, in some cases, viewers define how Web-page elements will appear. DIAL will also work with the W3C's proposed DISelect (Content Selection for Device Independence) standard to permit authors and device owners to specify and fine-tune content that will be delivered to multiple mobile platforms. DISelect is based on criteria such as device and network capabilities and even user preferences. Authors could thus specify that parts of a document should not appear on certain types of devices. For example, a cellular phone, which has a small screen, might display only the headline and the first few paragraphs of a news article.

SYSTEM SETUP

Various methods are used to implement mobile web content and there are substantial differences between them. For example, using JDBC to access databases is totally different from using PHP to access databases, but both methods are commonly used for mobile content implementation. Therefore, the systems and utilities used for mobile content implementation must be clearly specified. This section discusses the systems and software used for handheld programming that will be applied in the rest of Section B: Server-Side Handheld Computing and Programming.

Systems and Tools

The systems and tools used for server-side handheld programming are as follows:

- A server hosting the Oracle9i DBMS and file systems:
  o *Hardware*: Sparc processor and SUNW, Ultra-4 platform,
  o *Operating system*: SunOS 5.9, and
  o *Provider*: Sun Microsystems.
- A server hosting the Apache web server and utilities such as a Perl interpreter:
  o *Hardware*: i686 and
  o *Operating system*: Linux 2.6.5-1-686-smp.
- A database management system: Oracle9i Enterprise Edition Release 9.2.0.1.0—64bit Production.
- A host language with embedded SQL: Oracle JDBC Drivers release 9.2.0.
- CGI script language: Perl 5.6.1 built for i386-linux.
- Microbrowser script language: WML 2.0.
- A web server: Apache /1.3.26 (Unix) Debian GNU/Linux PHP/4.1.2
- Microbrowsers:
  o WinWAP 3.2.1.28 and
  o TagTag (tagtag.com, n.d.) online microbrowser emulator.

In order to use the above tools and systems, it may be necessary to set up correct environment variables. These are system-dependent, so programmers are likely to have systems and utilities that differ considerably from the above list, which is intended as a guide only. Those attempting to implement such a system may need to check the references or consult their local system administrators in order to duplicate the programming.

Microbrowser Emulators

Although the WML 2.0 specification was originally proposed by the WAP Forum (http://www.wapforum.org/) in 2001, most microbrowsers are still not fully compatible with the specification, either by not supporting some features, having their own particular features, or both. A microbrowser emulator accepts the same inputs and

Table 5.1. Features of five popular microbrowser emulators

	Mobile Content Viewer	Mobile Explorer Emulator	Opera Mini Simulator	TTemulator	WinWAP for Windows
Vendor	ACCESS	Microsoft	Opera	Inetis	WinWAP Technology
Needs to be downloaded?	Yes	Yes	No	No	Yes
Free?	Yes	Yes	Yes	Yes	No
Supports HTML?	Yes	Yes	Yes	No	No
Supports WML?	No	Most	Yes	Most	Most
Supports WMLScript?	No	No	Not all	Not all	Not all

produces the same outputs as a microbrowser. Table 5.1 lists the five most popular microbrowser emulators and summarizes their features. A more detailed description of each is provided below.

NetFront Mobile Content Viewer

NetFront Mobile Content Viewer, from the Access Co., Ltd. (2005), is a microbrowser emulator used to confirm how content created for NetFront will be displayed on NetFront-equipped mobile terminals. It includes the following features:

1. Shows Internet content in the same way as an ordinary microbrowser.
2. The screen size, font size, etc. can be set according to the terminal specifications.
3. Performs the same key operations as a mobile terminal.
4. Shows web content created from authoring tools such as Adobe GoLive and Macromedia Dreamweaver.

NetFront can display mobile content in HTML 4.01, XHTML 1.1, Parts of CSS 1 and 2, ECMAScript 262 3rd Edition (JavaScript 1.5 equivalent), DOM Level 1, Level 2, and part of Dynamic HTM, and conforms to SMIL Basic 2.0 and SVG Tiny. The operating environment must be Windows 2000 or Windows XP. Figure 5.1 shows a screenshot of the NetFront Mobile Content Viewer.

Figure 5.1. A screenshot of NetFront Mobile Content Viewer © 2008 ACCESS Co. Ltd.

Mobile Explorer Emulator

Microsoft Mobile Explorer (Microsoft Corp, 1999) can be used to simulate the activity of using a browser on a mobile phone on a desktop PC. The image of the mobile phone device in the emulator window can be used to:

- View local contents under development, allowing programmers to assess how the content will look on an actual mobile phone.
- Browse Wireless Markup Language (WML), HTML, or Compact HTML (cHTML) content stored on a desktop computer or from a remote site and display that content on the device screen.

Opera Mini Simulator

Opera Software ASA (n.d.a) has developed the Opera web browser, a multi-platform product that can be used with a wide range of platforms, operating systems, and embedded Internet products. There are three kinds of Opera browsers:

Figure 5.2. A screenshot of Microsoft Mobile Explorer Emulator © 2008 Microsoft Corp.

- **Opera for Windows:** This is a relatively fast system to use because the full-featured Opera browser comes in a compact 3.5 MB download compared with the 14.8 MB required by Internet Explorer 7.1 and the 18.3 MB for Netscape Navigator 8.1.
- **Opera Mobile:** This lets users surf the "full" web on their mobile phones. Equipped with Opera's Small-Screen Rendering technology, the Opera Mobile browser can be used to access any site on the Internet, just as on a computer.
- **Opera for Devices:** This is based on the same core engine as the Opera desktop browser and delivers web functions to set-top boxes, portable media players, and other devices. It is used to bring full web browsing to connected devices, or as a powerful execution environment for Ajax, Widgets, Web applications and dynamic user interfaces.

Opera Mini is a fast and easy alternative to Opera's mobile browser, allowing users to access the web on mobile phones that would normally be incapable of running a web browser. This includes the vast majority of today's WAP-enabled phones. Opera Mini uses a remote server to pre-process web pages before sending them to a phone, compressing web content in order to reduce the size of data transferred, thus enabling it to be handled on simpler phones and creating fast browsing at low costs. Opera Mini microbrowser provides the following features:

- **Receive RSS news:** Subscribers to RSS news feeds can receive updates every time they connect with Opera Mini, sorted by feed source or by date.
- **Point, snap, publish:** A picture can be shared from any location at any time using a mobile phone equipped with Opera Mini's photo sharing feature. Photos can be uploaded to a blog or forum, or as an e-mail attachment.
- **Right to the point:** The content folding feature shrinks lengthy menus to save scrolling. Users can easily inspect hidden content by touching the button next to it.
- **Safe and sound:** Secure connections allow users to safely access secured sites such as e-mail, bank sites, and online stores with no risk of exposing personal details.
- **Rapid browsing:** All subsequent requests to a server within a session are faster as Opera Mini keeps an open connection between server and client, thus reducing overhead TCP set-up times.

Opera Mini recognizes the user's phone's capabilities and optimizes web pages accordingly for fast and easy browsing. Figure 5.3 shows a screenshot of the Opera Mini Simulator.

Figure 5.3. A screenshot of the Opera Mini Simulator © 2008 Opera Software ASA

Figure 5.4. An example of Opera's Small-Screen Rendering technology © 2008 Opera Software ASA

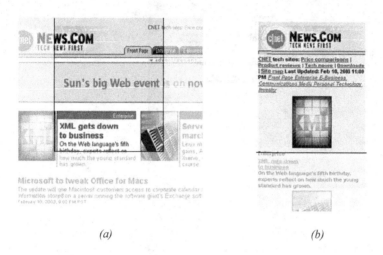

(a)   (b)

Opera Software claims this its new software will help transform the wireless Web into a reality. Most sites are written for, and tested exclusively on desktop computers with large color monitors, and it has been a challenge to adequately present Web pages on the much smaller screens of mobile wireless devices. Most sites are designed with fixed widths that make them hard to navigate on small handheld devices; for example, most news sites have a center column where the main article text is located. This column is usually 468 pixels wide (due to the standard ad-banner sizes) and the text is set to fill this width, so to read an article it is necessary to scroll back and forth for every line of text [Figure 5.4.(a)]. Opera's Small-Screen Rendering technology (Opera Software ASA, n.d.c) intelligently reformats web sites to fit inside the screen width, thereby eliminating the need for horizontal scrolling and enabling users to easily read Internet content [Figure 5.4.(b)]. The content and functionality are still available, and only the layout of the page that is changed. This innovation is a key enabler for surfing on a mobile device.

TTemulator

The *TTemulator* is an online emulator for WAP microbrowsers that offers visitors an easy way to surf WAP sites (Inetis Ltd., n.d.). A screenshot of the TTemulator is shown in Figure 5.5. It is free for non-commercial use and offers a stand-alone product that can be licensed for use on any Web site. TTemulator reads a WAP site

Figure 5.5. A screenshot of the TTemulator © 2008 Inetis Ltd.

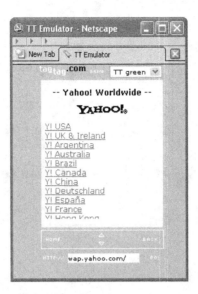

page, converts it to HTML format and sends it back to the browser, allowing users to browse WAP sites with their existing browser, thus avoiding the need to buy a real WAP device. Its implementation features include:

- **Application type:** developed in C++ language and using the CGI technology.
- **Platforms supported:** Windows, Solaris, and Linux.
- **Special features:**
  - No download is required for site visitors.
  - Plain HTML data are transferred because a WML to HTML converter is used.
  - Phone skins can be changed to suit users' needs.
  - Location for home button can be changed.
- Most WML elements are supported, including:
  - forms,
  - text formatting (all),
  - links (a, anchor),
  - pictures (wbmp and color),
  - variables (all, attribute for URL escaping var: e is ignored),
  - tasks (all—go, prev, refresh, noop),
  - events (all except onenterbackward),

- o timer,
- o templates, and
- o user input (both tags, `input` and `select`); `input` tag attributes supported: `name`, `type`, `value`, `title`; `select` tag: `iname` and `ivalue` are not supported.
- Some WMLScript elements are supported.

WinWAP for Windows

The WinWAP Technologies Oy. (n.d.) provides three WAP microbrowser emulators for mobile content development and browsing:

- **WinWAP for Windows:** This allows users to use WAP services on their Windows PCs.
- **WinWAP for Pocket PC:** This allows users to use WAP services on their Windows Pocket PC and Windows mobile devices.
- **WinWAP Smartphone browser emulator:** This allows users to use WAP services on their Windows PCs and looks like a smartphone on the desktop PC.

The WAP browser is a mobile Internet browser that allows users to access mobile Internet services. WinWAP for Windows 3.2 supports the Wireless Markup Language (WML 1.3), and WinWAP for Windows 4.0 for full WAP 2.0 supports WML and xHTML-MP. A screenshot of WinWAP for Windows is shown in Figure 5.6. The *WinWAP3.2* technology has been applied to a number of platforms and consists of discrete modules that have each been optimized for the task they are expected to perform. The WAP protocol stack that is an essential part of the WAP technology is available for a number of platforms, and can easily be ported to further platforms. The different modules can be licensed either as parts or as full WAP browsing technology (for smartphones, PDA's or testing/assurance applications). The WAP client protocol's current features are as follows:

- Source code, variable and cookie viewing utility,
- Launched automatically when Internet Explorer receives WML content,
- Navigation using the Tabulator key without a mouse or other pointing device,
- File cache that makes browsing quick,
- Dragging and dropping files on WinWAP to open,
- Command line parameters [/AUTODIAL:'Dial-up connection name'], [/NO-MENU] and [/NOTOOL] to enable kiosk mode

Figure 5.6. A screenshot of WinWAP for Windows © 2008 WinWAP Technologies Oy.

- Select size and font of the screen
- Preconfigured aveAccess WAP Gateway for gateway mode
- Open sites with HTTP or via a WAP Gateway or from your own hard drive
- Has WBMP and color image support (GIF, animated GIF and JPG)
- Supports WMLScript
- Supports HTTP cookies
- Supports secure modes (WTLS and HTTPS)
- Supports bango.net numbers
- Has the feel and look of a normal web browser (easy to use)
- Has the functionality of a normal web browser, including printing, bookmarks, remembering locations, resizing windows, opening in a new window, sounds, backgrounds, proxy, http & WAP gateway authentication, dial-up connections, saving (text, wml or html), viewing source code and variables, selecting and copying text, and finding text.
- Search engine
- View size as Nokia 7110/6210, Ericsson R320, Ericsson MC218, Motorola Timeport
- Costs less then any WAP enabled device
- No size limits for the decks
- Connects to WAP Gateways

Traditional web-services are provided in HTML format, and mobile services (WAP) in WML or xHTML-MP (Mobile Profile). Traditional web browsers such as MS Internet Explorer or Mozilla Firefox do not fully support the WAP format, so in order to access WAP pages it is necessary to have a WAP enabled browser. WinWAP is especially designed to provide a comfortable and user-friendly experience when browsing mobile content. WAP gateway connection features include:

- Connection-less and oriented mode
- Secure connection-less and oriented mode (WTLS)
- Gateway authentication
- Compatible with all the popular gateways

A CASE STUDY: ADAPTIVE VIEWING OF MOBILE CONTENT

Using Internet-enabled mobile handheld devices to access the World Wide Web is a promising addition to traditional e-commerce on the Web. Mobile handheld devices provide convenience and portable access to the huge amount of information available on the Internet for mobile users from anywhere and at anytime. However, traditional web pages are primarily designed for viewing on desktop or notebook computers and usually do not work well with handheld devices because the pages, especially large text files, cannot be properly displayed on a microbrowser due to its limited screen size, narrow network bandwidth, small memory capacity, and low computing power.

A great deal of effort has been devoted to solving this problem. For example, Opera's *Small-Screen Rendering* technology intelligently reformats web pages to fit the smaller screen width, thereby eliminating the need for horizontal scrolling (Figure 5.7). This technology enables users to access all the content available on the Internet and is a key enabler for surfing on a mobile device.

This case study investigates an approach to large text summarization for mobile handheld devices. Here, web usage mining technology—web navigation pattern discovery and applications—is applied to adaptive mobile web browsing. An experimental example is given to illustrate the method. Regardless of the potential of mobile commerce, its prosperity and popularity will be assured only if information can be properly and speedily displayed. Traditional web pages are designed for desktop or notebook computers and loading and visualizing large text documents on handheld devices is often an arduous task. The approach described in this case study is designed to improve the readability and download speed of existing web pages on mobile devices.

Figure 5.7. Screenshots without (a) and with (b) adaptive viewing

(a)

(b)

Adaptive Web Browsing Using Web Mining Technologies

HTML web pages usually do not work well on Internet-enabled mobile handheld devices because the pages cannot be displayed quickly and readably on the devices' microbrowsers due to:

- small screen size,
- narrow network bandwidth,
- low memory capacity, and
- limited computing power and resources.

In an effort to alleviate this problem, this case study describes a way of applying web usage mining technologies to web page summarization for handheld devices.

Web Usage Mining

World Wide Web data mining includes content mining, hyperlink structure mining, and usage mining. All three approaches are designed to extract knowledge from the web, allowing users to achieve useful results from the knowledge extracted, and then apply the results to particular real-world problems. The first two approaches apply

Figure 5.8. A web usage mining system structure

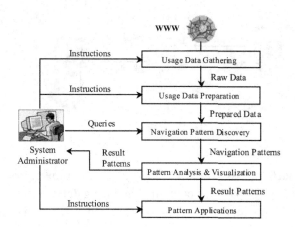

data mining techniques to the content of web pages and their hyperlink structures, respectively. The third approach, web usage mining, which is the method used here, applies data mining techniques to the usage logs of large web data repositories in order to produce results that can be applied to many practical subjects, such as improving web sites/pages, making additional topic or product recommendations, or conducting user/customer behavior studies.

A variety of implementations and realizations are employed by web usage mining systems. Figure 5.8 shows a generalized structure of a typical Web usage mining system (Hu *et al.*, 2005). A web usage mining system performs the following five major tasks:

1. **Usage data gathering:** Web logs, which record user activities on Web sites, provide the most comprehensive, detailed Web usage data. A log file can be located in three different places: (i) web servers, (ii) web proxy servers, and (iii) client browsers, as shown in Figure 5.9.

2. **Usage data preparation:** Log data are normally too raw to be used by mining algorithms. This task restores the users' activities that are recorded in the web server logs in a reliable and consistent way. This phase should at least achieve the following four major tasks: (i) removing undesirable entries, (ii) distinguishing among users, (iii) building sessions, and (iv) restoring the content viewed in a session.

Figure 5.9. Three web log file locations

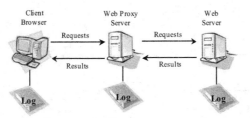

3. **Navigation pattern discovery:** This part of a usage mining system looks for any interesting usage patterns contained in the log data. Most algorithms use the method of sequential pattern generation, while the remaining methods tend to be rather ad hoc.
4. **Pattern analysis and visualization:** Navigation patterns show the facts of web usage, but these require further interpretation and analysis before they can be applied to yield useful results.
5. **Pattern applications:** The navigation patterns discovered can be applied to the following major areas, among others: (i) improving the page/site design, (ii) making additional product or topic recommendations, and (iii) web personalization. Learning user/customer behavior and web caching, although less important applications for navigation patterns, are also worth considering.

A Case Study

This case study shows how to apply web usage mining technologies to adaptive web browsing for handheld devices. Figure 5.10 shows a typical HTML page—in this case, the World Health Organization of the United Nations—which is too large to be properly displayed on the microbrowser of a mobile handheld device. An HTML page can provide the following information:

- **Content:** Web page content provides the most accurate and full-text information. However, it is also the least-used information for a search engine, since content extraction is far less practical than other methods.
- **Descriptions:** Web page descriptions can either be constructed from the metatags or submitted by Webmasters or reviewers. A metatag is an HTML tag that provides information (e.g., author, expiration date, a list of keywords, etc.) about a web page.
- **Hyperlinked text:** Hyperlink text is normally a title or brief summary of the target page.

Figure 5.10. The About page of the World Health Organization

- **Hyperlinks:** Hyperlinks often contain high-quality semantic clues to a page's topic (Chakrabarti *et al.*, 1999). A hyperlink to a Web page also represents an implicit endorsement of the page being pointed to. However, exploiting this link information is challenging because it is highly noisy.
- **Keywords:** Keywords can be extracted from full-text documents or metatags. Before obtaining keywords from a full-text document, filtering operations are normally applied to the document. Typical operations would include the removal of common words using a list of stopwords, the transformation of uppercase letters to lowercase letters, and word ranking (Korfhage, 1997).
- **Page structure:** An HTML page is usually organized as a tree, in which top-level nodes are normally more important than lower-level nodes.
- **Page title:** The title tag, which is only valid in a head section, defines the title of an HTML document. A title is usually chosen that makes sense with no context.
- **Text with different fonts:** Emphasized text is usually given a different font to highlight its importance.
- **The first sentence:** The first sentence of a Web document is likely to give crucial information related to the document, as it is usually an introduction or an abstract.

Based on the above HTML page information and the web usage mining technologies, the following three major steps are applied to achieve adaptive web browsing for handheld devices:

1. The first sentence of each paragraph is retained because the sentence usually contains important information or an introduction about the paragraph.
2. The rest of the paragraph is ignored. By doing this, the page size can be reduced significantly.
3. The hyperlinks are sorted based on popularity from the web usage mining results. The system may, for example, install a counter on each web page so each page visit increases the counter by one. A popular page will have a higher number in its counter.

Figure 5.11 shows three microbrowser screen dumps from different parts of the same page obtained by applying the above methods to the page shown in Figure 5.10. Note that these methods are still in the very early stage of development, and this is probably the best result currently achievable by this method. The major reason for this inadequate summarizing of a web page for handheld devices is the high complexity of web pages, many of which are not made up simply of text written by humans. Instead, they are generated from software such as Dreamweaver or include a variety of scripts such as JavaScript and ASP (Active Server Pages).

Figure 5.11. Screen dumps of the results after applying the proposed methods to the page in Figure 5.10

WHO

About WHO
WHO is the directing and coordinating authority for health within the United Nations system.

In the 21st century, health is a shared responsibility, involving equitable access to essential care and collective defence against transnational threats.

---

transnational threats.

The WHO agenda A six-point agenda to improve public health

The role of WHO in public health The Organization's core functions

Governance of WHO World Health Assembly, Executive Board and Constitution

---

WHO and historical resources

People and offices The Organization's structure and presence

Resources and planning Budget, fund sources and expenditures

Our greatest concern must always rest with disadvantaged and vulnerable groups

FUTURE TRENDS

Many methods have been proposed for rendering web pages for microbrowsers. This approach used web usage mining technologies to summarize web pages and then display the results on microbrowsers. Other promising methods include:

- **A block importance model:** This method extracts and presents more condensed web search results to mobile users by using a block importance model (Xie *et al.*, 2005), which assigns importance values to different segments of a web page.
- **Link analysis:** Yin and Lee (2004) proposed a ranking algorithm similar to Google's *PageRank* algorithm to rank the content objects within a web page. The PageRank model assumes the reputation of a page on a topic is proportional to the sum of the reputation weights of the pages pointing to it that are devoted to the same topic. Thus, links from pages with high reputations are weighted more heavily. This allows the extraction of only important parts of web pages for delivery to mobile devices, saving wireless traffic and reducing download times while still providing a satisfactory reading experience on the mobile device.
- **Page and form summarization:** This method (Buyukkokten *et al.*, 2002) breaks each web page into text units that can be either hidden, partially displayed, made fully visible, or summarized. A variety of methods can be used to summarize the text units. In addition, HTML forms can also be summarized by displaying just the text labels that prompt the user for input.
- **Page reformatted:** This method changes the page format, but not its content. Two commercial products use this method:
  - *ACCESS*: NetFront Browser includes Smart-Fit Rendering technology (ACCESS, n.d.) intelligently adapts standard web pages to fit the screen width of any mobile device, enabling an intuitive and rapid vertical scrolling process without degrading the quality or usability of the pages being browsed. The following processes are performed:
  - Images larger than the screen width are scaled down to fit the screen width.
  - Tables larger than the screen width are split and laid out vertically, as shown in Figure 5.12.
  - *Opera*: Opera's *Small-Screen Rendering* technology (n.d.a) reformats web pages to fit inside the screen width and eliminate the need for horizontal scrolling. All the content and functionality is still available, and only the layout of the page is changed.

Figure 5.12. A web page table split by ACCESS' NetFront Browser

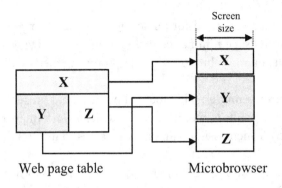

Web page table   Microbrowser

- *Page structure*: One example of this method analyzes the structure of an existing web page and splits it into small and logically related units that fit the screen of a mobile device. For example, Chen, Ma, and Zhang (2005) organize a web page into a two level hierarchy with a thumbnail representation at the top level that provides a global view, along with an index to a set of sub-pages at the bottom level for more detailed information.
- *Visitor's context*: This method displays the web content based on the visitor's context, such as their location, information interests, and device capabilities. For example, the nearest gas stations or affordable motels can be displayed based on a mobile user's location and preferences. Pashtan, Kollipara, and Pearce (2003) proposed a method adapting web content to a user's dynamic context for Motorola Lab's web-enabled museum system.

At the time of writing, it is almost impossible to predict which methods will prevail in the future because each device and microbrowser manufacturer uses their own technology.

SUMMARY

Although mobile commerce is a field offering enormous potential, development in this field is constrained by device limitations and there are still considerable barriers waiting to be overcome. One of the major barriers is the inconvenience of browsing large text web pages using handheld devices. Without the ability to effectively view complex web pages, mobile commerce cannot be raised to a higher level. This case study examined how web usage mining technologies can be applied to adaptive web viewing for handheld devices. The application of data mining techniques to the usage logs of large web data repositories can be used to produce results that are potentially useful for many practical subjects, such as improving web sites/pages, making additional topic or product recommendations, user/customer behavior studies, etc. A web usage mining system must be able to perform five major functions: (i) data gathering, (ii) data preparation, (iii) navigation pattern discovery, (iv) pattern analysis and visualization, and (v) pattern applications. This approach can be used to improve the readability and download speed of web pages for handheld mobile devices.

REFERENCES

ACCESS Co., Ltd. (2005). *NetFront Mobile Content Viewer.* Retrieved September 11, 2006, from http://www.access.co.jp/develop/en/index.html

ACCESS Co., Ltd. (n.d.). *NetFront Browser 3.4.* Retrieved September 10, 2006, from http://www.access-us-inc.com/Products/client-side/Prod_NetFront_nf.html

ACCESS Co., Ltd. (n.d.). *Small-Fit Rendering.* Retrieved June 14, 2007, from http://www.access-company.com/products/netfrontmobile/contentviewer/mcv_tips.html#Anchor-Smar-45765

Buyukkokten, O., Kaljuvee, O., Garcia-Molina, H., Paepcke, A., & Winograd, T. (2002). Efficient web browsing on handheld devices using page and form summarization. *ACM Transactions on Information Systems*, 20(1), 82-115.

Chakrabarti, S., Dom, B.E., Kumar, S.R., Raghavan, P., Rajagopalan, S., Tomkins, A., Gibson, D., & Kleinberg, J. (1999). Mining the web's link structure, *IEEE Computer*, 32(8), 60-67.

Chen, Y., Ma, W.-Y., & Zhang, H.-J. (2005). Adaptive web pages for small-screen devices. *IEEE Internet Computing*, 9(1), 50-56.

Hu, W.-C., Yang, H.-J., Lee, C.-w., & Yeh, J.-h. (2005). World Wide Web usage mining. In John Wang, editor, *Encyclopedia of Data Warehousing and Mining*, pages 1242-1248, Idea Group, Inc.

Korfhage, R.R. (1997). *Information Storage and Retrieval.* John Wiley & Sons, pages 105-144.

Microsoft Corp. (1999). *Mobile Explorer Emulator.* Retrieved July 17, 2006, from http://www.devhood.com/tools/tool_details.aspx?tool_id=52

Open Mobile Alliance. (2001). *Wireless Markup Language (WML), Version 2.0.* Retrieved June 28, 2004 from http://www.openmobilealliance.org/tech/affiliates/wap/wap-238-wml-20010911-a.pdf

Opera Software ASA. (n.d.a). *Opera's Small-Screen Rendering.* Retrieved June 23, 2007, from http://www.opera.com/products/mobile/smallscreen/

Opera Software ASA. (n.d.b). *About Opera.* Retrieved November 19, 2006, from http://www.opera.com/company/about/

Opera Software ASA. (n.d.c). *Opera Mini Simulator.* Retrieved September 15, 2006, from http://www.opera.com/products/mobile/operamini/demo.dml

Pashtan, A., Kollipara, S., & Pearce, M. (2003). Adapting content for wireless web services. *IEEE Internet Computing, 7*(5), 79-85.

Inetis Ltd. (n.d.). *TTemulator.* Retrieved from February 14, 2004, from http://tagtag.com/site/info.php3?p=tt

W3C (World Wide Web Consortium). (1998). *Compact HTML for Small Information Appliances.* Retrieved July 02, 2006, from http://www.w3.org/TR/1998/NOTE-compactHTML-19980209/

W3C (World Wide Web Consortium). (1999). *HTML 4.01 Specification.* Retrieved May 12, 2006, from http://www.w3.org/TR/REC-html40/

W3C (World Wide Web Consortium). (2006). *Device Independent Authoring Language (DIAL).* Retrieved June 12, 2006, from http://www.w3.org/TR/dial/

WinWAP Technologies Oy. (n.d.). *WinWAP for Windows (Version 3.2).* Retrieved August 21, 2006, from http://www.winwap.com/products_2_1.php

Wireless Application Protocol Forum, Ltd. (2001). *Wireless Markup Language (Version 2.0).* Retrieved September 07, 2006, from http://www.wapforum.org/tech/documents/WAP-238-WML-20010911-a.pdf#search=%22Wireless%20Markup%20Language%20%20version%20Specification%22

Xie, X., Miao, G., Song, R., Wen, J.-R., & Ma, W.-Y. (2005). Efficient browsing of web search results on mobile devices based on block importance model. In *Proceedings of the 3rd IEEE International Conference on Pervasive Computing and Communications (PerCom 2005)*, March 2005, Kauai Island, Hawaii.

Yin, X. & Lee, W. (2004). Using link analysis to improve layout on mobile devices. In *Proceedings of the 13ᵗʰ International conference on World Wide Web*, New York City, pages 338-344, New York City.

Chapter VI
WML
(Wireless Markup Language)

INTRODUCTION

Wireless application protocol (WAP) (Open Mobile Alliance, 2003) is a suite of network protocols that specifies ways of sending data across the airwaves. A wireless device is said to be WAP-compatible if, and only if, it has software that is fully capable of handling all WML 1.1 DTD entities. *WML (Wireless Markup Language)* (Open Mobile Alliance, 2001) is the XML-based language that is used in conjunction with WAP to format documents. As with all such protocol suites, WAP is organized hierarchically. At the bottom there are low-level protocols that are used for basic operations such as establishing connections, coding alphanumeric characters, and so on. At the top are the high-level protocols such as WML, which passes on page information. For more information on other WAP protocols, please visit http://www.wapforum.org/. WML script writing and applications will be discussed in Chapters VI through IX:

- **Chapter VI:** The current chapter introduces fundamental WML components such as tables and images.
- **Chapter VII:** Advanced WML, especially dynamic WML pages using CGI (Common Gateway Interface), will be introduced.

- **Chapter VIII:** WMLScript, a lightweight JavaScript language used in conjunction with WML, is explained.
- **Chapter IX:** The construction of a database-driven mobile web site using WML is explained step-by-step.

Background

From inception, WAP has been designed to take into account the limitations inherent in handsets and networks. Because networks are slow, and handsets are unable to carry significant amounts of either memory or power, it is important that all of its elements are as efficient as possible. It is not yet clear whether this has been achieved at the cost of functionality; this will only become apparent when fast mobile networks are commonplace and handset technology has improved. However, it seems reasonable to expect that WAP's efficiency will continue to contribute towards its success. WAP protocols are not the same as web (HTTP) protocols, although WML content can be stored on Web servers. WML content is served up to mobile phones (and other portables) through 'gateways' that stand at the borders of WAP and Web networks. These gateways act as intermediaries between the two types of network, translating from one system to the other and as they are provided by the mobile phone network providers WML developers do not need to install gateway software into their products.

WML is the language now used to write content for WAP phones; the alternative, HDML (Handheld Device Markup Language), has effectively become obsolete. WML is a markup language, which means that WML pages are written and saved as text files using tags like those found in HTML [W3C (World Wide Web Consortium), 1999]. Programmers familiar with HTML should find learning WML fairly easy. There are, however, some important general differences between HTML and WML. These stem from the fact that WML is specified in XML (eXtensible Markup Language) [W3C (World Wide Web Consortium), 2004] and XML specifies a general way to define different types of markup languages, with the following quirks:

- XML-specified languages are case sensitive. For example, the tag <Wml> is different from the tag <wml>. In HTML, case is generally ignored.
- XML-specified languages are strict. Most HTML editors are very forgiving about badly coded HTML pages, and do their best to show some content, but WML editors will simply report an error if given a badly coded WML page.
- All the attributes of elements must be contained within either double (") or single (') quotes. This is slightly different from HTML, where attributes need not be contained within quotation marks for most browsers.

- One way in which WML is strict is that all tags require closure: an opening <wml> tag must have a closing </wml> tag. Some tags do not come in pairs and are allowed to close themselves; these must have a forward slash at the end of their text, for example

WML is all about text. Tags that would slow down communications with hand-held devices are not a part of the WML standard, and the use of tables and images is strongly restricted. Since WML is an XML application, all tags are case sensitive (<wml> is not the same as <WML>), and all tags must be properly closed.

Terminology

Most of the *terminology* for WML comes from XML because WML is an extension of XHTML, which in turn is based on XML and HTML. All the REQUIRED attributes are in bold, while the default attribute value of an attribute, if one exists, is in italics. The following gives notations used by XML:

- **CDATA:** Character Data, part of an SGML or XML document, is not parsed and may therefore contain almost any character sequence. A CDATA-Section begins with "<![CDATA[" and ends with "]]>".
- **PCDATA:** Parsed Character Data. Entities should be expanded by the processing application (web browser, search engine, etc) and any markup encountered should be treated as markup and processed.
- **NMTOKEN:** An NMTOKEN (name token) is any mixture of name characters.
- **ID:** Values of type ID must match the Name production. A name must not appear more than once in an XML document as a value of this type; i.e., ID values must uniquely identify the elements that bear them.

If WML2 (Open Mobile Alliance, 2001) includes WML1 (Open Mobile Alliance, 2000) elements and attributes, WML1 features cannot be expressed in XHTML and CSS. These elements are included using the WML namespace, identified by the "wml:" prefix.

WML SCRIPTS

Every WML document begins with prologue statements:

```
<xml version='1.0'>
<!doctype wml public "-//WAPFORUM//DTD WML 1.2//EN"
http://www.wapforum.org/DTD/wml _ 1.2.xml>
```

Following this prologue is the WML document itself, which in enclosed between the `<wml>` and `</wml>` tags. The WML document uses a deck of cards concept to describe its contents. Each WML document can be thought of as a deck, and each agent/user interaction is described as a card, delimited by the `<card>` and `</card>` WML tags. A `card` tag can specify `id` and `title` attributes for this card. For example,

```
<card id="card0045" title="Help">
```

where the value of `id` is used to provide a unique name for the card and the value of `title` is a text header that can be displayed at the top of an interaction window. Thus, a basic skeleton for a WML document is

```
<xml version='1.0'>
<!doctype wml public "-//WAPFORUM//DTD WML 1.2//EN"
  http://www.wapforum.org/DTD/wml _ 1.2.xml>
<wml>
 <card id="Card1" title="Card1">
 … contents of Card1 …
 </card>
 <card id="Card2" title="Card2">
 … contents of Card2 …
 </card>
 <card id="Card3" title="Card3">
 … contents of Card3 …
 </card>
</wml>
```

A card in a WML document can contain ordinary text, images, links to other WML documents or other cards in this document, input-fields, buttons, calls to procedures, and other elements to support user interactions.

If a WML document has several cards, they are all downloaded from the WAP server as parts of the same document. Navigation between this card in this deck can then be done with no further need for service from the WAP server, although the server's services will be needed if an interaction with a card causes a server-side task to be executed. The WAP protocol is the leading standard for information services on wireless terminals like digital mobile phones. WML is the language used to create pages to be displayed in a WAP browser. WAP homepages are not very different from HTML homepages. The markup language used for WAP is WML, which uses tags, just like HTML, although but the syntax is stricter and conforms to the XML 1.0 standard. WML pages have the extension `*.WML`, just as HTML pages have the extension `*.HTML`.

As noted earlier, WML pages are called `decks` and are constructed as a set of cards, related to each other with links. When a WML page is accessed from a mobile phone, all the cards in the page are downloaded from the WAP server. Navigation between the cards is done by the computer inside the phone without the need for extra access trips to the server. Figure 6.1 gives a WML script of cards where (a) is Card 1 and (b) is Card 2. As the example shows, the WML document is an XML document. The `DOCTYPE` is defined to be `wml`, and the DTD is accessed at http://www.wapforum.org/DTD/wml_1.2.xml. The document content is inside the `<wml>...</wml>` tags, each card in the document is inside `<card>...</card>` tags, and actual paragraphs are inside `<p>...</p>` tags. Each card element has both an `id` and a `title`.

ELEMENT FORMATTING

This section explains how to format WML elements, including paragraphs, line breaks, and text formatting. The `p` tag is primarily used as a container for text and other WML tags; it is important to remember that text in WML cannot stand alone but must be contained in an element. This tag also causes a line break to occur, where the flow of text and images is halted on one line and resumes on the next. Thus, each `p` element starts on a new line in the display. Note that no additional blank line is inserted as for the HTML `p` tag, so this is not a true paragraph break.

The `<br>` tag ends the flow of text and images on the current line and starts a new line at the left margin of the display, which is commonly referred to as a line break. This is a self-closing tag. A WML card can be set up to display the text formatting functions of WML.

- The `<em>` tag renders the specified text in an emphasized font format.
- The `<strong>` tag renders the specified text in some sort of strongly emphasized font format.
- The `<b>` tag renders the specified text in a bold font format.
- The `<i>` tag renders the specified text in an italic font format.
- The `<u>` tag causes the specified text to be underlined.
- The `<big>` tag renders the specified text in a larger than normal font size.

Figure 6.1. A WML script of cards and its corresponding screenshots, where (a) is Card 1 and (b) is Card 2

A WML Script of Cards	Screenshots

```<?xml version="1.0"?>```
 ```<!DOCTYPE wml PUBLIC "-//WAPFORUM//DTD WML 1.2//EN"```
 ```"http://www.wapforum.org/DTD/wml_1.2.xml">```
 	
 ```<wml>```
 ```<card id="card1" title="NBA">```
 ```<do type="NFL">```
 ```<go href="#card2"/>```
 ``</do>
 	
``
 ```NBA is National Basketball Association.```
 ```</card>```
 	
 ```<card id="card2" title="NFL">```
 ```<do type="NBA">```
 ```<go href="#card1"/>```
 ``</do>
 	
``
 ```NFL is National Football League.```
 ```</card>```
 ```</wml>```
	-- NBA --
	 [NFL]
	 NBA is National Basketball Association.
	
	 (a)
	
	 -- NFL --
	 [NBA]
	 NFL is National Football League.
	
	 (b)

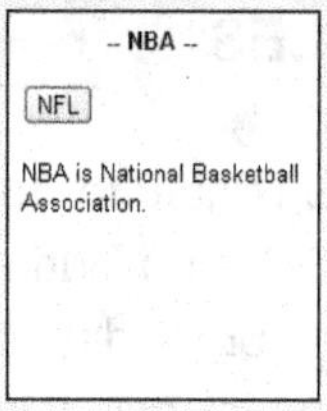

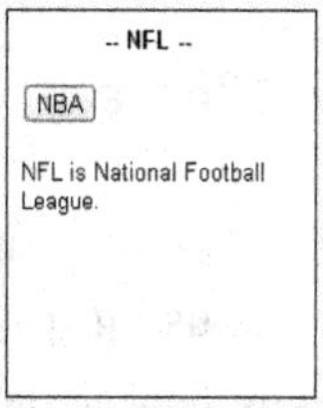

Table 6.1. Some attributes of the element p

Attribute	Value	Description
align	'left'|'right'|'center'	The position of the data or images in the columns
class	NMTOKENS	A class name for the element
id	ID	An identifier for the element
title	CDATA	A title for the element
xml:lang	NMTOKEN	The language used in the element
wml:mode	'wrap'|'nowrap'	Line wrapping or no line wrapping

- The <small> tag renders the specified text in a smaller than normal font size.

TABLES

WML is able to display tables using five elements borrowed from the XHTML [W3C (World Wide Web Consortium), 2002] table module: (i) table, (ii) tr, (iii) td, (iv) th, and (v) caption. The XHTML table module allows authors to arrange data, which may take the form of text, preformatted text, images, links, forms, form fields, or even other tables, into rows and columns of cells. Each table may have an associated caption that provides a short description of the table's purpose.

Table Element

The table tag is used to specify a *table*. A table is a structured presentation of data cells using rows and columns, which are constructed using the tr and td tags. The data cells contain data or information that can be composed of letters,

Figure 6.2. A WML script of element formatting and its corresponding screenshot

A WML Script of Element Formatting	Screenshot

``xml
<?xml version="1.0"?>
<!DOCTYPE wml PUBLIC "-//WAPFORUM//DTD WML 1.2//EN"
 "http://www.wapforum.org/DTD/wml_1.2.xml">
 	
<wml>
 <card title="Formatting">
 normal
 	
 <em>emphasized</em>
 	
 <strong>strong</strong>
 	
 <b>bold</b>
 	
 <i>italic</i>
 	
 <u>underline</u>
 	
 <big>big</big>
 	
 <small>small</small>
 </card>
</wml>
``
	-- Formatting --
	normal
	emphasized
	strong
	bold
	italic
	<u>underline</u>
	big
	small

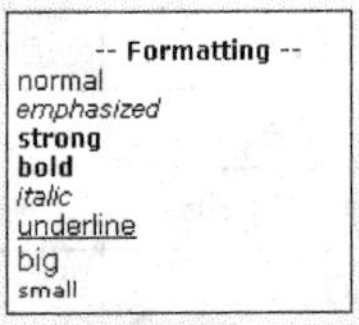

Table 6.2. Some attributes of the element table

Attribute	Value	Description
align	C | D | L | R	The position of the data or images in the columns
class	NMTOKENS	A class name for the element
columns	CDATA	The number of columns in a table. It must be an integer greater than zero.
id	ID	An identifier for the element
title	CDATA	A title for the element
xml:lang	NMTOKEN	The language used in the element

images, links, numbers, strings, and text that are to be displayed in the table. The structure of a table is as follows:

```
<table columns="a number">
 ..<tr>..
  ..<td>..</td>..
 ..</tr>..
</table>
```

where the columns attribute must be used. Table 6.2 gives the attribute list of the table element, where c: center, d: default, l: left, and r: right.

tr Element

This tag is used to create a row in a table element and there can be as many rows as necessary. Each row (tr element) can contain one or more data cells, each of which is a td element that can contain data composed of letters, images, links, numbers, strings, and text that are to be displayed in the table. The structure of a row is as follows:

```
..<tr>..
 ..<td>..</td>..
..</tr>..
```

where the tr elements must appear inside a table element. Table 6.3 shows the attribute list for the v element.

Table 6.3. Some attributes of the element `tr`

Attribute	Value	Description
class	NMTOKENS	A class name for the element
id	ID	An identifier for the element

Table 6.4. Some attributes of the element `td`

Attribute	Value	Description
class	NMTOKENS	A class name for the element
colspan	CDATA	Allows a cell to horizontally span two or more columns
id	ID	An identifier for the element
rowspan	CDATA	Allows a cell to extend down two or more rows
xml:lang	NMTOKEN	The language used in the element

td Element

The `td` tag is used to create a container element to hold a single data cell within a row of a table. The data cell contains data or information that can be composed of letters, images, links, numbers, strings, and text. The structure of a cell is as follows:

```
..<td>..</td>..
```

where the `td` elements must appear inside a `tr` element. Table 6.4 lists some attributes of the element `td`.

th Element

This tag is used to create a header cell for a row of cells in a table element. The purpose of the header is to provide a caption, name, or information related to the column of cells and the header text will be displayed in a bold font style. The coding sequence is

```
<tr><th> ... header ... </th></tr>
```

Table 6.5. Some attributes of the element th

Attribute	Value	Description
align	left | center | right	The horizontal alignment of the cell contents
colspan	CDATA	Allowing a header to horizontally span two or more columns
rowspan	CDATA	Allowing a cell to extend down two or more rows
valign	top | middle | bottom	The vertical alignment of the cell contents

Table 6.6. Some attributes of the element caption

Attribute	Value	Description
class	NMTOKENS	A class name for the element
id	ID	An identifier for the element
style	CDATA	Style sheet properties to the element
title	CDATA	A title for the element
xml:lang	NMTOKEN	The language used in the element

Table 6.5 lists some attributes of the element th.

caption Element

The caption tag allows programmers to place a comment or caption with a table. This caption will not appear inside the table, but rather outside the table either at the top (default) or the bottom and by default will be centered on the table. This tag must occur immediately after the table tag and only one caption is allowed per table. The text that composes the caption may contain HTML tags and style sheet properties. Table 6.6 lists some attributes of the element caption.

A Code Example

Figure 6.3 gives a code example of WML tables and shows its corresponding display on a microbrowser. The exact presentation of the table in the display will be browser dependent.

Figure 6.3. WML Script of a table and its corresponding screenshot

WML Script of a Table	Screenshot
```<?xml version="1.0"?><!DOCTYPE wml PUBLIC "-//WAPFORUM//DTD WML 1.2//EN" "http://www.wapforum.org/DTD/wml_1.2.xml"><wml> <card title="A Table"> <table columns="2" border="1"> <caption>A 3×2 Table</caption> <tr> <th>Column 1</th> <th>Column 2</th> </tr> <tr> <td align="center">Cell 11</td> <td align="center">Cell 12</td> </tr> <tr> <td align="left">Cell 21</td> <td align="right">Cell 22</td> </tr> <tr> <td align="center"> </td> <td align="center"></td> </tr> </table> </card></wml>```	-- A Table -- A 3×2 Table Column 1 / Column 2 Cell 11 / Cell 12 Cell 21 / Cell 22

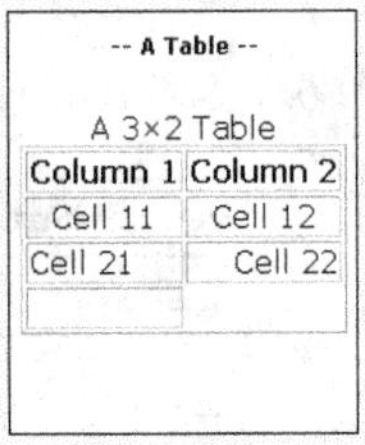

IMAGES

The `img` tag is used to place an image in the text. The black-and-white, one-bit-per-pixel, and compression-free `.wbmp` (wireless bitmap) format is used to code images for wireless display. Programs such as WapTiger's online bmp2wbmp converter (Infotiger Group, n.d.), obtainable at http://www.waptiger.com/bmp2wbmp/, can be used to convert `.bmp`, `.gif`, or `.jpg` files into `.wbmp` format. Many browsers impose an upper size limit on the image, for example, 44 pixels high by 96 pixels wide, and images can also be used as hyperlinks and appear in tables. This is a self-closing tag. Note that

- `.wbmp` is the only image type that can be displayed in a WAP browser such as WinWAP(Slob-Trot Software Oy Ab., n.d.), whereas the TagTag microbrowser (Inetis Ltd., n.d.) only accepts `.bmp` files due to emulation, and

Table 6.7. Some attributes of the element img

Attribute	Value	Description
align	bottom | middle | top	The image alignment with regard to the baseline of the text
alt	CDATA	An alternative string to be displayed if the image can not be displayed
class	NMTOKENS	The class name for the element
height	px | %	The image height
hspace	px | %	The amount of white space to be inserted on both the right and left sides of the image
id	ID	The identifier for the element
wml:localsrc	CDATA	An alternative internal representation for the image
src	URL	The URL address of the image
vspace	px | %	The amount of white space to be inserted both above and below the image
width	px | %	The image width
xml:lang	NMTOKEN	The language used in the element

- the image is not displayed if the script is located in the directory cgi-bin.

Table 6.7 shows the attribute list for the img element, where px is the image pixel. The localsrc attribute specifies an alternative internal representation for the image. If an alternative is specified, it is used by default; otherwise the image is downloaded from the URI specified in the src attribute. Figure 6.5 gives a code example of the img img element and shows its corresponding display on a microbrowser.

LINKS

A WML card can be set up to display the anchor functions (links) of WML including two elements, anchor and a. The anchor tag is used to set a hypertext link and always includes the following tasks, which define what to do when a user selects the link:

- go: navigates to the specified URL.
- noop: dictates that no operation should be performed.

Figure 6.5. WML script of an image and its corresponding screenshot

WML Script of an Image	Screenshot

<pre><?xml version="1.0"?>
<!DOCTYPE wml PUBLIC "-//WAPFORUM//DTD WML 1.2//
EN"
 "http://www.wapforum.org/DTD/wml_1.2.xml">
 	
<wml>
 <card title="Grand Forks Map">
 This is a map of GF, ND.
 <img src="GF.wbmp" align="middle" alt="GF map" />
 </card>
</wml></pre>	

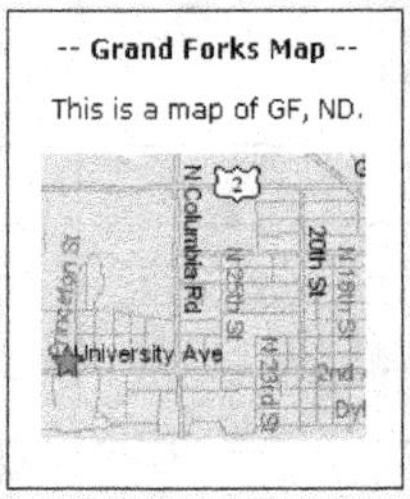

Table 6.8. Some attributes of the element `anchor`

Attribute	Value	Description
class	NMTOKENS	The class name of the element
id	ID	The identifier of the element
style	CDATA	Style sheet properties to the element
title	CDATA	The title offor the element
xml:lang	NMTOKEN	The language used in the element

- `prev`: navigates back to the previous URL in the history stack.
- `refresh`: updates the current display.

When the user activates the `anchor` tag, the user agent must execute the associated task. Some attributes of the element `anchor` are listed in Table 6.8.

The a tag is used with the mandatory `href` attribute to set a hypertext link, which allows users to travel from one XML card or deck to another. The `anchor` tag with the `go` tag can perform the same task as the a tag does. Whenever it is possible, use the a tag instead of the `anchor` tag because the former tag is simple and easy. Some attributes of the element a are given in Table 6.9. An example of a WML script using the elements `anchor` and a, and the corresponding screenshot is shown in Figure 6.6.

Table 6.9. Some attributes of the element a

Attribute	Value	Description
class	NMTOKENS	The class name of the element
href	URL	The URL that is to be loaded when the user selects the link
id	ID	The identifier of the element
style	CDATA	Style sheet properties to the element
title	CDATA	The title offor the element
xml:lang	NMTOKEN	The language used in the element

Figure 6.6. WML script of links and its corresponding screenshot

WML Script of Links	Screenshot
``` <?xml version="1.0"?> <!DOCTYPE wml PUBLIC "-//WAPFORUM//DTD WML 1.2//EN" "http://www.wapforum.org/DTD/wml_1.2.xml"> <wml> <card title="Links"> Google's <anchor>Mobile Homepage <go href="http://wap.google.com/" /> </anchor> NBA's <a href="http://wap.nba.com/"> Mobile Homepage </a> </card> </wml> ```	-- Links -- Google's Mobile Homepage NBA's Mobile Homepage

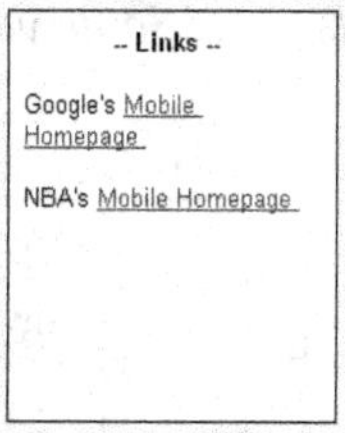

INPUT

The input tag defines an input field, which is a text field where the user can enter some text. Table 6.10 lists some attributes of the element input. The value entered by the user will be assigned to the variable named in the mandatory name attribute after submitted. Validity is based upon the input mask set by the optional format attribute, whose some of permitted values are shown in Table 6.11. For example, if the input mask is form="*N", then the text typed by the user must be any number of any numeric characters.

Table 6.10. Some attributes of the element `input`

Attribute	Value	Description
`checked`	`Checked`	Checked field
`class`	`NMTOKENS`	The class name for the element
`id`	`ID`	The identifier for the element
`name`	`CDATA`	The name of the variable that will be assigned the value of the string or text entered by the user
`size`	`CDATA`	An integer number that sets the character width of the input field
`type`	`text	password	checkbox	radio	submit	reset	hidden`	Input type
`Value`	`CDATA`	The default value for the variable named in the mandatory `name` attribute
`wml:format`	`CDATA`	Input mask
`xml:lang`	`NMTOKEN`	The language used in the element

Table 6.11. Some values of the attribute `format` *of the element* `input`

Value	Description
`A`	Any uppercase alphabetic or punctuation character
`A`	Any lowercase alphabetic or punctuation character
`N`	Any numeric character
`*N`	Any number of any numeric characters
`X`	Any uppercase character
`X`	Any lowercase character
`M`	Any character, treated as uppercase for date entry
`*M`	Any number of any characters, treated as uppercase for date entry
`M`	Any character, treated as lowercase for data entry
`*f`	Any number of any type of characters
`N f`	Any n integer number of any characters
`\c`	Display the character after the slash in the display

Figure 6.7. WML script of input and its corresponding screenshot

A WML Script of Input	Screenshot
```<?xml version="1.0"?> <!DOCTYPE wml PUBLIC "-//WAPFORUM//DTD WML 1.2//EN" "http://www.wapforum.org/DTD/wml_1.2.xml"> <wml> <card title="A Video Game"> Title: <input name="title" size="16" type="text" /> ID: <input name="ID" size="12" type="text" /> Quantity: <input name="quantity" size="4" format="*N" /> </card> </wml>```	-- A Video Game -- Title: Final Fantasy XII ID: B000BL1FZM Quantity: 2

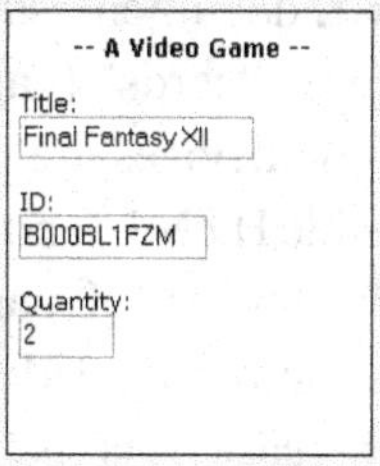

An example of a WML script with `input` tag and the corresponding screenshot is shown in Figure 6.7. This script is virtually useless for all practical purposes because the user data cannot be saved. The next chapter will discuss a CGI method for receiving and saving the user data from the mobile Web interface.

SUMMARY

WML (Wireless Markup Language) is an XML language that is used to specify content and user interfaces for WAP devices such as smartphones. WML documents are XML documents that validate entries against the WML (currently version 2.0) DTD (Document Type Definition). The W3C Markup Validation Service can be accessed at http://validator.w3.org/ in order to validate WML documents. For example, the following WML page could be saved as `example.wml`:

```
<?xml version="1.0"?>
<!DOCTYPE wml PUBLIC "-//PHONE.COM//DTD WML 1.1//EN"
 "http://www.phone.com/dtd/wml11.dtd">
<wml>
 <card id="main" title="First Card">
  <p mode="wrap">This is a sample WML page.</p>
 </card>
</wml>
```

WML pages are stored on a web server. They are accessed via a WAP gateway, which sits between mobile devices and the World Wide Web and passes pages from one to the other much like a proxy. The WAP gateway translates pages into a form suitable for handheld devices. WML is similar to HTML in that it provides navigational support, data input, hyperlinks, text and image presentation, and forms. A WML document is known as a "deck," and data in the deck is structured into one or more "cards" (pages), each which represents a single interaction with the user. Mobile devices are moving towards support for greater amounts of XHTML (eXtensible HTML) and even standard HTML. Currently, most microbrowsers are able to display HTML pages with some limitations and the number of WML pages is not increasing tremendously. As the available processing power in handsets continues to increase, it is likely that at some point WML will no longer be necessary.

REFERENCES

Inetis Ltd. (n.d.). *TTemulator*. Retrieved August 21, 2006, from http://tagtag.com/site/info.php3?p=tt

Infotiger Group. (n.d.) *Online bmp2wbmp Converter*. Retrieved June 30, 2006, from http://www.waptiger.com/bmp2wbmp/

Open Mobile Alliance. (2000). *Wireless Markup Language Specification, Version 1.3*. Retrieved December 21, 2005, from http://www.openmobilealliance.org/tech/affiliates/wap/wap-191-wml-20000219-a.pdf

Open Mobile Alliance. (2001). *Wireless Markup Language Specification, Version 2.0*. Retrieved December 28, 2005, from http://www.openmobilealliance.org/tech/affiliates/wap/wap-238-wml-20010911-a.pdf

Open Mobile Alliance. (2003). *WAP (Wireless Application Protocol)*. Retrieved November 21, 2006, from http://www.wapforum.org/

Slob-Trot Software Oy Ab. (n.d.). *WinWAP 3.1 Pro*. Retrieved July 01, 2004, from http://www.winwap.org/winwap/download.shtml

W3C (World Wide Web Consortium). (1999). *HTML 4.01 Specification*. Retrieved May 12, 2004, from http://www.w3.org/TR/REC-html40/

W3C (World Wide Web Consortium). (2002). *XHTML 1.0 The Extensible HyperText Markup Language*. Retrieved June 5, 2004, from http://www.w3.org/TR/xhtml1/

W3C (World Wide Web Consortium). (2004). *Extensible Markup Language (XML) 1.0 (Third Edition)*. Retrieved December 12, 2005, from http://www.w3.org/TR/REC-xml/

Chapter VII
Advanced WML

INTRODUCTION

Chapter VI discusses the creation of static web pages, which have a fixed content at all times. In order to change static web pages to dynamic ones, it is necessary to implement advanced WML, the subject of this chapter, which requires support from external programs containing procedural languages. There are several methods available for calling external programs the two most common being:

- **PHP (Hypertext Preprocessor):** PHP is a server-side, cross-platform, HTML embedded scripting language that allows programmers to create dynamic web pages. In an HTML document, PHP script (with a similar syntax to that of Perl or C) is enclosed within special PHP tags. Because PHP is embedded within tags, it is possible to jump between HTML and PHP (as in ASP and Cold Fusion) rather than relying on heavy amounts of code to output HTML. PHP is executed on the server, so the client cannot view the PHP code. PHP can perform any task that a CGI program can, and PHP-enabled Web pages can be created and edited just like regular HTML pages.
- **ASP.NET (Active Server Pages):** ASP.NET is a free technology from Microsoft that allows programmers to create dynamic web applications. An ASP.

NET file can contain text, HTML tags and scripts. Scripts in an ASP.NET file are executed on the server. ASP can be used to create web applications ranging from small, personal websites through to large, enterprise-class web applications.

This chapter will focus on applications that use CGI because of its simplicity.

CGI (COMMON GATEWAY INTERFACE)

CGI [W3C (World Wide Web Consortium), 1999] is a standard for running external programs from a World Wide Web HTTP server. CGI specifies how to pass arguments to the executing program as part of the HTTP request and defines a set of environment variables. For most mobile commerce applications, the program generates WML pages that are then passed back to the browser. CGI allows the returned WML (or other document types) to depend in any arbitrary way on the request, and a CGI program can be any program that can accept command-line arguments. Perl is a common choice for writing CGI scripts because it is good at string processing and most Web applications are string-related. Some HTTP servers require CGI programs to reside in a special directory, often "/cgi-bin/ ."

A CGI Script

Figure 7.1 shows the top part of a CGI script, which performs the following two tasks:

1. Informs the Web server about the script type and content type, and prints the WML header information, and
2. Retrieves the user entry data from the Web and converts it into $FORM variables.

The remainder of the CGI script can be made up of any kind of processing or could call other programs. It usually calls a program of a host language with embedded-SQL, such as JDBC, or a 3G language, such as C.

CGI Script Anatomy

The best way to clarify a concept is by giving an example. This section explains how CGI is used by studying the script in Figure 7.1 line by line.

Figure 7.1. A sample of the top part of a CGI script

```
#!/usr/bin/perl

# Send Content-type and header info.
print <<EndofWML;
Content-type: text/vnd.wap.wml \n\n
<?xml version="1.0"?>
<!DOCTYPE wml PUBLIC "-//WAPFORUM//DTD WML 1.2//EN"
   "http://www.wapforum.org/DTD/wml_1.2.xml">;
EndofWML

# Retrieve Web argument values.
read(STDIN, $buffer, $ENV{'CONTENT_LENGTH'});
@pairs = split(/&/, $buffer);
foreach $pair (@pairs) {
  ($name, $value) = split(/=/, $pair);
  $value =~ tr/+/ /;
  $value =~ s/%([a-fA-F0-9][a-fA-F0-9])/pack("C", hex($1))/eg;
  $value =~ s/~!/ ~!/g;
  $FORM{$name} = $value;
}
```

#!/usr/bin/perl

This command tells the server, a Unix server in this case, three things:

1. This is a Perl script.
2. The Perl interpreter is located at /usr/bin/perl. Users can use the Unix command which , locating a command, to find where the Perl interpreter is located, for example,

```
prompt> which perl
   /usr/bin/perl
```

3. Interpret this script.

Note that the character '#' must be in the first column of the first line of the script.

print "Content-type: text/vnd.wap.wml \n\n";

Standard output from CGI scripts will be redirected to the browser, which returns a MIME (Multipurpose Internet Mail Extensions) version of the document. MIME is a standard used for multi-part, multimedia electronic mail messages and World-

Wide Web hypertext documents on the Internet. MIME makes it possible to transfer non-textual data, such as graphics, audio and fax. If the CGI is to generate a WML page, the above command appears in the script before anything can be printed. This command is a content header that tells the receiving web browser what sort of data it is about to receive—in this case, a WML file.

```
read(STDIN, $buffer, $ENV{'CONTENT_LENGTH'});
```

This input stream (web INPUT data) is coming in over STDIN (standard input), and the read function stores the data in the scalar variable $buffer. The environment variable $ENV{'CONTENT_LENGTH'} specifies the length of data to be read. Note that the OFFSET is the offset of the variable SCALAR rather than of the FILEHANDLE. In order to pass data about the information request from the Web server to the script, the server uses command line arguments as well as CGI environment variables. These variables are set when the server executes the gateway program. Environment variables are stored in an associative array called %ENV. These variables include:

- CONTENT _ LENGTH: The length of the submitted data
- GATEWAY _ INTERFACE: The version of the CGI specification used by the server, e.g., CGI/1.1
- HTTP _ HOST: The hostname of the server, e.g., www.cs.und.edu
- HTTP _ REFERED: The URL of the page that called the script, e.g., http://people.cs.und.edu/~wenchen/wml/test.wml
- PATH: The system path the server is running under, e.g., /usr/bin
- QUERY _ STRING: The query string, e.g., query=environment
- REMOTE _ ADDR: The visitor's IP address, e.g., 134.129.216.100
- REMOTE _ HOST: The hostname of the visitor, e.g., www.und.edu
- REQUEST _ METHOD:
  - *GET:* The input values from the form are sent as part of the URL, and saved in the QUERY _ STRING environment variable. The advantage of the GET method is the page can be retrieved again by entering the URL. For example, after submit the keywords: CGI and Perl, to the Yahoo, the URL is changed to the following string:

    http://search.yahoo.com/bin/search?p=cgi%20perl

  - *POST:* Data is sent as a standard input stream to the program. For example, if the input type names are email, password, and button, the standard input may contain the following string after users enter the requested information and submit:

```
email=userid%40cs.und.edu&password=399/
501&button=customer
```

- `SCRIPT _ FILENAME:` The full pathname of the current CGI, e.g., `/home/Agassiz/wenchen/public _ html/cgi-bin/ecs/week8/env.pl`
- `SCRIPT _ NAME:` The interpreted pathname of the current CGI (relative to the document root), e.g., `~wenchen/cgi-bin/ecs/week8/env.pl`
- `SERVER _ NAME:` The server's fully qualified domain name, e.g., `people.aero.und.edu`
- `SERVER _ SOFTWARE:` The name of the information server software answering the request (and running the gateway), e.g., `Apache 1.3.23`
- `SERVER _ PORT:` The port number the server is listening on, e.g., `80`
- `SERVER _ PROTOCOL:` The name of the information protocol this request came in with, e.g., `HTTP/1.1`

```
@pairs = split(/&/, $buffer);
```

Consider the example given above of an input string from the POST method:

```
email=userid%40cs.und.edu&password=399/501&button=customer
```

The variable `$buffer` contains the above string after the `read`. The GET method is not a secure method of sending data since the data is passed through as part of the URL and it will therefore show up in the Web server's logfile.

```
$value =~ tr/+/ /;
```

Consider another example of part of an input string from the POST method:

```
Internet-Enabled+Mobile+Commerce+and+Computing
```

The above code translates every '+' sign back to a space:

```
Internet-Enabled Mobile Commerce and Computing
```

```
$value =~ s/%([a-fA-F0-9][a-fA-F0-9])/pack("C",
hex($1))/eg;
```

QUERY _ STRING is the information that follows the '?' in the URL referenced by this script and represents the query information. The specification for URLs (Berners-Lee, Masinter, & McCahill, 1994) poses a problem, in that it limits the use of allowed characters in URLs to only a limited subset of the ASCII character set:

```
...Only alphanumerics [0-9a-zA-Z], the special characters "$-
_ .+!*'()," [not including the quotes], and reserved characters
used for their reserved purposes may be used unencoded within
a URL.
```

HTML, on the other hand, allows the entire range of the ISO-8859-1 (ISO-Latin) character set to be used in documents; non-ISO-8859-1 characters cannot be used in URLs. To remove any confusion, the URL encoding scheme was created. Any spaces are converted into plus '+' signs to avoid semantic ambiguities. In addition, special characters or 8-bit values are converted into their hexadecimal equivalents and prefaced with a percentage sign '%'. For example, the string

```
Kids Next Door <kids@cs.und.edu>
```

is encoded as

```
Kids+Next+Door+%3Ckids%40cs.und.edu%3E
```

Some commonly encoded characters are given in Table 7.1.
Now consider another part of the input string from the POST method:

```
userid%40cs.und.edu
```

A regular expression that substitutes every %HH hexadecimal pair back to its equivalent ASCII character using the pack() function produces:

```
userid@cs.und.edu
```

Table 7.1. Some encoded characters used in HTML

Normal Character	\t (tab)	\n (return)	/	~	:	;	@	&
URL Encoded String	%09	%0A	%2F	%7E	%3A	%3B	%40	%26

Table 7.2. An example of the execution results of the CGI script in Figure 7.1

Execution	1ˢᵗ	2ⁿᵈ	3ʳᵈ
Variable	$FORM{email}	$FORM{password}	$FORM{button}
Value	userid@cs.und.edu	Secret	CustomerEnter

Some options provided by the Perl substitution operator s include:

- Option g indicates that all occurrences of the pattern are to be replaced.
- Option i indicates that matching is to be done in a case-insensitive manner.
- Option e indicates that the replacement string is to be evaluated as an expression rather than just as a double-quoted string.
- If the pattern is only to be compiled after the variable has been interpolated for the first time, add an o at the end.

```
$value =~ s/~!/ ~!/g;
```

This adds an extra space before the error message.

```
$FORM{$name} = $value;
```

This stores the values into an associative array called %FORM. Applying this to the same example of an input string from the POST method:

```
email=userid%40cs.und.edu&password=secret&button=CustomerEnter
```

After the assignment, the %FORM contents in each execution of the loop are as shown in Table 7.2.

CGI POST and GET Methods

Figure 7.1 shows the script for the CGI POST method, in which data is sent as a standard input stream to the program. For example, if the input type names are email, password, and button the standard input may contain the following string after a user enters the requested information and submits:

```
email=userid%40cs.und.edu&password=399/501&button=customer
```

Figure 7.2. The top part of the CGI Perl script using the GET method

```perl
#!/usr/bin/perl

# Send Content-type and header info.
print <<EndofWML;
Content-type: text/vnd.wap.wml \n\n
<?xml version="1.0"?>
<!DOCTYPE wml PUBLIC "-//WAPFORUM//DTD WML 1.2//EN"
  "http://www.wapforum.org/DTD/wml_1.2.xml">;
EndofWML

# Retrieve information from the variable $ENV{'QUERY_STRING'}.
@pairs = split(/&/, $ENV{'QUERY_STRING'});
foreach $pair (@pairs) {
  ($name, $value) = split(/=/, $pair);
  $value =~ tr/+/ /;
  $value =~ s/%([a-fA-F0-9][a-fA-F0-9])/pack("C", hex($1))/eg;
  $value =~ s/~!/ ~!/g;
  $FORM{$name} = $value;
}
```

For the CGI GET method, the input values from the form are sent as part of the URL, and saved in the QUERY _ STRING environment variable. The advantage of the GET method is that the page can be retrieved again by entering the URL. For example, after submitting the keywords CGI Perl to Yahoo! the URL may be changed to the following string:

```
http://search.yahoo.com/bin/search?p=cgi%20perl
```

where the hexadecimal 20 is an ASCII code for a space and the string %20 thus represents a space according to the URL-encoding, as explained previously. The string "p=cgi%20perl" is then saved in the variable $ENV{`QUERY _ STRING'} and sent to the server to process.

TASKS

WML (Open Mobile Alliance, 2001) is a markup language, which applies speci-fications (for example, HTML or SGML) for marking or tagging a document that indicate its logical structure (such as paragraphs) and gives instructions for its layout on the page for electronic transmission and display. Without the help of a programming language, the functions of a markup language are very limited. This section introduces additional WML elements that require assistance from server-side programs by using CGI. The script in Figure 6.7 is almost useless because the user data cannot be received by host computers. The tasks defined in WML can solve this problem. A task specifies what action to perform when an event, for example entering a card or selecting a link, occurs. Section 6.6 defined four basic tasks in WML: `go`, `noop`, `prev`, and `refresh`.

do Element

The `do` element provides a general mechanism for the user to activate a task, which is performed in response to an event. This is typically performed by the user clicking on a word or phrase in the display. A `do` element can be nested inside the following two elements:

- *The `template` element on the deck-level*: The `do` element will apply to all cards in the deck.
- *The `card` element*: A do element in a card will override the do element in the surrounding deck if both elements are given the same name.

Some attributes of the element `do` and some permitted values for the attribute `type` are given in Tables 7.3 and 7.4, respectively.

go Element

The `go` element specifies the destination URL. The `go` element can contain one or more of the following two elements:

- *`postfield` elements*: These elements specify information to be submitted to the origin server during the request.

Table 7.3. Some attributes of the element do

Attribute	Value	Description
class	NMTOKENS	The class name for the element
id	ID	The identifier for the element
label	CDATA	The string label for the element
type	CDATA	Information about the intent of the element
xml:lang	NMTOKENS	The language used in the element

Table 7.4. Some permitted values of the attribute `type` *of the element* `do`

Type	Description
`Accept`	Acknowledge acceptance
`Delete`	Delete item
`Help`	Request help
`Options`	Provide options or additional operations
`Prev`	Backward navigation
`Reset`	Clearing or reset
`X-*n or x-*n`	Experimental
`Vnd*` Any mix of upper or lower case	Vendor specific

Table 7.5. Some attributes of the element `go`

Attribute	Value	Description
`class`	NMTOKENS	The class name for the element
`href`	URL	The URL for the link's destination
`id`	ID	An identifier for the element
`method`	`post	get`	The HTTP submission method, which includes only two permitted values, `get` and `post`
`xml:lang`	NMTOKEN	The language used in the element

- `setvar` *elements*: They are used to set variables to specified values without requiring destination limitations on passing information as the `postfield` elements.

Table 7.5 lists some attributes of the element `go`.

`postfield` Element

The `postfield` tag contains information to be sent to the server during a URL request. It includes two required attributes:

- the *name* attribute specifies the field name, and
- the *value* attribute specifies the field value.

Table 7.6. Some attributes of the element `postfield`

Attribute	Value	Description
id	ID	The identifier for the element
class	NMTOKENS	The class name for the element
name	CDATA	Part of the name/value pair
value	CDATA	Part of the name/value pair

A `go` element can contain one or more `postfield` elements. Table 7.6 lists some attributes of the element `postfield`.

A Code Example

Figure 7.4 shows a code example of WML tasks and Figure 7.5 gives the CGI script for `Task.pl`. As explained in the previous section, CGI (Common Gateway Interface) is a standard used for running external programs from a World Wide Web HTTP server. CGI specifies how to pass arguments to the executing program as part of the HTTP request. The script `Task.pl` performs the following two tasks:

1. Receives the user input values from the Web.
2. Prints the input values.

This script simply prints the input values without further processing. The CGI and advanced processing of the input values, such as saving them in a database, will be discussed in detail in Chapter VIII.

Figure 7.5 shows the CGI Perl script `Task.pl` activated when the button "Enter a Game" in Figure 7.4 is clicked. This prints the values of the three input arguments to show how a task is performed. This script is provided solely as a demonstration; most server-side scripts perform more complicated tasks, such as accessing databases.

SELECTIONS

A select list offers a series of choices from which the user chooses one or more items. It is similar to the radio buttons, checkboxes, and pull-down menus provided in HTML.

Figure 7.4. A task example and its display on a microbrowser

A WML Page of a Task Example	Screenshot

``<?xml version="1.0"?>
<!DOCTYPE wml PUBLIC "-//WAPFORUM//DTD WML 1.2//EN"
  "http://www.wapforum.org/DTD/wml_1.2.xml">
 	
<wml>
 <card title="A Video Game">
  <p>
   Title: <input name="title" size="13" type="text" />
   ID: <input name="ID" size="12" type="text" />
   Quantity: <input name="quantity" size="4" type="*N" />
 	
   <do type="accept" label="Enter a Game">
    <go href="http://people.cs.und.edu/~wenchen/cgi-
bin/device/Task.pl" method="post">
     <postfield name="title" value="$(title)"/>
     <postfield name="ID" value="$(ID)"/>
     <postfield name="quantity" value="$(quantity)"/>
    </go>
   </do>
  </p>
 </card>
</wml>```
	-- A Video Game --
	
	Title: Final Fantasy VII
	
	ID: B000BL1FZM
	
	Quantity: 2
	
	[! Enter a Game]

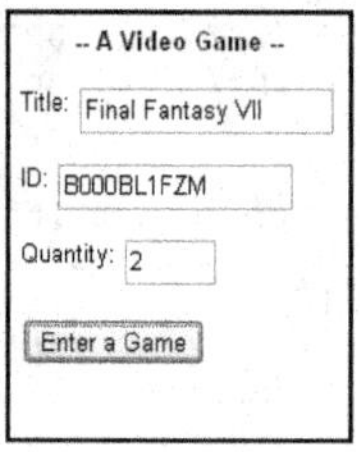

select Element

The select tag defines a selectable list and the option tag is used to define the options in the selectable list. Table 7.7 lists some attributes of the element select. Some of the attributes are explained as follows:

- The name attribute specifies the name of the variable to set with the result of the selection.
- The value attribute specifies the default-selected option element.
- The iname attribute specifies the name of the variable to be set with the index of the selection.
- The ivalue attribute specifies the index of the default-selected option element.

option Element

The option tag defines an option in a selectable list, which is defined by the select tag. Related option elements can be grouped into sub-listings using optgroup elements. Table 7.8 lists some attributes of the element option.

Figure 7.5. The CGI Perl script Task.pl and its output on a microbrowser

The CGI Perl Script `Task.pl`	Screenshot
| ```
#!/usr/bin/perl

# Send Content-type and header info.
print <<EndofWML;
Content-type: text/vnd.wap.wml \n\n
<?xml version="1.0"?>
<!DOCTYPE wml PUBLIC "-//WAPFORUM//DTD WML 1.2//EN"
  "http://www.wapforum.org/DTD/wml_1.2.xml">;
EndofWML

# Retrieve Web input values.
read(STDIN, $buffer, $ENV{'CONTENT_LENGTH'});
@pairs = split(/&/, $buffer);
foreach $pair (@pairs)  {
  ($name, $value) = split(/=/, $pair);
  $value =~ tr/+/ /;
  $value =~ s/%([a-fA-F0-9][a-fA-F0-9])/pack("C",
hex($1))/eg;
  $value =~ s/~!/ ~!/g;
  $FORM{$name} = $value;
}

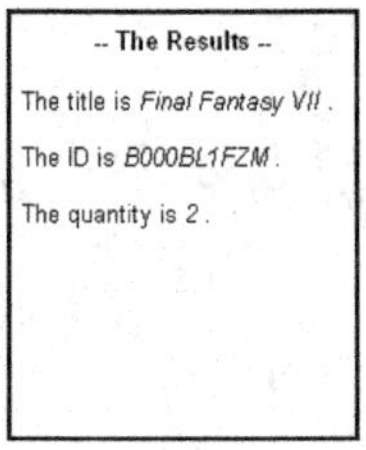

print( "<wml><card title=\"The Results\"><p>" );
print( "The title is <i>$FORM{title}</i>.<br /><br />" );
print( "The ID is <i>$FORM{ID}</i>.<br /><br />" );
print( "The quantity is <i>$FORM{quantity}</i>.<br />" );
print( "</p></card></wml>" );
``` | **-- The Results --**<br><br>The title is *Final Fantasy VII*.<br><br>The ID is *B000BL1FZM*.<br><br>The quantity is *2*. |

Table 7.7. Some attributes of the element `select`

Attribute	Value	Description
`id`	`ID`	The identifier for the element
`iname`	`NMTOKEN`	The name of the variable that is set with the index result of the selection
`ivalue`	`CDATA`	The pre-selected option element
`class`	`NMTOKEN`	The class name for the element
`multiple`	`true	false`	Single or multiple item in the select list
`name`	`CDATA`	The name of the variable to which the results of the selection will be assigned
`title`	`CDATA`	A string for additional information about the element
`value`	`CDATA`	Default value of the variable in the `name` attribute
`xml:lang`	`NMTOKEN`	The language used in the element
```

Table 7.8. Some attributes of the element `option`

Attribute	Value	Description
class	NMTOKENS	The class name for the element
id	ID	The identifier for the element
value	CDATA	The value associated with the element
wml:onpick	URL	The URL that is to be loaded when the item is selected or unselected
xml:lang	NMTOKEN	The language used in the element

Code Examples

Figure 7.6 shows a code example of single-item selection similar to the radio buttons of HTML. This example offers three video games from which a user can select one, and only one game. The selection specifies a single item if the value of the attribute `multiple` is `false`. Once the button "Select a Game" is clicked, this activates a CGI Perl script at http://people.cs.und.edu/~wenchen/cgi-bin/Single.pl, which receives an argument `$(item)` showing which item has been selected.

Figure 7.7 shows the CGI script `single.pl` that is activated when the submission button, in this case "Select a Game," is clicked. If the third game, Underground, is selected the CGI variable `$buffer` will include the substring "item=3." The loop in the script then produces a variable `$FORM{item}` containing the value 3 and the `if` statement displays the title of the selected game.

Fgure 7.8 shows another code example of multiple-item selection similar to the checkboxes of HTML. This example allows users to select more than one game from among the three options presented. The selection allows multiple items if the value of the attribute `multiple` is `true`. Once the button "Select Games" is clicked, this activates a CGI Perl script at http://people.cs.und.edu/~wenchen/cgi-bin/Multiple.pl, which receives an argument `$(items)` showing which items have been selected.

Figure 7.9 shows the CGI script `Multiple.pl` activated when the submission button, once again "Select Games" in this example, is clicked. If the first and third games, Final Fantasy XII and Underground, are selected, the CGI variable `$buffer` will include the substring "items=1;3." The first loop in the script then produces a variable `$FORM{items}` containing a string "1;3." The following command

```
@items = split(/;/, $FORM{items});
```

then assigns the values 1 and 3 to `$items[0]` and `$items[1]`, respectively. `@itmes` is an array name for Perl and `$items[0]` is the first element of the array,

Figure 7.6. A single-item selection example and its display on a microbrowser

The WML Page of Single-Item Selection	Screenshot

<pre><?xml version="1.0"?>
<!DOCTYPE wml PUBLIC "-//WAPFORUM//DTD WML 1.2//EN"
  "http://www.wapforum.org/DTD/wml_1.2.xml">
 	
<wml>
 <card title="Selecting Single Item">
  <p>
   <select name="item" title="item" multiple="false">
    <option value="1">Final Fantasy XII</option>
    <option value="2">Grand Theft Auto</option>
    <option value="3">Underground</option>
   </select>
 	
   <do type="accept" label="Select a Game">
    <go href="http://people.cs.und.edu/~wenchen/cgi-
bin/device/Single.pl" method="post">
     <postfield name="item" value="$(item)"/>
    </go>
   </do>
  </p>
 </card>
</wml></pre>
	-- Selecting Single Item --
	
	Underground
	
	Select a Game

$items[1] is the second element, and so on. The second loop prints the titles of the selected games.

A CASE STUDY: A MOBILE WEB SEARCH ENGINE USING A TOPIC-SPECIFIC KNOWLEDGE BASE

Using Internet-enabled mobile handheld devices to access the World Wide Web is a promising new addition for Web and traditional e-commerce retailers. Mobile handheld devices provide convenient and portable access to the huge amount of information on the Internet for mobile users from any location and at any time. However, choosing appropriate queries for web search engines is never an easy task and the search results may or may not be relevant to what users are really looking for. Also, the constraints inherent in handheld devices, such as slow communication, low storage capacity, and awkward input methods must be considered. Due to the above factors, information discovery using handheld devices is currently both impractical and inconvenient.

This case study investigates a new, innovative focused search method for handheld devices that uses a topic-specific knowledge base instead of the entire Web.

Figure 7.7. The CGI Perl script `Single.pl` *and its output on a microbrowser*

The CGI Perl Script **Single.pl**	Screenshot
``#!/usr/bin/perl

Send Content-type and header info.
print <<EndofWML;
Content-type: text/vnd.wap.wml \n\n
<?xml version="1.0"?>
<!DOCTYPE wml PUBLIC "-//WAPFORUM//DTD WML 1.2//EN"
  "http://www.wapforum.org/DTD/wml_1.2.xml">;
EndofWML

# Retrieve Web input values.
read(STDIN, $buffer, $ENV{'CONTENT_LENGTH'});
@pairs = split(/&/, $buffer);
foreach $pair (@pairs) {
  ($name, $value) = split(/=/, $pair);
  $value =~ tr/+/ /;
  $value =~ s/%([a-fA-F0-9][a-fA-F0-9])/pack("C",
hex($1))/eg;
  $value =~ s/~!/ ~!/g;
  $FORM{$name} = $value;
}

print("<wml><card title=\"The Results\"><p>");
if ($FORM{item} == 1) {
  $item = "Final Fantasy XII";
}
elsif ($FORM{item} == 2) {
  $item = "Grand Theft Auto";
}
elsif ($FORM{item} == 3) {
  $item = "Underground";
}
else {
  $item = "Not found";
}
print("The game <i>$item</i> is selected.");
print("</p></card></wml>");``` | The game **Underground** is selected. |

The system performs the following three tasks:

1. Autonomous crawlers are sent to the (mobile) Internet to collect topic-specific data. Two kinds of data storage, a knowledge base on a server and persistent storage on a device, are updated accordingly to reflect the latest content.
2. Users are then able to search the data stored in the persistent storage on the devices off-line, thus receiving the results instantly.
3. If the results from the local searches do not produce the information being sought, users can then search the entire knowledge base on the server.

Figure 7.8. A multiple-item selection example and its display on a microbrowser

WML Page of Multiple-Item Selection	Screenshot

<pre><?xml version="1.0"?>
<!DOCTYPE wml PUBLIC "-//WAPFORUM//DTD WML 1.2//EN"
  "http://www.wapforum.org/DTD/wml_1.2.xml">
 	
<wml>
  <card title="Selecting Multiple Items">
    <p>
     <select name="items" title="items" multiple="true">
      <option value="1">Final Fantasy X</option>
      <option value="2">Grand Theft Auto</option>
      <option value="3">Underground</option>
     </select>
 	
     <do type="accept" label="Select Games">
      <go href="http://people.cs.und.edu/~wenchen/cgi-
bin/device/Multiple.pl" method="post">
       <postfield name="items" value="$(items)"/>
      </go>
     </do>
    </p>
  </card>
</wml></pre>
	-- Selecting Multiple Items --
	
	 ☑ Final Fantasy X
	 ☐ Grand Theft Auto
	 ☑ Underground
	
	 [Select Games]

Also, query formulation assistance for query composition can be provided to help users more effectively find information and proper user interfaces developed to show the search results. This approach has been proved to greatly improve both the speed and the quality of the results returned for mobile searches.

The Development of a Focused Search Engine

A mobile web focused search system based on this approach was proposed by Bemgal (2006). Figure 7.10 shows the system structure of a typical search engine (Hu *et al.*, 2004), which traditionally consists of three major components: (i) the crawler, (ii) the indexing software, and (iii) the search and ranking software:

- A crawler is a program that automatically scans various web sites and collects web documents from them. Crawlers follow the links on a site to find other relevant pages. Two search algorithms, breadth-first searches and depth-first searches, are widely used by crawlers to traverse the Web.
- Automatic indexing is the process of algorithmically examining information items to build a data structure that can be quickly searched. Traditional search engines utilize the following information, provided by HTML scripts, to locate the desired web pages: (i) content, (ii) descriptions, (iii) hyperlink,

Figure 7.9. The CGI Perl script `Multiple.pl` *and its output on a microbrowser*

The CGI Perl Script `Multiple.pl`	Screenshot
<pre>#!/usr/bin/perl

Send Content-type and header info.
print <<EndofWML;
Content-type: text/vnd.wap.wml \n\n
<?xml version="1.0"?>
<!DOCTYPE wml PUBLIC "-//WAPFORUM//DTD WML 1.2//EN"
"http://www.wapforum.org/DTD/wml_1.2.xml">;
EndofWML

# Retrieve Web input values.
read(STDIN, $buffer, $ENV{'CONTENT_LENGTH'});
@pairs = split(/&/, $buffer);
foreach $pair (@pairs) {
  ($name, $value) = split(/=/, $pair);
  $value =~ tr/+/ /;
  $value =~ s/%([a-fA-F0-9][a-fA-F0-9])/pack("C",
hex($1))/eg;
  $value =~ s/~!/ ~!/g;
  $FORM{$name} = $value;
}

print("<wml><card title=\"The Results\"><p>");
@items = split(/;/, $FORM{items});
foreach $item (@items) {
  if ($item == 1) {
    $game = "Final Fantasy XII";
  }
  elsif ($item == 2) {
    $game = "Grand Theft Auto";
  }
  elsif ($item == 3) {
    $game = "Underground";
  }
  else {
    $game = "Not found";
  }
  print("<i>$game</i> is selected.

");
}
print("</p></card></wml>");</pre> | -- The Results --

Final Fantasy X is selected.

Underground is selected. |

(iv) hyperlink text, (v) keywords, (vi) page title, (vii) text with a different font, and (viii) the first sentence.

- Query processing is the activity of analyzing a query and comparing it to indexes to find relevant items. A user enters a keyword or keywords, along with Boolean modifiers such as "and," "or," or "not," into a search engine, which then scans indexed Web pages for the keywords. To determine in which order to display pages to the user, the engine uses an algorithm to rank pages that contain the keywords.

Figure 7.10. System structure of a generic web search engine

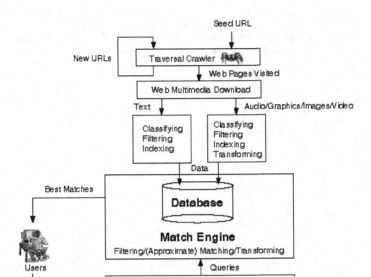

Details of the three components of the proposed focused web search engine are given next.

The Crawler

Crawlers, also known as robots or agents, are the programs that automatically explore the World Wide Web by first retrieving a document and then recursively retrieving some or all the documents that are referenced in it (Menczer, Pant, & Srinivasan, 2004). Crawlers follow the links on a site to find other relevant pages. There are generally two algorithms involved in crawlers: one is a depth-first search and the other is a breadth-first search. A breadth-first search is applied in this example. Figure 7.11 shows the crawler structure, where an "array" is used for the queue for storing the URLs. Initially, a seed URL, provided by the system administrator, is stored in the queue, which forms the basis for the crawler to explore the Web. The crawler takes one URL at a time and retrieves its content. The content is then parsed and the keywords are collected and saved. The URLs referred by this page are added to the end of the queue and the process is repeated for each URL in turn.

Figure 7.11. A crawling procedure

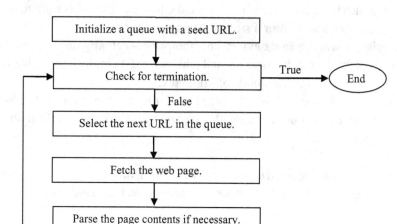

In this way, the information for the knowledge base is collected. The crawling stops when the queue is empty.

Indexing Using a Knowledge Base

A knowledge base such as the one used in this case study is a repository storing web data for searches. Information about a topic of interest can be represented either as a set of thematically related URLs or as a set of queries (Aridor *et al.*, 2001). The first approach is applied in this system, where a seed URL is provided to initiate the crawler's exploration of the Web. The knowledge base constructed is comprised of topic-related terms and URLs. This knowledge base should facilitate the retrieval of topic-related information, as it is constructed using related information only. The crawler is responsible for knowledge acquisition. In general, several crawlers are used to acquire data. Knowledge acquisition is considered as an evolutionary process, with the knowledge base evolving by iteratively collecting URLs from the Web starting with a seed URL. Once the data has been collected, it is processed, indexed, and stored in the knowledge base. Many indexing strategies may be used to organize the data that is gathered; this case study uses a web-document index created based on the URLs and hyperlinked text in a document. The indexed data is stored in three places:

- **A knowledge base residing on the server:** This includes a set of database tables, which store the retrieved URLs and URL text. Its size is limited to the few megabytes allowed for a student account.
- **A persistent storage in a device:** This footprint is actually implemented using files in the server. It stores a small part of the data in the knowledge base and is limited to a few hundreds of kilobytes.
- **A cache in a device:** This is simulated by creating a space of tens of kilobytes in the server. It contains only a small part of the data held in either the footprint or knowledge base.

Though simulation is applied to the last two methods, this should not pose a problem if the storage is based on the memory available in actual handheld devices.

Searching and Ranking

When a user submits a query, the search engine will search the indexes to find relevant web pages and display the results on the screen. The order of the displayed results is based on the use of a ranking methodology. This case study uses query formulation assistance to facilitate mobile data search and entry, usually a problem for mobile users, by providing users with a list of related terms using the lexicon stored in the knowledge base. As an alternative to entering a series of query keywords, users can pick related terms from the list to help the system perform better searches and reduce the amount of data entry required. Once the query has been formulated and submitted, the search engine performs the matching and displays the search results according to the number of keywords matched. Various search filtering operations, such as stopword deletion and space removal, can also be implemented.

Experiments

This section shows some screenshots that demonstrate various information discoveries used in this research. There are, however, some factors that should be considered when implementing the entire system:

- The first is the number of URLs stored in the knowledge base. Due to the limited capacity of an Oracle student account, only a relatively few URLs are stored, though a large number of URLs are generated. The page content is not stored, which could be useful.
- Second, several WAP browsers are available for mobile application testing and implementation (Slob-Trot Software Oy Ab., n.d.). One of the most popular, "TTEmulator," is used here. This is an online WAP emulator hosted at http://www.tagtag.com/ (Inetis Ltd., n.d.).

- Finally, there is the issue of mobile interface usability (Buchanan *et al.*, 2001). Mobile interfaces are usually small and inconvenient for users. This case study used an innovative mobile interface designed to make the entire system feasible and easy to use.

Experimental Results

Initially, a predetermined set of topics was presented to users as a drop-down list, along with another option that allowed users to create their own topics of interest. The topics were hosted by a knowledge base stored in the backend server. A small part of the knowledge base was also stored in the persistent storage of a device. Users then performed searches either directly on the knowledge base or via the footprint on the device. Query formulation assistance was also provided in this system. Users were allowed to refine their queries for better results. Since there was also access to the knowledge base available on the device, albeit only a limited portion, searches could initially be performed off-line. If the search results from the footprint were not of interest to the users, then the entire knowledge base was available for searching on-line. Users were also able to cache their search results and perform searches on the cached results later. The following two demonstrations show the strength of this system.

Figure 7.12 illustrates searching the web pages of Sun Microsystems at http://www.sun.com/ using the knowledge base:

a.   The system entry page allowed users to select one of the three demonstrations: UND, Sun Microsystems, and Yahoo Sports.
b.   A list of relevant terms was displayed next, which consisted of the hyperlinked text.
c.   The query formulation interface then came up, which allowed users to provide additional information to supplement the original query.
d.   Finally, the search results generated from the knowledge base were listed.

The above demonstration shows the results of searches on the pre-set data. The system also allowed users to dynamically collect and search data. Figure 7.13 gives another demonstration showing dynamic knowledge collection and searching:

a.   The interface allowed users to enter a seed URL for knowledge collection.
b. & c.
    After the knowledge base had been constructed, users were able to start performing searches using the system's query formulation assistance function.

Figure 7.12. A demonstration of searching the "Sun Microsystems" knowledge base

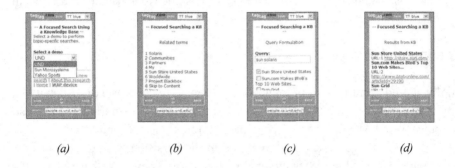

(a)   (b)   (c)   (d)

d. Finally, the search results from the knowledge base were displayed.

Users were again able to perform their searches off-line using the footprint or cache in the device itself.

Comparisons

These experimental results show that the new methods described in this case study increase the search speed and improve the relevance between the search results and the original query. All search results produced were related to the query either directly or indirectly and no irrelevant results were displayed. This sub-section compares these search results to the results from a Google WAP Search (Google, n.d.). Figure 7.14 shows the screen dumps from both systems for the query "sun solaris":

Figure 7.13. Second demonstration showing dynamic knowledge collection and searching

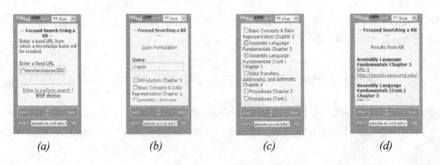

(a)   (b)   (c)   (d)

Figure 7.14. Search results from the proposed new method and Google

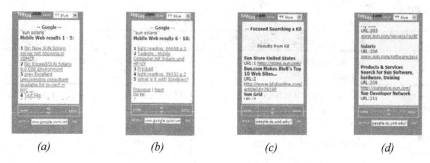

| (a) | (b) | (c) | (d) |

- Figures 7.14.a and 7.14.b show the top-10 search results from the Google WAP Search and
- Figures 7.14.c and 7.14.d show the top-6 search results from the new system.

Although Google provided more search results, several of the top results were not related to the query. The search method described in the case study produced fewer results, but all were related to the query.

Table 7.9 summarizes the differences between the new approach and Google's WAP Search. The above experimental results indicate that this approach tends to benefit from increased relevance between the search results and the original query compared to commercial search engines. Though the search engine implemented may not be able to compete with commercial search engines in scale, this case study shows the effectiveness of methods and concepts designed with the limitations of handheld devices in mind. The main disadvantage of using Google's WAP Search or any other search engines is that irrelevant results are frequently displayed, a major irritant on the small screen of a handheld device.

Case-Study Conclusion

This case study described a new approach for mobile information retrieval, applying a focused search to a topic-specific knowledge base with topics are selected by system administrators. The advantages and disadvantages of using this system were as follows:

- **Advantages:**
  - The users did not need to search the entire (mobile) Internet to find relevant information. Instead, they were able to select a topic of interest and

Table 7.9. Comparisons between the approach used in the case study and Google's WAP search

	Case Study	**Google**
Result Relevancy	Results closely related to the query	Some results related to the query but some not
Number of Results	Fewer, but all related to the query directly or indirectly	More, but after the first few results the relevance decreasing
Search Speed	Fast, because of using query formulation assistance	Slow, because of the lack of query formulation
Options	Caching results and checking related URLs and terms	No advanced features available

perform a search only on information related to that topic.

o   In the absence of wireless access, information could still be searched and retrieved since a small footprint was included in the device.

o   Navigation and browsing were greatly improved with the help of the new interfaces.

o   Query formulation assistance was provided and found to greatly facilitate searching and date entry.

- **Disadvantages:**

o   Since server-side methodology was used here, unforeseen difficulties may arise if the approach is implemented using handheld devices on the client side.

o   Because of the small storage space available, the indexed topics and data are limited. For example, the information requested might not be stored at all.

Though only server-side handheld computing was examined in this case study, it should be possible to extend this approach to client-side devices. Several environments/languages are currently used in client-side handheld computing, including BREW, J2ME, Palm OS, Symbian, and Windows Mobile. The data could be stored in the persistent storage of a handheld device, such as the Record management system in J2ME. Future improvements are expected to include:

- Extending this approach to different types of handheld devices.
- Implementing and strengthening the system on a large scale using both client-side and server-side handheld computing.

- Saving more information in the knowledge base, such as the text of web pages and their audio/video contents, thus further improving mobile information retrieval.

With more people using handheld devices, mobile information discovery becomes crucial. While current devices may not possess sufficient memory or processing capabilities to apply the methods used in the case study, hopefully in the near future these devices will gain additional, enhanced features that will enable them to handle the proposed methods and many other complex tasks in the near future.

SUMMARY

The previous chapter introduced the fundamentals of WML (Wireless Markup Language) and this chapter extended this by looking at advanced features of WML. The technology of CGI (Common Gateway Interface), used to created dynamic WML pages, was also considered in this chapter. Two advanced topics, tasks and selections, using CGI were explained, giving examples. A case study was then used to describe a new approach for mobile information retrieval, applying a focused search to a topic-specific knowledge base with topics selected by system administrators. The knowledge base was located on a server and could be accessed using wireless communication. Users were able to select one of several topics and start searching the knowledge base. A small part of the knowledge base could also be downloaded to the persistent storage in a device and searches conducted locally in a disconnected mode. If the users did not receive useable results from local searches, they were then able to extend their search to the entire knowledge base.

REFERENCES

Aridor, Y., Carmel, D., Lempel, R., Maarek, Y. S., & Soffer, A. (2001). Knowledge encapsulation for focused search from pervasive devices. In *Proceedings of the WWW10 Conference*, pp. 754-764.

Bemgal, J. (2006). *A Focused Search Using a Topic-Specific Knowledge Base for Web-Enabled Mobile Handheld Devices*. Unpublished master's thesis, University of North Dakota.

Berners-Lee, T., Masinter, L. & McCahill, M. (1994). *RFC 1783: Uniform Resource Locators (URL)*. Retrieved April 07, 2003, from http://www.rfc-editor. org/rfc/rfc1738.txt

Buchanan, G., Farrant, S., Jones, M., Thimbleby, H., Marsden, G., & Pazzani, M. (2001). Improving mobile Internet usability. In *Proceedings of the 10th International WWW Conference,* Hong-Kong.

Google. (n.d.) *Google's WAP Search.* Retrieved March 23, 2007, from http://www.google.com/wml/

Hu, W.-C., Yang, H.-J., Yeh, J.-h., & Lee, C.-w. (2004). World Wide Web search technologies. In Mehdi Khosrow-Pour, editor, *Encyclopedia of Information Science and Technology*, I(V), pages 3111-3117, IRM Press.

Inetis Ltd. (n.d.). *TT Emulator.* Retrieved September 18, 2006, from http://www.inetis.com/index.php?module=ttemulator

Menczer, F., Pant, G., & Srinivasan, P. (2004). Crawling the Web. In M. Levene and A. Poulovassilis, editors, *Web Dynamics: Adapting to Change in Content, Size, Topology and Use,* Springer-Verlag.

Open Mobile Alliance. (2001). *Wireless Markup Language Specification, Version 2.0.* Retrieved December 28, 2005, from http://www.openmobilealliance.org/tech/affiliates/wap/wap-238-wml-20010911-a.pdf

Slob-Trot Software Oy Ab. (n.d.). *WinWAP 3.1 Pro.* Retrieved July 01, 2004, from http://www.winwap.org/winwap/download.shtml

W3C (World Wide Web Consortium). (1999). *CGI: Common Gateway Interface.* Retrieved May 12, 2007, from http://www.w3.org/CGI/

WinWap Technologies. (n.d.). *WinWAP Browsers.* Retrieved September 14, 2006, from http://www.winwap.com/products_2.php

Chapter VIII
WMLScript

INTRODUCTION

WML is a markup language used for text formatting and displaying (Open Mobile Alliance, 2001). However, the functions of a markup language are limited if there is no support from other programming languages. Two kinds of programming languages can help to extend the functions of WML:

1. server-side scripts such as CGI Perl running on servers, and
2. client-side scripts such as WMLScript running on handheld devices.

This chapter focuses on WMLScript, building on the descriptions of WML and CGI provided in the previous two chapters. *WMLScript* (Open Mobile Alliance, 2000a) is a light JavaScript language (Netscape Communications Corporation, n. d.) that must be compiled into byte code on a server before it can run on a handheld device. It is based on ECMAScript but has been modified to better support low bandwidth communication and thin clients. WMLScript can be used in conjunction with WML to provide intelligent content to clients, but can also be used as a stand alone tool.

WMLSCRIPT ACTIVATION

Unlike JavaScripts, which are embedded in HTML pages, WMLScripts are not embedded in WML pages. To activate a WMLScript from a WML page, the page contains references to the URL of the WMLScript. Figure 8.1 shows how to call a WMLScript from a WML page. The example shown is a single-item selection for displaying the selected sports page. Assume the WML script in Figure 8.1 is located at http://people.cs.und.edu/~userid/handheld/wmls/Activate.wml. Once the "Display" label is clicked, the external WMLScript function goto in Functions. wmls in Figure 8.2 will be activated. The actual URL of functions.wmls is located at http://people.cs.und.edu/~userid/handheld/wmls/Functions.wmls. The activation uses the href attribute of the go element to find the destination WMLScript and sends an argument $(item) storing the item selected.

The WMLScript function goto in Figure 8.2 is in a file called Functions. wmls and the function uses the extern keyword. When using this keyword, the function can be called by other functions or WML events outside the .wmls file. To keep a function private, the extern keyword must be dropped. The optional extern keyword can be used to specify a function to be externally accessible. Such functions can be called from outside the compilation unit in which they are defined. There must be at least one externally accessible function in a compilation

Figure 8.1. The WML script Activate.wml *showing how to activate a WMLScript*

The WML Script Activate.wml	Screenshot
| ```
<?xml version="1.0"?>
<!DOCTYPE wml PUBLIC "-//WAPFORUM//DTD WML 1.2//EN"
  "http://www.wapforum.org/DTD/wml_1.2.xml">

<wml>
 <card title="Call WMLScript">
  <p>
   <select name="item" title="item" multiple="false">
    <option value="MLB">MLB</option>
    <option value="NBA">NBA</option>
    <option value="NFL">NFL</option>
    <option value="NHL">NHL</option>
   </select><br />

   <do type="accept" label="Display">
    <go href="Functions.wmls#goto($(item))"/>
   </do>
  </p>
 </card>
</wml>
``` | -- Call WMLScript -- <br><br> MLB ▾ <br><br> Display |
```

Figure 8.2. The function goto *activated by the WML page in Figure 8.1*

The WMLScript External Function goto	Screenshot of an Output of the Function goto
| ```
extern function goto( item )  {

  if ( item == "NBA" )  {
    WMLBrowser.go( http://wap.nba.com/ );
  }
  else {
    if (item == "NFL")  {
      WMLBrowser.go( http://wap.nfl.com/ );
    }
    else {
      alert( "Not found!" );
    }
  }
}
``` | NBA<br>I Love This Game!<br>**ⓈNBA** |

unit. This function checks whether the item, for example NBA or NFL, is selected. If it is, the corresponding homepage is displayed; if not, the message "Not found" is shown. It uses three features of WMLScript, which will be explained in more detail later:

1. if statement,
2. the go function of the WMLBrowser library, which goes to a new card, specified by the new URL, and returns an empty string, and
3. the alert function of the Dialog library, which displays a message, waits for a confirmation, and then returns an empty string.

STATEMENTS

WMLScript statements consist of expressions and keywords used with the appropriate syntax. A single statement may span multiple lines and multiple statements may occur on a single line. The following sections define the statements: for, if... else, return, var, and while.

If Statement

This statement is used to specify conditional execution of statements. Its syntax is as follows:

```
IfStatement :
```
```

```
if ( Expression ) Statement else Statement
if ( Expression ) Statement
```

It works as follows:

1. The Expression (condition) can be any WMLScript expression that is found to be a boolean or invalid value.
2. If the condition is judged to be true, the first statement is executed.
3. If condition is found to be false or invalid, the second (optional) else statement is executed.

The Statement can be any WMLScript statement and the else is always tied to the closest if. Figure 8.2 shows an example using the if statement.

While Statement

A loop is created by using this statement, whose syntax is as follows:

WhileStatement:
while (Expression) Statement

The statement execution includes the following steps:

1. Evaluate the Expression (condition), which can be any WMLScript expression that is found to be a boolean or invalid value.
2. If the condition is found to be true, execute the Statement.
3. When the condition is judged to be false or invalid, execution continues with the statement following Statement.
4. The loop repeats as long as the specified condition is true.

Figure 8.3 shows an example of using a while statement. The page receives an input of a nonnegative integer n from the user and then calls a function series in a file functions.wmls to calculate the sum of the sequence 1, 2, 3, ..., n. The function takes one input argument, $(n), which is the user input, and returns one output argument, $(result), which is the result (sum).

Figure 8.4 shows the series function in the file Functions.wmls. It performs the actual calculation of the arithmetic series using a while statement. The result is set using the function WMLBrowser.setVar(destination, value) and the interface is updated based on the current content by the function WMLBrowser.

Figure 8.3. An example of a `while` *statement calculating the sum of a sequence and its display on a microbrowser*

The WML Page of Using a WMLScript `while` Statement	Screenshot

``
<?xml version="1.0"?>
<!DOCTYPE wml PUBLIC "-//WAPFORUM//DTD WML 1.2//EN"
   "http://www.wapforum.org/DTD/wml_1.2.xml">
 	
<wml>
 <card title="While Statement">
  <p>
   1 + 2 + 3 + ... + <input name="n" size="3" type="*N"
/> = $(result)
 	
   <do label="Add">
    <go href="Functions.wmls#series($(n), 'result')"/>
   </do>
  </p>
 </card>
</wml>
``
	-- While Statement --
	
	1 + 2 + 3 + ... + [ ] =
	
	[Add]

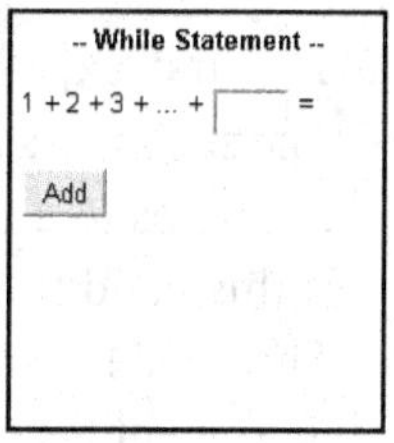

Figure 8.4. The function `series` *in the file* `Functions.wmls` *and its display on a microbrowser*

The WMLScript External Function `series`	Screenshot

``
extern function series(n, result) {
 	
   var total = 0, i = 1;
 	
   while (i <= n) {
      total += i++;
   }
   WMLBrowser.setVar(result, total);
   WMLBrowser.refresh( );
 	
}
``
	-- While Statement --
	
	1 + 2 + 3 + ... + [10] = 55
	
	[Add]

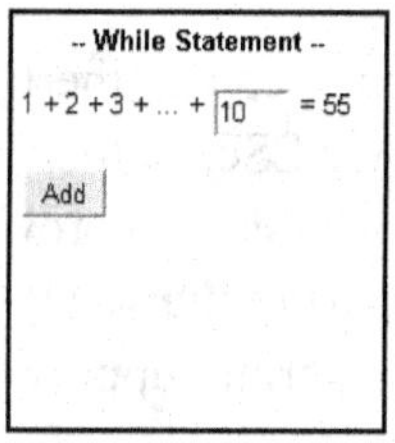

`refresh( )`. An example of the updated interface is shown on the right hand side of Figure 8.4 with an input value of 10 and a result of 55.

For Statement

This statement is also used to create a loop. The syntax is as follows:

```
ForStatement:
    for ( Expressionopt; Expressionopt; Expressionopt )
       Statement
```

for (**var** VariableDeclarationList; Expressionopt; Expressionopt)
    Statement

It consists of three optional expressions enclosed in parentheses and separated by semicolons, followed by the statement that is to be executed in the loop. This statement works as follows:

1.   The first Expression is typically used to initialize a counter variable.
2.   The second Expression (condition) can be any WMLScript expression that evaluates to a boolean or an invalid value.
3.   If this condition is found to be true, the Statement is performed.
4.   The third Expression (increment-expression) is generally used to update or increment the counter variable. Statement is executed as long as the condition continues to be true.

Figure 8.5 gives another version of the function series using a for statement. This function works the same as the function series in Figure 8.4, except the while statement is replaced by a for statement.

STANDARD LIBRARIES

This section specifies the library interfaces for the standard set of libraries supported by WMLScript that provide access to the core functionality of a WAP client. WMLScript is used to provide programmed functionality to WAP based applications. It is part of the WAP platform (Open Mobile Alliance, n.d.) and can also be used to add script support to the client. Table 8.1 lists the libraries provided by

Figure 8.5. The function series *calculating the sum of a series using a* for *statement*

```
extern function series( n, result ) {

  var total = 0;

  for ( var i = 1;  i <= n;  i++ ) {
    total += i;
  }
  WMLBrowser.setVar( result, total );
  WMLBrowser.refresh( );
}
```

Table 8.1. The libraries provided by WMLScript

Library	Description
Lang	Closely related to the WMLScript language core
Float	Typical arithmetic floating-point functions that are frequently used by applications
String	A set of string functions
URL	Handles both absolute URLs and relative URLs
WMLBrowser	A set of functions by which WMLScript can access the associated WML context
Dialogs	Typical user interface functions

WMLScript (Open Mobile Alliance, 2000b). The following sections describe the set of libraries defined to provide access to the core functionality of a WAP client. This means that all libraries, except `Float`, are present in the client's scripting environment. The `Float` library is optional and only supported with clients that can support floating-point arithmetic operations.

String Library

This library contains a set of string functions. A string is an array of characters, each of which has an index. The first character in a string has an index of zero. The length of the string is the number of characters in the array. Table 8.2 lists some functions provided by the `String` library.

The next example shows the applications of several `String` functions and the calling sequence: WML page ⇒ WMLScript ⇒ CGI Perl script. Technically the calling sequence is not necessary, but it is included to demonstrate the capability of calling a CGI script from a WMLScript. Figure 8.6 shows how a WML page goes about abbreviating a state name, e.g., from "New York" to "NY," and its corresponding display on a microbrowser. The button "Abbreviate" activates a WMLScript function `abbreviate` in a file `Functions.wmls` with an argument `$(state)`, which stores the user input string, in this case the name of a state.

Once the button "Abbreviate" is clicked, it will activate the WMLScript function `abbreviate`, which is shown in Figure 8.7. It takes the following steps:

1. Remove leading and trailing spaces using the function `trim( )`.
2. Reduce all white spaces to single spaces using the function `squeeze( )`.
3. Find the position of a space using the function `find( )` and assign the position to a variable `index`.

Table 8.2. The functions provided by the `String` *library*

Function	Description
charAt(string, index)	Returns a new string of length one containing the character at the specified `index` of the given `string`.
Compare(string1, string2)	The return value indicates the lexicographic relation of `string1` to `string2`.
elementAt(string, index, separator)	Searches string for the element enumerated by `index`, elements being separated by `separator`, and returns the corresponding element.
Elements(string, separator)	Returns the number of elements in the given `string` separated by the given `separator`.
Find(string, substring)	Returns the index of the first character in the `string` that matches the requested `subString`.
Format(format, value)	Converts the given value to a string by using the given formatting provided as a format string.
insertAt(string, element, index, separator)	Returns a string with the `element` and the corresponding `separator` inserted at the specified element `index` of the original `string`.
isEmpty(string)	Returns a boolean `true` if the string length is zero; otherwise returns a boolean `false`.
length (string)	Returns the length of the given `string`.
removeAt(string, index, separator)	Returns a new `string` where the element and the corresponding `separator` with the given `index` are removed from the given `string`.
Replace(string, oldSubString, newSubString)	Returns a new string resulting from replacing all occurrences of `oldSubString` in this string with `newSubString`.
replaceAt(string, element, index, separator)	Returns a string with the current element at the specified `index` replaced with the given `element`.
Squeeze(string)	Reduces all white spaces to single spaces.
substring(string, startIndex, length)	Returns a new string that is a substring of the given `string`.
toString(value)	Returns a string representation of the given `value`.
Trim(string)	Returns a string without leading and trailing spaces.

Figure 8.6. A WML page abbreviating a state name and its display on a micro-browser

A WML Page Using the WMLScript `String` Library	Screenshot

<pre><?xml version="1.0"?>
<!DOCTYPE wml PUBLIC "-//WAPFORUM//DTD WML 1.2//EN"
  "http://www.wapforum.org/DTD/wml_1.2.xml">
 	
<wml>
 <card title="String Library">
  <p>
   State: <input name="state" size="10" />
   <do type="accept" label="Abbreviate">
    <go href="functions.wmls#abbreviate($(state))"/>
   </do>
  </p>
 </card>
</wml></pre>
	-- String Library --
	
	State: New York
	
	Abbreviate

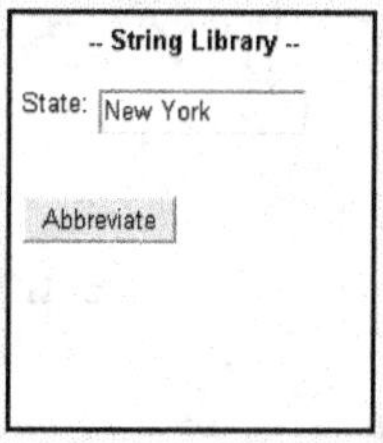

4. If a space cannot be found (`index` is equal to -1), the state name has only one word and the first two letters are retrieved. Otherwise, it has at least two words and the two first letters from the first two words are retrieved. The retrieval uses the function `subString( )`, and the position of the first letter of the second word is `index+1`.

5. Calls a CGI Perl script to display the abbreviation by using the `go` function of the `WMLBrowser` library. The CGI `GET` method is used to send the abbreviation to the CGI script. The string concatenation operator for the WMLScript is the plus symbol '+.'

Note that this example will not correctly abbreviate all the state names; Alabama and Alaska will both be abbreviated to "AL," for example, which is incorrect for the latter whose correct abbreviation should be "AK."

Figure 8.8 shows the CGI Perl script `PrintAbbr.pl` displaying the abbreviation of the state produced by the WMLScript function `abbreviate`. This script simply retrieves the abbreviation and prints it out. The abbreviation is sent to the script via the CGI `GET` method.

URL Library

This library contains a set of functions for handling URLs. Table 8.3 shows a list of the functions. The general URL syntax used in the functions is as follows:

```
<scheme>://<host>:<port>/<path>;<params>?<query>#<fragment>
```

Figure 8.7. The WMLScript function `abbreviate`

```
extern function abbreviate( state ) {

  var  abbr  = String.trim( state );
       abbr  = String.squeeze( abbr );
  var  index = String.find( abbr, " " );

  if ( index != -1 ) {
    index = index + 1;
  }
  else {
    index = 1;
  }
  var abbr1 = String.subString( abbr, 0, 1 );
  var abbr2 = String.subString( abbr, index, 1 );

  WMLBrowser.go( "http://people.cs.und.edu/~wenchen/cgi-
bin/device/PrintAbbr.pl?state=" + abbr1 + abbr2 );
```

WMLBrowser Library

This library contains functions by which WMLScript can access the associated WML context. These functions must not have any side effects and they must return `invalid` if the system does not have a WML browser or if the WMLScript interpreter was not invoked by the WML browser. Table 8.4 lists the functions provided by the `WMLBrowser` library.

Dialogs Library

This library contains a set of typical user interface functions. Table 8.5 lists three functions provided by this library.

Figure 8.11 shows one application of the function `alert( )`. When a user enters an ID into the page this activates a WMLScript `checkID( )` to determine whether or not the ID is valid.

Figure 8.12 shows the WMLScript `checkID( )` that determines whether or not the user has entered a valid ID. A valid ID contains digits only. If a character is not a digit, the script removes it and reports an error using the function `alert( )`.

Figure 8.13(a) shows a pop-up error message created by the function `alert( )`. In this example the error message will be created four times, once for each non-digit character of the input `B00005TNI6`. The user needs to click the "OK" button on the pop-up message four times in order to find the final valid ID, which is shown in Figure 8.13(b).

Figure 8.8. The CGI Perl script PrintAbbr.pl *and a microbrowser display of its output*

A CGI Perl Script **PrintAbbr.pl**	Screenshot
``#!/usr/bin/perl

Send Content-type.
print "Content-type: text/vnd.wap.wml \n\n";

Send WML header information.
print "<?xml version=\"1.0\"?>\n";
print "<!DOCTYPE wml PUBLIC \"-//WAPFORUM//DTD WML
1.2//EN\""
   . " \"http://www.wapforum.org/DTD/wml_1.2.xml\">\n";

Retrieve information from the variable
$ENV{'QUERY_STRING'}.

@pairs = split(/&/, $ENV{'QUERY_STRING'});
foreach $pair (@pairs) {
  ($name, $value) = split(/=/, $pair);
  $value =~ tr/+/ /;
  $value =~ s/%([a-fA-F0-9][a-fA-F0-9])/pack("C",
hex($1))/eg;
  $value =~ s/~!/ ~!/g;
  $FORM{$name} = $value;
}

Define a minimal deck
print <<EndOfWML;
<wml>
 <card title="State Abbreviation">
  <p>
   You have entered a state:
       <b>$FORM{state}</b>
  </p>
 </card>
</wml>
EndOfWML``` | -- State Abbreviation --

You have entered a state:

NY |

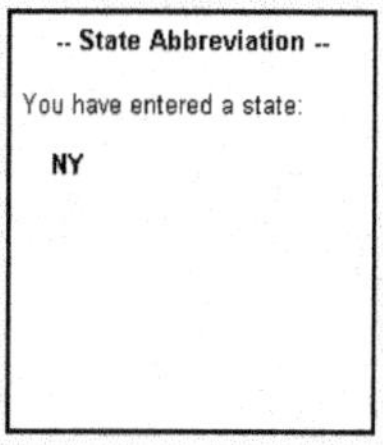

Table 8.3. The functions provided by the URL *library*

Function	Description
escapeString(string)	Computes a new version of a string value in which special characters have been replaced by a hexadecimal escape sequence.
gerReferer( )	Returns the URL to the resource that called the current file.
getBase( )	Returns an absolute URL .
getFragment(URL)	Returns the fragment used in the given URL.
getHost(URL)	Returns the host specified in a URL.

continued on following page

Table 8.3. continued

getParameters(URL)	Returns the parameters used in the given URL.
getPath(URL)	Returns the path specified in the given URL.
getPort(URL)	Returns the port number specified in the given URL.
getQuery(URL)	Returns the query part in a URL.
getScheme(URL)	Returns the scheme in a URL.
isValid(URL)	Returns true if a URL has the right syntax, and false if not.
loadString(URL, contentType)	Returns the content and the content type of a specified URL.
Resolve(baseURL, embeddedURL)	Returns an absolute URL from a base URL and a relative URL.
unescapeString(string)	Replaces the escape sequences in a URL with characters.

Table 8.4. The functions provided by the WMLBrowser *library*

Function	Description
getCurrentCard( )	Returns the URL specifying the current card.
getVar(name)	Returns the value of the variable with the given name.
Go(URL)	Loads the given URL.
newContext( )	Clears the current WML browser context.
Prev( )	Goes back to the previous WML card.
Refresh( )	Refreshes the current card.
setVar(name, value)	Sets the variable name to the given value value.

Table 8.5. The functions provided by the Dialogs *library*

Function	Description
Prompt	Displays the given message and prompts for user input.
confirm	Displays the given message and two reply options: ok and cancel.
Alert	Displays the given message to the user.

Figure 8.11. The WML page for users entering an ID

The WML Page Using the WMLScript **Dialogs** Library	Screenshot

<pre><?xml version="1.0"?>
<!DOCTYPE wml PUBLIC "-//WAPFORUM//DTD WML 1.2//EN"
  "http://www.wapforum.org/DTD/wml_1.2.xml">
 	
<wml>
 <card title="Dialogs Library">
  <p>
   ID: <input name="ID" size="10" />

   The ID should be $(result)

 	
   <do type="accept" label="Check ID">
    <go href="functions.wmls#checkID($(ID),'result')" />
   </do>
  </p>
 </card>
</wml></pre>
	-- Dialogs Library --
	
	ID: B00005TNI6
	
	The ID should be
	
	Check ID

Figure 8.12. The WMLScript checkID( ) *checking the validity of a user ID*

```
extern function checkID( ID, result ) {

  var  newID = "";

  for ( var i = 0;  i < String.length(ID);  i++ ) {
    if ( (String.charAt(ID,i) >= "0") && (String.charAt(ID,i) <= "9") ) {
      newID += String.charAt( ID, I );
    }
    else {
      Dialogs.alert( "Illegal character: " + String.charAt(ID,i) );
    }
  }
  WMLBrowser.setVar ( result, newID );
  WMLBrowser.refresh( );
}
```

Figure 8.13. (a) A pop-up error message and (b) the final valid ID.

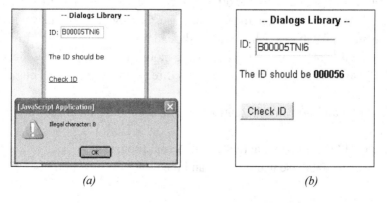

(a)   (b)

A CASE STUDY: USING HANDHELD DEVICES TO ACCESS INTERNET-ENABLED GENOME DATABASES

Agriculture genome researchers currently use desk- or lap-top computers to perform genomic research, including consulting on-line genome databases provided by data acquisition centers such as NCBI and TAIR. However, researchers may sometimes need to work in a field, literally, or in other remote locations away from their offices or labs. In this case, the genome databases cannot be easily reached, hampering their research. The emergence of wireless and mobile networks has made it possible to extend web-enabled databases to wider applications and research areas. This case study is based on the use of a new method to facilitate on-line searching of genome databases using mobile handheld devices such as personal digital assistants (PDAs) and smart phones while in the field. The technologies involved include web services, WAP, WML, and handheld computing. These mobile applications have the potential to not only substantially improve agriculture genome research, but also to provide more convenient services for researchers in other areas. Mobile commerce applications are also likely to benefit as a result of the technologies developed to address the issues involved in consulting very large databases using handheld devices.

Genome research frequently requires on-line searching of the latest genome information from public databases such as those provided by the NCBI (National Center for Biotechnology Information) and TAIR (The Arabidopsis Information Resource). However, researchers may not always be able to access the Internet to search for genome information when they need it. Recent developments in wireless and mobile communications, coupled with advances in web technology, have made it possible to access genome databases using handheld devices. BioWAP (Riikonen et al., 2001, 2002) was the first reported wireless bioinformatics application for handheld devices. It provides on-line genome searches on more than twenty different databases at the same time. WiGID (Ursing, 2003), a by-product of BioWAP, was also developed specifically for mobile Internet bioinformatics applications.

Some handheld devices, such as those using Microsoft Pocket PC, can send and accept HTTP requests, while other devices may only be able to accept WML (Wireless Markup Language). In the latter case, the devices have no way to access HTML genome databases. This case study examines a new method to facilitate on-line searching of genome databases using mobile handheld devices that can use both HTTP and WML. The case study uses three steps to make this possible:

- Simplify and convert the entry page of a genome database into a WML page.
- Use CGI technology to activate an external program.
- Access the database using PERL and the tool *lynx*, a text browser.

The technologies involved include web services, Wireless Application Protocol (WAP), WML, and handheld computing. Genome databases are usually huge, containing over a billion and in some cases up to a trillion records. Handling such large amounts of data is not trivial in itself; server performance is degraded and database maintenance is costly and hard to perform. The technologies proposed by this research can be applied to most public genome databases, which is preferable to having users develop and maintain their own databases.

Internet-Enabled Genome Databases

The NCBI (National Center for Biotechnology Information) provides web services that use Simple Object Access Protocol (SOAP) to access all their databases (NCBI, n.d.). So far, the web service has been tested in Java, MS SOAP toolkit, MS Word Visual Basic, and Visual Studio .NET. Programmers can develop Windows applications and Web applications, as well as mobile web application using this service. Genome databases such as TAIR (The Arabidopsis Information Resource) (n.d.) do not currently use mobile web services, but it is possible to develop mobile application access to TAIR using WML and either PERL or another programming language associated with a mobile standard. This case study demonstrates how to implement such a mobile system.

The Proposed Technologies

Most web-enabled genome databases use HTML (HyperText Markup Language), but mobile handheld devices such as smart phones and PDAs are often only able to display WAP pages in WML. Although some advanced devices have the ability to display HTML pages, the results are not very satisfactory because of the inherent limitations of handheld devices. This section discusses a way to facilitate accessing web-enabled plant genome databases using handheld devices.

The Converter for Internet-Enabled Plant Genome Databases

There are three major limitations of handheld devices compared to desktop PCs or notebooks, namely their:

- small screen size,
- low network bandwidth, and
- limited computing power and resources such as memory.

Figure 8.14. The role of the case study converter in plant genome database access

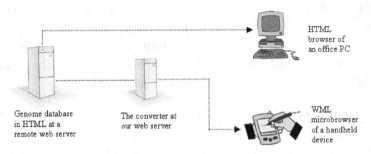

The low network bandwidth prevents the display of most multimedia on a microbrowser. Though the Wi-Fi and 3G networks go some way toward addressing this problem, the wireless bandwidth is inevitably far below the bandwidth of wired networks. The problem of limited computing power and resources is gradually being solved as the technologies improve and new methods are constantly being introduced. The problem of small screen size is addressed by the converter developed for use in this case study, which performs three major tasks:

- allows mobile users to access Internet-enabled plant genome databases,
- alleviates the problems that arise due to the small screen size of a handheld, and
- converts HTML to WML.

Figure 8.14 shows the role of the converter in plant genome database applications.

Implementation

The following three steps must be taken in order to implement the case study's new converter:

1. *Simplify and convert the entry page of a plant genome database into a WML page.* For example, Figure 8.15 shows the corresponding WML page of the Functional Genomics Characterization of Arabidopsis Genes at *http://www. arabidopsis.org/info/2010_projects/,* whose HTML interface is shown at the top of the left hand side of Figure 8.17.
2. *CGI (Common Gateway Interface) technology is used to activate an external program.* CGI is a standard for running external programs from a World-Wide

Figure 8.15. The WML page corresponding to the HTML page at http://www.arabidopsis.org/info/2010_projects/

```
File Name: ~userid/public_html/wcca/Genome.wml
<?xml version="1.0"?>
<!DOCTYPE wml PUBLIC "-//WAPFORUM//DTD WML 1.2//EN"
"http://www.wapforum.org/DTD/wml_1.2.xml">
<wml>
 <card title="Functional Genomics">
  Query Text: <input name="qstring" size="23" format="text" value="At2g41140" />
  <select name="stype">
   <option value="any">Any</option>
   <option value="accession">Genbank Accession #</option>
   <option value="locus">Locus Name</option>
   <option value="other_gene_names">Other Gene Names</option>
   <option value="lead_pi">PI Name</option>
   <option value="proposal">Proposal Title</option>
  </select>
  <do type="accept" label="Submit">
   <go href="http://www.und.edu/~userid/cgi-bin/wcca/Genome.pl" method="post">
    <postfield name="cgi_qstring" value="$(qstring)"/>
    <postfield name="cgi_stype" value="$(stype)"/>
   </go>
  </do>
  <do type="accept" label="Help">
   <go href="http://www.und.edu/~userid/cgi-bin/wcca/Help.pl" method="post">
   </go>
  </do>
 </card>
</wml>
```

Web HTTP server. CGI specifies how to pass arguments to the executing program as part of the HTTP request.

3. *PERL (Practical Extraction and Report Language) and the tool lynx are used to access the database.* Figure 8.16 shows the corresponding CGI PERL script for the WML page in Figure 8.15. The script includes a *lynx* command

   lynx -dump 'http://www.arabidopsis.org/cgibin/2010_projects/2010_search.pl?qstring=At2g41140&stype=all'

Figure 8.16. The CGI Perl script for the WML script in Figure 8.15

```
File Name: ~userid/public_html/cgi-bin/wcca/Genome.pl
#!/usr/bin/perl
print "Content-type: text/vnd.wap.wml \n\n";
print "<?xml version=\"1.0\"?>\n";
print "<!DOCTYPE wml PUBLIC \"-//WAPFORUM//DTD WML 1.2//EN\""
  . " \"http://www.wapforum.org/DTD/wml_1.2.xml\">\n";
read(STDIN, $buffer, $ENV{'CONTENT_LENGTH'});
@pairs = split(/&/, $buffer);
foreach $pair (@pairs) {
  ($name, $value) = split(/=/, $pair);
  $value =~ tr/+/ /;
  $value =~ s/%([a-fA-F0-9][a-fA-F0-9])/pack("C", hex($1))/eg;
  $value =~ s/~!/ ~!/g;
  $FORM{$name} = $value;
}
$command  = "lynx -dump 'http://www.arabidopsis.org/cgi-bin/2010_projects/2010_search.pl?";
$command .= "qstring=" . $FORM{cgi_qstring} . "&stype=" . $FORM{cgi_stype} . "'";
system( "$command > out.txt" );
print ( "<wml><card title='Results'>" );
# convert is an application program for further processing the lynx output file out.txt.
system( "./convert out.txt; cat out.txt" );
print ( "</card></wml>" );
```

where "At2g41140" and "all" are input field values from the web. *Lynx* is a text browser for the World Wide Web and can be downloaded from http://lynx. browser.org/ (n.d.).

Experimental Results

This section describes the system requirements for this case study and gives the experimental results.

System Requirements

The systems and utilities required for this case study include:

- A server for hosting the Apache web server, a file system, and utilities such as a PERL interpreter:
  - o   Hardware: i686
  - o   Operating system: Linux 2.6.5-1-686-smp.
- CGI script language: Perl 5.6.1 built for i386-linux.
- Microbrowser script language: WML 2.0.
- A Web server: Apache /1.3.26 (Unix) Debian GNU/Linux PHP/4.1.2.
- Microbrowsers: The *TTemulator* is a WAP microbrowser online emulator that offers an easy way to surf WAP sites (Inetis Ltd, n.d.).

To use the above tools and systems, readers may need to set up correct environment variables, which are system-dependent; it is recommended that those seeking to apply this case study using their own systems should check the references carefully and consult their local system administrator.

A Demonstration

The method used in this case study can be applied to most Internet-enabled plant genome databases such as the *http://www.ncbi.nlm.nih.gov/blast/Genome/PlantBlast.shtml?10* of the NCBI (National Center for Biotechnology Information, n.d.). This demonstration uses the functional genomics characterization of Arabidopsis genes at http://www.arabidopsis.org/info/ 2010_projects/. Figure 8.17 shows a demonstration where the figure shows, in turn:

a.   the HTML page with the address *http://www.arabidopsis.org/info/2010_projects/,*

Figure 8.17. Screen shots of browser (left) and microbrowser (right) showing the application of an on-line plant genome database at TAIR

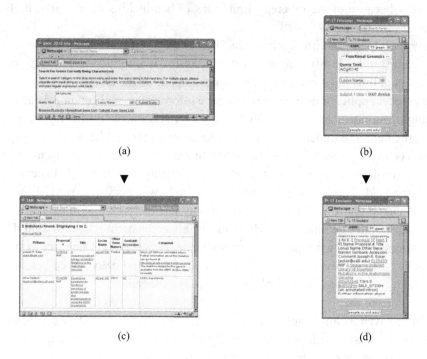

b. the WML page corresponding to (a),
c. the result HTML page after submitting the query at (a), and
d. the result WML page after submitting the query at (b).

Although limited in scope, this demonstration may be the best the case study method is currently able to achieve, as many important details, such as automatic conversion of the HTML-form to the WML-form, have yet to be accomplished.

Case-Study Conclusion

Agriculture genome researchers frequently need to access on-line genome databases, such as those provided by the NCBI and TAIR, while working away from their offices in locations with no Internet service. The emergence of wireless and mobile networks has made it possible to extend web-enabled databases to wider applications and research areas. However, most of those databases use an HTML interface to enable users to access their data and many mobile handheld devices such as smart phones and PDAs are so far only able to display WAP pages in WML. Even for advanced devices that are capable of displaying HTML pages, the results are not satisfactory because of the inherent limitations of handheld devices, particularly their small screen sizes.

Many mobile agriculture applications such as SureHarvest (http://www.sure-harvest.com/ prods2.html) and Fruit AdVisor (http://www.ento.vt.edu/Fruitfiles/FruitAdVisor.html) have been extensively developed. Also, several applications, such as breeder applications incorporating gene information, and genome database searching using portable real-time PCR and DNA sequences to identify viruses while in the field, are under construction. The demand for mobile agriculture applications is therefore already present. This case study has described a new method to facilitate on-line searching genome databases by using mobile handheld devices while in the field. The technologies involved include web services, WAP, WML, and handheld computing. This approach not only has the potential to extensively improve agriculture genome research, it also offers convenient access to vital databases to researchers wherever they happen to be. However, this research is still in the early stage of development and many issues need to be addressed before it can be incorporated into a practical application. For example:

- Various web technologies such as ASP.NET and PHP are used by public genome databases, each of which is likely to require its own treatment.
- It may not be possible to display some results, such as images, that are generated by the databases on the small screens of microbrowsers.
- Some handheld devices do not use WML. For example, i-mode devices use cHTML.

SUMMARY

This chapter introduced WMLScript, a client-side script language for mobile content, and described a case study where a handheld device is used to access an Internet-enabled genome database. As handheld device technology matures and new approaches are developed to deal with these problems, mobile commerce will also benefit from these innovations. The WMLScript topics covered in this chapter included the use of statements and standard libraries. The case study examined a new method to facilitate on-line searching of genome databases using mobile handheld devices for researchers working in the field, in locations with no Internet access. The method, which can be applied to any large database, was implemented using three steps:

1. Simplify and convert the entry page of a genome database into a WML page.
2. Use CGI technology to activate an external program.
3. Access the database using PERL and the tool *lynx*, a text browser.

REFERENCES

Inetis Ltd. (n.d.). *TT Emulator.* Retrieved April 30, 2006, from http://tagtag.com/site/info.php3?p=tt

lynx.browser.org. (n.d.). *lynx.* Retrieved May 25, 2006, from http://lynx.browser.org/

NCBI. (n.d.). *National Center for Biotechnology Information.* Retrieved January 13, 2006, from http://www.ncbi.nih.gov/

Netscape Communications Corporation. (n. d.). *JavaScript Central.* Retrieved July 21, 2004, from http://devedge.netscape.com/central/javascript/

Open Mobile Alliance Ltd. (n.d.). *WAP Forum Releases.* Retrieved May 12, 2006, from http://www.openmobilealliance.org/tech/affiliates/wap/wapindex.html

Open Mobile Alliance. (2000a). *WMLScript Language Specification, Version 1.2.* Retrieved June 28, 2004, from http://enrico.seven.it/mans/wml/WAP-193-WMLScript-20000324-a.pdf

Open Mobile Alliance. (2000b). *Wireless Application Protocol WMLScript Standard Libraries Specification, Version 1.3.* Retrieved July 09, 2004, from http://www.wapforum.org/tech/documents/WAP-194-WMLScriptLibs-20000324-a.pdf

Open Mobile Alliance. (2001). *Wireless Markup Language (WML), Version 2.0.* Retrieved June 28, 2004, from http://www.openmobilealliance.org/tech/affiliates/wap/wap-238-wml-20010911-a.pdf

Riikonen, P., Boberg, J., Salakoski, T., & Vihinen, M. (2001). BioWAP, mobile Internet service for bioinformatics. *Bioinformatics,* 17(9), pages 855-856.

Riikonen, P., Boberg, J., Salakoski, T., & Vihinen, M. (2002). Mobile access to biological databases on the Internet. *IEEE Transactions on Biomedical Engineering,* 49(12), 1477-1479.

TAIR. (n.d.) *The Arabidopsis Information Resource.* Retrieved January 21, 2006, from http://www.arabidopsis.org/index.jsp

Ursing, B. M. (2003). WiGID: wireless genome information database. *Bioinformatics*, 19(3), 439-440.

Chapter IX
Database–Driven Mobile Web Content Construction

INTRODUCTION

Numerous server-side handheld applications are available for devices. Some popular applications include:

- *Instant messages*, which require service providers to relay the messages,
- *Mobile web content*, which consists of web content that can be viewed via handheld devices and can be implemented using markup languages such as HTML, WML, cHTML, and DIAL,
- *On-line games*, which are video games playable on the Internet that allow remote players to play the games together, and
- *Telephony*, which is the most common operation performed by smartphone users and requires the telecommunication company to provide the service.

Among the various mobile applications, mobile web content is the most popular application and this chapter will be devoted to a detailed consideration of the construction of database-driven mobile web content. The term "handheld programming" is used here to refer to mobile-commerce programming for Internet-enabled mobile handheld devices, which requires various programming and markup languages and utilities. As in previous chapters, the concepts involved in handheld programming are illustrated using a case study, in this case the construction of a B2C, mobile, online video-game store.

A database-driven mobile web site is often implemented using a `three-tiered client-server architecture` consisting, as the name suggests, of three layers:

1. **User interface:** This runs on a mobile handheld device (the client) and uses a standard graphical user interface (GUI).
2. **Function module:** This level actually processes data and may consist of one or more separate modules running on a workstation or an application server. This tier may be multi-tiered itself, in which case the overall architecture is called an `n-tier architecture`.
3. **Database management system (DBMS):** A DBMS on a host computer stores the data required by the middle tier.

The three-tier design offers many advantages over traditional two-tier or single-tier designs, the chief one being that the modular structure makes it easier to modify or replace one tier without affecting the others. Figure 9.1 shows a generalized system structure of database-driven mobile web sites. Note that web and database servers are not hardware; they are the processes running on host computers that manage web pages and databases, respectively.

Many approaches can be used to create a database-driven mobile web site; the following list suggests the construction steps for a typical approach:

1. system setup,
2. database design and implementation,

Figure 9.1. A generalized system structure of database-driven mobile web content

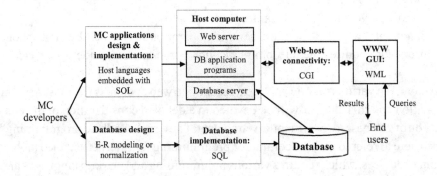

3. mobile web user interface construction,
4. web and host-computer connection such as CGI, and
5. database accesses and management using host languages with embedded SQL such as JDBC.

These five steps are not definite, nor are they unique. Other approaches may also be used. An example of a B2C video-game store construction will be used in this chapter to demonstrate the above steps, except for Step 1, which was discussed in Chapter V.

DATABASE DESIGN AND IMPLEMENTATION

This section shows how to design and implement a video-game store, *MicroGames. com*, using a database. MicroGames is a hypothetical online, B2C (business-to-customer), mobile video-game store with the following features:

- It has many video games for sale.
- Each customer has a name and a customer ID.
- Each video game has a title, a game ID, and a quantity on hand.
- A customer can select and buy copies of video games from the store.

Database Design

When designing a database, the database designers study the basic properties and interrelationships between data objects in the real world that are part of the enterprise to be modeled, where a data model is a mathematical formalism with a notation for describing data structures and a set of operations used to manipulate and validate that data. The aim of database design is to provide faithful representation of such objects as columns in relational tables. Database design usually applies one of two methods: entity-relationship modeling or normalization (O'Neil & O'Neil, 2000).

Entity-Relationship (E-R) Modeling

This approach was proposed by P. Chen in 1967. It is based on the intuitive recognition of certain real-world data classifications. This design divides a database into two logical parts, entities (such as "customer" or "game") and relations (such as "buys" or "teaches"). Figure 9.2 shows the E-R diagram that can be constructed

Figure 9.2. The entity-relationship diagram for MicroGames.com

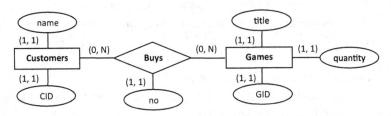

based on the functional description of MicroGames.com given above. This diagram includes two entities: Customers and Games and one relationship: Buys.

- Customers: This entity includes two attributes: name and CID (customer identification).
- Games: This entity includes three attributes: title, GID (game identification), and quantity (on hand).
- Buys: This relationship relates the entity Customers to the other entity Games and includes one attribute no, which is the number of copies of the video game bought by the customer.

According to the E-R diagram in Figure 9.2, the final database includes three tables, customers, games, and buys, as shown in Figure 9.3. Further details of this approach are available in database textbooks (see, for example, Elmasri and Navathe, 2003).

Normalization

This approach implements a series of steps to obtain a database design that allows for efficient access and storage of data in a relational database (O'Neil & O'Neil, 2000). The following steps are applied to MicroGames.com:

1. The data items are listed according to the problem:
    - name, CID
    - title, GID, quantity
    - no

    The functional dependencies are given according to the problem:

- CID → name
- GID → name quantity

Figure 9.3. The schema of the final database, including three tables: customers, games, *and* buys, *based on the E-R modeling approach*

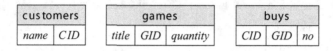

- CID GID → no

  Initially, therefore, the universal table is constructed with the following headings:

- name, CID, title, GID, quantity, no

2. The above functional dependencies are replaced with a minimal cover that is the same as the original functional dependencies.
3. The universal table is then decomposed into a set of small tables, whose headings are:
    - CID name
    - GID name quantity
    - CID GID no

The final database thus includes three tables with the headings shown in Step 3. Note that the final database structure is the same as that obtained using E-R modeling and shown in Figure 9.3.

Database Implementation

The two database designs described above, E-R modeling and normalization, are used for relational database management systems (RDBMSs). In contrast, Oracle9i is an object-relational database management system (ORDBMSs) that puts an object-oriented front end on a relational database. When applications interface to an object-relational database, it will normally interface as though the data are stored as objects. However, the system will convert the object information into data tables with rows and columns and handle the data in the same way as for a relational database. Likewise, when the data is retrieved it must be reassembled from simple data into complex objects. Oracle9i expands current data types and adds new data types that support larger data and openness in the database:

Figure 9.4. Database implementation for MicroGames.com

```
server> sqlplus userid/password

SQL*Plus: Release 9.2.0.1.0 - Production on Thu Feb 2 15:41:20 2006

Copyright (c) 1982, 2002, Oracle Corporation.  All rights reserved.
Connected to:
Oracle9i Enterprise Edition Release 9.2.0.1.0 - 64bit Production
With the Partitioning, OLAP and Oracle Data Mining options
JServer Release 9.2.0.1.0 - Production

SQL> create type customer_typ as object (
  2     name   varchar(32),
  3     CID    char(10) );
  4  /

Type created.


SQL> create table customers of customer_typ (
  2     primary key (CID) );

Table created.


SQL> create type game_typ as object (
  2     title     varchar(32),
  3     GID       char(12),
  4     quantity  integer );
  5  /

Type created.


SQL> create table games of game_typ (
  2     primary key (GID),
  3     check (quantity >= 0) );

Table created.


SQL> create type buy_typ as object (
  2     customer  ref  customer_typ,
  3     game      ref  game_typ,
  4     no        integer );
  5  /

Type created.


SQL> create table buys of buy_typ (
  2     scope for (customer) is customers,
  3     scope for (game) is games,
  4     check (no > 0) );

Table created.
```

- User-defined types or object types,
- Collection types such as VARRAY (varying array) and TABLE (nested table),
- Relationships such as REF (reference), and
- Large object types such as BLOB (binary large object), CLOB (character large object), and BFILE (binary file).

In order to take advantage of the object-relational features of Oracle9i, object tables are implemented rather than relational tables. Figure 9.4 shows an example of the database implementation for MicroGames.com using the Oracle9i object-relational SQL.

SQL (Structured Query Language) is the most popular language for database implementation. The following comments refer to the above example:

- Italic text is entered by users and regular text is automatically generated by Unix or Oracle9i.
- server> is the Unix prompt for user input.
- SQL*Plus, the Oracle interface, enables users to manipulate SQL commands and PL/SQL blocks.
- SQL> is the Oracle9i prompt for user input.
- Object reference (REF) is a system-generated value that locates a persistent object, which is a pair of the object identifier with the user-defined data type value.
- SCOPE FOR scope _ table _ name restricts the scope of the column REF values to scope _ table _ name. The REF values for the column must come from REF values obtained from the object table specified in the clause.

MOBILE WEB USER INTERFACE CONSTRUCTION

Several markup languages such as WML and cHTML can be used to create mobile Web user interfaces. This chapter uses WML (Wireless Markup Language), which is the authoring language used to create documents on the World Wide Web. WML defines the structure and layout of a mobile Web document using a variety of tags and attributes. WML INPUT is used to select different kinds of user input. A form is an area that can contain form elements, which in turn allow the user to enter information (for example, text fields, text area fields, drop-down menus, radio buttons, and checkboxes) in a form. Figure 9.5 shows the WML script of the MicroGames. com entry page and its display on a microbrowser. Clicking the button "Customer

Figure 9.5. The WML script of the MicroGames.com entry page and its display on a microbrowser

The WML Script of the MicroGames.com Entry Page	The Microbrowser Screenshot

``xml
<?xml version="1.0"?>
<!DOCTYPE wml PUBLIC "-//WAPFORUM//DTD WML 1.2//EN"
  "http://www.wapforum.org/DTD/wml_1.2.xml">
<wml>
 <card title="MicroGames.com">
  <p>
   Name: <input name="name" size="12" />
 	
   ID: <input name="ID" size="9" format="*N" />
 	
   <do type="accept" label="Customer Enters">
    <go href="http://people.cs.und.edu/~wenchen/cgi-
bin/device/CustomerEnter.pl" method="post">
     <postfield name="name" value="$(name)" />
     <postfield name="ID"   value="$(ID)" />
    </go>
   </do>
  </p>
 </card>
</wml>
``
	-- MicroGames.com --
	
	Name: Powerpuff Girls
	
	ID: 123456789
	
	[Customer Enters]

Enters" activates the CGI Perl script `CustomerEnter.pl`, which then receives two parameters: customer name and customer ID.

WEB AND HOST COMPUTER CONNECTION

Several methods are available for Web and host computer connectivity, including ASP (Active Server Pages) and PHP (Hypertext Preprocessor). Most of these methods are actually based on programming languages, which each have their own syntax and semantics. To reduce the level of complexity, here we will use the CGI (Common Gateway Interface) technology because it is coded in Perl and its implementation is fairly straightforward.

A CGI Script

CGI is a standard used for running external programs from a World Wide Web HTTP server. CGI specifies how to pass arguments to the executing program as part of the HTTP request and also defines a set of environment variables. For further information, please refer to Chapter VII in this book. Figure 9.5 shows the CGI script `CustomerEnter.pl`, which is activated when the button "Customer

Enters" on the MicroGames.com entry page in Figure 9.5 is clicked. It performs the following tasks:

1. Informs the Web server about the script and content types and prints the WML header information.
2. Retrieves the user entry data from the Web.
3. Calls a program with embedded-SQL such as JDBC or a 3G language such as C to enter the user information into a database
4. Prints the next interface by using the Perl *HERE document* to print a block of script. The HERE document is a long (usually multi-line) string value, but it is quoted in an unusual way. An simple example is as follows:

```
$a = <<EndofScript;
Some stuff
goes here.
EndofScript
```

Another way to achieve the same result is:

```
$a = "Some stuff\ngoes here.\n";
```

Note that in the first example the string value is written across two separate lines. The key to this is the <<END token. The << says "this is a string value, beginning at the start of the next line, and going until we find the end marker." In this case, the end marker is literally "END", which must be on a line by itself later in the program. All the characters between the start of the following line, and the end marker, including the last newline before the end marker, are considered to be part of the value. Note that <<END is followed by a semicolon.

Because the code of the output WML page is embedded in the Perl script, it is not easy to see the whole code at one time. Figure 9.7 shows the output page of the JDBC code in Figure 9.6 and the corresponding WML code for the same output page.

CGI GET Method

Once the user has registered with MicroGames, the following interfaces and transactions have to know who the current user is. One way to achieve this is to use the CGI GET method, where the input values from the form are sent as part of the URL, and saved in the QUERY _ STRING environment variable. The advantage of the GET method is that the page can be retrieved again by entering the URL. For example,

Figure 9.6. The CGI Perl script `CustomerEnter.pl`

```
#!/usr/bin/perl

# Send Content-type and header info.
print <<EndofWML;
Content-type: text/vnd.wap.wml \n\n
<?xml version="1.0"?>
<!DOCTYPE wml PUBLIC "-//WAPFORUM//DTD WML 1.2//EN"
  "http://www.wapforum.org/DTD/wml_1.2.xml">;
EndofWML

# Retrieve Web argument values.
read(STDIN, $buffer, $ENV{'CONTENT_LENGTH'});
@pairs = split(/&/, $buffer);
foreach $pair (@pairs)  {
  ($name, $value) = split(/=/, $pair);
  $value =~ tr/+/ /;
  $value =~ s/%([a-fA-F0-9][a-fA-F0-9])/pack("C", hex($1))/eg;
  $value =~ s/~!/ ~!/g;
  $FORM{$name} = $value;
}

# For security, remove some Unix metacharacters from the web input.
$FORM{name} =~ s/;|>|>>|<|\*|\?|\&|\|//g;
$FORM{ID}   =~ s/;|>|>>|<|\*|\?|\&|\|//g;

# Use the system function to call a JDBC program.
system( "/usr/bin/java  CustomerEnter '$FORM{name}' '$FORM{ID}'" );

# Print the next interface.
print <<EndofWML;
<wml>
 <card title="Welcome $FORM{name}">
  <p>
   A title word:<br />
   <input name="title" size="16" /><br />

   <do type="accept" label="List Games">
    <go href="http://people.cs.und.edu/~wenchen/cgi-
bin/device/ListGames.pl?name=$FORM{name}&ID=$FORM{ID}" method="post">
     <postfield name="title" value="\$(title)" />
    </go>
   </do>
  </p>
 </card>
</wml>
EndofWML
```

after submitting the keywords: `CGI Perl`, to `Yahoo! Search`, the current URL may be changed to the following string:

`http://search.yahoo.com/bin/search?p=cgi%20perl`

where the hexadecimal 20 is an ASCII code for a space and the string %20 represents a space according to the URL-encoding, which is explained in Chapter 7. The server

Figure 9.7. The output of the JDBC program in Figure 9.6 and its corresponding WML script

The Microbrowser Screenshot of an Output of the Figure 9.6	The Corresponding WML Script of the Screenshot

-- Welcome Powerpuff Girls --
 	
 A title word:
 Fantasy
 	
 List Games
	<?xml version="1.0"?>
	<!DOCTYPE wml PUBLIC "-//WAPFORUM//DTD WML 1.2//EN"
	  "http://www.wapforum.org/DTD/wml_1.2.xml">
	<wml>
	 <card title="Welcome Powerpuff Girls">
	  <p>
	  A title word:
	
	  <input name="Title" size="16" />
	
	  <do type="accept" label="List Games">
	   <go href="http://people.cs.und.edu/~wenchen/cgi-bin/device/ListGames.pl?name=Powerpuff Girls&ID=123456789" method="post">
	    <postfield name="title" value="$(title)" />
	   </go>
	  </do>
	  </p>
	 </card>
	</wml>

then receives the keywords via the URL and passes them to the next interface. Using the concepts of the GET method, the user's name and ID can be passed to the next interface by appending them to the URL of the `go` element:

```
<go href="http://people.cs.und.edu/~wenchen/cgi-
    bin/device/ListGames.pl?name=$FORM{name}&ID=$FORM{ID}"
    method="post">
    <postfield name="title" value="\$(title)" />
</go>
```

It is important to note that the GET method is not a secure method of sending data; the data is passed through as part of the URL so it will show up in the Web server's logfile.

CGI Security Concerns

The Perl function `system(list)` sends the argument `list` to the host Unix machine for parsing by the standard and job control shell and command interpreter such as "`/bin/sh -c`." However, this approach may have security flaws. For example, a user may enter the following value into the web input element:

```
Dragonball Z'; ls
```

where it is saved in a Perl variable $FORM{identifier}. If the variable is used in the system argument list and the host machine using Unix, a security breach may occur because the symbol ';' is a command separator for Unix and the command ls lists the directory contents for Unix. This input value will reveal the owner's information if no proper protection is taken. To avoid potential security attacks, the following command

```
$FORM{identifier} =~ s/;|>|>>|<|\*|\?|\&|\|//g;
```

may be inserted before calling a system function with an argument containing $FORM{identifier} variable. The Perl substitution operator s removes Unix metacharacters:

- ;: command separator,
- >: output redirection,
- >>: output redirection (appending),
- <: input redirection,
- *: matching any string of characters including the null string,
- ?: matching any single character,
- &: running as a background process, and
- |: pipe.

from the variable $FORM{identifier}, which stores the web input. If the metacharacters are required for the input, other methods have to be used in order to keep them. Of course, if the variable is not part of the argument of the function system, the operation is not needed. There may also be other potential security threats that affect CGI, and it is recommended that programmers consult their local system administrators for advice before using it. However, in spite of CGI's security issues, it is widely used because of its simplicity.

DATABASE ACCESSES

SQL (Structured Query Language) is used to access most databases. Since SQL is an interactive query language, it must be embedded in a host language to effectively access databases. Several host languages with embedded SQL, such as SQLJ and OraPerl, are available. JDBC is used here because it is probably the most popular host language at present. JDBC (Java Database Connectivity) is JavaSoft's database connectivity specification (Sun Microsystems, Inc., n.d.). This is a Java API (Application Program Interface), the interface (calling conventions) application program used for accessing the services provided by lower-level modules and for communicating with databases in a uniform manner, and thus enables Java programs to execute SQL statements and allows Java programs to interact with any SQL-compliant database. JDBC is particularly useful for two reasons:

- nearly all relational database management systems (DBMSs) support SQL and
- Java itself runs on most platforms.

JDBC makes it possible to write a single database application that can run on different platforms and interact with different DBMSs. JDBC is similar to ODBC (Open Database Connectivity), but is designed specifically for Java programs, whereas ODBC is language-independent. It is based on *X/Open SQL Call Level Interface*, as is ODBC.

Typical Steps for a JDBC Program

To connect to and query a database from a client using JDBC, the following steps are usually followed (Oracle Corporation, 2002):

1. Import database-related packages.
2. Register the JDBC drivers.
3. Open a connection to the database.
4. Create a statement object.
5. Execute a query and return a result set object.
6. Process the result set.
7. Close the result set and statement objects.
8. Make changes to the database.
9. Commit changes.
10. Close the connection.

These steps are not definite, nor are they unique and other steps may also be used. If an Oracle database is used, Oracle driver-specific information must be supplied for the first three steps, which allow programs to use the JDBC API to access a database. For the other steps, standard JDBC Java code can be used, as for any Java application.

A JDBC Program

The rest of this section discusses each of the above ten steps in turn. To illustrate the steps, the JDBC program `CustomerEnter.java` is shown in Figure 9.8. The program is activated by the CGI Perl script `CustomerEnter.pl`, when the customer name and ID are entered and stored in the files `$FORM{name}` and `$FORM{ID}`, respectively, into a database. The SQL query for the insertion is

```
insert into customers values(
    customer _ typ( '$FORM{name}', '$FORM{ID}' ) );
```

Importing Packages

In order to access and update databases, some database-related packages must be imported into JDBC programs. The following list shows some of the most commonly imported packages:

- `Java.sql.*`: This is one of the most commonly imported of all the JDBC programs and provides the API for accessing and processing the data stored in a database. Figure 9.9 shows the class hierarchy of the package `java.sql.*`, whose classes and interfaces include the following functions:
  - o Making a connection with the database,
  - o Sending SQL statements to the database,
  - o Retrieving and updating the results of a query,
  - o Mapping an SQL value to the standard mapping in the Java programming language,
  - o Custom mapping an SQL user-defined type to a class in the Java programming language,
  - o Providing information about the database and the columns of a `Result-Set` object,
  - o Throwing exceptions, and
  - o Providing security.
- `java.math.*`: This package provides classes for performing arbitrary-precision integer arithmetic (`BigInteger`) and arbitrary-precision decimal arithmetic (`BigDecimal`). BigInteger is analogous to Java's primitive integer types except that it provides arbitrary precision, hence operations on BigIntegers do not overflow or lose precision. BigDecimal provides arbitrary-precision signed decimal numbers suitable for currency calculations and the like. BigDecimal gives the user complete control over rounding behavior, allowing the user to choose from a comprehensive set of eight rounding modes.

Figure 9.8. The JDBC program `CustomerEnter.java`

```
// Need to import the java.sql package to use JDBC.
import  java.sql.*;

class  CustomerEnter {
 public static void  main( String args[ ] )  throws SQLException {

  // Load the Oracle JDBC driver.
  DriverManager.registerDriver( new oracle.jdbc.driver.OracleDriver( ) );
  // Connect to the database.  You can put a database
  // name after the @ sign in the connection URL.
  Connection conn = DriverManager.getConnection(
   "jdbc:oracle:thin:@cs.und.edu:1521:device", "userid", "password" );

  try {
  // Create and compose a statement.
  Statement stmt = conn.createStatement( );
  String    query    = "insert into customers values( customer_typ('" +
args[0].trim( ) + "', '" + args[1].trim( ) + "') )";
  // Insert the information into the customers table.
  stmt.executeUpdate( query );
  stmt.close( );
  }
  catch( SQLException ex ) {
  // Send a minimal deck.
  System.out.println( "<wml><card><p>" + ex + "</p></card></wml>" );
  }
  // Commit and close the connection.
  conn.commit( );
  conn.close ( );
 }
}
```

Figure 9.9. The class hierarchy of the package `java.sql.*`

Java.sql			
DriverManager	Connection		Array
DriverPropertyInfo	Driver		Blob
Types	DatabaseMetaData		Clob
SQLException	BatchUpdateException		Ref
	SQLWarning	DataTransaction	SQLData
Statement	PreparedStatement	CallableStatement	SQLInput
Data	ResultSet		SQLOutput
Time	ResultSetMetaData		Struct
Timestamp			

- `oracle.jdbc.*` and `oracle.sql.*`: These two packages provide extended functionality for Oracle drivers only.

Registering the JDBC Drivers

The JDBC program must include the code needed to register the installed driver. This registration uses the static `registerDriver( )` method of the JDBC `DriverManager` class, for example:

```
DriverManager.registerDriver (
    new oracle.jdbc.driver.OracleDriver( ) );
```

The `DriverManager` class is used to open a connection to a database via a JDBC driver, which must be registered with the `DriverManager`. `DriverManager` chooses from a given list of available drivers to suit the explicit type of database connection. Three major methods included in this class are

- `public static void registerDriver(Driver driver) throws SQLException`: Registers the given driver with the `DriverManager`. A newly-loaded driver class should call the method `registerDriver` to make itself known to the `DriverManager`.
- `public static Connection getConnection (String driver, String userid, String password) throws SQLException`: Attempts to establish a connection to the given database URL. The `DriverManager` attempts to select an appropriate driver from the set of registered JDBC drivers.
- `public static Driver getDriver(String url) throws SQLException`: Attempts to locate a driver that understands the given URL. The `DriverManager` attempts to select an appropriate driver from the set of registered JDBC drivers.

Using one of Oracle's JDBC drivers declares a specific driver name string to `registerDriver( )`. The driver is registered only once in each Java application.

Opening a Connection to a Database

The static `getConnection( )` method of the JDBC `DriverManager` class is used to open a connection to a database. This method returns an object of the JDBC `Connection` class that requires as input a user name, a password, a connect string that identifies the JDBC driver to use, and the name of the database that the user wants to connect to. The following signature takes the URL, user name, and password as separate parameters:

```
getConnection(String URL, String user, String password);
```

where the URL is of the form

```
jdbc:oracle:<drivertype>:@<database>
```

One example is

```
Connection conn = DriverManager.getConnection (
    "jdbc:oracle:thin:@cs.und.edu:1521:device",
    "scott", "tiger" );
```

The above example connects user `scott` with password `tiger` to a database with `INSTANCE _ NAME device` through port 1521 of host `agassiz.cs.und. edu`, using the `Thin` driver. Following the database connection, one common task is to set the database commit automatically. By default, JDBC commits each SQL statement as it is sent to the database. However, for more robust error handling, it is possible to set up a `Connection` object so it issues a series of changes that have no effect on the database until a commit is explicitly sent. The following command sets whether `auto-commit` is enabled or disabled on the specified connection object:

```
conn.setAutoCommit( false );
```

Each `Connection` is separate, and a commit on one has no effect on the statements included in the other.

Creating a Statement Object

Once the user connects to the database and, in the process, creates a `Connection` object, the next step is to create a `Statement` object. The `createStatement( )` method of a JDBC `Connection` object returns an object of the JDBC `Statement` interface. Below is an example of how to create the `Statement` object:

```
Statement stmt = conn.createStatement( );
```

Note that there is nothing Oracle-specific about this statement; it follows standard JDBC syntax. When the `Connection` object is first created, it simply provides a direct link to the database. A `Connection` object is used to generate implementations of `java.sql.Statement` that are tied to the same database transaction. `java.sql.Statement` contains methods to execute SQL statements directly against the database and to obtain the results. Only one `ResultSet` object per `Statement` object can be open at any point in time. Therefore, if the reading of one `ResultSet` object is interleaved with the reading of another, each must have been generated by different `Statement` objects. All statement execute methods implicitly close a statement's current `ResultSet` object if an open one exists.

Executing a Query

A simple database transaction uses only one of the three execution methods in the `Statement Interface`:

- `public ResultSet executeQuery(String sql) throws SQLException:`

This executes an SQL statement that returns a single `ResultSet` object. This method should be used for any SQL calls that expect to return data from the database. For example,

```
ResultSet rset = stmt.executeQuery (
    "select * from customers" );
```

- `public int executeUpdate(String sql) throws SQLException:`

This executes an SQL `INSERT`, `UPDATE`, or `DELETE` statement. In addition, SQL statements that return nothing, such as SQL DDL (Data Definition Language) statements, can be executed. This method returns the number of affected rows. For example,

```
stmt.executeUpdate( "insert into customers values (
    customer_typ( 'Powerpuff Girls', '123456789' )" );
```

- `public boolean execute(String sql) throws SQLException:`

This is for situations where it is not known whether the SQL being executed is a query or an update. For example,

```
try {
```

```
    stmt.execute( "drop table customers" );
    stmt.execute( "drop type customer _ typ force" );
    stmt.execute( "drop type game _ typ force" );
}
  catch( SQLException e ) {
  System.out.println( e );
  }
```

This usually happens when the application is executing dynamically created SQL statements.

Processing the Result Set

A table of data representing a database result set is usually generated by executing a statement that queries the database. A ResultSet object maintains a cursor pointing to its current row of data, which initially is positioned before the first row. The next method moves the cursor to the next row, and because it returns false when there are no more rows in the ResultSet object, it can be used in a while loop to iterate through the result set. For example, the following code will iterate through the ResultSet object rset and will retrieve and print each entry of the first column, which is a string:

```
while ( rset.next( ) )
    System.out.println( rset.getString( 1 ) );
```

A default ResultSet object is not updatable and has a cursor that moves forward only. The ResultSet interface provides getXXX methods for retrieving column values from the current row. Values can be retrieved using either of the following two methods:

- **The index number of the column:** In general, using the column index will be more efficient. Columns are numbered from 1. For maximum portability, result set columns within each row should be read in left-to-right order, and each column should be read only once.
- **The name of the column:** Column names used as input to getXXX methods are case insensitive. When a getXXX method is called with a column name and several columns have the same name, the value of the first matching column will be returned. The column name option is designed to be used when column names are used in the SQL query that generated the result set.

Closing the Result Set and Statement Objects

The ResultSet and Statement objects must be explicitly closed after users have finished using them. This applies to all ResultSet and Statement objects created when using the Oracle JDBC drivers. The drivers do not have finalizer methods, so cleanup routines are performed by the close( ) method of the ResultSet and Statement classes. If users fail to explicitly close ResultSet and Statement objects, serious memory leaks could occur. It is also possible to run out of cursors, as closing a result set or statement releases the corresponding cursor in the database. For example, if a ResultSet object is rset and a Statement object is stmt, the result set and statement can be closed with these lines:

```
rset.close( );
stmt.close( );
```

When a Statement object is closed that a given Connection object has created, the connection itself remains open.

Making Changes to the Database

To write changes to the database, such as for INSERT or UPDATE operations, typically a PreparedStatement object is created. This makes it possible to execute a statement with varying sets of input parameters. The prepareStatement( ) method of a JDBC Connection object allows a statement to be defined that takes variable binding parameters, and returns a JDBC PreparedStatement object with the statement definition. setXXX( ) methods are used on the PreparedStatement object to bind data into the prepared statement that is to be sent to the database.

Committing Changes

By default, DML (Data Manipulation Language) operations (INSERT, UPDATE, DELETE) are committed automatically as soon as they are executed. This is known as auto-commit mode. It is, however, possible to disable auto-commit mode by using the following method call on the Connection object:

```
conn.setAutoCommit( false );
```

Disabling auto-commit mode means that users must manually commit or roll back changes with the appropriate method call on the Connection object:

```
conn.commit( );
```

or

```
conn.rollback( );
```

A COMMIT or ROLLBACK operation affects all the DML statements executed since the last COMMIT or ROLLBACK. Note that:

- If auto-commit mode is disabled and the connection is closed without explicitly committing or rolling back the last changes, then an implicit COMMIT operation is executed.
- Any DDL (Data Definition Language) operation, such as CREATE or ALTER, always includes an implicit COMMIT. If auto-commit mode is disabled, this implicit COMMIT will not only commit the DDL statement, but also any pending DML operations that had not yet been explicitly committed or rolled back.

Closing the Connection

JDBC programs must close their connection to the databases once they are finished. The close( ) method of the Connection object can be used to do this:

```
conn.close( );
```

Typically, the close( ) statements are placed in a final clause.

A CASE STUDY: MICROGAMES.COM

The code described in the previous section only shows parts of the MicroGames. com implementation. The store's customers are still not able to purchase video games. This section completes the programming for this case study.

Listing Video Games

After a MicroGames user enters their information into the system, their next step is to search and list the video games available for purchasing. Figure 9.10 shows the CGI Perl script listGames.pl for the target link of the button "List Games" in Figure 9.7. It performs the following tasks:

1.   The first loop retrieves the web input value, a keyword for each video-game title, that is submitted via the CGI POST method. The second loop retrieves the customer name and ID sent via the CGI GET method.
2.   Print the next interface.
3.   Call a JDBC program `listGames.java` (shown in Figure 9.11) to list the video games queried by the user.
4.   If the user is not satisfied with the search results, a back button is also provided for them to return to the previous interface.

Figure 9.11 is the JDBC program `ListGames.java` used for listing video games, which contains a substring of the input keywords of each of the video-game titles. The following SQL command is used to find the video games:

```
select g.title, g.GID, g.quantity from games g
    where g.title like '%args[0]%' order by g.title;
```

where the command-line argument `args[0]` contains the input keyword. The output interface includes a multiple-item selection for users to purchase video games. The script for each item is

```
<option value="rset.getString(2).trim( )">
rset.getString( 1 )
</option>
```

where `rset.getString(2)` is the game ID and `rset.getString(1)` is the game title. The function `trim( )` removes the trailing spaces. The item's value, a game ID, will be sent to the CGI script if the item is selected by the user.

Figure 9.12 shows the script for the target link of the "Back" button in Figure 9.13. A specific "Back" button is included because using the default back buttons provided by the devices may result in an error:

```
java.sql.SQLException: ORA-00001: unique constraint
(USERID.SYS _ C004971) violated
```

because it causes the device to try to re-execute the previous CGI script. For example, it could try to enter the user information twice.

Figure 9.13 shows the output interface of the button "List Games" in Figure 9.7. The WML script of the interface is embedded in the CGI Perl script and the JDBC program. It is not easy to read the whole script at once, so Figure 9.13 also shows the corresponding WML script for the interface.

Purchasing Video Games

The user can then examine the video-game list produced by the search results. If they do not like the results, they can then use the back button to return to the previous page and submit another search. If the results are satisfactory, the user may proceed and purchase video games. This includes the following tasks:

1.   Print the customer name.
2.   Print the titles of the video games purchased by the customer.
3.   Subtract one from the quantity of that video game in the store's inventory.
4.   Update the purchase record. If the record is already in the database, increase the number by one, otherwise insert a new record into the database.

Figure 9.10. The CGI Perl script `ListGames.pl`

```
#!/usr/bin/perl

# Send Content-type and header info.
print <<EndofWML;
Content-type: text/vnd.wap.wml \n\n
<?xml version="1.0"?>
<!DOCTYPE wml PUBLIC "-//WAPFORUM//DTD WML 1.2//EN"
"http://www.wapforum.org/DTD/wml_1.2.xml">;
EndofWML

# Retrieve Web argument values.
read(STDIN, $buffer, $ENV{'CONTENT_LENGTH'});
@pairs = split(/&/, $buffer);
foreach $pair (@pairs) {
  ($name, $value) = split(/=/, $pair);
  $value =~ tr/+/ /;
  $value =~ s/%([a-fA-F0-9][a-fA-F0-9])/pack("C", hex($1))/eg;
  $value =~ s/~!/ ~!/g;
  $FORM{$name} = $value;
}

# Print the top part of the next interface.
print <<EndofWML;
<wml>
 <card title="A Game List">
  <p>
   <select name="items" title="items" multiple="true">
EndofWML

# For security, remove some Unix metacharacters.
$FORM{title} =~ s/;|>|>>|<|\*|\?|&|\|//g;

# Call a JDBC program to retrieve and print games.
system( "/usr/bin/java  ListGames '$FORM{title}'" );
```

continued on following page

Figure 9.10. continued

```
# Retrieve information from the variable $ENV{'QUERY_STRING'}.
@pairs = split(/&/, $ENV{'QUERY_STRING'});
foreach $pair (@pairs) {
  ($name, $value) = split(/=/, $pair);
  $value =~ tr/+/ /;
  $value =~ s/%([a-fA-F0-9][a-fA-F0-9])/pack("C", hex($1))/eg;
  $value =~ s/~!/ ~!/g;
  $FORM1{$name} = $value;
}

# Print the last part of the next interface.
print <<EndofWML
    </select><br />

    <do type="accept" label="Purchase Games">
     <go href="http://people.cs.und.edu/~wenchen/cgi-
bin/device/PurchaseGames.pl?name=$FORM1{name}&ID=$FORM1{ID}" method="post">
      <postfield name="items" value="\$(items)"/>
     </go>
    </do>

    <do type="accept" label="Back">
     <go href="http://people.cs.und.edu/~wenchen/cgi-
bin/device/Interface2.pl?name=$FORM1{name}&ID=$FORM1{ID}" method="post">
     </go>
    </do>
   </p>
  </card>
</wml>
EndofWML
```

Figure 9.14 shows the CGI Perl script `PurchaseGames.pl`, which includes three loops. These are responsible for performing the following tasks:

1. Retrieving the selected items from the previous interface via the CGI POST method.
2. Retrieving the customer name and ID entered from the entry page via the CGI GET method.
3. Calling the JDBC program `PurchaseGames.java` to process each selected video games.

A "Main Page" button is provided in this interface, so the user can easily return to the entry page.

Figure 9.15 shows the JDBC program `PurchaseGames.java`, which employs four SQL queries:

Figure 9.11. The JDBC program `ListGames.java`

```
// Need to import the java.sql package to use JDBC.
import  java.sql.*;

class  ListGames {
 public static void  main( String args[ ] ) throws SQLException {
  // Load the Oracle JDBC driver.
  DriverManager.registerDriver( new oracle.jdbc.driver.OracleDriver( ) );
  // Connect to the database.  You can put a database
  // name after the @ sign in the connection URL.
  Connection  conn = DriverManager.getConnection(
   "jdbc:oracle:thin:@cs.und.edu:1521:device", "userid", "password" );

  try {
   // Create and compose a statement.
   Statement stmt = conn.createStatement( );
   String query = "select g.title, g.GID, g.quantity from games g ";
   // Do the matching on the titles.
   query += "where g.title like '%" + args[0].trim( );
   query += "%' order by g.title";
   // Retrieve games from the GAMES table.
   ResultSet rset = stmt.executeQuery( query );

   // Iterate through the results and print the games.
   while (rset.next( )) {
    String  str = rset.getString( 2 );
    System.out.println( "<option value=\"" + str.trim( ) + "\">" );
    str = rset.getString( 1 );
    System.out.println( str + "</option>" );
   }
   // Close the ResultSet and Statement.
   rset.close( );
   stmt.close( );
  }
  catch( SQLException ex ) {
   // Send a minimal deck.
   System.out.println( "<wml><card><p>" + ex + "</p></card></wml>" );
  }
  // Close the Connection.
  conn.close( );
 }
}
```

- update games g set g.quantity = g.quantity - 1

where g.GID = 'GID';

where `args[1]` is the identifier of the game purchased by the customer. This update command subtracts one from the quantity on hand of that game.

- select title from games where GID = 'GID';

Figure 9.12. The CGI script `Interface2.pl`

```perl
#!/usr/bin/perl

# Retrieve information from the variable $ENV{'QUERY_STRING'}.
@pairs = split(/&/, $ENV{'QUERY_STRING'});
foreach $pair (@pairs) {
  ($name, $value) = split(/=/, $pair);
  $value =~ tr/+/ /;
  $value =~ s/%([a-fA-F0-9][a-fA-F0-9])/pack("C", hex($1))/eg;
  $value =~ s/~!/ ~!/g;
  $FORM{$name} = $value;
}

print <<EndofWML;
Content-type: text/vnd.wap.wml \n\n
<?xml version="1.0"?>
<!DOCTYPE wml PUBLIC "-//WAPFORUM//DTD WML 1.2//EN"
 "http://www.wapforum.org/DTD/wml_1.2.xml">;

<wml>
 <card title="Welcome $FORM{Name}">
  <p>
   A title word:<br />
   <input name="title" size="16" /><br />

   <do type="accept" label="List Games">
    <go href="http://people.cs.und.edu/~wenchen/cgi-
bin/device/ListGames.cgi?name=$FORM{name}&ID=$FORM{ID}" method="post">
     <postfield name="title" value="\$(title)" />
    </go>
   </do>
  </p>
 </card>
</wml>
EndofWML
```

Figure 9.13. An output of the JDBC program in Figure 9.12 and its corresponding WML script

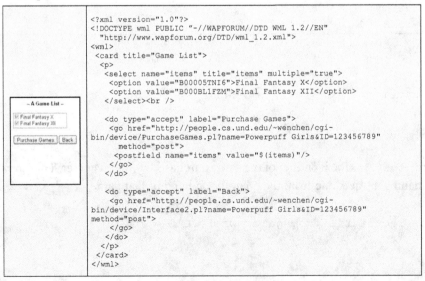

```
<?xml version="1.0"?>
<!DOCTYPE wml PUBLIC "-//WAPFORUM//DTD WML 1.2//EN"
 "http://www.wapforum.org/DTD/wml_1.2.xml">
<wml>
 <card title="Game List">
  <p>
   <select name="items" title="items" multiple="true">
    <option value="B00005TNI6">Final Fantasy X</option>
    <option value="B000BL1FZM">Final Fantasy XII</option>
   </select><br />

   <do type="accept" label="Purchase Games">
    <go href="http://people.cs.und.edu/~wenchen/cgi-
bin/device/PurchaseGames.pl?name=Powerpuff Girls&ID=123456789"
        method="post">
     <postfield name="items" value="$(items)"/>
    </go>
   </do>

   <do type="accept" label="Back">
    <go href="http://people.cs.und.edu/~wenchen/cgi-
bin/device/Interface2.pl?name=Powerpuff Girls&ID=123456789"
method="post">
    </go>
   </do>
  </p>
 </card>
</wml>
```

Figure 9.14. The CGI Perl script `PurchaseGames.pl`

```perl
#!/usr/bin/perl

# Retrieve Web argument values.
read(STDIN, $buffer, $ENV{'CONTENT_LENGTH'});
@pairs = split(/&/, $buffer);
foreach $pair (@pairs) {
  ($name, $value) = split(/=/, $pair);
  $value =~ tr/+/ /;
  $value =~ s/%([a-fA-F0-9][a-fA-F0-9])/pack("C", hex($1))/eg;
  $value =~ s/~!/ ~!/g;
  $FORM{$name} = $value;
}

# Retrieve information from the variable $ENV{'QUERY_STRING'}.
@pairs = split(/&/, $ENV{'QUERY_STRING'});
foreach $pair (@pairs) {
  ($name, $value) = split(/=/, $pair);
  $value =~ tr/+/ /;
  $value =~ s/%([a-fA-F0-9][a-fA-F0-9])/pack("C", hex($1))/eg;
  $value =~ s/~!/ ~!/g;
  $FORM1{$name} = $value;
}

# Print the top part of the next interface.
print <<EndofWML;
Content-type: text/vnd.wap.wml \n\n
<?xml version="1.0"?>
<!DOCTYPE wml PUBLIC "-//WAPFORUM//DTD WML 1.2//EN"
  "http://www.wapforum.org/DTD/wml_1.2.xml">;
<wml>
 <card title="Purchasing List">
  <p>
   Customer <b>$FORM1{name}</b> has purchased<br /><br />
EndofWML

# For security, remove some Unix metacharacters.
$FORM{ID} =~ s/;|>|>>|<|\*|\?|\&|\|//g;

@items = split( /;/, $FORM{items} );
foreach $item ( @items ) {
 # For security, remove some Unix metacharacters.
 $item =~ s/;|>|>>|<|\*|\?|\&|\|//g;
 system( "/usr/bin/java  PurchaseGames '$FORM{ID}' '$item'" );
}

print <<EndofWML;
   <do type="accept" label="Main Page">
    <go href="http://people.cs.und.edu/~wenchen/device/MicroGames.wml">
    </go>
   </do>
  </p>
 </card>
</wml>
EndofWML
```

This query finds the title of the game purchased by the customer. The titles are printed later.

```
•    select * from buys b

where b.customer.CID = 'CID' and
  b.game.GID = 'GID';
```

where `args[0]` is the identifier of the customer performing the purchase. This query checks whether or not the record has already been created in the purchasing records.

```
•    update buys b set b.no = b.no + 1

where b.customer.CID = 'args[0]' and
  b.game.GID = 'args[1]';
```

If the record has already been created in the purchasing records, increase the value of the attribute `no` of the record by one.

```
•    insert into buys select ref(c), ref(g), 1

from customers c, games g
  where c.CID = 'args[0]' and g.GID = 'args[1]';
```

If the record is not in the purchasing records, insert a new record.

SUMMARY

There are a number of approaches available for database-driven mobile website construction. This chapter explains a CGI approach composed of five steps:

1. **System setup:** Various tools and software are involved with the construction, which need to be set up before they can be used.
2. **Database design and implementation:** Entity-relationship modeling or normalization is used for database design and SQL (Structured Query Language) is for database implementation.

3. **Mobile web user interface construction:** Mobile web interface can be created by using WML or HTML.

4. **Web and host-computer connection:** The CGI technology is used to connect the web interface and host program.

5. **Database accesses and management:** JDBC, a Java language with embedded SQL, is used to access and manage a database.

Figure 9.15. The JDBC program `PurchaseGames.java`

```
// Need to import the java.sql package to use JDBC.
import  java.sql.*;

class  PurchaseGames {
 public static void  main( String args[ ] ) throws SQLException {
  // Load the Oracle JDBC driver.
  DriverManager.registerDriver( new oracle.jdbc.driver.OracleDriver( ) );
  // Connect to the database.  You can put a database
  // name after the @ sign in the connection URL.
  Connection conn = DriverManager.getConnection(
   "jdbc:oracle:thin:@cs.und.edu:1521:device", "userid", "password" );

  try {
   // Create and compose a statement.
   Statement  stmt = conn.createStatement( );
   // Subtract one from the video game's quantity.
   String query = "update games g set g.quantity = g.quantity - 1 ";
   // Do the matching on the ID.
   query += "where g.GID = '" + args[1].trim( ) + "'";
   // Execute the update.
   stmt.executeUpdate( query );

   // Print the titles of the purchased games.
   query = "select title from games where GID = '" + args[1].trim( ) + "'";
   ResultSet  rset = stmt.executeQuery( query );
   while ( rset.next( ) ) {
    String  str = rset.getString( 1 );
    System.out.println( "     " + str + "<br />" );
   }

   // Check whether or not the purchasing record is in the database.
   query  = "select * from buys b where b.customer.CID='";
   query += args[0].trim( ) + "' and b.game.GID='" + args[1].trim( ) + "'";
   rset = stmt.executeQuery( query );

   if ( rset.next( ) ) {
    // The record has already been in the database.
    query  = "update buys b set b.no = b.no + 1 where b.customer.CID='";
    query += args[0].trim( ) + "' and b.game.GID='" + args[1].trim( ) + "'";
   }
   else {
    // The record is not in the database.
    query  = "insert into buys select ref(c), ref(g), 1 from customers c,
```

continued on following page

Figure 9.15. continued

```
games g where c.CID='";
    query += args[0].trim( ) + "' and g.GID='" + args[1].trim( ) + "'";
  }
  stmt.executeUpdate( query );

  // Close the result set and statement.
  rset.close( );
  stmt.close( );
}
catch( SQLException ex ) {
  // Send a minimal deck.
  System.out.println ( "<wml><card><p>" + ex + "</p></card></wml>" );
}
// Close the Connection.
conn.close( );
}
}
```

Figure 9.16. An output of the JDBC program in Figure 8.15 and its corresponding WML script

The Microbrowser Display of the Output of Figure 9.15	The Corresponding WML Script of the Display

-- A Purchasing List --
 	
Customer **Powerpuff Girls** has purchased
 	
Final Fantasy X
Final Fantasy XII
 	
Main Page
	```<?xml version="1.0"?>```
	```<!DOCTYPE wml PUBLIC "-//WAPFORUM//DTD WML 1.2//EN"```
	``` "http://www.wapforum.org/DTD/wml_1.2.xml">```
	
	```<wml>```
	``` <card title="Purchasing List">```
	``` <p>```
	`` Customer <b>Powerpuff Girls</b> has brought
	``
	`` Final Fantasy X
	``
	`` Final Fantasy XII
	``
	
	``` <do type="accept" label="Main Page">```
	``` <go href="http://people.cs.und.edu/~wenchen/device/```
	```MicroGames.wml">```
	``` </go>```
	``` </do>```
	``` </p>```
	``` </card>```
	```</wml>```

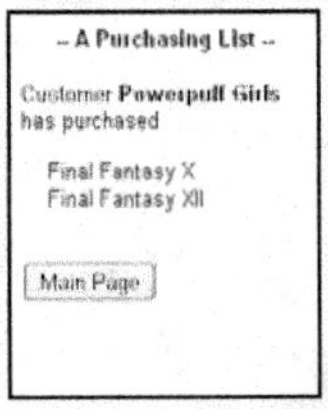

REFERENCES

Chen, P. (1976). The entity-relationship model: Toward a unified view of data. *ACM Transactions on Database Systems*. 1(1), 9-36.

Elmasri, R. & Navathe, S. B. (2003). *Fundamentals of Database Systems, 4ᵗʰ Edition*. Pearson Addison Wesley.

O'Neil, P. & O'Neil, E. (2000). *Database—Principles, programming, performance, 2ⁿᵈ Edition*. Morgan Kaufmann.

Oracle Corporation. (2002). *Oracle9i JDBC Developer's Guide and Reference, Release 2 (9.2)*. Retrieved June 13, 2006, from http://download-west.oracle.com/docs/cd/B10501_01/java.920/a96654/toc.htm

Sun Microsystems, Inc. (n.d.). *Java 2 Platform, Standard Edition, V 1.3.1, API Specification*. Retrieved from July 13, 2006, from http://java.sun.com/j2se/1.3/docs/api/overview-summary.html

Sun Microsystems, Inc. (n.d.). *JDBC Technology*. Retrieved July 16, 2005, from http://java.sun.com/products/jdbc/

Section III
Client–Side Mobile Handheld Computing and Programming

Chapter X
Client–Side Handheld Computing and Programming

INTRODUCTION

There are two kinds of handheld computing and programming, namely client- and server- side handheld computing and programming. The most popular applications of the latter are used with database-driven mobile web content, whose construction steps were described in the previous section. The remainder of this book will be devoted to client-side handheld computing and programming, whose applications do not need the support of server-side programs. Client-side handheld applications are varied and numerous, covering a wide range of everyday activities. Popular application examples include:

- *address books*, which store personal information such as addresses, telephone numbers, and email addresses in an accessible format,
- *appointments*, which allow users to edit, save, and view times reserved for business meetings and visits to the doctor,
- *calculators*, which may be a standard 4-function pocket calculator or a multi-function scientific calculator,

- *datebooks/calendars*, which allow users to enter hourly activities and show a daily or weekly schedule, or a simple monthly view,
- *expenses*, which allow users to track and record common business expenses such as car mileage, per diems, air fees, and hotel bills,
- *mobile office functions*, which include viewing and processing documents, spread sheets, presentations, and inventory.
- *multimedia*, which includes playing music and videos, photography, and personal albums.
- *note pads*, which allow users to save, view, and edit text notes,
- *to-do lists*, which allow users to enter a list of tasks to be performed, and
- *video games*, in addition to those on-line video games that require the support of server-side programs.

HANDHELD PROGRAMMING ENVIRONMENTS/LANGUAGES

Various mobile programming environments/languages are applied to client-side handheld programming and computing. Handheld devices are inconvenient for handheld application development because of their small sizes and screens and awkward input methods, so handheld application programmers generally develop software with the aid of handheld emulators, which run on regular PCs and laptops but are configured to accept the same inputs and produce the same outputs as the handheld device being modeled. Once the applications are fully developed and tested, they are then synchronized to the actual devices. Figure 10.1 shows a generic development cycle for client-side handheld applications. Several popular mobile programming environments/languages for client-side handheld computing and programming are listed below:

Figure 10.1. A generic development cycle for client-side handheld applications

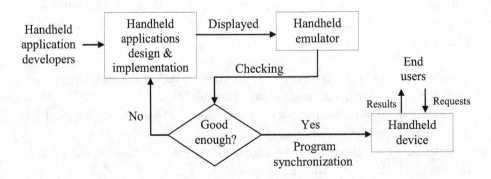

- *Android*, an open and free mobile platform proposed by the Open Handset Alliance, which is made up of more than 30 technology and mobile phone companies,
- *BREW (Binary Runtime Environment for Wireless)*, an application development platform from Qualcomm Inc. for CDMA-based mobile phones,
- *Java ME (Java Platform, Micro Edition)*, which was developed by Sun Microsystems Inc. and provides an environment for applications running on consumer devices such as mobile phones, PDAs, and TV set-top boxes, as well as a broad range of embedded devices,
- *Palm OS*, originally developed by Palm Source, Inc., but then acquired by ACCESS in 2005, and is now a fully ARM-native, 32-bit operating system running on handheld devices,
- *Symbian*, from Symbian Ltd., a software licensing company that develops and supplies the open, standard operating system—Symbian OS—for data-enabled mobile phones, and
- *Windows Mobile*, a compact operating system for mobile devices based on the Microsoft Win32 API that is designed to be similar to desktop versions of Windows.

All these programming languages and environments apply different approaches to accomplishing the same goal, namely to develop new handheld applications. Table 10.1 compares these six handheld programming environments/languages, and in the rest of this chapter they will each be introduced in more detail. The final four

Table 10.1. A comparison among six handheld programming environments/languages

	Android	BREW	Java ME	Palm OS	Symbian OS	Windows Mobile
Creator	Open Handset Alliance	Qualcomm Inc.	Sun Microsystems Inc.	PalmSource Inc.	Symbian Ltd.	Microsoft Corp.
(L)anguage/ (E)nvironment	E	E	L	E	E	E
Market Share (PDA) as of 2005	N/A	N/A	N/A	3rd	4th	1st
Market Share (Smartphone) as of 2006	N/A	?	N/A	4th	1st	5th
Primary Host Language	Java	C/C++	Java	C/C++	C++	C/C++
Target Devices	Phones	Phones	PDAs & phones	PDAs	Phones	PDAs & phones

chapters of the book will discuss Java ME programming (using Java) and Palm OS programming (using C/C++), chosen because Java and C/C++ are the two major handheld programming languages.

ANDROID

Programming for desktop PCs or laptops are relatively easy compared to programming for handheld devices because the operating systems of PCs are dominated by Microsoft Windows. PC programmers develop applications on Windows and the applications can be deployed and will run on most PCs. In contrast, handheld programmers face a greater challenge because no single handheld operating system yet dominates the market; applications developed on Symbian will not work on cellphones using Microsoft Windows Mobile. The Android project, sponsored by the *Open Handset Alliance* (n.d.), is an attempt to solve this problem by providing a uniform, open mobile platform. Android is a software stack for mobile devices that includes an operating system, middleware and key applications.

Features

Android includes the following features:

- *Application framework*, which enables reuse and replacement of components,
- *Dalvik virtual machine*, which optimizes operations for mobile devices,
- *Integrated browser*, which is based on the open source WebKit engine,
- *Optimized graphics*, which is powered by a custom 2D graphics library; 3D graphics based on the OpenGL ES 1.0 specification (hardware acceleration optional),
- *SQLite,* **which allows** structured data storage,
- *Media support*, which supports common audio, video, and still image formats (MPEG4, H.264, MP3, AAC, AMR, JPG, PNG, GIF),
- *GSM Telephony* (hardware dependent),
- *Bluetooth, EDGE, 3G, and WiFi* (hardware dependent),
- *Camera, GPS, compass, and accelerometer* (hardware dependent), and
- *Rich development environment,* **which** includes a device emulator, tools for debugging, memory and performance profiling, and a plugin for the Eclipse IDE.

Figure 10.2. The Android architecture

Level	Components				
Applications	Home	Contacts	Phone	Browser	...
Application Framework	Activity Manager	Window Manager	Content Providers	View System	Notification Manager
	Package Manager	Telephony Manager	Resource Manager	Location Manager	XMPP Service
Libraries	Surface Manager	Media Framework	SQLite	*Android Runtime*	
	OpenGLjES	FreeType	WebKit	Core Libraries	
	SGL	SSL	Libc	Dalvik Virtual Machine	
Linux Kernel	Display Driver	Camera Driver	Bluetooth Driver	Flash Memory Driver	Binder (IPC) Driver
	USB Driver	Keypad Driver	WiFi Driver	Audio Drivers	Power Management

Architecture

Figure 10.2 shows the major components of the Android operating system, which is composed of four layers, (i) *Applications*, (ii) *Application Framework*, (iii) *Libraries/Android Runtime*, and (iv) *Linux Kernel*:

- **Applications:** Android will ship with a set of core applications including an email client, SMS program, calendar, maps, browser, contacts, and others. All applications are written using the Java programming language.
- **Application framework:** Developers have full access to the same framework APIs used by the core applications. The application architecture is designed to simplify the reuse of components; any application can publish its capabilities and any other application may then make use of those capabilities (subject to security constraints enforced by the framework). This same mechanism allows components to be replaced by the user.
- **Libraries:** Android includes a set of C/C++ libraries used by various components of the Android system. These capabilities are exposed to developers through the Android application framework. Some of the core libraries are listed below:
  - *System C library*, which is a BSD-derived implementation of the standard C system library (`libc`), tuned for embedded Linux-based devices,

- o *Media libraries*, which are based on PacketVideo's OpenCORE; the libraries support playback and recording of many popular audio and video formats, as well as static image files, including MPEG4, H.264, MP3, AAC, AMR, JPG, and PNG,
- o *Surface manager*, which manages access to the display subsystem and seamlessly composites 2D and 3D graphic layers from multiple applications,
- o *LibWebCore*, which is a modern web browser engine which powers both the Android browser and an embeddable web view,
- o *SGL*, which is the underlying 2D graphics engine,
- o *3D libraries*, which are an implementation based on OpenGL ES 1.0 APIs; the libraries use either hardware 3D acceleration (where available) or the included, highly optimized 3D software rasterizer,
- o *FreeType*, which is for bitmap and vector font rendering, and
- o *SQLite*, which is a powerful and lightweight relational database engine available to all applications.
- **Android runtime:** Android includes a set of core libraries that provides most of the functionality available in the core libraries of the Java programming language.
- **Linux kernel:** Android relies on Linux version 2.6 for core system services such as security, memory management, process management, network stack, and driver model. The kernel also acts as an abstraction layer between the hardware and the rest of the software stack.

BREW (BINARY RUNTIME ENVIRONMENT FOR WIRELESS)

BREW is an application development platform developed by Qualcomm Inc. (2003) for CDMA (Code Division Multiple Access) -based mobile phones. CDMA is a digital wireless telephony transmission technique that allows multiple frequencies to be used simultaneously. It is capable of providing the higher data transfer speeds required by 3G devices and forms the foundation for the two most widely adopted 3G standards—CDMA2000 and WCDMA (UMTS). BREW is used for wireless application development, device configuration, application distribution, and billing and payment. The complete BREW platform includes:

- BREW SDK (software development kit) for application developers,
- BREW client software and porting tools for device manufacturers, and
- the BREW Distribution System (BDS), which is controlled and managed by

operators and enables them to easily transfer applications from developers to market and coordinate the billing and payment process.

BREW benefits from the following special features:

- The BREW platform was designed from the chip out rather than by scaling down a product originally developed for PCs or PDAs.
- It supports other languages in addition to native C/C++, including alternative execution environments such as Java and XML.

The BREW client software serves as a common denominator across all types and tiers of devices, exposing a common set of application programming interfaces (APIs) for standardized development of wireless applications. The BREW client can act as an extended platform for other environments (such as VMs) and allow any type of browser (HTML, WAP, cHTML, etc.) to run on BREW as an application.

JAVA ME (JAVA PLATFORM, MICRO EDITION)

Java ME (previously known as J2ME) provides an environment for applications running on consumer devices such as mobile phones, PDAs, and TV set-top boxes, as well as a broad range of embedded devices. Java ME, along with the other Java products listed below, was developed by Sun Microsystems, Inc. (2002a,b, 2004):

- **Java EE (Java Platform, Enterprise Edition):** Java EE (formerly known as J2EE) defines the standard for developing component-based multitier enterprise applications. Building on the foundation of Java SE, Java EE provides web services, component model, management, and communications APIs for implementing enterprise-class service-oriented architecture (SOA) and next-generation web applications.
- **Java SE (Java Platform, Standard Edition):** Java SE (formerly known as J2SE) allows users to develop and deploy Java applications on desktops and servers, as well as in both embedded and real-time environments. Java SE includes classes that support the development of Java web services and provides the foundation for Java EE.
- **Java Card:** Java Card technology enables smart cards and other devices with limited memory to run small applications, known as applets, that utilize Java technology. Multiple applications can be deployed on a single card, and new ones can be added even after the card has been issued to the end user. Appli-

Figure 10.3. The four Java programming environments from Sun Microsystem, Inc.

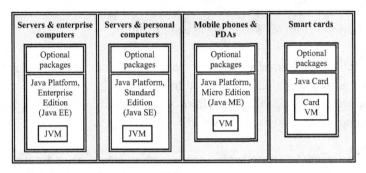

cations written in the Java programming language can be executed securely on cards from different vendors.

Figure 10.3 shows the four Java programming environments. Java ME includes Java virtual machines and a set of standard Java APIs, which have been defined through the Java Community Process by expert groups made up of device manufacturers, software vendors, and service providers.

The Java ME Architecture

The Java ME architecture comprises a variety of configurations, profiles, and optional packages that implementers and developers can choose from and combine to construct a complete Java runtime environment that closely matches the requirements of a particular range of devices and a target market. There are two sets of Java ME packages, which target different devices:

- **High-end devices:** These include *Connected Device Configuration (CDC)*, Foundation, and Personal Profile.
- **Entry-level devices and smart phones:** These include *Connected Limited Device Configuration (CLDC)* and *Mobile Information Device Profile (MIDP)*.

Figure 10.4 shows the Java ME architecture. The configurations and profiles are defined as follows:

- *Configurations* are composed of a virtual machine and a minimal set of class libraries and provide the base functionality for a particular range of devices

Figure 10.4. The Java ME architecture

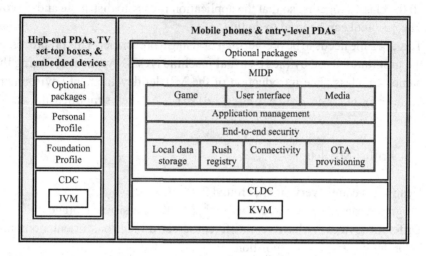

that share similar characteristics, such as network connectivity and memory footprint.

*   *Profiles* provide a complete runtime environment for a specific device category.

Recent updates to the J2ME Platform include MIDP 2.0, MMA (Mobile Media API), and WMA (Wireless Messaging API). This section discusses some of their features, including:

*   MIDlet signing,
*   Testing MIDlet deployment Over The Air (OTA),
*   Creating MIDlets for sending and receiving SMS (Short Message Service) messages, and
*   Developing MIDlets with multimedia functionality.

A *MIDlet* application is a Java program for embedded devices that is written for MIDP (Mobile Information Device Profile). MIDlet applications are subclasses of the `javax.microedition.midlet.MIDlet` class that is defined by MIDP. A MIDlet must fulfill the following requirements in order to run on a mobile phone:

*   The main class must be a subclass of `javax.microedition. midlet.MIDlet`.

- If an application consists of multiple classes, a `.jar` file must be used to group all the classes together so that the application is easy to distribute and deploy. The `jar` tool can be used to do this.
- The `.jar` file needs to be pre-verified by using a preverifier. This preprocesses the program for use by the K virtual machine (KVM) without changing the name of a class. The introduction of the MIDlet development environment `KToolbar` of `J2ME Wireless Toolkit 2.3` has simplified the above steps.

When writing MIDlets:

- Heap sizes can be very small, around 200KB.
- Programs cannot expect to use more than 20KB persistent storage.
- Different devices can have very different screen dimensions, orientations, and color depths, so absolute positions cannot be used.
- Not all devices have keypads or pointers, so programs must be able to use either. Key layouts also vary, so it is best to use `Game Actions` for `up-down-left-right-action` style events.
- Do not white list devices. If the program has not been tested on a specific device, assume it will work. Never attempt to block the user from trying it.
- Use an `obfuscator` such as `Proguard` to compress the MIDlet size.

PALM OS

Palm OS was created by Palm, Inc, which split into two companies in 2002, PalmOne and PalmSource, with the latter being responsible for Palm OS development and its licenses (PalmSource, Inc., 2002, 2004a, 2004b, 2004c). PalmSource was then acquired in 2005 by ACCESS, a global provider of advanced software technologies to the mobile and beyond-PC markets. Principal ACCESS technologies include:

- *Garnet OS*, the advanced version of Palm 5.0,
- *ACCESS Linux Platform*, a software platform that combines the functionality of Garnet OS with a Linux core,
- *NetFront Mobile Client Suite*, a client software suite for mobile devices, and
- *NetFront*, an Internet browser.

Palm OSs and Application Types

The first Palm OS was released in 1996 and the most recent Palm OS, Palm OS Cobalt, was introduced in 2004. So far, no hardware products run Palm OS Cobalt and all devices use Palm OS Garnet. Probably as a result of Palm OS Cobalt's lack of adoption, PalmSource has shifted to developing Palm OS Cobalt's APIs on top of a Linux kernel. The following list shows different Palm OS versions:

- *Palm OS Version 1.0*, which was present on the original Pilot 1000 and 5000 and required 128K and 512K of RAM, respectively.
- *Palm OS Version 2.0*, which was introduced with the PalmPilot Personal and Professional and used 512K and 1M of RAM, respectively.
- *Palm OS Version 30*, which was introduced with the launch of the Palm III series and used 2M of RAM. Incremental upgrades occurred with the release of versions 3.1, 3.3 and 3.5, adding support for color, multiple expansion ports, new processors and sundry other additions.
- *Palm OS Version 4.0*, which was released with the m500 series, and later made available as an upgrade for older devices. This added a standard interface for external file system access (such as Secure Digital Memory cards) and improved telephony libraries, security and UI improvements.
- *Palm OS Version 5.0*, which was introduced with the Tungsten T and was the first version released to support ARM devices.
- *Palm OS Garnet*, which is an enhanced version of Palm OS 5 and provides features such as dynamic input area, improved network communication, and support for a broad range of screen resolutions including QVGA.
- *Palm OS Cobalt*, which is also referred to as Palm OS 6, focuses on enabling faster and more efficient development of smartphones and integrated wireless (WiFi/Bluetooth) handhelds. However, as yet few devices use Palm OS Cobalt.

Currently, there are three Palm OS application types:

- *Palm OS 68K applications* span all Palm OS releases. The 68K API allows application code compiled for Dragonball processors to access the capabilities of Palm OS, while Palm OS Garnet and Palm OS Cobalt are designed for handhelds with ARM-based processors. Both incorporate *PACE (Palm Application Compatibility Environment)*, which enables 68K applications to also run on the following Palm OS versions:
  - o   *68K*, the family of Motorola 68000 processors.

o   *ARM,* the family of *Advanced RISC Machine* processors. An ARM processor is a type of 4-byte RISC processor, and is available from many sources.

- *Palm OS 68K application with PACE Native Objects* allows 68K developers to take advantage of the ARM CPUs that power Palm OS Garnet and Cobalt handhelds. PACE Native Object (PNO) is an ARM-native subroutine that 68K application calls using the `PceNativeCall( )` function.
- *Palm OS Protein application* is an ARM-native application written using the Palm OS Protein APIs that takes full advantage of the new features introduced in Palm OS Cobalt. In addition to their other features, Palm OS Protein applications can
  o   be multithreaded,
  o   access schema and extended databases, and
  o   employ Palm OS Cobalt's multimedia framework.

Palm OS Protein applications only run on Palm OS Cobalt and later, so in order to develop applications that will span all Palm OS releases, developers must use 68K API.

Palm OS Built-in Applications

One of the major advantages of Palm OS is the number of applications available. Palm OS licensees decides which applications are included on their Palm OS devices and can also customize the applications. The following list gives some of the most common Palm applications included with the Palm OS:

- **Address books/contact:** The Palm's *Address* program stores personal information, keyed by any of several user-definable categories. Entries are displayed and sorted in last name, first name order (this can be changed only to Company, Last Name order). There are five slots for phone or e-mail, each of which may be designated Work, Home, Fax, Other, E-mail, Main, Pager, or Mobile. Figure 10.5 shows a screenshot of the Palm address book.
- **Calculator:** *Calc* turns the Palm into a standard 4-function pocket calculator. It also includes a menu option to switch to an advanced mode, which features several button layouts that pertain to specific jobs. These modes include, for example, Math, Trig, Finance, Logic, Statistics, Weight/Tmp, Length, Area, and Volume. Figure 10.6 shows a screenshot of the Palm calculator.
- **Date book/calendar:** Date Book shows a daily or weekly schedule, or a simple monthly view. The daily schedule has one line per hour, between user-selected begin and end times. Clicking on an empty line creates a new appointment.

Figure 10.5. A screenshot of the Palm address book © 2008 ACCESS Co., Ltd.

Figure 10.6. A screenshot of the Palm calculator © 2008 ACCESS Co., Ltd.

Figure 10.7. A screenshot of the Palm date book © 2008 ACCESS Co., Ltd.

An appointment can be signaled by an alarm, any number of minutes, hours or days before it is due to begin. Appointments can recur in a specified number of days, weeks, months or years—and can contain notes. Figure 10.7 shows a screenshot of the Palm date book.

- **Expense:** The Expense application allows a user to track common business expenses. No totals are calculated on the Palm, and the user must sync with a host computer and view the expense data in a worksheet. Templates for Microsoft Excel are supplied.
- **HotSync:** The HotSync application provides integration with the user's PC. Usually activated by a press of the physical HotSync button on the Palm's cradle (a docking station), this application communicates with various conduits

Figure 10.8. A screenshot of Palm HotSync © 2008 ACCESS Co., Ltd.

Figure 10.9. A screenshot of Palm Memo pad © 2008 ACCESS Co., Ltd.

Figure 10.10.

on the desktop PC to install software, backup databases, or merge changes made on the PC or the handheld to both devices. A Backup conduit included with the HotSync software backs up (and restores, if necessary) most of the data on a Palm OS device. This allows users to hard reset their Palm, thus clearing all of the data, with few noticeable consequences. This also allows users to migrate to new Palm devices of the same Palm OS version easily, a feature that is particularly helpful for those who have lost or damaged their device. Some models of Palm keep their data storage in volatile memory and require constant power to maintain their memory, while later Palms use

Figure 10.11. A screenshot of a Palm to-do list © 2008 ACCESS Co., Ltd.

NVRAM (Non-Volatile RAM) or microdrive for storage. Figure 10.8 shows a screenshot of Palm HotSync.

- **Memo Pad:** This can hold notes of up to 4,000 characters, keyed to user-configurable categories. Memos can be ordered in two ways: alphabetically or manually, with the user choosing the order of the memos in the latter case. Memo Pad is intended for text, not for drawings, so text in Memo Pad must be entered using the Graffiti application. Figure 10.9 shows a screenshot of Palm Memo Pad.

- **Note Pad:** This is intended primarily for drawings, `although` up to 10 words per page can be shown. Generally, however, it is best to use `Memo Pad for text`. Three sizes of drawing crayon are provided, plus an eraser and a background color change feature. Note Pad can be used to draw a very simple map, for example. Figure 10.9 shows a screenshot of Palm Note Pad.

- **To do list/tasks:** Also referred to as `Task List`, this is a convenient place to create personal reminders and prioritize activities. Each `To Do List` item may also have a priority, the ability to organize and view items in logical groups, and attached Notes that add more information about the task. Figure 10.11 shows a screenshot of a Palm to-do list.

Many applications can be installed on a Palm OS device. As of August 2005, more than 20,000 third-party applications were available for the Palm OS platform, with various licensing types including open-source, freeware, shareware, and traditional commercial applications. Palm OS Garnet applications are primarily coded in C/C++. Two popular compilers are

- a commercial product, Metrowerks' CodeWarrior, and
- an open source tool chain called PRC-Tools, based on GCC.

Although CodeWarrior has been criticized for being expensive and is no longer being developed, PRC-Tools lacks many of CodeWarrior's features. A version of

Figure 10.12. Palm OS 5 block diagram

Palm Applications	
PACE: Palm Application Compatibility Environment	
Core Palm OS	Licensee libraries
DAL: Device Abstraction Layer	
HAL: Hardware Abstraction Layer	

PRC-Tools is included in Palm OS Developer Suite and higher level development tools are also available.

Palm OS Architecture

Palm OS is a fully ARM-native, 32-bit operating system designed for used on Palm handhelds and other third-party devices. It has many advantages, such as long battery life, support for a wide variety of wireless standards, and the abundant software available. The plain design of the Palm OS has resulted in a long battery life, approximately twice that of its rivals. It supports many important wireless standards, including Bluetooth and 802.11b local wireless and GSM, Mo-bitex, and CDMA wide-area wireless networks (PalmSource Inc., 2002). Figure 10.12 shows the structure of Palm OS 5, which consists of five layers:

1. **Applications:** include all the built-in Palm OS applications, such as the address book, date book, and memo pad.
2. **PACE (Palm Application Compatibility Environment):** provides a 68K application environment that is equivalent to Palm OS 4.1. PACE handles the data translation required for a 68K application to run on Palm OS 5. For example, 68K applications read and write data in big-endian mode, but Palm OS 5 views data in little-endian mode. When a 68K application calls a Palm OS function, PACE handles the translation of the parameters, objects, and structure layouts so that existing applications do not have to be updated to handle the change of endianness. PACE creates "shadow structures" for the 68K application's data that allow the 68K application to run under Palm OS 5.
3. **Core Palm OS and Licensee Libraries:** This layer includes two functions:
    *   **Palm OS runtime services:** requests the desktop system library files (DLLs). These DLLs are located in the Palm OS directory, and are loaded when the code that they contain needs to be executed.

- **Communication stacks:** accesses the communication stacks for NetLib and Telephony components. Palm OS can optionally redirect NetLib calls to the host machine TCP/IP stack.

4. **DAL (Device Abstraction Layer):** is responsible for insulating Palm OS from the underlying system and hardware.
5. **HAL (Hardware Abstraction Layer):** allows a computer operating system to interact with a hardware device at a general or abstract level rather than at a detailed hardware level.

SYMBIAN OS

Symbian is a software licensing company that develops and supplies the open operating system, Symbian OS, for data-enabled mobile phones (Symbian Ltd., 2006). Symbian was established as a private independent company in June 1998 and is an independent, for-profit company aiming to establish Symbian OS as the world standard for mobile digital data systems, primarily for use in cellular telecoms. It is owned by Ericsson (15.6%), Nokia (47.9%), Panasonic (10.5%), Samsung (4.5%), Siemens (8.4%) and Sony Ericsson (13.1%). Headquartered in the UK, it has more than 1300 staff with offices in Japan, Sweden, UK and the USA and a development centre in Bangalore in 2006. It is the most popular mobile operating system for smartphones. The market share (in a descending order) of smartphone operating systems in the first quarter of 2006 was (1) Symbian OS, (2) Linux, (3) RIM (Research In Motion), (4) Palm OS, (5) Windows Mobile-based Smartphone, and (6) others. Cumulative shipments of Symbian OS phones since Symbian's formation reached 70.5 million phones in 2006. Key features of Symbian OS include:

- **Suite of application engines:** Contacts, schedule, messaging, browsing, utility and system control; appointments and business cards; integrated APIs for data management, text, clipboard and graphics.
- **Browsing:** A WAP stack, with support for WAP 1.2.1 .
- **Messaging:** Multimedia messaging, enhanced messaging and SMS; Internet mail; attachments; fax.*Multimedia*: Audio and video support for recording, playback and streaming; image conversion.
- **Graphics:** Direct access to screen and keyboard for high performance; graphics accelerator API.
- **Communications protocols:** Wide-area networking stacks including TCP/IP and WAP, personal area networking support including infrared, Bluetooth wireless technology and USB.

- **Mobile telephony:** GSM circuit switched voice and data and packet-based data; CDMA circuit switched voice, data and packet-based data; SIM, RUIM and UICC Toolkit.
- **International support:** Conforms to the Unicode Standard version 3.0.
- **Data synchronization:** SyncML; PC-based synchronization over serial, Bluetooth wireless technology, Infrared and USB.
- **Security:** Full encryption and certificate management, secure protocols, WIM framework and certificate-based application installation.
- **Developing for Symbian OS:** Content development options include: C++, Java MIDP 2.0 and PersonalJava 1.1.1a, and WAP.
- **User inputs:** Full keyboard, numeric mobile phone keypad, voice, handwriting recognition, and predictive text input.

Symbian OS Architecture

Symbian OS is designed for the specific requirements of advanced 2.5G and 3G mobile phones. It combines the power of an integrated applications environment with mobile telephony, bringing advanced data services to the mass market. Symbian OS supports a wide range of device categories with several user interfaces, including Nokia S60, UIQ and the NTT DoCoMo common software platform for 3G FOMA handsets. Symbian OS includes the following features:

- a multi-tasking kernel,
- integrated telephony support,
- communications protocols,
- data management,
- advanced graphics support,
- a low-level graphical user interface framework, and
- a variety of application engines.

Figure 10.13 shows the Symbian OS architecture (Symbian Ltd., 2005), which includes five layers:

1. *User interface framework*, which includes two key components:
   - *Uikon*, a generic core UI framework, which is present on all Symbian OS phones, and
   - *Product UI*, UI libraries developed by a Symbian OS licensee for a particular phone or range of phones.

2. *Application services*, which provide network operators with leading edge services such as email based on POP3/IMAP4/SMTP including attachment support, contacts, management, calendaring, and bookmarks.

3. *OS services*, which include generic OS, communication, multimedia & graphics, and connectivity services.

4. *Base services*, which are the lowest level of user-side services and extend the OS kernel into a useable (but minimal) system.

5. *Kernel services & hardware interface*, which contain the OS kernel itself, device drivers, and similar low-level components.

MICROSOFT WINDOWS MOBILE

In 1996, Microsoft launched Windows CE, a version of the Microsoft Windows operating system designed specifically for a variety of embedded products, including handheld devices. However, it was not well received, primarily because of its battery-hungry functions and because it was difficult to use. The latter problem is possibly due to the way that Windows CE was adapted for handheld devices from other Microsoft 32-bit desktop operating systems. A handheld operating system

Figure 10.13. Symbian OS architecture © 2004 Symbian Ltd or its Licensors

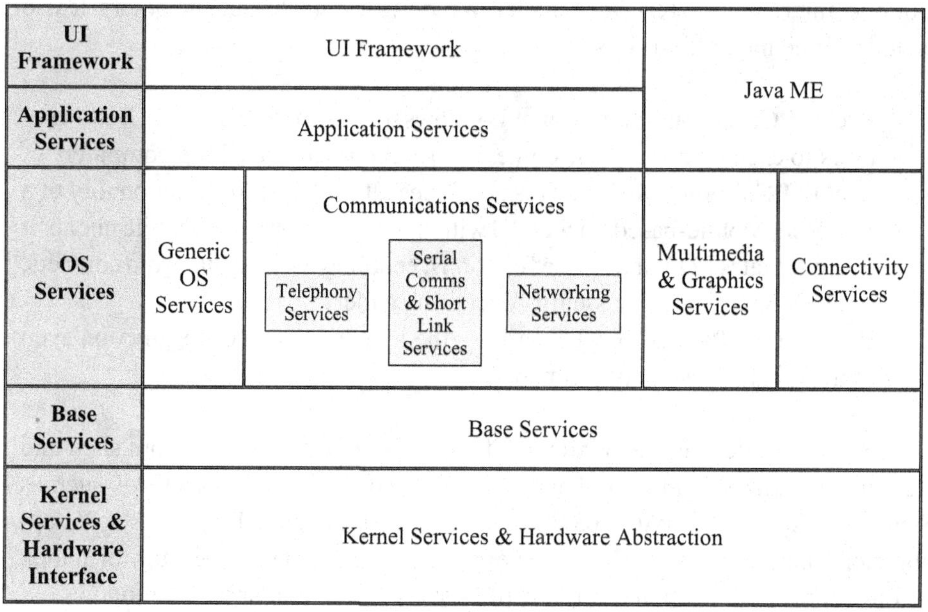

UI Framework	UI Framework					Java ME	
Application Services	Application Services						
OS Services	Generic OS Services	Communications Services				Multimedia & Graphics Services	Connectivity Services
		Telephony Services	Serial Comms & Short Link Services	Networking Services			
Base Services	Base Services						
Kernel Services & Hardware Interface	Kernel Services & Hardware Abstraction						

adapted from a desktop one is a diminutive version of a desktop operating system, and may not meet the special needs of handheld devices. Windows Mobile is a compact operating system for mobile devices based on the Microsoft Win32 API that is powered by Windows CE 5.x and uses the .NET Compact Framework 2.0, an environment for programs based on .NET (Microsoft Corp., 2005). Windows Mobile includes three major kinds of software:

- **Windows Mobile-based Pocket PC:** This was intended to put the power of Windows software into a pocket PC, enabling users to store and retrieve e-mail, contacts, appointments, games, exchange text messages with MSN Messenger, and browse the Web.
- **Windows Mobile-based Smartphone:** In addition to supplying the functions of a mobile phone, this also integrates PDA-type functionality, such as emails, instant messages, music, and Web surfing, into a voice-centric handset.
- **Windows Mobile-based Portable Media Center:** This allows users to access recorded TV programs, movies, home videos, music, and photos transferred from Microsoft Windows XP-based PC on their handheld devices.

Windows Mobile-Based Pocket PCs

Windows Mobile-based Pocket PCs were designed with better service for mobile users in mind, offering far more computing power than Windows CE. Scaled-down versions of many popular desktop applications are provided, including Microsoft Outlook, Internet Explorer, Word, Excel, Windows Media Player, and others. It also includes three major kinds of software:

- **Pocket PC:** This puts the power of Windows software into a Pocket PC, allowing users to exchange, or synchronize, information with a desktop computer.
- **Pocket PC Phone Edition:** This combines all the standard functionality of a Windows Mobile-based Pocket PC with that of a feature-rich mobile phone. It also integrates PDA and phone functions, enabling users to dial from contacts, send SMS messages, or identify incoming callers.
- **Ruggedized Pocket PC:** This allows the handheld devices to function even in the toughest user environments.

A Pocket PC device is a Windows Mobile-based PDA with a custom shell and a set of customized applications written by Microsoft but sold by OEMs such as Siemens (SX66), HP (iPAQ h6340) and Casio (Cassiopeia E115). Pocket PC applications must conform to a strict set of requirements that enforce a uniform look and feel for the applications. Figure 10.14 shows the modularity of Windows CE

Figure 10.14. Windows CE architecture

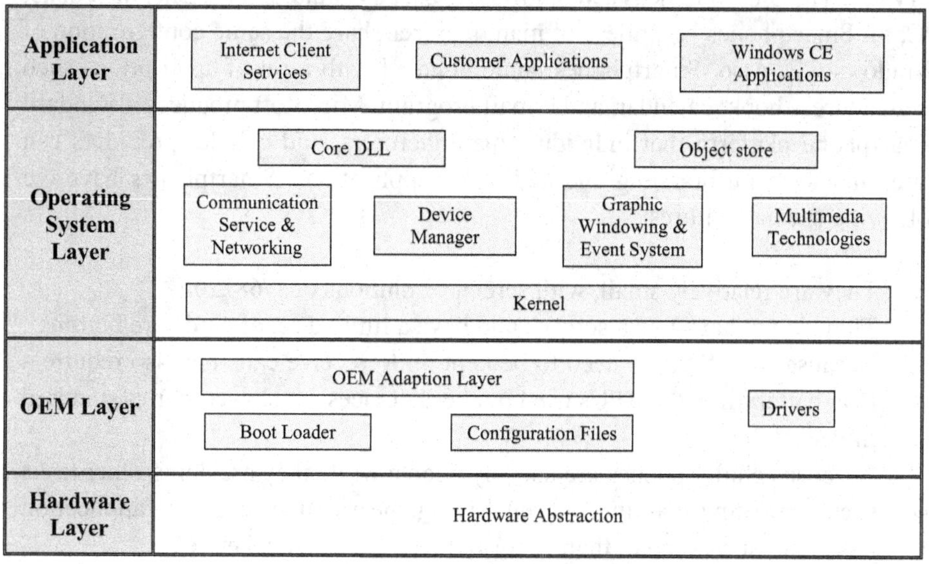

Application Layer	Internet Client Services		Customer Applications		Windows CE Applications	
Operating System Layer	Core DLL			Object store		
	Communication Service & Networking	Device Manager		Graphic Windowing & Event System	Multimedia Technologies	
	Kernel					
OEM Layer	OEM Adaption Layer				Drivers	
	Boot Loader		Configuration Files			
Hardware Layer	Hardware Abstraction					

4.20. Pocket PCs were built on top of Windows CE, which was itself built using a modular approach. As a result, the core operating system contains modules and services that can be used when building new instances of the operating system.

Windows CE is optimized for devices that have minimal storage—a Windows CE kernel may run in under a megabyte of memory. Devices are often configured without disk storage, and may be configured as a "closed" system that does not allow for end user extension; for instance, it can be burned into a ROM. Windows CE conforms to the definition of a real-time operating system, with a deterministic interrupt latency. It supports 256 priority levels and permits priority inversion. Unlike Unix-like operating systems, the fundamental unit of execution is the thread, allowing simpler, faster concurrent programming. A Pocket PC application is still a Windows application, however, so it has a message loop, a main window, and window procedures.

Windows Mobile-Based Smartphones

Smartphone supplies the functions of a mobile phone, but also integrates PDA-type functionality such as emails, instant messages, music, and Web surfing, into a voice-centric handset comparable in size to a mobile phone. It is designed for one-handed operation with keypad access to both voice and data features and is optimized for voice and text communication, although it also allows wireless access to Outlook information and encrypted browsing to corporate and Internet information and services. The Smartphone is a Windows CE-based cellular phone. Like the Pocket PC, all Smartphones regardless of manufacturer share the same configuration of Windows CE. Also, Smartphones come bundled with a set of applications such as an address book, calendar, and e-mail program. Microsoft produces a standard Smartphone platform that individual manufacturers, and cellular providers can then enhance with branding and additional applications. Smartphones have the following special features:

- They are relatively small, with screen resolutions of 176×220.
- They do not have touch screens and have a limited set of hardware buttons.
- Because Smartphones need to be kept on to receive calls but also require a long battery life, the CPUs used by these devices are slower than is standard in Pocket PCs.
- Because cellular phones are used by people while they are doing other tasks such as working, walking, or even driving, the user interface of the application has to be much simpler than is normal on a PC or a Pocket PC.

Other Smartphone functions include voice, SMS, and Instant Messaging services; email that can be received from sources such as the Outlook messaging and collaboration client, Exchange, IMAP, and POP3 services; and Personal Information Management (PIM) applications such as calendar and contacts.

Figure 10.15 shows the Smartphone architecture, which provides a core set of services that will abstract a variety of underlying links for both voice and data services. The primary Smartphone architecture consists of four layers:

1. **Applications/UI:** The top level includes the Smartphone shell and customer-level applications such as Pocket Internet Explorer, the Inbox, the control panel, and the phone dialer.
2. **Logic:** This level contains system application logic that can be used by the application layer. Examples of this include the control of network connections and synchronization capabilities.
3. **Core APIs:** This level provides the interfaces between the low-level architecture components and the application/logic layers. By developing applications targeted at this layer and the one above, developers do not need to know the underlying low level details in order to take full advantage of their capabilities.
4. **Radio Stack:** The bottom level refers, in general, to the architectural components responsible for voice and data control and data transmission.

Figure 10.15. The structure of Windows Mobile-based Smartphone

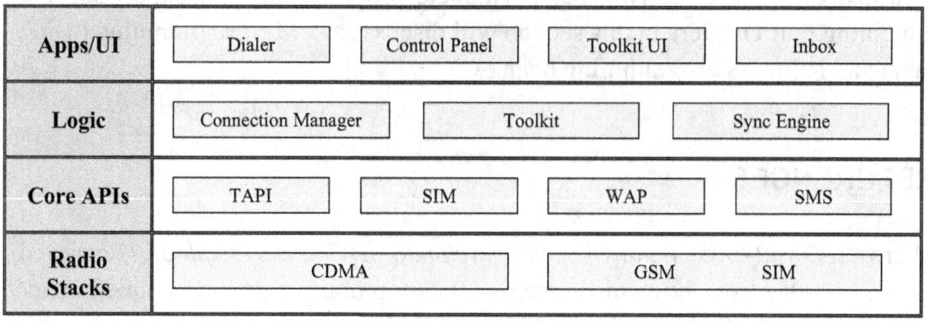

Apps/UI	Dialer	Control Panel	Toolkit UI	Inbox
Logic	Connection Manager	Toolkit	Sync Engine	
Core APIs	TAPI	SIM	WAP	SMS
Radio Stacks	CDMA		GSM SIM	

SUMMARY

Various mobile programming environments/languages may be applied to client-side handheld programming and computing. Handheld devices pose severe challenges for new handheld application development because of their small size and awkward input methods, so those developing new handheld applications work using emulators that accept the same inputs and produce the same outputs as the handheld devices. When the applications are fully developed, they are then synchronized to the devices. Six popular mobile programming environments/languages for client-side handheld computing and programming were described in this chapter:

- *Android*, a software stack for mobile devices that includes an operating system, middleware, and key applications such as contacts,
- *BREW (Binary Runtime Environment for Wireless)*, an application development platform from Qualcomm Inc. for CDMA-based mobile phones,
- *Java ME (Java Platform, Micro Edition)*, developed by Sun Microsystems Inc., provides an environment for applications running on consumer devices such as mobile phones, PDAs, and TV set-top boxes, as well as a broad range of embedded devices,
- *Palm OS*, developed by Palm Source Inc., is a fully ARM-native, 32-bit operating system running on handheld devices,
- *Symbian*, developed by Symbian Ltd., a software licensing company that develops and supplies the advanced, open, standard operating system Symbian OS for data-enabled mobile phones, and
- *Windows Mobile*, a compact operating system for mobile devices based on the Microsoft Win32 API that is designed to be similar to desktop versions of Windows.

Each of these applies a different approach to handheld application development. Java and C/C++ are the two major handheld programming languages, and the remaining four chapters in this section will discuss Java ME programming (using Java) and Palm OS programming (using C/C++).

REFERENCES

Microsoft Corp. (2005). *What's New for Developers in Windows Mobile 5.0?* Retrieved June 21, 2006, from http://msdn.microsoft.com/mobility/windowsmobile/howto/documentation/default.aspx?pull=/library/en-us/dnppcgen/html/whatsnew_wm5.asp

Open Handset Alliance. (n.d.). *Android—An Open Handset Alliance Project*. Retrieved November 21, 2007, from http://code.google.com/android/

PalmSource Inc. (2002). *Why PalmOS?* Retrieved June 23, 2006, from http://www.palmsource.com/palmos/Advantage/index_files/v3_document.htm

PalmSource Inc. (2004a). *Palm OS programmer's API reference*. Retrieved May 5, 2006, from http://www.palmos.com/dev/support/docs/palmos/PalmOSReference/ReferenceTOC.html

PalmSource Inc. (2004b). *Palm OS Programmer's Companion, Vol. I*. Retrieved August 12, 2006, from http://www.palmos.com/dev/support/docs/palmos/PalmOSCompanion/CompanionTOC.html

PalmSource Inc. (2004c). *Palm OS Programmer's Companion, Vol. II*. Retrieved February 21, 2006, from http://www.palmos.com/dev/support/docs/palmos/PalmOSCompanion2/Companion2TOC.html

Qualcomm Inc. (2003). *BREW and J2ME—A Complete Wireless Solution for Operators Committed to Java*. Retrieved February 12, 2006, from http://brew.qualcomm.com/brew/en/img/about/pdf/brew_j2me.pdf

Sun Microsystem Inc. (2002a). *Java 2 Platform, Micro Edition*. Retrieved January 12, 2006, from http://java.sun.com/j2me/docs/j2me-ds.pdf

Sun Microsystem Inc. (2002b). *Mobile Information Device Profile Specification 2.0*. Retrieved March 25, 2006, from http://jcp.org/aboutJava/communityprocess/final/jsr118/

Sun Microsystem Inc. (2004). *J2ME Wireless Toolkit 2.2—User's Guide*. Retrieved April 21, 2006, from http://java.sun.com/j2me/docs/wtk2.2/docs/UserGuide.pdf

Symbian Ltd. (2005). *Symbian OS Version 9.2*. Retrieved May 20, 2006, from http://www.symbian.com/technology/symbianOSv9.2_ds_0905.pdf

Symbian Ltd. (2006). *Fast Facts*. Retrieved June 12, 2006, from http://www.symbian.com/about/fastfacts/fastfacts.html

Chapter XI
Java ME
(Java Platform,
Micro Edition)
Programming

INTRODUCTION

Most client-side handheld programming uses either Java or C/C++. This chapter introduces *Java ME* (previously known as J2ME), which is a version of Java (Sun Microsystem Inc., 2004). Java ME is a collection of technologies and specifications used to develop a platform that fits the requirements of mobile devices such as consumer products, embedded devices, and advanced mobile devices. It creates a complete Java runtime environment tailored to fit the specific requirements of a particular device or market. Java ME includes user interfaces, security, built-in network protocols, and support for networked and offline applications that can be downloaded dynamically. Compared to other client-side handheld programming languages, Java ME is light-weight and easy to learn, although this also means that Java ME may not contain as many features as other languages. Advanced Java ME programming will be discussed in the next chapter. Chapters 13 and 14 will discuss Palm OS programming, which uses C/C++.

JAVA ME PROGRAMMING STEPS

Figure 11.1 shows the Sun Java Wireless Toolkit© used to develop wireless applications that are based on Java ME's CLDC and MIDP. The toolkit includes the emulation

Figure 11.1. A screenshot of KToolbar after launching © 2008 Sun Microsystems, Inc.

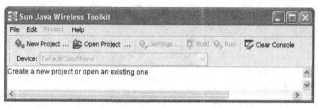

environments, performance optimization and tuning features, documentation, and examples that developers need to bring efficient and successful wireless applications to market quickly. The following steps show how to develop an MIDP application, in this case a simple "Hello, World!" program, under Microsoft Windows XP:

1. Download and install *Sun Java Wireless Toolkit 2.3 Beta*, which includes a set of tools and utilities and an emulator for creating Java applications that run on handheld devices, at the URL (http://java.sun.com/products/sjwtoolkit/download-2_3.html).
2. Run the development environment KToolbar of an MIDlet, an MIDP application, as shown in Figure 11.1 by selecting the following Windows options:

```
Start ⇒ All Programs ⇒ Sun Java Wireless Toolkit 2.3 Beta
       ⇒ KToolbar
```

3. Create a new project by giving a project name such as HelloSuite and a class name such as HelloMIDlet as shown in Figure 11.2. After the project HelloSuite is created, the KToolbar will display the message shown in Figure 11.3, which specifies where the Java source files, application resource files, and application library files are to be put.
4. Create a J2ME source program and place it in the directory of the local disk (C:\WTK23\apps\HelloSuite\src\). Figure 11.4 gives a J2ME example,

Figure 11.2. A screenshot of the pop-up window obtained after clicking on the button "New Project" of KToolbar © 2008 Sun Microsystems, Inc.

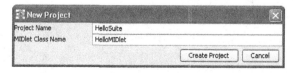

Figure 11.3. A screenshot of KToolbar after the project HelloSuite *is created*
© 2008 Sun Microsystems, Inc.

Figure 11.4. An example of a MIDlet program HelloMIDlet.java

```
C:\WTK23\apps\HelloSuite\src\HelloMIDlet.java

// This package defines MIDP applications and the interactions between
// the application and the environment in which the application runs.
import  javax.microedition.midlet.*;

// This package provides a set of features for user interfaces.
import  javax.microedition.lcdui.*;

public class HelloMIDlet  extends MIDlet  implements CommandListener {

  public void  startApp( ) {
    Display   display    = Display.getDisplay( this );
    Form      mainForm   = new  Form   ( "HelloMIDlet" );
    Ticker    ticker     = new  Ticker ( "Greeting, World" );
    Command   exitCommand = new  Command( "Exit", Command.EXIT, 0 );

    mainForm.append            ( "\n\n          Hello, World!" );
    mainForm.setTicker         ( ticker );
    mainForm.addCommand        ( exitCommand );
    mainForm.setCommandListener( this );
    display.setCurrent         ( mainForm );
  }

  public void  pauseApp ( ) { }

  public void  destroyApp( boolean unconditional ) {
    notifyDestroyed( );
  }

  public void  commandAction( Command c, Displayable s ) {
    if ( c.getCommandType( ) == Command.EXIT )
      notifyDestroyed( );
  }
}
```

Figure 11.5. The screenshot of an emulator displaying the execution results of Hel-loSuite © *2008 Sun Microsystems, Inc.*

which displays the text "Hello, World!" and a ticker with the message "Greeting, world."

5. Build the project by clicking on the "Build" button. The "Build" includes compilation and pre-verifying.

6. Run the project by clicking on the "Run" button. An emulator will be popped up that displays the execution results of the built project. For example, Figure 11.5 shows an emulator displays the execution results of HelloSuite.

7. Upload the application to the handheld device using USB cables, infrared ports, or Bluetooth wireless technology.

THE HELLO-WORLD MIDLET

The following list gives a line-by-line analysis of the program HelloMIDlet.java in Figure 11.4.

- `import javax.microedition.lcdui.*;`

The package javax.microedition.lcdui provides a set of features for implementing user interfaces for MIDP applications. The class hierarchy is

```
- java.lang.Object
  - javax.microedition.lcdui.AlertType
```

```
- javax.microedition.lcdui.Command
- javax.microedition.lcdui.Display
- javax.microedition.lcdui.Displayable
  - javax.microedition.lcdui.Canvas
  - javax.microedition.lcdui.Screen
    - javax.microedition.lcdui.Alert
    - javax.microedition.lcdui.Form
    - javax.microedition.lcdui.List
        (implements javax.microedition.lcdui.Choice)
    - javax.microedition.lcdui.TextBox
- javax.microedition.lcdui.Font
- javax.microedition.lcdui.Graphics
- javax.microedition.lcdui.Image
- javax.microedition.lcdui.Item
  - javax.microedition.lcdui.ChoiceGroup
      (implements javax.microedition.lcdui.Choice)
  - javax.microedition.lcdui.DateField
  - javax.microedition.lcdui.Gauge
  - javax.microedition.lcdui.ImageItem
  - javax.microedition.lcdui.StringItem
  - javax.microedition.lcdui.TextField
- javax.microedition.lcdui.Ticker
```

The interface hierarchy is

```
- javax.microedition.lcdui.Choice
- javax.microedition.lcdui.CommandListener
- javax.microedition.lcdui.ItemStateListener
```

• `import javax.microedition.midlet.*;`

The package `javax.microedition.midlet` defines MIDP applications and the interactions between the application and the environment in which the application runs. The class hierarchy is

```
- java.lang.Object
  - javax.microedition.midlet.MIDlet
- java.lang.Throwable
  - java.lang.Exception
  - javax.microedition.midlet.MIDletStateChangeException
```

- `public class HelloMIDlet extends MIDlet implements Com-mandListener {`

The class `javax.microedition.midlet.MIDlet` is an MIDP application. The application must extend this class to allow the application management software to control the MIDlet and to be able to retrieve properties from the application descriptor and notify and request state changes. The interface `javax.microedition.lcdui.CommandListener` is used by applications that need to receive high-level events from the implementation. An application will provide an implementation of a `Listener` and will then provide an instance of it on a `Screen` in order to receive high-level events on that screen.

- `private Display display;`

The class `javax.microedition.lcdui.Display` represents the manager of the display and input devices of the system. It includes methods for retrieving the properties of the device and for requesting the objects to be displayed.

- `private TextBox tbxMain;`

The class `javax.microedition.lcdui.TextBox` is a `Screen` that allows the user to enter and edit text.

- `private Command cmdExit;`

The class `javax.microedition.lcdui.Command` is a construct that encapsulates the semantic information of an action.

- `public HelloMIDlet( ) {`

The purpose of a constructor is to initialize the instance variables of a newly instantiated object. The *J2ME Application Manager (JAM)* is responsible for installing, running, and removing MIDlets from the handheld devices. When a user chooses to run a MIDlet, it is the JAM that creates an instance of the MIDlet class and runs methods on it. The sequence of methods that will be called in the MIDlet subclass is defined by the MIDlet life cycle, which is shown in Figure 11.6.

The application manager calls methods in the MIDlet to signify changes from one state to another. `startApp( )`, `pauseApp( )`, and `destroyApp( )` are the three life-cycle methods that every MIDlet must define.

Figure 11.6. The MIDlet life cycle

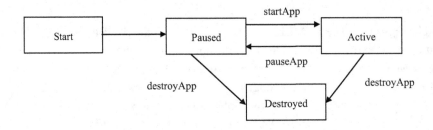

A MIDlet goes through the following states:

a. When the MIDlet is about to be run, an instance is created. The MIDlet's constructor is run, and the MIDlet is in the `Paused` state.
b. Next, the MIDlet enters the `Active` state after the application manager calls `startApp( )`.
c. While the MIDlet is `Active`, the JAM can suspend its execution by calling `pauseApp( )`, which puts the MIDlet back in the `Paused` state.
d. The application manager can terminate the execution of the MIDlet by calling `destroyApp( )`, at which point the MIDlet is `Destroyed` and patiently awaits garbage collection.

- `display = Display.getDisplay( this );`

The method `public static Display javax.microedition.lcdui.Display.getDisplay( MIDlet m )` gets the `Display` object that is unique to this MIDlet.

- `cmdExit = new Command( "Exit", Command.SCREEN, 1 );`

The constructor `public javax.microedition.lcdui.Command(String label, int commandType, int priority)` creates a new command object with the following parameters:

- o `label`—The label string is what the application requests be shown to the user to represent this command.
- o `commandType`—The command types include `BACK, CANCEL, EXIT, HELP, ITEM, OK, SCREEN,` or `STOP. public static final int SCREEN`

specifies an application-defined command that pertains to the current screen

- o   `priority`—The application uses the value to describe the importance of this command relative to other commands on the same screen.

- •   `tbxMain = new TextBox( "HelloMIDlet", "Hello, World!", 50, 0 );`

The constructor `public javax.microedition.lcdui.TextBox(String title, String text, int maxSize, int constraints)` creates a new `TextBox` object with the following parameters:

- o   `title`—The title text is to be shown with the display.
- o   `text`—The initial contents of the text editing area. If the text parameter is null, the `TextBox` is created empty.
- o   `maxSize`—The maximum capacity in characters, which must be greater than zero.
- o   `constraints`—The different constraints allow the application to request that the user's input be restricted in a variety of ways. Constant 0 is assigned to `public static final int ANY`, which allows users to enter any text. Other constraints can be found from the Field Summary of input constraints.

- •   `tbxMain.addCommand( cmdExit );`

The method `public void javax.microedition.lcdui.Displayable. addCommand( Command cmd )` adds a command to the `Displayable`. The implementation may choose, for example, to add the command to any of the available soft buttons or place it in a menu.

- •   `tbxMain.setCommandListener(this);`

The method `public void javax.microedition.lcdui.Displayable. setCommandListener( CommandListener l )` sets a listener for `Commands` to this `Displayable`, replacing any previous `CommandListener`.

- •   `public void startApp( ) {`

The MIDlet enters the `Active` state after the application manager calls `startApp( )` via clicking on the button `Launch`.

- ```
display.setCurrent(tbxMain);
```

When a MIDlet application is first started, there is no current `Displayable` object. It is the responsibility of the application to ensure that a `Displayable` is visible and can interact with the user at all times. Thus, the application should always call `setCurrent( )` as part of its initialization. The method `public void javax.microedition.lcdui.Display.setCurrent (Displayable nextDisplayable)` requests that a different `Displayable` object be made visible on the display.

- ```
public void pauseApp( ) { }
public void destroyApp( boolean unconditional ) { }
```

These two methods usually have empty bodies.

- ```
public void commandAction(Command c, Displayable s) {
```

This method implements the method `public void javax.microedition.lcdui.CommandListener.commandAction(Command c, Displayable d)`, which indicates that a command event has occurred on `Displayable d`.

- ```
if ( c == cmdExit ) {
```

This checks to see if the `Exit` command was selected.

- ```
destroyApp(false);
```

A MIDlet can destroy itself by calling the method `destroyApp( )`, which is empty in this case.

- ```
notifyDestroyed( );
```

The method `public final void javax.microedition.midlet.MIDlet.notifyDestroyed( )` notifies the application management software that it has entered into the `Destroyed` state. The JAM software will not call the MIDlet's `destroyApp` method, and all resources held by the MIDlet will be considered eligible for reclamation. The MIDlet must have performed the same operations (clean up, releasing of resources, etc.) as it would have if the `MIDlet.destroyApp( )` had been called.

USER INTERFACE

This section demonstrates how to create various GUI components. The MIDlet in the example shown here is used to test lists, forms, choices, gauges, text fields, and text boxes.

Lists

The method `startApp( )` starts the MIDlet by creating a list of items and associating the exit command with it.

The following list gives a line-by-line analysis of the program `GuiTests.java` shown in Figure 11.7.

- `List menu;`

The class `javax.microedition.lcdui.List` is a `Screen` containing a list of choices.

- `menu = new List( "Test Components", Choice.IMPLICIT );`

The constructor `public javax.microedition.lcdui.List.List( String title, int listType )` creates a new, empty `List` with the following two parameters:
  - `title` — the screen's title, and
  - `listType` — one of the following three field values:
    - `public static final int IMPLICIT`: This selects the currently highlighted item when a `Command` is initiated.
    - `pt public static final int EXCLUSIVE`: This specifies that only one element can be selected at a time.
    - `public static final int MULTIPLE`: This allows an arbitrary number of elements to be selected simultaneously.
- `menu.append( "Test TextBox", null );`

The method `public int javax.microedition.lcdui.List.append( String stringPart, Image imagePart )` appends an element to the `Choice`, which is an interface of the package `javax.microedition.lcdui` and defines an API for a user interface components implementing a selection from a predefined number of choices. The added element will be the last element of the `Choice`.

Figure 11.7. The script GuiTests.java

```
                              GuiTests.java

// This package defines MIDP applications and the interactions
// between the application and the environment in which the
// application runs.
import javax.microedition.midlet.*;

// This package provides a set of features for implementation
// of user interfaces.
import javax.microedition.lcdui.*;


public class  GuiTests
    extends  MIDlet
    implements  CommandListener {

  // display manager
  Display  display;

  // a menu with items; main menu
  List   menu;

  // list of choices
  List   choose;

  // textbox
  TextBox   input;

  // ticker
  Ticker   ticker = new Ticker( "Test GUI Components" );

  // alerts
  final Alert  soundAlert = new Alert( "sound Alert" );

  // date
  DateField  date = new DateField( "Today's date: ", DateField.DATE );

  // form
  Form  form = new Form( "Form for Stuff" );

  // today's form
  Form  today = new Form( "Today's date" );

  // gauge
  Gauge  gauge = new Gauge( "Progress Bar", false, 20, 9 );

  // text field
  TextField  textfield = new TextField( "TextField Label", "abc", 50, 0 );

  // command
  static final  Command backCommand     = new Command( "Back", Command.BACK,
0 );
  static final  Command mainMenuCommand = new Command( "Main",
Command.SCREEN, 1 );
  static final  Command exitCommand     = new Command( "Exit", Command.STOP,
```

continued on following page

Figure 11.7. continued

```
                          GuiTests.java
2 );
  String  currentMenu;


  // constructor.
  public  GuiTests( ) { }


  /**************************************************************
   *                                                          *
   *     Start the MIDlet by creating a list of items         *
   *     and associating the exit command with it.            *
   *                                                          *
   **************************************************************/

  public void  startApp( )
       throws  MIDletStateChangeException {
    display = Display.getDisplay( this );
    menu = new List( "Test Components", Choice.IMPLICIT );
    menu.append( "Test TextBox", null );
    menu.append( "Test List", null );
    menu.append( "Test Alert", null );
    menu.append( "Test Date", null );
    menu.append( "Test Form", null );
    menu.addCommand( exitCommand );
    menu.setCommandListener( this );
    menu.setTicker( ticker );
    mainMenu( );

    // form
    form.append( gauge );
    form.append( textfield );

    // today
    today.append( date );
  }


  public void  pauseApp( ) {
    display   = null;
    choose    = null;
    menu      = null;
    ticker    = null;
    form      = null;
    today     = null;
    input     = null;
    gauge     = null;
    textfield = null;
  }


  public void  destroyApp( boolean unconditional ) {
    notifyDestroyed( );
```

continued on following page

Figure 11.7. continued

```
                              GuiTests.java

}


  // main menu
  void  mainMenu( ) {
    display.setCurrent( menu );
    currentMenu = "Main";
  }


  /***********************************************************
   *                                                         *
   *      Test the TextBox component.                        *
   *                                                         *
   ***********************************************************/

  public void  testTextBox( ) {
    input = new TextBox( "Enter Some Text:", "", 10, TextField.ANY );
    input.setTicker( new Ticker( "Testing TextBox" ) );
    input.addCommand( backCommand );
    input.setCommandListener( this );
    input.setString( "" );
    display.setCurrent( input );
    currentMenu = "input";
  }


  /***********************************************************
   *                                                         *
   *      Test the List component.                           *
   *                                                         *
   ***********************************************************/

  public void  testList( ) {
    choose = new List( "Choose Items", Choice.MULTIPLE );
    choose.setTicker( new Ticker( "Testing List" ) );
    choose.addCommand( backCommand );
    choose.setCommandListener( this );
    choose.append( "Item 1", null );
    choose.append( "Item 2", null );
    choose.append( "Item 3", null );
    display.setCurrent( choose );
    currentMenu = "list";
  }


  /***********************************************************
   *                                                         *
   *      Test the Alert component.                          *
   *                                                         *
   ***********************************************************/

  public void  testAlert( ) {
```

continued on following page

Figure 11.7. continued

GuiTests.java

```
  soundAlert.setType( AlertType.ERROR );

  //soundAlert.setTimeout( 20 );
  soundAlert.setString( "** ERROR **" );
  display.setCurrent( soundAlert );
}


/****************************************************************
 *                                                            *
 *     Test the DateField component.                          *
 *                                                            *
 ****************************************************************/

public void  testDate( ) {
  java.util.Date  now = new java.util.Date( );
  date.setDate( now );
  today.addCommand( backCommand );
  today.setCommandListener( this );
  display.setCurrent( today );
  currentMenu = "date";
}


/****************************************************************
 *                                                            *
 *     Test the Form component.                               *
 *                                                            *
 ****************************************************************/

public void  testForm( ) {
  form.addCommand( backCommand );
  form.setCommandListener( this );
  display.setCurrent( form );
  currentMenu = "form";
}


/****************************************************************
 *                                                            *
 *     Handle events.                                         *
 *                                                            *
 ****************************************************************/

public void  commandAction( Command c, Displayable d ) {
  String  label = c.getLabel( );
  if ( label.equals( "Exit" ) ) {
    destroyApp( true );
  }
  else if ( label.equals( "Back" ) ) {
    if ( currentMenu.equals( "list" ) || currentMenu.equals( "input" ) ||
         currentMenu.equals( "date" ) || currentMenu.equals( "form" ) ) {
      // go back to menu
```

continued on following page

Figure 11.7. continued

GuiTests.java

```
            mainMenu( );
      }
   }
   else {
      List  down = (List) display.getCurrent( );
      switch( down.getSelectedIndex( ) ) {
         case 0: testTextBox( );   break;
         case 1: testList( );      break;
         case 2: testAlert( );     break;
         case 3: testDate( );      break;
         case 4: testForm( );      break;
      }
    }
  }
}
```

Figure 11.8: The method startApp( )

startApp( )

```
public void  startApp( )
     throws  MIDletStateChangeException {
   display = Display.getDisplay( this );
   menu = new List( "Test Components", Choice.IMPLICIT );
   menu.append( "Test TextBox", null );
   menu.append( "Test List", null );
   menu.append( "Test Alert", null );
   menu.append( "Test Date", null );
   menu.append( "Test Form", null );
   menu.addCommand( exitCommand );
   menu.setCommandListener( this );
   menu.setTicker( ticker );
   mainMenu( );

   // form
   form.append( gauge );
   form.append( textfield );

   // today
   today.append( date );
 }

 ...

 // main menu
 void  mainMenu( ) {
   display.setCurrent( menu );
   currentMenu = "Main";
 }
```

Figure 11.9. The first two interfaces from the project GuiSuite

Click on "Launch" ⇨

⇦ Click on "Exit"

- Ticker ticker = new Ticker("Test GUI Components");

The class javax.microedition.lcdui.Ticker implements a "ticker-tape," a piece of text that runs continuously across the display. The direction and speed of scrolling are determined by the implementation. While animated, the ticker string scrolls continuously. The constructor public Ticker(String str) constructs a new Ticker object, given its initial contents string.

- menu.setTicker(ticker);

The method public void javax.microedition.lcdui.Screen.set-Ticker (Ticker ticker) sets a ticker for use with this Screen, replacing any previous ticker.

- Gauge gauge = new Gauge("Progress Bar", false, 20, 9);

The class javax.microedition.lcdui.Gauge implements a bar graph display of a value intended for use in a form. The constructor public Gauge(String label, boolean interactive, int maxValue, int initialValue) creates a new Gauge object with the following parameters:

- o label: the Gauge's label,
- o interactive: interactive or non-interactive mode. In interactive mode, the user is allowed to modify the value.
- o maxValue: the maximum value must be greater than zero.
- o initialValue: the initial value must be within the range zero to max-Value, inclusive.

For example, consider a `Gauge` object that has a range of values from zero to 99, running on a device that displays the `Gauge`'s approximate value using a set of one to ten bars. The device might show one bar for values zero through nine, two bars for values ten through 19, three bars for values 20 through 29, and so forth.

- ```
  TextField textfield = new TextField( "TextField Label",
  "abc", 50, 0 );
  ```

The class `javax.microedition.lcdui.TextField` is an editable text component that may be placed into a `Form`. The constructor `public TextField( String label, String text, int maxSize, int constraints )` creates a new `TextField` object with the following parameters:

- o `label`: the item label.
- o `text`: the initial contents, or null if the `TextField` is to be empty.
- o `maxSize`: the maximum capacity in characters.
- o `constraints`: constant 0 allows users to enter any text. Other values can be found from the `Field Summary` of input constraints.

- ```
  Form form = new Form("Form for Stuff");
  ```

The class `javax.microedition.lcdui.Form` is a `Screen` that contains an arbitrary mixture of items: images, read-only text fields, editable text fields, editable date fields, gauges, and choice groups. The constructor `public Form( String title )` creates a new, empty `Form`.

- ```
  form.append(gauge);
  form.append(textfield);
  ```

The method `public int javax.microedition.lcdui.Form.append(Item item)` adds an `Item` into the `Form`. An `Item` is a superclass for components that can be added to a `Form` and `Alert`.

- ```
  DateField date = new DateField( "Today's date: ", DateField.
  DATE );
  ```

The class `javax.microedition.lcdui.DateField` is an editable component for presenting date and time (calendar) information that may be placed into a `Form`. The constructor `public DateField(String label, int mode)` creates a `DateField` object with the following parameters:

o   `label`: the item label.
o   `mode`: the input mode, one of the following three modes:
  ➤ `DATE`: allows only date information to be set.
  ➤ `TIME`: allows only time information (hours, minutes) to be set.
  ➤ `DATE _ TIME`: allows both clock time and date values to be set.
• `List down = (List) display.getCurrent( );switch(down.getSe-`
  `lectedIndex( )) {`

The method `public int getSelectedIndex( )` returns the index number of an element in `Choice` that has been selected. For `Choice` types `EXCLUSIVE` and `IMPLICIT` there is at most one element selected, so this method is useful for determining the user's selection.

Other Interfaces

Figure 11.10 shows screenshots of other interfaces from the project `GuiSuite`.

• `final Alert soundAlert = new Alert( "sound Alert" );`

The class `javax.microedition.lcdui.Alert` is a screen that shows data to the user and waits for a certain period of time before proceeding to the next screen. An alert is an ordinary screen that can contain text and image, and which handles events like other screens. The constructor `public Alert( String title )` constructs a new, empty `Alert` object with the given title.

• `soundAlert.setType( AlertType.ERROR );`

The method `public void setType( AlertType type )` sets the type of the `Alert`. The handling and behavior of specific `AlertTypes` is described in `AlertType`. An `ERROR` `AlertType` is designed to alert the user to an erroneous operation.

• `soundAlert.setString( "** ERROR **" );`

The method `public void setString( String str )` sets the text string used in the `Alert`.

• `java.util.Date now = new java.util.Date( );`

The class `java.util.Date` represents a specific instant in time, with millisecond precision. The constructor `public Date( )` allocates a `Date` object and initializes

Figure 11.10. Screenshots of other interfaces from `GuiSuite`

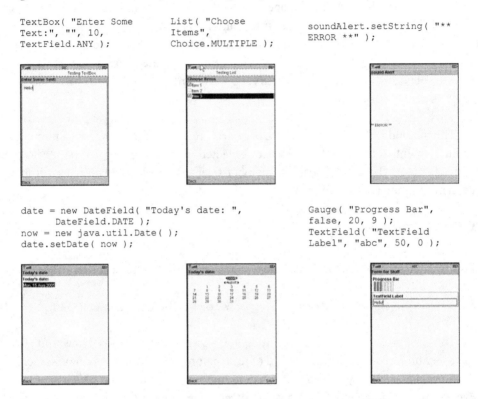

```
TextBox( "Enter Some
Text:", "", 10,
TextField.ANY );
```

```
List( "Choose
Items",
Choice.MULTIPLE );
```

```
soundAlert.setString( "**
ERROR **" );
```

```
date = new DateField( "Today's date: ",
    DateField.DATE );
now = new java.util.Date( );
date.setDate( now );
```

```
Gauge( "Progress Bar",
false, 20, 9 );
TextField( "TextField
Label", "abc", 50, 0 );
```

it to represent the current time specified number of milliseconds since the standard base time known as "the epoch," namely January 1, 1970, 00:00:00 GMT.

- `date.setDate( now );`

The method `public  void  javax.microedition.lcdui.DateField.` `setDate( Date date )` sets a new value for this field.

SUMMARY

A number of mobile operating systems with small footprints and reduced storage capacity have emerged to support the computing-related functions of mobile devices. For example, Research In Motion Ltd's BlackBerry 8700 smartphone uses RIM OS and provides web access, as well as wireless voice, address book, and appointment applications (Research In Motion Ltd., 2005). Because handheld devices are small and have limited power and memory, the options for a mobile OS are restricted significantly compared to a desktop OS. Although a wide range of mobile handheld devices are commercially available, operating systems, the hub of the devices, are dominated by only a few major organizations. The operating systems used in the top brands of smart cellular phones and PDAs are, in descending order of market share:

- **Smart cellular phones:** Symbian OS, Microsoft Smartphone, Palm OS, Linux, and RIM OS (Symbian Ltd., n.d.).
- **PDAs:** Microsoft Pocket PC, Palm OS, RIM OS, and Linux (WindowsForDevices, 2004).

However, the market share of each of these changes constantly and claims concerning market share vary enormously. It is almost impossible to predict which will be the ultimate winner in the battle between mobile operating systems.

REFERENCES

Research In Motion Ltd. (2005). *BlackBerry Application Control—An Overview for Application Developers*. Retrieved January 05, 2006, from http://www.blackberry.com/knowledgecenterpublic/livelink.exe/fetch/2000/7979/1181821/832210/BlackBerry_Application_Control_Overview_for_Developers.pdf?nodeid=1106734&vernum=0

Sun Microsystem Inc. (2004). *J2ME Wireless Toolkit 2.2—User's Guide*. Retrieved October 21, 2005, from http://java.sun.com/j2me/docs/wtk2.2/docs/UserGuide.pdf

Symbian Ltd. (n.d.). *Symbian Fast Facts*. Retrieved January 26, 2005, from http://www.symbian.com/about/fastfaqs.html

WindowsForDevices.com. (2004). *Windows CE Zooms Past Palm*. Retrieved August 23, 2005, from http://www.windowsfordevices.com/news/NS6887329036.html

Chapter XII
Advanced Java ME Programming

INTRODUCTION

Chapter XI introduced the basics of Java ME programming. This chapter will build on this, focusing on advanced Java ME programming. The following two major topics will be discussed:

- **Persistent storage:** This refers to the type of storage embedded in handheld devices. Random access memory loses its contents when the power is off, but the contents of persistent storage are preserved even when the power is off. Flash memory, and very occasionally hard disks, are usually used for this kind of storage.
- **Network connection:** Many client-side applications such as weather reports and location-based applications require a network connection. The generic `Connection` framework of MIDP can be used for this purpose.

Although these two chapters, Chapters XI and XII, introduce Java ME programming to readers, it is not possible to fully cover Java ME programming in only two chapters. For a deeper understanding, readers can consult the section on Java ME References provided later in this chapter for more information.

PERSISTENT STORAGE

For some applications, including address books and appointment diaries, it is necessary for the information to be retained even after the application that created them is switched off.

Persistent (non-volatile) storage is a storage device whose contents are preserved when its power is off.

Without persistent storage, objects and their states are destroyed when an application closes. If objects are saved to persistent storage, their lifetime is longer than the program that created them and they can later be retrieved for users to continue to work with them. The MIDP `Record Management System (RMS)` is a persistent storage method for MIDlets. It is a simple record-oriented database, which consists of a collection of records. Record stores (binary files) are platform-dependent because they are created in platform-dependent locations, and MIDlets within a single application (a MIDlet suite) can create multiple record stores with different names. The RMS APIs provide the following functionality:

- Allow MIDlets to manipulate records within a record store.
- Allow MIDlets in the same application to share records.

They do not, however, provide a mechanism for sharing records between MIDlets in different applications. Record store names are case sensitive, and cannot be more than 32 characters long. Also, a MIDlet cannot create two record stores with the same name in the same application, although a record store can be created with the same name as a MIDlet in another application. When a new record store is created it is stored under a directory called `appdb`. For example, assume that you are using the *Wireless Toolkit* and that it is installed under the directory (`C:\WTK23`). If your record store is `preferences`, the record store is located at the address of the local disk: (`C:\WTK23\appdb\DefaultColorPhone\run _ by _ class _ storage _ preferences.db`).

Record Management System

The MIDP RMS implementation ensures that all individual record store operations are atomic, synchronous, and serialized, so no corruption occurs with multiple access. However, if MIDlets use multiple threads to access a record store, it is the programmer's responsibility to synchronize this access. The RMS package consists of the following four interfaces, one class, and five exception classes:

- **Four interfaces:**
  - `RecordComparator`: Defines a comparator that can be used to compare two records.
  - `RecordEnumeration`: Represents a bidirectional record enumerator.
  - `RecordFilter`: Defines a filter that can be used to examine a record and check if it matches based on criteria defined by the application.
  - `RecordListener`: Receives records which have been added, changed, or deleted from a record store.
- **One class:**
  - `RecordStore`: Represents a record store.
- **Five exception classes:**
  - `InvalidRecordIDException`: Indicates the RecordID is invalid.
  - `RecordStoreException`: Indicates a general exception has been thrown.
  - `RecordStoreFullException`: Indicates the record store file system is full.
  - `RecordStoreNotFoundException`: Indicates the record store could not be found.
  - `RecordStoreNotOpenException`: Indicates an operation on a closed record store.

Programming with RMS

A record store consists of a collection of records that are uniquely identified by their record ID, which is always an integer value. The record ID is the *primary key* for the records. The first record has an ID of 1, and each additional record is assigned an ID that is the previous value plus one.

1. **Opening a record store:** To open a record store, use the `openRecordStore( )` static method:

```
import javax.microedition.rms.*;
RecordStore rs = null;
try {
  rs = RecordStore.openRecordStore( "myDBfile", true );
}
catch( RecordStoreNotFoundException e ) {
  // doesn't exist
}
```

```
catch( RecordStoreException e ) {
  // some other error
}
```

This creates a new database file named myDBfile. The second parameter, which is set to true, says that if the record store does not exist, create it.

2. **Creating a new record:** A record is an array of bytes. The DataInputStream, DataOutputStream, ByteArrayInputStream, and ByteArrayOutput-Stream classes can be used to pack and unpack data types into and out of the byte arrays. To add a record to the record store, use the addRecord( ) method as follows:

```
byte[ ] data = new byte[2];
data[0] = 0;    data[1] = 1;
try {
  int id = rs.addRecord( data, 0, data.length );
}
catch( RecordStoreFullException e ) {
  // no room left for more data
}
catch( RecordStoreNotOpenException e ) {
  // store has been closed
}
catch( RecordStoreException e ) {
  // general error
}
```

3. **Reading data from the record store:** To read a record from the record store, input streams are constructed instead of output streams. The getRecord method reads the contents of a record.

```
byte[ ] data = new byte[100];
int   id = ....;  // get the ID from somewhere
try {
  int numBytes = rs.getRecord( id, data, 0 );
}
catch( ArrayIndexOutOfBoundsException e ) {
  // record too big for the array
}
```

```
catch( InvalidRecordIDException e ) {
 // record doesn't exist
}
catch( RecordStoreNotOpenException e ) {
 // store has been closed
}
catch( RecordStoreException e ){
 // general error
}
```

4. **Deleting a record from the record store:** To delete a record from the record store, the record ID for the record must be known in order for it to be deleted. The deleteRecord( ) method takes an integer as a parameter, which is the record ID of the record to be deleted. There is no method to provide the record ID. To work around this limitation, every time a new record is created its record ID should be added to a vector as follows:

```
Vector recordIDs = new Vector( );
int lastID = 1;
//Add a record....parameters are missing here
db.addRecord( );
// Now add the ID to the vector
recordIDs.addElement( new Integer(++lastID) );
```

Now, to delete a record, first find its ID:

```
Enumeration IDs = recordIDs.elements( );
while( IDs.hasMoreElements( ) ) {
 int id = ((Integer) IDs.nextElement( )).intValue( );
 // Compare to see if this is the record you want by
 // invoking compare( ) which is shown next.
 // Then call db.deleteRecord( id );
}
```

5. **Comparing a record with records in the record store:** To search for the right record to delete, an application must implement the RecordComparator interface (by providing an implementation to the compare method) to compare two records. The compare method is called by RecordEnumeration to sort and return records in an application specified order. The return value indicates the ordering of the two records. The following code compares two strings that are retrieved from two records.

```
public someClass implements RecordComparator {
 public int compare( byte[ ] record1, byte[] record2 ) {
  ByteArrayInputStream bais1 =
    new ByteArrayInputStream( record1 );
  DataInputStream dis1 = new DataInputStream( bais1 );
  ByteArrayInputStream bais2 =
    new ByteArrayInputStream( record2 );
  DataInputStream dis2 = new DataInputStream( bais2 );

  String name1 = dis1.readUTF( );
  String name2 = dis.readUTF( );
  int num = name1.compareTo( name2 );
  if ( num > 0 ) {
   return RecordComparator.FOLLOWS;
  } else if ( num < 0 ) {
   return recordcomparator.PRECEDES;
  } else {
   return recordcomparator.EQUIVALENT;
  }
 }
}
```

The three constants are defined in the `RecordComparator` interface:

- o   FOLLOWS: This has a value of 1 and means that the left parameter follows the right parameter in terms of search or sort order.
- o   PRECEDES: This has a value of -1 and means that the left parameter precedes the right parameter in terms of search or sort order.
- o   EQUIVALENT: This has a value of 0 and means that the two parameters are the same.

6.   **Closing the record store:** To close the record store, use the `closeRecord-Store( )` method.

An Example

This MIDlet saves a user name and password in a `RecordStore`. Each time the MIDlet is used, it can load the user name and password from the `RecordStore` instead of requiring the user to reenter the same information. Its only screen is a

Form that contains fields for entering the user name and password. It uses a helper class, Preferences, to perform all the RecordStore work.

The entire RecordStore is encapsulated in the Preferences class. Preferences is a wrapper for a user name and password, stored as String member variables mUser and mPassword. A static method, get( ), provides access to a single Preferences object. Each time get( ) is called, the user name and password are loaded from a RecordStore.

The following gives a line-by-line analysis of the program Preferences.java in Figure 12.3.

* `import javax.microedition.rms.*;`

The package javax.microedition.rms allows MIDlets to persistently store data and later retrieve it. The class hierarchy is

```
- java.lang.Object
  - javax.microedition.rms.RecordStore
  - java.lang.Throwable
  - java.lang.Exception
    - javax.microedition.rms.RecordStoreException
      - javax.microedition.rms.InvalidRecordIDException
      - javax.microedition.rms.RecordStoreFullException
      - javax.microedition.rms.RecordStoreNotFoundException
      - javax.microedition.rms.RecordStoreNotOpenException
```

The interface hierarchy is

```
- javax.microedition.rms.RecordComparator
  - javax.microedition.rms.RecordEnumeration
  - javax.microedition.rms.RecordFilter
  - javax.microedition.rms.RecordListener
```

* `mForm.append( new StringItem( null, rse.toString( ) ) );`

The constructor public StringItem(String label, String text) creates a new javax.microedition.lcdui.StringItem object with the given label and textual content:

Figure 12.1. The script `RecordMIDlet.java`

```
                          RecordMIDlet.java

import   javax.microedition.midlet.*;
import   javax.microedition.lcdui.*;
import   javax.microedition.rms.RecordStoreException;

public class  RecordMIDlet
    extends  MIDlet
    implements  CommandListener {
  private static final String  kUser     = "user";
  private static final String  kPassword = "password";

  private Preferences  mPreferences;
  private Form         mForm;
  private TextField     mUserField, mPasswordField;

  public  RecordMIDlet( ) {
    try {
      mPreferences = new Preferences( "preferences" );
    }
    catch ( RecordStoreException  rse ) {
      mForm = new Form( "Exception" );
      mForm.append( new StringItem( null, rse.toString( ) ) );
      mForm.addCommand( new Command( "Exit", Command.EXIT, 0 ) );
      mForm.setCommandListener( this );
      return;
    }

    mForm = new Form( "Login" );
    mUserField     = new TextField(
      "Name", mPreferences.get( kUser ), 32, 0 );
    mPasswordField = new TextField(
      "Password", mPreferences.get( kPassword ), 32, 0 );
    mForm.append( mUserField );
    mForm.append( mPasswordField );
    mForm.addCommand( new Command( "Exit", Command.EXIT, 0 ) );
    mForm.setCommandListener( this );
  }

  public void  startApp( ) {
    Display.getDisplay( this ).setCurrent( mForm );
  }

  public void  pauseApp( ) { }

  public void  destroyApp( boolean unconditional ) {
    // Save the user name and password.
    mPreferences.put( kUser, mUserField.getString( ) );
    mPreferences.put( kPassword, mPasswordField.getString( ) );
    try {
      mPreferences.save( );
    }
    catch ( RecordStoreException  rse ) { }
  }
```

Figure 12.2. Screenshots of the execution results of the script in Figure 12.1

Click on "Launch" $\Rightarrow$

$\Leftarrow$ Click on "Exit"

Figure 12.3. The script `Preferences.java`

```
                          Preferences.java

import  java.util.*;
import  javax.microedition.lcdui.*;
import  javax.microedition.rms.*;

public class  Preferences {
  private String     mRecordStoreName;
  private Hashtable  mHashtable;

  public  Preferences( String recordStoreName )
      throws  RecordStoreException {
    mRecordStoreName = recordStoreName;
    mHashtable       = new Hashtable( );
    load( );
  }

  public String  get( String key ) {
    return  (String) mHashtable.get( key );
  }

  public void  put( String key, String value ) {
    if ( value == null )  value = "";
    mHashtable.put( key, value );
  }

  private void  load( )  throws  RecordStoreException {
    RecordStore        rs = null;
    RecordEnumeration  re = null;
```

continued on following page

Figure 12.3. continued

```
                          Preferences.java

   try {
     rs = RecordStore.openRecordStore( mRecordStoreName, true );
     re = rs.enumerateRecords( null, null, false );
     while ( re.hasNextElement( ) ) {
       byte[ ]  raw  = re.nextRecord( );
       String  pref  = new String( raw );
       // Parse out the name.
       int     index = pref.indexOf( '|' );
       String  name  = pref.substring( 0, index );
       String  value = pref.substring( index + 1 );
       put( name, value );
     }
   }
   finally {
     if ( re != null )  re.destroy( );
     if ( rs != null )  rs.closeRecordStore( );
   }
 }

 public void  save( )  throws  RecordStoreException {
   RecordStore         rs = null;
   RecordEnumeration   re = null;
   try {
     rs = RecordStore.openRecordStore( mRecordStoreName, true );
     re = rs.enumerateRecords( null, null, false );

     // First remove all records, a little clumsy.
     while ( re.hasNextElement( ) ) {
       int  id = re.nextRecordId( );
       rs.deleteRecord( id );
     }

     // Now save the preferences records.
     Enumeration  keys = mHashtable.keys( );
     while ( keys.hasMoreElements( ) ) {
       String  key   = (String) keys.nextElement( );
       String  value = get( key );
       String  pref  = key + "|" + value;
       byte[ ]  raw  = pref.getBytes( );
       rs.addRecord( raw, 0, raw.length );
     }
   }
   finally {
     if ( re != null )  re.destroy( );
     if ( rs != null )  rs.closeRecordStore( );
   }
 }
}
```

- o   `label`: the `Item` label, and
- o   `text`: the text contents.

- • `private Hashtable mHashtable;`

The class `java.util.Hashtable` implements a hashtable, which maps keys to values. To successfully store and retrieve objects from a hashtable, the objects used as keys must implement the `hashCode` method and the `equals` method.

- • `mHashtable.get( key )`

The method `public Object java.util.Hashtable.get(Object key)` returns the value to which the specified key is mapped in this hashtable. A value `null` is returned if the key is not mapped to any value in this hashtable.

- • `mHashtable.put( key, value );`

The method `public Object java.util.Hashtable.put( Object key, Object value )` maps the specified key to the specified value in this hashtable.

- • `RecordStore rs = null;`

The class `javax.microedition.rms.RecordStore` represents a record store consisting of a collection of records and remains persistent across multiple invocations of the MIDlet.

- • `RecordEnumeration re = null;`

The interface `javax.microedition.rms.RecordEnumeration` represents a bidirectional record store `Record` enumerator. `RecordEnumeration` logically maintains a sequence of the `recordId`'s of the records in a record store. The enumerator will iterate over all of the records in an order determined by an optional record comparator.

- o   By using an optional `RecordFilter`, a subset of the records can be chosen that match the supplied filter.
- o   By using an optional `RecordComparator`, the enumerator can index through the records in an order determined by the comparator.

- `rs = RecordStore.openRecordStore( mRecordStoreName, true );`

The method `public static RecordStore openRecordStore( String recordStoreName, boolean createIfNecessary )` opens a record store associated with the given MIDlet suite.

- `re = rs.enumerateRecords( null, null, false );`

The method `public RecordEnumeration enumerateRecords(RecordFilter filter, RecordComparator comparator, boolean keepUpdated)` returns an enumeration for traversing a set of records in the record store in an optionally specified order:

- `filter`: If non-null, this will be used to determine what subset of the record store records will be used.
- `comparator`: If non-null, this will be used to determine the order in which the records are returned.
- `keepUpdated`:
  - If true, the enumerator will keep its enumeration current with any changes in the records of the record store.
  - If false, the enumeration will not be kept current and may return `recordIds` for records that have been deleted or miss records that are added later.

If both the `filter` and `comparator` are `null`, the enumeration will traverse all records in the record store in an undefined order. The first call to `RecordEnumeration.nextRecord( )` returns the record data from the first record in the sequence. Subsequent calls to `RecordEnumeration.nextRecord( )` return the next consecutive record's data. To return the record data from the previous consecutive from any given point in the enumeration, call `previousRecord( )`. On the other hand, if after creation the first call is to `previousRecord( )`, the record data of the last element of the enumeration will be returned.

- `re.hasNextElement( )`

The method `public boolean javax.microedition.rms.RecordEnumeration.hasNextElement` returns true if more elements exist in the `next` direction.

- `byte[ ] raw = re.nextRecord( );`

The method `public byte[ ] javax.microedition.rms.RecordEnumeration.nextRecord` returns a copy of the next record in this enumeration, where next is defined by the comparator and/or filter supplied in the constructor of this enumerator. The byte array returned is a copy of the record, and any changes made to this array will NOT be reflected in the record store. After calling this method, the enumeration is advanced to the next available record.

- `re.destroy( );`

The method public void javax.microedition.rms.RecordEnumeration.destroy frees internal resources used by this `RecordEnumeration`. MIDlets should call this method when they have finished using a `RecordEnumeration`. If a MIDlet tries to use a `RecordEnumeration` after this method has been called, it will throw a `IllegalStateException`.

- `rs.closeRecordStore( );`

The method `public void javax.microedition.rms.RecordStore.closeRecordStore( )` is called when the MIDlet requests the record store be closed. Note that the record store will not actually be closed until `closeRecordStore( )` is called as many times as `openRecordStore( )` was called. In other words, the MIDlet needs to make a balanced number of close calls and open calls before the record store is closed. When the record store is closed, all listeners are removed. A `RecordStoreNotOpenException` is thrown if a MIDlet attempts to perform operations on the `RecordStore` object after it has been closed.

- `int id = re.nextRecordId( );`

The method `public int javax.microedition.rms.RecordEnumeration.nextRecordId( )` returns the `recordId` of the next record in this enumeration, where `next` is defined by the comparator and/or filter supplied in the constructor of this enumerator.

- `rs.deleteRecord( id );`

The method `public void javax.microedition.rms.RecordStore.deleteRecord(int recordId)` deletes the record from the record store.

   o   `recordId` — the ID of the record to delete

* `Enumeration keys = mHashtable.keys( );`

The method `public Enumeration java.util.Hashtable.keys` returns an `java.util.Enumeration` of the keys in this hashtable. An object that implements the `Enumeration` interface generates a series of elements, one at a time. Successive calls to the `nextElement` method return successive elements of the series.

* `keys.hasMoreElements( )`

The method `public boolean java.util.Enumeration.hasMoreElements( )` tests if this enumeration contains more elements.

* `keys.nextElement( )`

The method `public Object java.util.Enumeration.nextElement( )` returns the next element of this enumeration if this enumeration object has at least one more element to provide.

* `rs.addRecord( raw, 0, raw.length );`

The method `public int javax.microedition.rms.RecordStore.addRecord( byte[] data, int offset, int numBytes )` adds a new record to the record store:

   o   `data`: the data to be stored in this record. If the data length is zero, this parameter may be null.
   o   `offset`: the index into the data buffer of the first byte for this record.
   o   `numBytes`: the number of bytes of the data buffer to use for this record.

NETWORK CONNECTION

The section introduces the details of the generic `Connection` framework used in MIDP, and shows how to develop network applications using this framework.

The CLDC Connection Framework

The `java.io.*` and `java.net.*` packages of J2SE are not suitable for handheld devices with a small memory footprint. Instead, the `javax.microedition.io` CLDC package must be used as it contains classes for input/output (I/O), including networking I/O. To these CLDC classes, the MIDP adds the `HttpConnection` interface for HTTP protocol access, which defines the necessary methods and constants for an HTTP connection. In the CLDC generic `Connection` framework, all connections are created using the open static method from the `Connector` class. If successful, this method returns an object that implements one of the generic connection interfaces. Figure 12.4 shows how these interfaces form an *is-a* hierarchy. The `Connection` interface is the base interface such that `StreamConnection-Notifier` is a `Connection` and `InputConnection` is also a `Connection`.

- The `Connection` interface is the most basic connection type and can only be opened and closed.
- The `InputConnection` interface represents a device from which data can be read. Its `openInputStream` method returns an input stream for the connection.

Figure 12.4. The is-a hierarchy of CLDC generic `Connection` *framework*

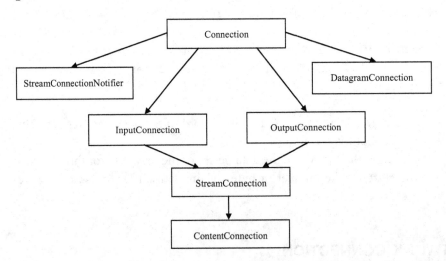

- The OuputConnection interface represents a device to which data can be written. Its openOutputStream method returns an output stream for the connection.
- The StreamConnection interface combines the input and output connections.
- The ContentConnection is a subinterface of StreamConnection and provides access to some of the basic meta data information provided by HTTP connections.
- The StreamConnectionNotified waits for a connection to be established. It returns a StreamConnection on which a communication link has been established.
- The DatagramConnection represents a datagram endpoint.

The open method of the Connector class has the following syntax, where the String parameter has the format "protocol:address;parameters."

```
Connector.open( String );
```

Below are a few examples:

- **HTTP connection:** Connector.open("http://java.sun.com/developer");
- **Datagram connection:** Connector.open("datagram://address:port#");
- **Communicate with a port:** Connector.open("comm:0;baudrate=9600');
- **Open files:** Connector.open("file:/myFile.txt");

MIDP Connectivity

HTTP can either be implemented using IP protocols (such as TCP/IP) or non-IP protocols (such as WAP and i-mode), because the MIDP extends CLDC connectivity to provide support for a subset of the HTTP protocol. For network programming using MIDP, reverting to the HTTP programming model allows applications to run on any MIDP device, whether it is a GSM phone with a WAP stack, a phone with i-mode, or a Palm VII wireless.

The HttpConnection Interface

The `HttpConnection` interface is part of the package `javax.microedition.io`. It defines the necessary methods and constants for an HTTP connection:

```
public interface HttpConnection
    extends javax.microedition.io.ContentConnection
```

The HTTP protocol is a request-response application protocol in which the parameters of the request must be set before the request is sent. The connection can be in one of the three following states:

- `Setup`: No connection yet.
- `Connected`: Connection has been made, the request has been sent, and some response is expected.
- `Closed`: Connection is closed.

In the `Setup` state, the following methods can be invoked:

```
public void setRequestMethod( String method )
public void setRequestProperty( String key, String value )
```

For example, suppose the connection state is:

```
HttpConnection c = ( HttpConnection )
 Connector.open( "http://java.sun.com/developer" );
```

The request method can be set to be of type `POST` as follows:

```
c.setRequestMethod( HttpConnection.POST );
```

HTTP/1.0 allows an open-ended set of methods to be used to indicate the purpose of a request:

- The GET method: Information from a form using the GET method is appended onto the end of the action URI being requested. It is important to note that this is not a secure way to transmit form data, since the form data is appended to a string of characters visible in the browser's "location" window, for example:

  ```
  scriptname.cgi?somedata=example&homephone=123-1234
  ```

- The HEAD method: used to ask only for information about a document, not for the document itself.
- The POST method: transmits all form input information immediately after the requested URI. The submitted data is not visible as it does not appear in the URL, unlike with the get method.

Similarly, it is possible to set some of the HTTP properties. The HTTP User-Agent (or browser ID) request header contains information about compatibility, the browser, and the platform name. For example,

```
c.setRequestProperty( "User-Agent",
  "Profile/MIDP-1.0 Configuration/CLDC-1.0" );
```

If there is a method that requires data to be sent or received from the server, there is a state transition from Setup to Connected. Examples of methods that cause the transition include:

```
openInputStream                    getLength
openOutputStream                   getType
openDataInputStream                getDate
openDataOutputStream               getExpiration
```

While the connection is open, some of these methods may be invoked:

```
                                   getHost
getURL                             getPort
getProtocol
```

Fetching a Page Using a StreamConnection

This example demonstrates how to write network applications to retrieve information across the network using the HTTP protocol. The contents of a file referenced by a URL are read using StreamConnection, and there is no HTTP-specific behavior needed. Connector.open opens a connection to the URL and returns a StreamConnection object, then an InputStream is opened through which to read the contents of the file, character by character, until the end of the file (-1). In the event an exception is thrown, both the stream and connection are closed.

- `StreamConnection c = null;`

The interface `javax.microedition.io.StreamConnection` defines the capabilities that a stream connection must have.

•   `InputStream s = null;`

The class `java.io.InputStream` is the superclass of all classes representing an input stream of bytes.

•   `StringBuffer b = new StringBuffer( );`

Figure 12.5. The script `FirstExample.java`

```
                        FirstExample.java

import java.io.*;
import javax.microedition.io.*;
import javax.microedition.lcdui.*;
import javax.microedition.midlet.*;

public class  FirstExample  extends MIDlet {
  private Display  display;
  String  url = "http://people.aero.und.edu/~wenchen/hello.txt";

  public  FirstExample( ) {
    display = Display.getDisplay( this );
  }


  /***************************************************************
  *         This will be invoked when we start the MIDlet.      *
  ***************************************************************/
  public void startApp( ) {
    try {
      getViaStreamConnection( url );
    } catch ( IOException e ) {
      //Handle Exceptions any other way you like.
      System.out.println( "IOException " + e );
      e.printStackTrace( );
    }
  }


  /***************************************************************
  *                 Pause, discontinue ....                     *
  ***************************************************************/
  public void  pauseApp( ) { }


  /***************************************************************
  *              Destroy must cleanup everything.               *
  ***************************************************************/
```

continued on following page

Figure 12.5. continued

```
                            FirstExample.java

public void  destroyApp( boolean unconditional ) { }


   /*******************************************************************
    *                   Read url via stream connection.             *
    *******************************************************************/
   void  getViaStreamConnection( String url ) throws IOException {
      StreamConnection   c = null;
      InputStream        s = null;
      StringBuffer       b = new StringBuffer( );
      TextBox            t = null;

      try {
         c = (StreamConnection) Connector.open( url );
         s = c.openInputStream( );
         int  ch;
         while ( (ch = s.read( )) != -1 ) {
           b.append( (char) ch );
         }
         System.out.println( b.toString( ) );
         t = new TextBox( "hello....", b.toString( ), 1024, 0 );
      } finally {
         if ( s != null ) {
           s.close( );
         }
         if ( c != null ) {
           c.close( );
         }
      }
      // Display the contents of the file in a text box.
      display.setCurrent( t );
   }
}
```

The class `java.lang.StringBuffer` implements a mutable sequence of char-acters. A string buffer is like a `String`, but can be modified. At any point in time it contains some particular sequence of characters, but the length and content of the sequence can be changed through certain method calls.

- `c = (StreamConnection) Connector.open( url );`

  o The class `javax.microedition.io.Connector` is a factory for creat-ing new `Connection` objects.
  o The method `public static Connection open(String name) throws IOException` creates and opens a `Connection`, where the parameter `name` is the URL for the connection.
  o The interface `javax.microedition.io.Connection` is the most ba-sic type of generic connection. Only the `close` method is defined; the

Figure 12.6. Screenshots of the execution results of the script in Figure 12.5

`open` method is not defined here because opening is always done using the `Connector.open( )` methods.

- `s = c.openInputStream( );`

The method `public InputStream javax.microedition.io.InputConnection.openInputStream( ) throws IOException` opens and returns an input stream for a connection.

- `System.out.println( b.toString( ) );`

The method `public String toString( )` converts to a string representing the data in this string buffer.

Fetching a Page Using an Http Connection

Similar to the last example, this example fetches a page, but instead uses an `Http-Connection`. The `Connector.open` method opens a URL and returns an `Http-Connection` object. When the input stream is opened the connection also opens and the HTTP headers are read. The `c.getLength` gets the content length; if the content type is also needed, the `c.getType` method can be used.

The following list gives a line-by-line analysis of the program SecondExample.java in Figure 12.7.

- `HttpConnection c = null;`

Figure 12.7. The script SecondExample.java

```
                        SecondExample.java

import   java.io.*;
import   javax.microedition.midlet.*;
import   javax.microedition.io.*;
import   javax.microedition.lcdui.*;


/*********************************************************************
 *    An example MIDlet to fetch a page using an HttpConnection     *
 *********************************************************************/

public class  SecondExample  extends MIDlet {
  private Display  display;
  private String   url = "http://people.aero.und.edu/~wenchen/hello.txt";

  public  SecondExample( ) {
    display = Display.getDisplay( this );
  }


  /*********************************************************************
   *         startApp is invoked when the MIDlet is activated.        *
   *********************************************************************/
  public void  startApp( ) {
    // The specified URL is overridden in the descriptor.
    try {
      downloadPage( url );
    } catch( IOException e ) {
      // Handle the exception.
    }
  }


  private void  downloadPage( String url )  throws IOException {
    StringBuffer      b = new StringBuffer( );
    InputStream       is = null;
    HttpConnection    c = null;
    TextBox           t = null;
    try {
      long len = 0 ;
      int   ch = 0;
      c   = (HttpConnection) Connector.open( url );
      is  = c.openInputStream( );
      len = c.getLength( );
      if( len != -1 ) {
        // Read exactly Content-Length bytes.
        for ( int i = 0;  i < len;  i++ ) {
          if ( (ch = is.read( )) != -1 ) {
            b.append( (char) ch );
          }
        }
```

continued on following page

Figure 12.7. continued

SecondExample.java

```
    } else {
      // Read until the connection is closed.
      while ( (ch = is.read( )) != -1 ) {
        len = is.available( );
        b.append( (char) ch );
      }
    }
    t = new TextBox( "hello again....", b.toString( ), 1024, 0 );
  } finally {
    is.close( );
    c.close( );
  }
  display.setCurrent( t );
}


/******************************************************************
*                      Pause, discontinue....                    *
******************************************************************/
public void  pauseApp( ) { }


/******************************************************************
*                  Destroy must cleanup everything.              *
******************************************************************/
public void  destroyApp( boolean unconditional ) { }
}
```

Figure 12.8. Screenshots of the execution results of the script in Figure 12.7

The interface `javax.microedition.io.HttpConnection` defines the necessary methods and constants for an HTTP connection. HTTP is a request-response protocol in which the parameters of request must be set before the request is sent. The connection exists in one of the three states: `Setup`, `Connected`, and `Closed`.

- `len = c.getLength( );`

The interface `javax.microedition.io.ContentConnection` defines the stream connection over which content is passed. The method `public long javax.microedition.io.ContentConnection.getLength( )` returns the length of the content which is being provided. For example, if the connection is via HTTP, then the value of `content-length` header field is returned.

- `while ( (ch = is.read( )) != -1 ) {`

The method `public abstract int java.io.InputStream.read( )` reads the next byte of data from the input stream. The value byte is returned as an integer in the range 0 to 255. If no byte is available because the end of the stream has been reached, the value -1 is returned. This method blocks until input data is available, the end of the stream is detected, or an exception is thrown.

- `b.append( (char) ch );`

The method `public StringBuffer java.lang.StringBuffer.append(char c)` appends the string representation of the `char` argument to this string buffer, increasing its length by one.

- `len = is.available( );`

The method `public int java.io.InputStream.available( )` returns the number of bytes that can be read from this input stream without being blocked by the next caller of a method for this input stream.

JAVA ME REFERENCES

Table 12.1 shows a list of the packages provided by MIDP (Sun Microsystems Inc., 2002a, 2002b, 2004). The packages labeled `javax.*` are extensions to standard Java packages and are not included in the JDK (Java Development Kit) or JRE (Java Runtime Environment). They must be downloaded separately.

Table 12.1. Mobile Information Device Profile (MIDP) package list

Package	Classes and Description
User Interface	`javax.microedition.lcdui`: The UI API provides a set of features for implementing user interfaces for MIDP applications.
	`javax.microedition.lcdui.game`: The Game API package provides a series of classes that enable the development of rich gaming content for wireless devices.
Persistence	`javax.microedition.rms`: This provides a mechanism for MIDlets to persistently store data and later retrieve it.
Application Lifecycle	`javax.microedition.midlet`: The MIDlet package defines MIDP applications and the interactions between the application and the environment in which the application runs.
Networking	`javax.microedition.io`: The MID Profile includes networking support based on the `Generic Connection` framework from the *Connected, Limited Device Configuration*.
Audio	`javax.microedition.media`: The MIDP 2.0 Media API is a directly compatible building block of the Mobile Media API (JSR-135) specification.
	`javax.microedition.media.control`: This package defines the specific Control types that can be used with a `Player`.
Public Key	`javax.microedition.pki`: Certificates are used to authenticate information for secure Connections.
Core	`java.io`: Provides classes for input and output through data streams.
	`java.lang`: MID Profile Language Classes included from Java 2 Standard Edition.
	`java.util`: MID Profile Utility Classes included from Java 2 Standard Edition.

Additional information is available in Hu *et al.* (2004) and Wilson (2005), and from companies such as Microsoft Corp. (2005), Qualcomm Inc. (2003), Research In Motion Ltd. (2005), and Symbian Ltd. (2005, n.d.).

SUMMARY

This chapter built on the introduction to Java ME programming provided in Chapter XI, discussing in detail two aspects of particular importance for handheld devices:

- **Persistent storage:** The MIDP `Record Management System (RMS)` is a persistent storage method for MIDlets. It is a simple record-oriented database, which consists of a collection of records.
- **Network connection:** The generic `Connection` framework of MIDP can be used for network connection.

JavaME is a huge topic in its own right and its coverage here was necessarily limited due to space constraints, so a section of the chapter was devoted to a survey of MIDP packages. References to sources of further information were also provided.

REFERENCES

Hu, W.-C., Lee, C.-w., & Yeh, J.-h. (2004). Mobile commerce systems. Shi Nansi, editor, *Mobile Commerce Applications*, pages 1-23, Idea Group Publishing.

Microsoft Corp. (2005). *What's New for Developers in Windows Mobile 5.0?* Retrieved August 29, 2005, from http://msdn.microsoft.com/mobility/windows-mobile/howto/documentation/default.aspx?pull=/library/en-us/dnppcgen/html/whatsnew_wm5.asp

Qualcomm Inc. (2003). *BREW and J2ME—A Complete Wireless Solution for Operators Committed to Java.* Retrieved February 12, 2006, from http://brew.qualcomm.com/brew/en/img/about/pdf/brew_j2me.pdf

Research In Motion Ltd. (2005). *BlackBerry Application Control—An Overview for Application Developers.* Retrieved January 05, 2006, from http://www.blackberry.com/knowledgecenterpublic/livelink.exe/fetch/2000/7979/1181821/832210/BlackBerry_Application_Control_Overview_for_Developers.pdf?nodeid=1106734&vernum=0

Sun Microsystem Inc. (2002a). *Java 2 Platform, Micro Edition.* Retrieved January 12, 2006, from http://java.sun.com/j2me/docs/j2me-ds.pdf

Sun Microsystem Inc. (2002b). *Mobile Information Device Profile Specification 2.0.* Retrieved February 25, 2006, from http://jcp.org/aboutJava/communityprocess/final/jsr118/

Sun Microsystem Inc. (2004). *J2ME Wireless Toolkit 2.2—User's Guide.* Retrieved October 21, 2005, from http://java.sun.com/j2me/docs/wtk2.2/docs/UserGuide.pdf

Symbian Ltd. (2005). *Symbian OS Version 9.2*. Retrieved December 20, 2005, from http://www.symbian.com/technology/symbianOSv9.2_ds_0905.pdf

Symbian Ltd. (n.d.). *Symbian Fast Facts*. Retrieved January 26, 2005, from http://www.symbian.com/about/fastfaqs.html

Wilson, J. (2005). *What's New for Developers in Windows Mobile 5.0*. Retrieved February 24, 2006, from http://msdn.microsoft.com/smartclient/default.aspx?pull=/library/en-us/dnppcgen/html/whatsnew_wm5.asp&print=true

Chapter XIII
Palm OS Programming

INTRODUCTION

Programming for Palm devices is not a trivial task and it is especially hard for beginners starting their first assignment. This chapter is not intended to be a comprehensive Palm programming guide, but rather to give an overview of what a Palm program is and how it works. For details of how to create Palm OS application programs, extensive coverage of this topic is provided by the Palm OS Developer Documentation at the URL (http://www.palmos.com/dev/support/docs/) (PalmSource, Inc. (2004a,b,c). The following steps for getting started with Palm OS programming are taken from PalmSource Inc. (2006):

1. **Join the Palm OS Developer Program:** Enroll as a member of Palm OS Developer Program at the URL (https://www.developerpavilion.com/palmos/page.asp?page_id=175) in order to download tools such as Palm OS Developer Suite and receive updates of Palm information.
2. **Choose a core platform:** There are two versions of the Palm OS core platform:

- Palm OS Garnet (above Palm OS 5.3) and
- Palm OS Cobalt (Palm OS 6).

and three Palm OS application types:

- Palm OS 68K applications,
- Palm OS 68K applications with PACE Native Objects, and
- Palm OS Protein applications.

3. **Choose a programming language and tools:** Although most Palm OS applications are written in C, development environments are available that will let developers create Palm OS applications in a number of different languages including C, C++, Visual Basic, or Java.

4. **Learn the basics of Palm OS programming:** Basic documentation related to Palm OS programming includes:
   - *Introduction to Palm OS Development Suite*, which is a conceptual introduction to all of the tools delivered with Garnet OS Development Suite. It can be found at at the URL (http://www.access-company.com/developers/documents/docs/dev_suite/PalmOSDevSuite/ToolsTOC.html)
   - *Garnet OS 68K SDK Documentation*, which contains documentation on the 68K software development kit. It can be found at the URL (http://www.access-company.com/developers/documents/palmos/index.html).

Also, there are several considerations that developers need to keep in mind as they design and build their applications:

- Small screen size.
- Usage patterns: for example, a handheld may be turned on 40 times in 1 hour.
- Limited input methods.
- Various wireless connectivity.
- Limited computing power.
- Short battery life. Actions such as wireless communications, sound, extended animation, or other tasks that occupy the CPU for long periods of time consume a great deal of power.
- Small memory. Expansion is often limited to the capacity of an SD card.
- Persistent data storage.
- Backward compatibility.

5. **Consider wireless-enabling applications:** Palm powered devices can connect with networks and with each other in an increasing number of ways,

including infrared, Bluetooth, Wi-Fi, and cellular telephony. Programmers can benefit from exploring these opportunities, discovering new grab tips, tools, and insights and learning how PalmSource can help test new applications and deploy them in the wireless marketplace.

6. **Tailor solutions to specific devices:** Although Palm OS forms the core of every Palm powered device, some devices have features that are specific to that device from a Palm OS licensee.

PALM OS PROGRAMMING

The best way to show how to program an application using a specific programming language or environment is to give a simple example. The following list is the step-by-step procedure involved in developing a Palm OS application, a simple "Hello, Mobile world!" program, under Microsoft Windows XP:

1. download and install the Palm OS Developer Suite,
2. create a new project,
3. create a Palm program,
4. use the Palm OS Resource Editor to manage resources,
5. build the project,
6. use the Palm OS Emulator to test the new application, and
7. synchronize the application with the handheld device(s) it is to run on.

Details of each step are given next.

Download and Install the Palm OS Developer Suite

The first step involved in developing a Palm application is to download *Palm OS Developer Suite* from the PalmSource Inc. website (http://www.palmos.com/dev/tools/dev_suite.html). The Palm OS Developer Suite is the official development environment and tool chain supplied by PalmSource Inc. It serves as a complete IDE (Integrated Development Environment) for two kinds of Palm applications:

- **Protein applications (all ARM-native code) for Palm OS Cobalt:** The term *ARM* processor refers to the family of `advanced RISC machine` processors, which are a type of 4-byte RISC processors.
- **68K applications for all versions that have been shipped of the Palm OS:** The term *68K* processor refers to the family of Motorola 68000 processors.

Create a New Project

The Eclipse IDE for the Palm OS Developer Suite, shown in Figure 13.1 under the Windows XP environment, can be activated by selecting the following options:

```
Start ⇒ All Programs ⇒ PalmSource ⇒ Palm OS Developer
Suite
```

The Eclipse IDE (IBM Corp., 2006) is supplied by the Eclipse Foundation, Inc., which is an open source community whose projects are focused on providing an extensible development platform and application frameworks for building software. The first-time user may select a default workspace at the address of local disk (C:\ Program Files\PalmSource\Palm OS Developer Suite\workspace).

Create a new project by selecting a *wizard*, which is an interactive computer program that acts as an interface to lead a user through a complex task using dialog steps. As mentioned earlier, there are three Palm OS application types:

- *Palm OS 68K Applications,*
- *Palm OS 68K Applications with PACE Native Objects*, and
- *Palm OS Protein Applications.*

PACE Native Objects (PNO) are ARM-native subroutines used to accelerate key performance bound portions of a 68K application. There are also two kinds of `makefiles,` which automate the compilation of programs whose files are dependent on each other:

Figure 13.1. A screenshot of the Palm OS Developer Suite © 2008 ACCESS Co., Ltd.

Figure 13.2. A screenshot showing Palm OS application and make types © 2008 ACCESS Co., Ltd.

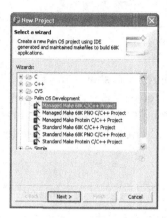

- **Standard make:** provides a generic set of makefiles that can be modified and tailored for a specific application build.
- **Managed make:** dynamically generates a makefile based on the contents of specific project folders.

Create a Palm Program

Once a Palm OS C program is created it is placed in a directory of the local disk, for example, (C:\Program Files\PalmSource\Palm OS Developer Suite\workspace\ HelloWorld\) in Figure 13.3. The Palm code example in the figure displays the text "Hello, Mobile world!," an image, and a button "OK" on a Palm device.

In order to display the current status on the Eclipse IDE, it may be necessary to constantly *refresh* the project HelloWorld by right clicking on the project name, as shown in Figure 13.4.

Use Palm OS Resource Editor

A Palm OS software resource is a data structure that describes the characteristics of an application element. For example, user interface elements such as forms, dialogs, or text strings are all resources and code segments are also stored in resources. A Palm OS software application uses resources to present something to the user. All resources are assigned an integer resource ID. For applications, resource IDs should be less than 9999. Resource IDs of 10000 or above are reserved for use by

Palm OS. If the project includes resources (`.xrd`) such as buttons and images, the Palm OS Resource Editor at

```
Start ⇒ All Programs ⇒ PalmSource ⇒ Tools
       ⇒ Palm OS Resource Editor
```

can be used to create the resources, as shown in Figure 13.5. Palm OS Resource Editor is a visual resource editor that is used to create and edit XML resource description (XRD) files for Palm OS applications. Palm OS Resource Editor is designed to work with the family of Palm OS resource tools. All of the resource

Figure 13.3. An example of a Palm OS program `HelloWorld.c`

```
                    C:\Program Files\PalmSource\Palm OS Developer
                      Suite\workspace\HelloWorld\HelloWorld.c

// This header is from the Palm SDK and contains the needed reference
// materials for the use of Palm API and its defined constants.
#include  <PalmOS.h>

// The following IDs are from using Palm Resource Editor.
#define   Form1   1000
#define   OK      1003

// -----------------------------------------------------------------
// PilotMain is called by the startup code and implements a simple
// event handling loop.
// -----------------------------------------------------------------
UInt32  PilotMain( UInt16 cmd, void *cmdPBP, UInt16 launchFlags ) {
    short       err;
  EventType   e;
  FormType    *pfrm;

  if ( cmd == sysAppLaunchCmdNormalLaunch ) {
    // Displays the Form with an ID 1000.
    FrmGotoForm( Form1 );


    //  Main event loop
    while( 1 ) {
      // Doze until an event arrives or 100 ticks are reached.
      EvtGetEvent( &e, 100 );
      // System gets first chance to handle the event.
      if ( SysHandleEvent( &e ) )  continue;
      if ( MenuHandleEvent( (void *) 0, &e, &err ) )  continue;

      switch ( e.eType ) {
        case ctlSelectEvent:
          if ( e.data.ctlSelect.controlID == OK )
            goto _quit;
          break;
```

continued on following page

Figure 13.3. continued

```
      C:\Program Files\PalmSource\Palm OS Developer
         Suite\workspace\HelloWorld\HelloWorld.c
```

```c
        case frmLoadEvent:
          FrmSetActiveForm( FrmInitForm( e.data.frmLoad.formID ) );
          break;

        case frmOpenEvent:
          pfrm = FrmGetActiveForm( );
          FrmDrawForm( pfrm );
          break;

        case menuEvent:
          break;

        case appStopEvent:
          goto _quit;
          break;

        default:
          if ( FrmGetActiveForm( ) )
            FrmHandleEvent( FrmGetActiveForm( ), &e );
          break;
      }
    }
_quit:
    FrmCloseAllForms( );
  }
  return 0;
}
```

Figure 13.4. A screenshot of the Palm OS Developer Suite after the project HelloWorld is created © 2008 ACCESS Co., Ltd.

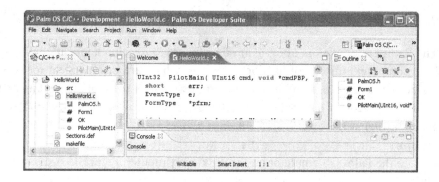

Figure 13.5. A screenshot of the Palm OS Resource Editor © 2008 ACCESS Co., Ltd.

tools operate on XRD files. An XRD file is an XML resource description file that contains XML tags that represent the resources needed by an application.

Build the Project

Build the project HelloWorld by right clicking on the mouse on the project name and selecting the option "Build Project."

Use the Palm OS Emulator to Test the New Application

Activate the *Palm OS emulator* by selecting

```
Start ⇒ All Programs ⇒ PalmSource ⇒ Tools ⇒ Palm OS Emulator
```

The Palm OS emulators allow Palm developers to develop applications using desktop computers instead of handheld devices, which are inconvenient for software development because of severe limitations such as their small screens and keyboards. The icon of the application to be tested, in this case Hello.prc (Palm Application file) at the local disk (C:\Program Files\PalmSource\Palm OS Developer Suite\workspace\HelloWorld\Debug\HelloWorld.prc), is dragged to the Palm OS emulator on the desktop computer. Figure 13.6 shows the execution result of the project HelloWorld.

Figure 13.6. A screenshot of the execution results of the project HelloWorld © 2008 ACCESS Co., Ltd.

Synchronize the Application with the Handheld Device(s)

If the application is finalized, synchronize the application to the handheld device or devices it is to be used on by selecting

```
Start ⇒ All Programs ⇒ Palm Desktop ⇒ Palm Desktop
```

after downloading the *Palm Desktop* as shown in Figure 13.7 at the URL (http://www.palmos.com/dev/tools/desktop/). Click on the "Quick Install" button and open the application file that will be installed into the device. If the Palm device is connected to the PC via a USB cable, clicking on the HotSync icon will start the synchronization.

THE HELLO-WORLD PROGRAM

The following list shows a line-by-line analysis of the Hello-World Palm program in Figure 13.3.

- `#include <PalmOS.h>`

PalmOS.h is an include file that contains most of the standard Palm OS include files. It is from the Palm SDK and contains the reference materials needed to use the Palm API and its defined constants.

Figure 13.7. A screenshot of the Palm Desktop © 2008 ACCESS Co., Ltd.

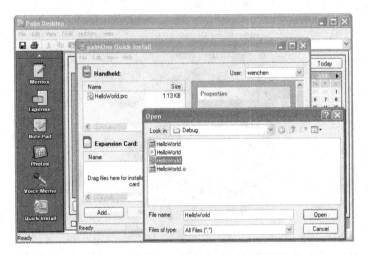

- `UInt32 PilotMain(UInt16 cmd, void *cmdPBP, UInt16 launch-Flags) {`

The function `PilotMain( )` is equivalent to the `main( )` procedure of C. It returns `errNone` if the application processed the launch code successfully, or an appropriate error code if there was a problem. The arguments are somewhat similar to C's:

- o `argc`: This contains the number of parameters added to the command line.
- o `argv`: If `argc` is greater than 0, then the contents of the argument variables (`argv[1]`, `argv[2]`, etc.) are evaluated; These specify which event fired the application.
- o `UInt32`: An integer value that is stored in 4 bytes.
- o `PilotMain`: The entry point for all Palm OS applications, this function's sole purpose is to receive and respond to launch codes.
- o `UInt16`: An integer value that is stored in 2 bytes.
- o `cmd`: The `Launch Code` to which the application is to respond.
- o `cmdPBP`: This points to any structures containing launch-command-specific parameters, or is `NULL` if the launch code has none. See the description of each launch code for a description of the parameter structure that accompanies it, if any.

o   `LaunchFlags`: When an application is launched with any launch command, it includes a set of `Launch Flags` that indicate:

   ➢   whether the application's global variables are available,

   ➢   whether the application is now the active application,

   ➢   whether the application was already active, and so on.

•   `EventType event;`

Events are structures that the system passes to the application when the user interacts with the graphical user interface. The `struct EventType` contains all the data associated with a system event. All event types have some common data, and most events also have data specific to those events. The specific data uses a union that is part of the `EventType` data structure. The `Event Reference` section gives details on the important data associated with each type of event.

```
Typedef struct {
  eventsEnum eType;
  Boolean penDown;
  UInt8 tapCount;
  Int16 screenX;
  Int16 screenY;
  union {
    ...
  } data;
} EventType;
```

where the fields are:

o   `eType`: One of the `eventsEnum` constants; this specifies the type of the event.

o   `penDown`: This is `true` if the pen was down at the time of the event, otherwise `false`. When the handheld is in doze mode, an interrupt is generated when the pen is first brought down on the screen. After a pen down is detected, the system software polls the pen location periodically (every 20 ms) until the pen is again raised. Most applications never need to call the `Pen Manager` directly because any pen activity is automatically returned to the application in the form of events.

o   `tapCount`: The number of taps received at this location. This value is used mainly by fields. When the user taps in a text field, two taps selects a word, and three taps selects the entire line.

- o   `screenX`: Window-relative position of the pen in pixels (number of pixels from the left bound of the window).
- o   `screenY`: Window-relative position of the pen in pixels (number of pixels from the top left of the window).
- o   `data`: The specific data for an event, if any.

- •   `if ( cmd == sysAppLaunchCmdNormalLaunch ) {`

An application launches when it receives a launch code. `Launch  Codes` are a means of communication between the Palm OS and the application (or between two applications). Each launch code may be accompanied by two types of information:

- o   `A parameter block`, which acts as a pointer to a structure that contains several parameters that contain information necessary to handle the associated launch code.
- o   `Launch flags`, which indicate how the application should behave; for example, a flag could be used to specify whether or not the UI should be displayed. An application typically launches when a user presses one of the buttons on the device or selects an application icon from the application launcher screen. When this happens, the system generates the launch code `sysAppLaunchCmdNormalLaunch`, which tells the application to perform a full launch and display its user interface.

- •   `WinDrawChars( "Hello, world!", 13, 55, 60 );`

A window defines a drawing region. This region may be on the display or in a memory buffer. All forms are windows, but not all windows are forms. The `Window` object is the portion of the `Form` object that determines how the form's window looks and behaves. A window object contains viewing coordinates of the window and clipping bounds. The function

`void WinDrawChars( const Char *chars, Int16 len, Coord x, Coord y )`

draws the specified characters in the draw window.

- o   `chars`: acts as a pointer indicating which characters to draw.
- o   `len`: the length in bytes of the characters to draw.
- o   x: the x coordinate of the first character to draw (left bound).
- o   y: the y coordinate of the first character to draw (top bound).

- `EvtGetEvent( &event, evtWaitForever );`

An event is a software message that indicates something has happened.

- o Traditional programs follow their own control flow pattern, occasionally changing course at branch points.
- o Event-driven programs are preprogrammed with an event loop to look repeatedly for information to process (for example, a keyboard or mouse operation) and then perform a trigger function to process it.

The function `void EvtGetEvent( EventType *event, Int32 timeout )` returns the next available event.

- o `event`: is a pointer telling the structure to hold the event returned.
- o `timeout`: the maximum number of ticks to wait before an event is returned (`evtWaitForever` means wait indefinitely).

Pass `evtWaitForever` acts as the timeout in most instances. When running on the device, this makes the CPU go into doze mode until the user provides input.

- `SysHandleEvent( &event );`

The function `Boolean SysHandleEvent( EventPtr eventP )` handles defaults for system events such as hard and soft key presses. It returns `true` if the system handled the event. Applications should call this routine immediately after calling `EvtGetEvent( )`.

- o `eventP`: once again, this points to an event.

- `} while ( event.eType != appStopEvent );`

When the system wants to launch a different application than the one currently running, the event manager sends this event to request the current application to terminate by using the event reference `appStopEvent`. In response, an application has to exit its event loop, close any open files and forms, and exit.

PALM OS RESOURCE TOOLS

Palm OS Resource Editor is designed to work with the family of Palm OS resource tools. All of the resource tools operate on XRD files. An XRD file is an XML resource description file and contains XML tags that represent the resources needed by an application. Figure 13.10 provides a graphical representation of how Palm OS resource tools are used to create resources for a Palm OS application:

- GenerateXRD converts existing Palm OS PRC files and Macintosh RSRC files into XRD files.
- Palm OS Resource Editor creates and edits XRD files.
- PalmRC compiles XRD files into TRC files. TRC is the file extension for the Debug support file associated with Power CTrace.

PRCMerge takes the compiled output from PalmRC and merges it with the code resources (BIN) to produce a Palm OS application (PRC). Palm OS Resource Editor uses a collection of files as a convenient way to manage resource definitions. Resource Editor uses the concept of a workspace for organizing resource files. A workspace is simply a collection of resource files that are loaded, saved, and closed as a group. Physically, a workspace file is a document containing a list of resource files that are collected together. Workspace files have the extension XRW.

Figure 13.10. Palm OS resource tools for creating resources for a Palm OS application

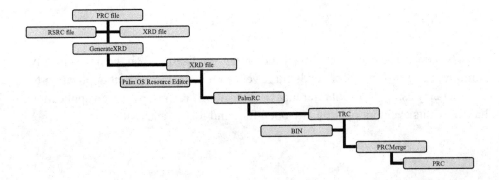

Palm OS resource description files use XML structure and text encoding to specify application resources. These XML resource description files are commonly called XRD files. There is a one-to-one correspondence between Palm OS resources and XML resource descriptions in the XRD file, so for every resource in the Palm OS application, an XML resource element name and associated attributes must be specified. Resource Editor streamlines the creation of XRD files. Rather than directly editing an XML-based text file, visual layout windows are used to create XRD files. The XRD file format allows for a special type of resource called a custom resource. Using a custom resource type element allows programmers to create a new XML-based format for resources that are not already defined. Custom resource type description files must have an XRT file extension.

Palm OS Resource Editor

As explained earlier in the chapter, Palm OS Resource Editor is a visual resource editor that is used to create and edit XML resource description (XRD) files for Palm OS applications. A Palm OS software resource is a data structure that describes the characteristics of an application element. User interface elements, such as forms, dialogs, or text strings are all resources; in addition, code segments are also stored in resources.

Resource Editor does not currently support creating a C header file for the resources defined in XRD files. If an application needs a C header file with preprocessor definitions for resources, it is necessary to create the header file independently. Palm OS resource types include:

- **Forms and form objects:** These include form, form title, buttons, form label, form checkbox, form field, form graffiti state, form list, form table, form

Figure 13.9. A screenshot of the Palm OS Resource Editor

Table 13.1. User interface elements of Palm OS Resource Editor © 2008 ACCESS Co., Ltd.

UI Element and Functionality	Example	Resource(s)
Alert—A warning, error, or confirmation message	**Memo Delete** — (?) Do you really want to delete this memo? (OK) (Cancel)	Alert (Talt)
Application icon—Icon to display in Launcher		Application icon (tAIB) Application icon family (taif)
Bitmap—A bitmap		Form bitmap (tFBM) Bitmap (Tbmp) Bitmap family (tbmf)
Command button—Executes a command.	(OK)	Button (tBTN) Graphic button (tgbn)
Check box—Toggle on or off	☑ Show Due Dates ☐ Show Priorities	Checkbox (tCBX)
Form—Window that displays other UI objects	**Address** ▼ All — Dugger, Mark 555-555-5555 W; Gossett, Brent 555-555-5555 W; Liu, Clif 555-555-5555 W; Maas, Brian 555-555-5555 W; Extrem, Jean 555-555-5555 W; Parker, Dennis 555-555-5555 W; Parrett, JB 555-555-5555 W; Rathjens, Lisa 555-555-5555 W; Schaller, Anna 555-555-5555 W; Schneider, Susan 555-555-5555 W; Wilson, Greg 555-555-5555 W — Look Up: (New)	
Gadget—Custom control		Gadget (tGDT)
Shift Indicator—Shift status	↑	Shift Indicator (tGSI)
Label—Noneditable text	**Set Date:**	Label (tLBL)
List—A series of items	**Edit Memo** — Horse of different color; Ruby slippers; Yellow brick road ... (Done)	List (tLST)
Menu—Executes commands.	**Record Edit Options** — Delete Item... /D; Attach Note /A; Delete Note... /O; Purge... /E; Beam Item /B; Beam Category	Menu Bar (MBAR) Menu (MENU)

continued on following page

Table 13.1. continued

UI Element and Functionality	Example	Resource(s)
Pop-up list—Chooses a setting from a list.	▼ Unfiled / Business / Personal / Unfiled / Edit Categories...	Pop-up trigger (tPUT) Pop-up list (tPUL) List (tLST)
Push button—Selects a value.	R A Ā	Push button (tPBN) Graphic push button (tgpb)
Repeating button—Increment/decrement values or scroll	◆	Repeating button (tREP) Graphic repeating button (tgrb)
Scroll bar—Scrolls fields or tables.			Scroll bar (tSCL)
Selector trigger—Invokes dialog that changes text of the control.	Selector	Selector trigger (tSLT)
Slider—Adjusts a setting.	◁▭▭▭▭◻▭▭▭▷	Slider (tsld) Feedback slider (tslf)
Table—Columns of data		Table (tTBL)
Text field—Text (single or multiple lines)	Text	Field (tFLD)

popup, form popup trigger, form selector trigger, form slider, form feedback slider, form scrollbar, and window constraints.

- **Menus:** These include menu bars.
- **Character strings, string lists, and category names:** For an application these include the default category, extended preferences, icon name, info strings, preferences, launch preferences, and version, as well as strings and string lists.
- **Alerts.**
- **Icons and bitmaps:** These include the bitmaps for the application icon and forms, as well as the color table.
- **Fonts:** These include regular and extended fonts, and TrueType fonts.
- **Sounds:** These include MIDI and wave sound.
- **Data types:** These include lists for byte integers, DWord integers and word integers, as well as raw, soft and constant data.

The Palm OS development environment provides a set of resource templates that application developers can use to implement the buttons, dialogs, and other UI elements. Table 13.1 maps user interface elements to resources.

SUMMARY

This chapter introduced the basic concepts involved in Palm OS programming, illustrating its operation by following in detail a step-by-step procedure of a simple Palm application development. The Palm OS Developer Suite is used to develop applications for Palm devices by handheld programmers. Further details of how this can be used for more sophisticated applications are given in the next chapter.

REFERENCES

IBM Corp. (2006). *Eclipse Platform Technical Overview.* Retrieved June 2, 2006, from http://www.eclipse.org/articles/Whitepaper-Platform-3.1/eclipse-platform-whitepaper.html

PalmSource Inc. (2004a). *Palm OS Programmer's API Reference.* Retrieved June 5, 2006, from http://www.palmos.com/dev/support/docs/palmos/PalmOSReference/ReferenceTOC.html

PalmSource Inc. (2004b). *Palm OS Programmer's Companion, Vol. I.* Retrieved February 21, 2006, from http://www.palmos.com/dev/support/docs/palmos/PalmOSCompanion/CompanionTOC.html

PalmSource Inc. (2004c). *Palm OS Programmer's Companion, Vol. II.* Retrieved June 21, 2006, from http://www.palmos.com/dev/support/docs/palmos/PalmOSCompanion2/Companion2TOC.html

PalmSource Inc. (2006). *Getting Started.* Retrieved March 15, 2006, from http://www.palmos.com/dev/start/

Chapter XIV
Advanced Palm OS Programming

INTRODUCTION

The introduction to Palm OS programming given in the previous chapter provided an overview of its structure and basic concepts. This chapter examines an advanced aspect of Palm OS programming, focusing on one major subject that is particularly relevant for handheld devices: forms. User interfaces such as check boxes and radio buttons can be contained in a form, allowing users to enter data that is, typically, then sent to a server for processing. It is important to note that this topic was selected to allow the reader to become familiar with how Palm OS operates; for other Palm OS topics such as databases and menus, readers may check the section later in this chapter on Palm OS References for further information.

- In Palm OS, every file is a database, which is similar to the persistent storage of J2ME. A Palm database does not correspond to a "relational database" but is actually closer to a structured, flexible, and mobile binary data file.
- A menu bar is displayed whenever the user taps a menu icon. The menu bar is also displayed when the user taps in a form's titlebar. The menu bar, a horizontal list of menu titles, appears at the top of the screen in its own window, above all the application windows.

FORMS

This section is divided into three sub-sections:

1. Screenshots of execution results of the application `Forms` are given first to illustrate how the application is used before the programming details are discussed.
2. User interface construction using Palm Resource Editor is then shown.
3. Finally, the Palm C program is given and explained line by line.

Execution Results of the Application Forms

The following emulator screenshots show the interfaces generated by the application `Forms`, which displays various kinds of user interface that may be contained in forms:

*   Figure 14.1 shows the default Palm Applications interface with a new icon `Forms`. The icon was created by the project `Forms`, which will be discussed later. Note that the default icon ⬤ is replaced by the image ⬤. The interface changes to the one shown in Figure 14.2 after the `Forms` icon is clicked.
*   Figure 14.2 shows the first interface of the application `Forms`, which includes various (disabled) buttons with/without (bold) frames. The interface changes to the interfaces shown in Figures 14.3 and 14.1 after the `Next` and `Exit` buttons are clicked, respectively.

Figure 14.1. The default Palm Applications interface including a new icon Forms

Figure 14.2. The first interface of the application Forms including various buttons

Figure 14.3. The second interface of the application Forms including grouped push buttons and checkboxes

- Figure 14.3 shows the second interface of the application Forms, which includes grouped push buttons and (grouped) checkboxes. The interface changes to the interfaces shown in Figures 14.2, 14.4, and 14.1 after the buttons Prev, Next, and Exit are clicked, respectively.
- Figure 14.4 shows the third interface of the application Forms, which includes a list, repeat buttons and field, and a bitmap image. The interface changes to the interfaces shown in Figures 14.3 and 14.1 after the buttons Prev and Exit are clicked, respectively.
- Figure 14.5 displays a help message for the application Forms reached by clicking on the letter 'i' in the top-right corner of each of the screens in Figures 14.2-4. The interface changes to the one shown in Figure 14.4 after the button Done is clicked.

Figure 14.4. The third interface of the application Forms including a list, repeat buttons and field, and a bitmap image

Figure 14.5. A help message for the application forms

Interface Creation for the Application Forms

Before the Palm OS Resource Editor was introduced, Palm OS programmers had to manually create the C header file Forms.h shown in Figure 14.6 and the Palm OS resource file Forms.rcp shown in Figure 14.7 for the interfaces in Figures 14.2-5. These two files are both trivial and hard to create and understand, so the ability to use Palm OS Resource Editor to avoid the need to deal with this is very helpful. Programmers can visually create the user interfaces shown in the previous section as follows:

1.   The application icon is created with an ID 1000 showing in the *Files* pane, as shown in Figure 14.8.
2.   Next, a bitmap image is created with an ID 1000 showing in the Files pane, as shown in Figure 14.9.

Figure 14.6. The C header file `Forms.h` *for the interfaces in Figures 14.2-5*

```
                                    Forms.h

#define   FormFirst     1000
#define   Form1         1000
#define   Form2         1001
#define   Form3         1002
#define   FormLast      1002

#define   Form3Minus    2044
#define   Form3Count    2045
#define   Form3Plus     2046

#define   Prev          9000
#define   Next          9001
#define   Exit          9002

#define   Bitmap        1000
#define   Help1         1000
```

3. A string message is created with an ID 1000 for `Help`, as shown in Figure 14.10.

4. Then a form is created with an ID 1000, as shown in Figure 14.11.

5. The buttons in Form 1000, shown in Figure 14.12, are created with the following properties:
   - `Comment`: Name of the form object. This must be a valid C name—for instance, it cannot have spaces.
   - `ID`: Integer ID assigned by Resource Editor.
   - `Usable`: Uncheck this box if the object is not to appear on the screen initially. Nonusable objects can programmatically be set to usable.
   - `Enabled`: Uncheck this box if the user is not allowed to interact with the object initially. Non-enabled objects can programmatically be set to enabled.
   - `Text`: Text is displayed inside the button.
   - `Left Anchor`: This controls how the object resizes itself when its text label is changed. If checked, the left bound of the object is fixed; if unchecked, the right bound is fixed.
   - `Frame`: The `BUTTON _ FRAME` element is used to specify the frame used by the form object. The element may be specified as one of the following `enum` values: `NO _ BUTTON _ FRAME`, `STANDARD _ BUTTON _ FRAME`, `BOLD _ BUTTON _ FRAME`, and `RECTANGLE _ BUTTON _ FRAME`.

6. Moving on to create the next form, with an ID 1001, as shown in Figure 14.13.

Figure 14.7. The Palm OS resource file `Forms.rcp` *for the interfaces in Figures 14.2-5*

```
                              Forms.rcp

#include  "Forms.h"

FORM ID Form1 AT (2 2 156 156)
USABLE
MODAL
HELPID Help1
BEGIN
TITLE "Forms 1/4 (Modal)"

LABEL "This is a label" ID 2000 AT (CENTER 20) FONT 1

LABEL "Those are individual buttons" ID 2000 AT (CENTER PREVBOTTOM+10) FONT 1
BUTTON "Frame" ID 2001 AT (CENTER PREVBOTTOM+10 AUTO AUTO) FRAME
BUTTON "NoFrame" ID 2002 AT (CENTER PREVBOTTOM+4 AUTO AUTO) NOFRAME
BUTTON "BoldFrame" ID 2003 AT (CENTER PREVBOTTOM+4 AUTO AUTO) BOLDFRAME
BUTTON "Disabled" ID 2004 AT (CENTER PREVBOTTOM+4 100 AUTO) DISABLED

BUTTON "Next" ID Next AT (CENTER@50 PREVBOTTOM+10 AUTO AUTO)
BUTTON "Exit" ID Exit AT (CENTER@120 PREVTOP AUTO AUTO)
END

FORM ID Form2 AT (2 2 156 156)
USABLE
MODAL
HELPID Help1
BEGIN
TITLE "Forms 2/4 (Modal)"

LABEL "Those are GROUPED buttons" ID 2010 AT (CENTER 20) FONT 1
PUSHBUTTON "1st" ID 2011 AT (CENTER@40 PREVBOTTOM+2 AUTO AUTO) GROUP 1
PUSHBUTTON "2nd" ID 2012 AT (CENTER@80 PREVTOP AUTO AUTO) GROUP 1
PUSHBUTTON "3rd" ID 2013 AT (CENTER@120 PREVTOP AUTO AUTO) GROUP 1

LABEL "Now single checkboxes..." ID 2020 AT (CENTER PREVBOTTOM+8) FONT 1
CHECKBOX "Unchecked" ID 2021 AT (CENTER@50 PREVBOTTOM+2 AUTO AUTO)
CHECKBOX "Checked" ID 2022 AT (CENTER@110 PREVTOP AUTO AUTO) CHECKED
CHECKBOX "Disabled" ID 2023 AT (CENTER PREVBOTTOM+2 AUTO AUTO) DISABLED

LABEL "... And grouped ones" ID 2030 AT (CENTER PREVBOTTOM+8) FONT 1
CHECKBOX "1st" ID 2031 AT (CENTER@40 PREVBOTTOM+2 AUTO AUTO) GROUP 1
CHECKBOX "2nd" ID 2032 AT (CENTER@80 PREVTOP AUTO AUTO) GROUP 1
CHECKBOX "3rd" ID 2033 AT (CENTER@120 PREVTOP AUTO AUTO) GROUP 1

BUTTON "Prev" ID Prev AT (CENTER@40 PREVBOTTOM+10 AUTO AUTO)
BUTTON "Next" ID Next AT (CENTER@80 PREVTOP AUTO AUTO)
BUTTON "Exit" ID Exit AT (CENTER@120 PREVTOP AUTO AUTO)
END

FORM ID Form3 AT (2 2 156 156)
USABLE
HELPID Help1
BEGIN
TITLE "Forms 3/4 (Non Modal)"

LABEL "List" AUTOID AT (CENTER 20) FONT 1
LIST "English" "Spanish" "German" "French" ID 2042 AT
   (CENTER@120 PREVTOP 52 1) VISIBLEITEMS 2

LABEL "Repeat button & field" AUTOID AT (CENTER PREVBOTTOM+8) FONT 1
REPEATBUTTON "-" ID Form3Minus AT (CENTER@50 PREVBOTTOM+2 AUTO AUTO)
FIELD ID Form3Count AT (CENTER@80 PREVTOP 24 AUTO)
   NONEDITABLE UNDERLINED MAXCHARS 4
REPEATBUTTON "+" ID Form3Plus AT (CENTER@110 PREVTOP AUTO AUTO)
```

continued on following page

Figure 14.7. continued

```
                            Forms.rcp

LABEL "Bitmap" AUTOID AT (CENTER PREVBOTTOM+8) FONT 1
FORMBITMAP AT (80-(32/2) PREVBOTTOM+2) BITMAP Bitmap

BUTTON "Prev" ID Prev AT (CENTER@40 PREVBOTTOM+16 AUTO AUTO)
BUTTON "Next" ID Next AT (CENTER@80 PREVTOP AUTO AUTO)
BUTTON "Exit" ID Exit AT (CENTER@120 PREVTOP AUTO AUTO)
END


BITMAP ID Bitmap "forms.bmp"

STRING Help1 "This is a demonstration of forms programming for PalmOS."

ICON "forms.bmp"

SMALLICON "formssmall.bmp"

VERSION 1 "1.0.0"

LAUNCHERCATEGORY ID 1000 "Tutorial"
```

Figure 14.8. The application icon with an ID 1000

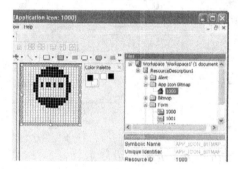

Figure 14.9. The bitmap image with an ID 1000

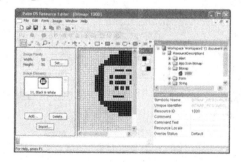

Figure 14.10. The string message with an ID 1000 for Help

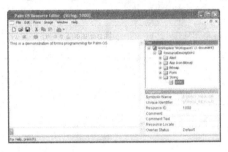

Figure 14.11. The form with an ID 1000

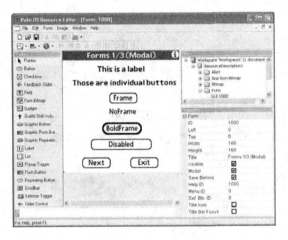

Figure 14.12. The buttons in Form 1000

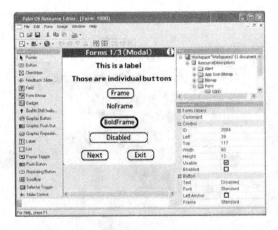

Figure 14.13. The form with an ID 1001

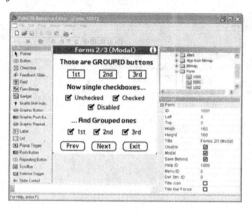

Figure 14.14. The push buttons in Form 1001

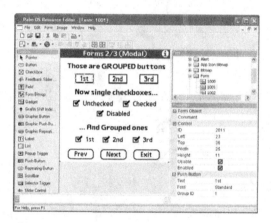

7. A push button is created in Form 1001, as shown in Figure 14.14. A push button object creates a push button and a group of push buttons represents a set of options where only one option can be selected at a time. Programmers typically create several push buttons that are aligned either horizontally or vertically:

   • Group ID: This has a nonzero value between 1 and 65535 that is used to identify the group. If it has a value of 0, the push button is not assigned to a group.

8. The checkbox in Form 1001 is created as shown in Figure 14.15. The check-box object creates a check box. Check boxes often appear in a group. If so,

Figure 14.15. The checkboxes in Form 1001

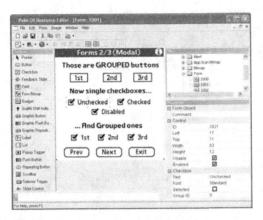

Figure 14.16. The form with an ID 1002

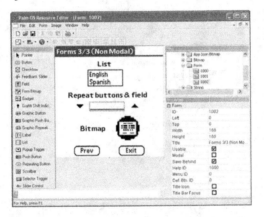

the group should be non-exclusive (so that the user can enable multiple check boxes) and can be aligned either vertically or horizontally. If the programmer wants to ensure that only one of a series of options is selected, push buttons or a list should be used instead of check boxes:

- Selected: This is the initial selection state of the check box. If this box is checked (the default), the check box is initially checked.

9. Now a form with an ID 1002 is created, as shown in Figure 14.16.

10. The list in Form 1002 is created as shown in Figure 14.17 and has the following properties:

- Usable: If a pop-up list is being created, uncheck this box.
- Num. Vis. Items: This specifies the number of items the list displays:

- o items for a full screen pop-up list
- o 11 items for a full screen stand-alone list (modeless form)
- o 10 items for a full screen stand-alone list (modal form)
- o 0 for the `Categories` pop-up list (its size is determined at runtime)

This should be set to the total number of items in the list if less than these numbers.

- `Num. Items`: This specifies the number of items in the list.

11. The repeating button in Form 1002 is created as shown in Figure 14.18. The repeating button object creates a repeating button, which may or may not look identical to command buttons. The difference between the two is that a repeating button sends events repeatedly as long as the user holds the pen down on the button, while command buttons wait until the user releases the pen and then send a single event. The most common use of repeating buttons is to draw the scroll buttons in the lower-right portion of a form. They are also often used as increment/decrement arrows:

- `Text`: Specifies the text that appears inside the repeating button: "\x01" specifies the scroll up button and "\x02" specifies the scroll down button.
- `Left Anchor`: This controls how the object resizes itself:
  - o `TRUE`—the object's left bound is fixed.
  - o `FALSE`—the object's right bound is fixed.

Figure 14.17. The list in Form 1002

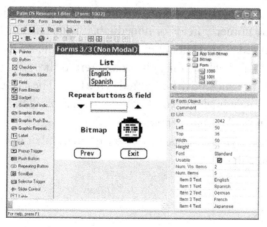

Figure 14.18. The repeating button in Form 1002

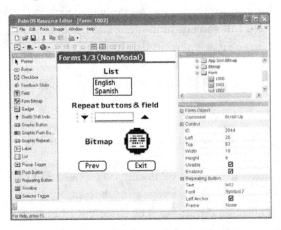

12. The field in Form 1002 is created as shown in Figure 14.19. The field object is used to create an editable text field that can be either a single-line long or multiple lines long or to create noneditable text that is displayed on the form. It is easier to use noneditable text fields than to use labels if the text of the label changes dynamically.

- `Editable`: If this box is checked, the field is editable. Noneditable fields do not accept user input but can be changed programmatically.
- `Underlined`: This box is checked for editable fields and unchecked for noneditable fields.
- `Single Line`: This box is checked for single-line fields so the field does not scroll horizontally and does not accept `Return` or `Tab` characters.
- `Max Chars`: This is the maximum number of bytes that the user can enter into an editable field.
- `Justification`: Editable single-line fields should be left justified and single-line numeric fields or noneditable fields used as labels should be right justified. This is not applicable to multi-line fields.
- `Numeric`: If checked, only the characters 0 through 9 and associated separators are allowed to be entered in the field. The associated separators are the thousands separator and the decimal character. Note that numeric fields do not allow plus signs.
- `Max. Vis. Lines`: This is the maximum number of lines visible for a multi-line entry field.

Figure 14.19. The field in Form 1002

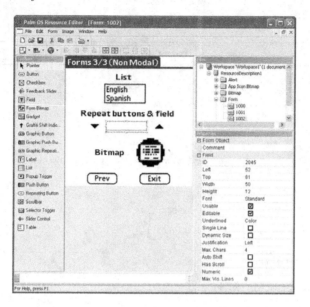

The resource editor will then automatically generate the resource description file `ResourceDescription1.xrd` (`.xrd` or `.txt`), shown in Appendix A, by selecting the following options:

```
File ⇒ Save As …
```

The C Program of the Application Forms

The C program `Forms.c` in Figure 14.20 is for the application in the previous discussion. The following list gives a line-by-line analysis of the program:

*   `#include <PalmCompatibility.h>`

Note that some header file names and the names used for basic types change in a legacy application with the Palm OS 3.5 or later SDK. For example, parameters previously declared as `Word` are now `UInt16` or `Int16`. In order to compile existing applications, it is necessary to incorporate these changes in the code or include the header file `PalmOSCompatibility.h`.

*   `case ctlRepeatEvent:`

Figure 14.20. The program Forms.c *of the application Forms*

```
                              Forms.c

#include  <PalmOS.h>
#include  <PalmCompatibility.h>
#include  "Forms.h"

#define   MAX_COUNT 9999
int       cnt = 1000;


UInt32  PilotMain( UInt16 cmd, MemPtr cmdPBP, UInt16 launchFlags ) {
  short       err;
  EventType   e;
  FormType    *pfrm;

  short  f = FormFirst;              // Start with 1st form 1st :)

  if ( cmd == sysAppLaunchCmdNormalLaunch ) {

    // Make sure only react to NormalLaunch, not Reset, Beam, Find, GoTo...
    FrmGotoForm( f );
    while ( 1 ) {
      EvtGetEvent( &e, 100 );
      if ( SysHandleEvent ( &e ) )    continue;
      if ( MenuHandleEvent( (void *) 0, &e, &err ) )   continue;

    switch ( e.eType ) {

      // if the Prev, Next, or Exit button is clicked on
      case  ctlSelectEvent:
        if ( e.data.ctlSelect.controlID == Prev ) {
          if ( f > FormFirst )  FrmGotoForm( --f );
        }
        else
          if ( e.data.ctlSelect.controlID == Next ) {
            if ( f < FormLast )   FrmGotoForm( ++f );
          }
          else
            if ( e.data.ctlSelect.controlID == Exit )   goto _quit;
          goto _default;

      // if the repeating button is clicked on
      case  ctlRepeatEvent:
        if ( e.data.ctlRepeat.controlID == Form3Minus ) {
          if ( cnt > 0 )   UpdateCount( -1 );
        }
        else
          if ( e.data.ctlRepeat.controlID == Form3Plus ) {
            if ( cnt < MAX_COUNT )   UpdateCount( +1 );
          }
        goto _default;

      case frmLoadEvent:
        FrmSetActiveForm( FrmInitForm( e.data.frmLoad.formID ) );
        break;
```

continued on following page

Figure 14.20. continued

```
        case  frmOpenEvent:
          pfrm = FrmGetActiveForm( );
          FrmDrawForm( pfrm );
          // Assign an initial value 1000 to the field value.
          if ( e.data.frmLoad.formID == Form3 )   UpdateCount( 0 );
          break;

        case menuEvent:
          break;

        case appStopEvent:
          goto _quit;

        default:
_default:
          if ( FrmGetActiveForm( ) )
             FrmHandleEvent( FrmGetActiveForm( ), &e );
      }
   }

_quit:
     FrmCloseAllForms( );
   }

   return 0;
}


/*******************************************************************
 *                                                                 *
 *       This function processes the increment and decrement of the *
 *           field value between the two repeating buttons.        *
 *                                                                 *
 *******************************************************************/
void  UpdateCount( UInt16 val ) {
  FormPtr     frm;
  FieldPtr    fld;
  UInt16      obj;
  CharPtr     p;
  VoidHand    h;

  cnt += val;
  frm = FrmGetActiveForm( );
  obj = FrmGetObjectIndex( frm, Form3Count );
  fld = (FieldPtr) FrmGetObjectPtr ( FrmGetActiveForm( ), obj );
  h   = (VoidHand) FldGetTextHandle( fld );




  if( h == NULL ) {
    h = MemHandleNew( FldGetMaxChars( fld )+10 );
    ErrFatalDisplayIf( !h, "No Memory" );
  }
  p = (CharPtr) MemHandleLock( h );
  StrIToA( p, cnt );
  MemHandleUnlock( h );
  FldSetTextHandle( fld, (Handle) h );
  FldDrawField( fld );
}
```

When the control routine `CtlHandleEvent( )` receives a `ctlEnterEvent` in a repeating button (`tREP`), it sends a `ctlRepeatEvent`. When `CtlHandleEvent` receives a `ctlRepeatEvent` in a repeating button, it sends another `ctlRepeatEvent` if the pen remains down within the bounds of the control for 1/2 second beyond the last `ctlRepeatEvent`. If `true` is returned in response to a `ctlRepeatEvent`, this stops the `ctlRepeatEvent` loop and no further `ctlRepeatEvents` are sent. For this event, the `data` field contains the following structure:

```
struct ctlRepeat {
   UInt16 controlID;
   struct ControlType *pControl;
   UInt32 time;
   UInt16 value;
} ctlRepeat;
```

- o `controlID`: Developer-defined ID of the control
- o `pControl`: Pointer to a control structure (`ControlType`)
- o `time`: System-ticks count when the event is added to the queue
- o `value`: Current value if the control is a feedback slider

- `obj = FrmGetObjectIndex( frm, Form3Count );`

This function `UInt16 FrmGetObjectIndex( const FormType *formP, UInt16 objID )` returns the index of an object in the form's objects list or `frmInvalidObjectId` if the supplied object ID is invalid.

- o `formP`: Pointer to the form object (`FormType` structure)
- o `objID`: ID of an object in the form

- `fld = (FieldPtr) FrmGetObjectPtr( FrmGetActiveForm( ), obj );`

The function `void *FrmGetObjectPtr( const FormType *formP, UInt16 objIndex )` returns a pointer to the data structure of an object in a form.

- o `formP`: Pointer to the form object (`FormType` structure)
- o `objIndex`: This is the index of an object in the form, which can be obtained by using `FrmGetObjectIndex( )`.

- `h = (VoidHand) FldGetTextHandle( fld );`

The function `MemHandle FldGetTextHandle( const FieldType *fldP )` returns a handle to the block that contains the text string of a field or `NULL` if no handle has been allocated for the field pointer.

- o   `fldP`: Pointer to a field object (`FieldType` structure)

- •   `h = MemHandleNew( FldGetMaxChars( fld )+10 );`

This function `UInt16 FldGetMaxChars( const FieldType *fldP )` returns the maximum number of bytes the `maxChars` field in `FieldType` accepts.

- o   `fldP`: Pointer to a field object (`FieldType` structure)

The function `MemHandle MemHandleNew( UInt32 size )` allocates a new movable chunk in the dynamic heap and returns a handle to it, or 0 if unsuccessful.

- o   `size`: The desired size of the chunk

- •   `ErrFatalDisplayIf( !h, "No Memory" );`

The macro `#define ErrFatalDisplayIf( condition, msg )` displays an error alert dialog if `condition` is `true` and error checking is set to partial or full.

- o   `condition`: A boolean value. If `true`, display the error.
- o   `msg`: Error message text as a string

- •   `p = (CharPtr) MemHandleLock( h );`

The function `MemPtr MemHandleLock( MemHandle h )` locks a chunk and obtains a pointer to the chunk's data.

- o   `h`: Chunk handle

- •   `StrIToA( p, cnt );`

The function `Char *StrIToA( Char *s, Int32 i )` converts an integer to ASCII.

- o s: Pointer to a string of size `maxStrIToALen` in which to store the results
- o i: Integer to convert

- `MemHandleUnlock( h );`

This function `Err MemHandleUnlock( MemHandle h )` unlocks a chunk given a chunk handle:

- o h: The chunk handle

- `FldSetTextHandle( fld, (Handle) h );`

The function `void FldSetTextHandle( FieldType *fldP, MemHandle textHandle )` sets the text value of a field to the string associated with the specified handle. It does not update the display

- o fldP: Pointer to a field object (`FieldType` structure)
- o textHandle: Unlocked handle of a field's text string

- `FldDrawField( fld );`

The function `void FldDrawField( FieldType *fldP )` draws the text of the field:

- o fldP: Pointer to a field object (`FieldType` structure)

The field's `usable` attribute must be `true` or the field will not be drawn.

PALM REFERENCES

Since this chapter was never intended to be a comprehensive Palm programming guide, this section provides interested readers with more Palm information for further reference. Table 14.3 describes the contents of four particularly useful documents in the Palm OS SDK (Software Development Kit). Further details of two of these documents, *Palm OS Programmer's API Reference* and *Palm OS Programmer's Companion,* are given below.

Palm OS Programmer's Companion

The *Palm OS Programmer's Companion* provides extensive conceptual and "how-to" development information, along with official reference information on Palm OS 68K functions and data structures. Table 14.4 gives an overview of the information available in each volume of the *Palm OS Programmer's Companion*.

Palm OS Programmer's API Reference

Table 14.5 gives an overview of the *Palm OS Programmer's API (Application Programming Interface) Reference* for Palm OS 68K SDK (PalmSource Inc., 2004a). It includes four major sections: (i) user interface, (ii) system management, (iii) communications, and (iv) libraries.

Table 14.3. Palm OS SDK documentation

Document	Description	URLs
Palm OS Programmer's API Reference	An API reference document that contains descriptions of all Palm OS function calls and important data structures.	http://www.palmos. com/dev/support/docs/ palmos/PalmOSReference/ ReferenceTOC.html
Palm OS Programmer's Companion, Vol. I & II	A multi-volume guide to application programming for the Palm OS. This guide contains conceptual and "how-to" information that complements the *Programmer's API Reference.*	http://www.palmos.com/ dev/support/docs/palmos/ PalmOSCompanion/ CompanionTOC.html and http://www.palmos.com/ dev/support/docs/palmos/ PalmOSCompanion2/ Companion2TOC.html
Constructor for Palm OS	A guide to using Constructor to create Palm OS resource files.	http://www.palmos.com/dev/ support/docs/constructor/ CGRTOC.html
Palm OS Programming Development Tools Guide	A guide to writing and debugging Palm OS applications with the various tools available.	http://www.palmos.com/ dev/support/docs/devguide/ ToolsTOC.html

Table 14.4. A overview of the Palm OS Programmer's Companion

Volume	Description
I	Gives fundamental knowledge of Palm OS programming such as event loop and user interface.
II	Describes the handheld's communications capabilities such as Bluetooth and network communication.

Table 14.5. An overview of the Palm OS Programmer's API Reference

Function	Description
User Interface	User interface APIs include events, notifications, attention, control, dialogs, forms, lists, menus, scroll bars, etc.
System Management	Provides largest number of functions such as alarm, debug, file streaming, graffiti, I/O, memory, pen, sound, time, windows, etc. for system management.
Communications	Provide various communication functions such as IR, modem, network, telephony, etc.
Libraries	Include miscellaneous libraries such as Internet, Bluetooth, cryptography, etc.

SUMMARY

Two major versions of Palm OS are currently under development:

- *Palm OS Garnet*: an enhanced version of Palm OS.
- *Palm OS Cobalt*: the Palm OS 6.

Building on the introduction to Palm OS programming given in the previous chapter, this chapter examined in detail how forms and menus are constructed. The use of the Palm OS Developer Suite was demonstrated, and its usefulness in developing applications for Palm devices was highlighted. As these two chapters have necessarily only provided an introduction to the basic concepts involved in Palm OS programming, the extensive documentation that has been developed by Palm to assist programmers was described, along with information on how to access it online.

REFERENCES

PalmSource Inc. (2004a). *Palm OS Programmer's API Reference*. Retrieved June 5, 2006, from http://www.palmos.com/dev/support/docs/palmos/PalmOSReference/ReferenceTOC.html

PalmSource Inc. (2004b). *Palm OS Programmer's Companion, Vol. I*. Retrieved May 21, 2006, from http://www.palmos.com/dev/support/docs/palmos/PalmOSCompanion/CompanionTOC.html

PalmSource Inc. (2004c). *Palm OS Programmer's Companion, Vol. II*. Retrieved February 21, 2006, from http://www.palmos.com/dev/support/docs/palmos/PalmOSCompanion2/Companion2TOC.html

PalmSource Inc. (2006). *Getting Started*. Retrieved March 15, 2006, from http://www.palmos.com/dev/start/

Appendix
The Resource
Description File:
ResourceDescription1.xrd

```
                        ResourceDescription1.xrd

<?xml version="1.0" encoding="UTF-8" standalone="yes"?>

<PALMOS_RESOURCE_FILE>

 <ALERT_RESOURCE RESOURCE_ID="1000">
  <ALERT_TYPE> INFORMATION_ALERT </ALERT_TYPE>
  <HELP_ID> 1000 </HELP_ID>
  <DEFAULT_BUTTON> 0 </DEFAULT_BUTTON>
  <TITLE> "About Forms" </TITLE>
  <MESSAGE> "Nothing special  :)" </MESSAGE>
  <BUTTONS>
   <TEXT> "OK" </TEXT>
  </BUTTONS>
 </ALERT_RESOURCE>

 <APP_ICON_BITMAP_RESOURCE RESOURCE_ID="1000">
  <BITMAPS>
   <BITMAP>
    <WIDTH> 22 </WIDTH>
    <HEIGHT> 22 </HEIGHT>
    <BIT_DEPTH> 1 </BIT_DEPTH>
    <BITMAP_COMPRESSION> BEST </BITMAP_COMPRESSION>
    <HAS_TRANSPARENCY> FALSE </HAS_TRANSPARENCY>
    <HAS_COLOR_TABLE> FALSE </HAS_COLOR_TABLE>
    <BITMAP_FILE> "AppIcon_Large_X1_1.bmp" </BITMAP_FILE>
   </BITMAP>
  </BITMAPS>
 </APP_ICON_BITMAP_RESOURCE>

 <BITMAP_RESOURCE RESOURCE_ID="1000">
  <BITMAPS>
   <BITMAP>
    <WIDTH> 50 </WIDTH>
    <HEIGHT> 50 </HEIGHT>
    <BIT_DEPTH> 1 </BIT_DEPTH>
    <BITMAP_COMPRESSION> BEST </BITMAP_COMPRESSION>
    <HAS_TRANSPARENCY> FALSE </HAS_TRANSPARENCY>
    <HAS_COLOR_TABLE> FALSE </HAS_COLOR_TABLE>
    <BITMAP_FILE> "Bitmap_1000_X1_1.bmp" </BITMAP_FILE>
   </BITMAP>
  </BITMAPS>
 </BITMAP_RESOURCE>

 <FORM_RESOURCE RESOURCE_ID="1000">
  <FORM_ID> 1000 </FORM_ID>
  <BOUNDS>
   <LEFT> 0 </LEFT>
   <TOP> 0 </TOP>
   <WIDTH> 160 </WIDTH>
   <HEIGHT> 160 </HEIGHT>
  </BOUNDS>
  <USABLE> TRUE </USABLE>
```

continued on following page

ResourceDescription1.xrd

```
  <FONT_ID> BOLD_FONT </FONT_ID>
  <TEXT> "This is a label" </TEXT>
 </FORM_LABEL>
 <FORM_LABEL>
  <ID> 2000 </ID>
  <LOCATION>
   <X> 13 </X>
   <Y> 36 </Y>
  </LOCATION>
  <USABLE> TRUE </USABLE>
  <FONT_ID> BOLD_FONT </FONT_ID>
  <TEXT> "Those are individual buttons" </TEXT>
 </FORM_LABEL>
 <FORM_BUTTON>
  <ID> 2001 </ID>
  <BOUNDS>
   <LEFT> 64 </LEFT>
   <TOP> 56 </TOP>
   <WIDTH> 36 </WIDTH>
   <HEIGHT> 12 </HEIGHT>
  </BOUNDS>
  <USABLE> TRUE </USABLE>
  <ENABLED> TRUE </ENABLED>
  <TEXT> "Frame" </TEXT>
  <LEFT_ANCHOR> FALSE </LEFT_ANCHOR>
  <FONT_ID> STD_FONT </FONT_ID>
  <BUTTON_FRAME> STANDARD_BUTTON_FRAME </BUTTON_FRAME>
 </FORM_BUTTON>
 <FORM_BUTTON>
  <ID> 2002 </ID>
  <BOUNDS>
   <LEFT> 63 </LEFT>
   <TOP> 74 </TOP>
   <WIDTH> 36 </WIDTH>
   <HEIGHT> 12 </HEIGHT>
  </BOUNDS>
  <USABLE> TRUE </USABLE>
  <ENABLED> TRUE </ENABLED>
  <TEXT> "NoFrame" </TEXT>
  <LEFT_ANCHOR> FALSE </LEFT_ANCHOR>
  <FONT_ID> STD_FONT </FONT_ID>
  <BUTTON_FRAME> NO_BUTTON_FRAME </BUTTON_FRAME>
 </FORM_BUTTON>
 <FORM_BUTTON>
  <ID> 2003 </ID>
  <BOUNDS>
   <LEFT> 55 </LEFT>
   <TOP> 96 </TOP>
   <WIDTH> 50 </WIDTH>
   <HEIGHT> 12 </HEIGHT>
  </BOUNDS>
  <USABLE> TRUE </USABLE>
  <ENABLED> TRUE </ENABLED>
  <TEXT> "BoldFrame" </TEXT>
  <LEFT_ANCHOR> FALSE </LEFT_ANCHOR>
  <FONT_ID> STD_FONT </FONT_ID>
  <BUTTON_FRAME> BOLD_BUTTON_FRAME </BUTTON_FRAME>
 </FORM_BUTTON>
 <FORM_BUTTON>
  <ID> 2004 </ID>
  <BOUNDS>
   <LEFT> 39 </LEFT>
   <TOP> 117 </TOP>
   <WIDTH> 80 </WIDTH>
   <HEIGHT> 12 </HEIGHT>
  </BOUNDS>
  <USABLE> TRUE </USABLE>
```

continued on following page

ResourceDescription1.xrd

```
  <ENABLED> FALSE </ENABLED>
 <TEXT> "Disabled" </TEXT>
 <LEFT_ANCHOR> FALSE </LEFT_ANCHOR>
 <FONT_ID> STD_FONT </FONT_ID>
 <BUTTON_FRAME> STANDARD_BUTTON_FRAME </BUTTON_FRAME>
</FORM_BUTTON>
<FORM_BUTTON>
 <ID> 9001 </ID>
 <BOUNDS>
  <LEFT> 27 </LEFT>
  <TOP> 141 </TOP>
  <WIDTH> 36 </WIDTH>
  <HEIGHT> 12 </HEIGHT>
 </BOUNDS>
 <USABLE> TRUE </USABLE>
 <ENABLED> TRUE </ENABLED>
 <TEXT> "Next" </TEXT>
 <LEFT_ANCHOR> FALSE </LEFT_ANCHOR>
 <FONT_ID> STD_FONT </FONT_ID>
 <BUTTON_FRAME> STANDARD_BUTTON_FRAME </BUTTON_FRAME>
</FORM_BUTTON>
<FORM_BUTTON>
 <ID> 9002 </ID>
 <BOUNDS>
  <LEFT> 92 </LEFT>
  <TOP> 141 </TOP>
  <WIDTH> 36 </WIDTH>
  <HEIGHT> 12 </HEIGHT>
 </BOUNDS>
 <USABLE> TRUE </USABLE>
 <ENABLED> TRUE </ENABLED>
 <TEXT> "Exit" </TEXT>
 <LEFT_ANCHOR> FALSE </LEFT_ANCHOR>
 <FONT_ID> STD_FONT </FONT_ID>
 <BUTTON_FRAME> STANDARD_BUTTON_FRAME </BUTTON_FRAME>
 </FORM_BUTTON>
 </FORM_OBJECTS>
</FORM_RESOURCE>


<FORM_RESOURCE RESOURCE_ID="1001">
 <FORM_ID> 1001 </FORM_ID>
 <BOUNDS>
  <LEFT> 0 </LEFT>
  <TOP> 0 </TOP>
  <WIDTH> 160 </WIDTH>
  <HEIGHT> 160 </HEIGHT>
 </BOUNDS>
 <USABLE> TRUE </USABLE>
 <MODAL> TRUE </MODAL>
 <SAVE_BEHIND> TRUE </SAVE_BEHIND>
 <HELP_ID> 1000 </HELP_ID>
 <MENU_ID> 0 </MENU_ID>
 <DEFAULT_BUTTON> 0 </DEFAULT_BUTTON>
 <TITLE_ICON> FALSE </TITLE_ICON>
 <TITLE_BAR_FOCUSABLE> FALSE </TITLE_BAR_FOCUSABLE>
 <FORM_OBJECTS>
  <FORM_TITLE>
   <TEXT> "Forms 2/3 (Modal)" </TEXT>
  </FORM_TITLE>
  <FORM_LABEL>
   <ID> 2010 </ID>
```

continued on following page

ResourceDescription1.xrd

```
 <LOCATION>
  <X> 10 </X>
  <Y> 18 </Y>
 </LOCATION>
 <USABLE> TRUE </USABLE>
 <FONT_ID> BOLD_FONT </FONT_ID>
 <TEXT> "Those are GROUPED buttons" </TEXT>
</FORM_LABEL>
<FORM_PUSH_BUTTON>
 <ID> 2011 </ID>
 <BOUNDS>
  <LEFT> 23 </LEFT>
  <TOP> 36 </TOP>
  <WIDTH> 25 </WIDTH>
  <HEIGHT> 11 </HEIGHT>
 </BOUNDS>
 <USABLE> TRUE </USABLE>
 <ENABLED> TRUE </ENABLED>
 <TEXT> "1st" </TEXT>
 <FONT_ID> STD_FONT </FONT_ID>
 <GROUP_ID> 1 </GROUP_ID>
</FORM_PUSH_BUTTON>
<FORM_PUSH_BUTTON>
 <ID> 2012 </ID>
 <BOUNDS>
  <LEFT> 72 </LEFT>
  <TOP> 36 </TOP>
  <WIDTH> 25 </WIDTH>
  <HEIGHT> 11 </HEIGHT>
 </BOUNDS>
 <USABLE> TRUE </USABLE>
 <ENABLED> TRUE </ENABLED>
 <TEXT> "2nd" </TEXT>
 <FONT_ID> STD_FONT </FONT_ID>
 <GROUP_ID> 1 </GROUP_ID>
</FORM_PUSH_BUTTON>
<FORM_PUSH_BUTTON>
 <ID> 2013 </ID>
 <BOUNDS>
  <LEFT> 117 </LEFT>
  <TOP> 36 </TOP>
  <WIDTH> 25 </WIDTH>
  <HEIGHT> 11 </HEIGHT>
 </BOUNDS>
 <USABLE> TRUE </USABLE>
 <ENABLED> TRUE </ENABLED>
 <TEXT> "3rd" </TEXT>
 <FONT_ID> STD_FONT </FONT_ID>
 <GROUP_ID> 1 </GROUP_ID>
</FORM_PUSH_BUTTON>
<FORM_LABEL>
 <ID> 2020 </ID>
 <LOCATION>
  <X> 22 </X>
  <Y> 55 </Y>
 </LOCATION>
 <USABLE> TRUE </USABLE>
 <FONT_ID> BOLD_FONT </FONT_ID>
 <TEXT> "Now single checkboxes..." </TEXT>
</FORM_LABEL>
<FORM_CHECKBOX>
 <ID> 2021 </ID>
 <BOUNDS>
  <LEFT> 17 </LEFT>
  <TOP> 71 </TOP>
  <WIDTH> 63 </WIDTH>
  <HEIGHT> 12 </HEIGHT>
```

continued on following page

ResourceDescription1.xrd

```
    </BOUNDS>
  <USABLE> TRUE </USABLE>
  <ENABLED> TRUE </ENABLED>
  <TEXT> "Unchecked" </TEXT>
  <FONT_ID> STD_FONT </FONT_ID>
  <GROUP_ID> 0 </GROUP_ID>
  <SELECTED> FALSE </SELECTED>
</FORM_CHECKBOX>
<FORM_CHECKBOX>
  <ID> 2022 </ID>
  <BOUNDS>
   <LEFT> 90 </LEFT>
   <TOP> 71 </TOP>
   <WIDTH> 53 </WIDTH>
   <HEIGHT> 12 </HEIGHT>
  </BOUNDS>
  <USABLE> TRUE </USABLE>
  <ENABLED> TRUE </ENABLED>
  <TEXT> "Checked" </TEXT>
  <FONT_ID> STD_FONT </FONT_ID>
  <GROUP_ID> 0 </GROUP_ID>
  <SELECTED> FALSE </SELECTED>
</FORM_CHECKBOX>
<FORM_CHECKBOX>
  <ID> 2023 </ID>
  <BOUNDS>
   <LEFT> 52 </LEFT>
   <TOP> 85 </TOP>
   <WIDTH> 53 </WIDTH>
   <HEIGHT> 12 </HEIGHT>
  </BOUNDS>
  <USABLE> TRUE </USABLE>
  <ENABLED> FALSE </ENABLED>
  <TEXT> "Disabled" </TEXT>
  <FONT_ID> STD_FONT </FONT_ID>
  <GROUP_ID> 0 </GROUP_ID>
  <SELECTED> FALSE </SELECTED>
  </FORM_CHECKBOX>
  <FORM_LABEL>
   <ID> 2030 </ID>
   <LOCATION>
    <X> 29 </X>
    <Y> 105 </Y>
   </LOCATION>
   <USABLE> TRUE </USABLE>
   <FONT_ID> BOLD_FONT </FONT_ID>
   <TEXT> "... And Grouped ones" </TEXT>
  </FORM_LABEL>
  <FORM_CHECKBOX>
   <ID> 2031 </ID>
   <BOUNDS>
    <LEFT> 21 </LEFT>
    <TOP> 122 </TOP>
    <WIDTH> 32 </WIDTH>
    <HEIGHT> 12 </HEIGHT>
   </BOUNDS>
   <USABLE> TRUE </USABLE>
   <ENABLED> TRUE </ENABLED>
   <TEXT> "1st" </TEXT>
   <FONT_ID> STD_FONT </FONT_ID>
   <GROUP_ID> 1 </GROUP_ID>
   <SELECTED> FALSE </SELECTED>
  </FORM_CHECKBOX>
  <FORM_CHECKBOX>
   <ID> 2032 </ID>
   <BOUNDS>
    <LEFT> 61 </LEFT>
```

continued on following page

ResourceDescription1.xrd

```
        </BOUNDS>
  <USABLE> TRUE </USABLE>
  <ENABLED> TRUE </ENABLED>
  <TEXT> "2nd" </TEXT>
  <FONT_ID> STD_FONT </FONT_ID>
  <GROUP_ID> 1 </GROUP_ID>
  <SELECTED> FALSE </SELECTED>
</FORM_CHECKBOX>
<FORM_CHECKBOX>
  <ID> 2033 </ID>
  <BOUNDS>
   <LEFT> 105 </LEFT>
   <TOP> 122 </TOP>
   <WIDTH> 33 </WIDTH>
   <HEIGHT> 12 </HEIGHT>
  </BOUNDS>
  <USABLE> TRUE </USABLE>
  <ENABLED> TRUE </ENABLED>
  <TEXT> "3rd" </TEXT>
  <FONT_ID> STD_FONT </FONT_ID>
  <GROUP_ID> 1 </GROUP_ID>
  <SELECTED> FALSE </SELECTED>
</FORM_CHECKBOX>
<FORM_BUTTON>
  <ID> 9000 </ID>
  <BOUNDS>
   <LEFT> 13 </LEFT>
   <TOP> 143 </TOP>
   <WIDTH> 36 </WIDTH>
   <HEIGHT> 12 </HEIGHT>
  </BOUNDS>
  <USABLE> TRUE </USABLE>
  <ENABLED> TRUE </ENABLED>
  <TEXT> "Prev" </TEXT>
  <LEFT_ANCHOR> FALSE </LEFT_ANCHOR>
  <FONT_ID> STD_FONT </FONT_ID>
  <BUTTON_FRAME> STANDARD_BUTTON_FRAME </BUTTON_FRAME>
</FORM_BUTTON>
<FORM_BUTTON>
  <ID> 9001 </ID>
  <BOUNDS>
   <LEFT> 61 </LEFT>
   <TOP> 143 </TOP>
   <WIDTH> 36 </WIDTH>
   <HEIGHT> 12 </HEIGHT>
  </BOUNDS>
  <USABLE> TRUE </USABLE>
  <ENABLED> TRUE </ENABLED>
  <TEXT> "Next" </TEXT>
  <LEFT_ANCHOR> FALSE </LEFT_ANCHOR>
  <FONT_ID> STD_FONT </FONT_ID>
  <BUTTON_FRAME> STANDARD_BUTTON_FRAME </BUTTON_FRAME>
</FORM_BUTTON>
<FORM_BUTTON>
  <ID> 9002 </ID>
  <BOUNDS>
   <LEFT> 109 </LEFT>
   <TOP> 143 </TOP>
   <WIDTH> 36 </WIDTH>
   <HEIGHT> 12 </HEIGHT>
  </BOUNDS>
  <USABLE> TRUE </USABLE>
  <ENABLED> TRUE </ENABLED>
  <TEXT> "Exit" </TEXT>
  <LEFT_ANCHOR> FALSE </LEFT_ANCHOR>
```

continued on following page

ResourceDescription1.xrd

```
    <FONT_ID> STD_FONT </FONT_ID>
   <BUTTON_FRAME> STANDARD_BUTTON_FRAME </BUTTON_FRAME>
  </FORM_BUTTON>
 </FORM_OBJECTS>
</FORM_RESOURCE>

<FORM_RESOURCE RESOURCE_ID="1002">
 <FORM_ID> 1002 </FORM_ID>
 <BOUNDS>
  <LEFT> 0 </LEFT>
  <TOP> 0 </TOP>
  <WIDTH> 160 </WIDTH>
  <HEIGHT> 160 </HEIGHT>
 </BOUNDS>
 <USABLE> TRUE </USABLE>
 <MODAL> FALSE </MODAL>
 <SAVE_BEHIND> TRUE </SAVE_BEHIND>
 <HELP_ID> 1000 </HELP_ID>
 <MENU_ID> 0 </MENU_ID>
 <DEFAULT_BUTTON> 0 </DEFAULT_BUTTON>
 <TITLE_ICON> FALSE </TITLE_ICON>
 <TITLE_BAR_FOCUSABLE> FALSE </TITLE_BAR_FOCUSABLE>
 <FORM_OBJECTS>
  <FORM_TITLE>
   <TEXT> "Forms 3/3 (Non Modal)" </TEXT>
  </FORM_TITLE>
  <FORM_LABEL>
   <ID> 1000 </ID>
   <LOCATION>
    <X> 64 </X>
    <Y> 20 </Y>
   </LOCATION>
   <USABLE> TRUE </USABLE>
   <FONT_ID> BOLD_FONT </FONT_ID>
   <TEXT> "List" </TEXT>
  </FORM_LABEL>
  <FORM_POPUP>
   <CONTROL_ID> 1001 </CONTROL_ID>
   <LIST_ID> 1001 </LIST_ID>
  </FORM_POPUP>
  <FORM_LIST>
   <ID> 2042 </ID>
   <BOUNDS>
    <LEFT> 50 </LEFT>
    <TOP> 35 </TOP>
    <WIDTH> 50 </WIDTH>
    <HEIGHT> 22 </HEIGHT>
   </BOUNDS>
   <USABLE> TRUE </USABLE>
   <FONT_ID> STD_FONT </FONT_ID>
   <NUM_VIS_ITEMS> 2 </NUM_VIS_ITEMS>
   <LIST_ITEMS>
    <TEXT> "English" </TEXT>
    <TEXT> "Spanish" </TEXT>
    <TEXT> "German" </TEXT>
    <TEXT> "French" </TEXT>
    <TEXT> "Japanese" </TEXT>
   </LIST_ITEMS>
  </FORM_LIST>
  <FORM_LABEL>
   <ID> 1001 </ID>
   <LOCATION>
    <X> 20 </X>
    <Y> 65 </Y>
   </LOCATION>
```

continued on following page

ResourceDescription1.xrd

```
<USABLE> TRUE </USABLE>
<FONT_ID> BOLD_FONT </FONT_ID>
<TEXT> "Repeat buttons & field" </TEXT>
</FORM_LABEL>
<FORM_REPEATING_BUTTON COMMENT="Scroll Up">
 <ID> 2044 </ID>
 <BOUNDS>
  <LEFT> 28 </LEFT>
  <TOP> 83 </TOP>
  <WIDTH> 18 </WIDTH>
  <HEIGHT> 8 </HEIGHT>
 </BOUNDS>
 <USABLE> TRUE </USABLE>
 <ENABLED> TRUE </ENABLED>
 <TEXT> "\x02" </TEXT>
 <LEFT_ANCHOR> TRUE </LEFT_ANCHOR>
 <FONT_ID> SYMBOL_7_FONT </FONT_ID>
 <BUTTON_FRAME> NO_BUTTON_FRAME </BUTTON_FRAME>
</FORM_REPEATING_BUTTON>
<FORM_FIELD>
 <ID> 2045 </ID>
 <BOUNDS>
  <LEFT> 52 </LEFT>
  <TOP> 81 </TOP>
  <WIDTH> 50 </WIDTH>
  <HEIGHT> 12 </HEIGHT>
 </BOUNDS>
 <USABLE> TRUE </USABLE>
 <EDITABLE> TRUE </EDITABLE>
 <SINGLE_LINE> FALSE </SINGLE_LINE>
 <DYNAMIC_SIZE> FALSE </DYNAMIC_SIZE>
 <UNDERLINE> COLOR_UNDERLINE </UNDERLINE>
 <JUSTIFICATION> LEFT_ALIGN </JUSTIFICATION>
 <AUTO_SHIFT> FALSE </AUTO_SHIFT>
 <HAS_SCROLLBAR> FALSE </HAS_SCROLLBAR>
 <NUMERIC> TRUE </NUMERIC>
 <MAX_CHARS> 4 </MAX_CHARS>
 <FONT_ID> STD_FONT </FONT_ID>
 <MAX_VISIBLE_LINES> 0 </MAX_VISIBLE_LINES>
</FORM_FIELD>
<FORM_REPEATING_BUTTON COMMENT="Scroll Up">
 <ID> 2046 </ID>
 <BOUNDS>
  <LEFT> 109 </LEFT>
  <TOP> 82 </TOP>
  <WIDTH> 18 </WIDTH>
  <HEIGHT> 8 </HEIGHT>
 </BOUNDS>
 <USABLE> TRUE </USABLE>
 <ENABLED> TRUE </ENABLED>
 <TEXT> "\x01" </TEXT>
 <LEFT_ANCHOR> TRUE </LEFT_ANCHOR>
 <FONT_ID> SYMBOL_7_FONT </FONT_ID>
 <BUTTON_FRAME> NO_BUTTON_FRAME </BUTTON_FRAME>
</FORM_REPEATING_BUTTON>
<FORM_LABEL>
 <ID> 1002 </ID>
 <LOCATION>
  <X> 38 </X>
  <Y> 113 </Y>
 </LOCATION>
 <USABLE> TRUE </USABLE>
 <FONT_ID> BOLD_FONT </FONT_ID>
 <TEXT> "Bitmap" </TEXT>
```

continued on following page

ResourceDescription1.xrd

```
</FORM_LABEL>
<FORM_BITMAP>
 <USABLE> TRUE </USABLE>
 <LOCATION>
  <X> 82 </X>
  <Y> 101 </Y>
 </LOCATION>
 <BITMAP_ID> 1000 </BITMAP_ID>
</FORM_BITMAP>
<FORM_BUTTON>
 <ID> 9000 </ID>
 <BOUNDS>
  <LEFT> 29 </LEFT>
  <TOP> 145 </TOP>
  <WIDTH> 36 </WIDTH>
  <HEIGHT> 12 </HEIGHT>
 </BOUNDS>
 <USABLE> TRUE </USABLE>
 <ENABLED> TRUE </ENABLED>
 <TEXT> "Prev" </TEXT>
 <LEFT_ANCHOR> FALSE </LEFT_ANCHOR>
 <FONT_ID> STD_FONT </FONT_ID>
 <BUTTON_FRAME> STANDARD_BUTTON_FRAME </BUTTON_FRAME>
</FORM_BUTTON>
<FORM_BUTTON>
 <ID> 9002 </ID>
 <BOUNDS>
  <LEFT> 95 </LEFT>
  <TOP> 145 </TOP>
  <WIDTH> 36 </WIDTH>
  <HEIGHT> 12 </HEIGHT>
 </BOUNDS>
 <USABLE> TRUE </USABLE>
 <ENABLED> TRUE </ENABLED>
 <TEXT> "Exit" </TEXT>
 <LEFT_ANCHOR> FALSE </LEFT_ANCHOR>
 <FONT_ID> STD_FONT </FONT_ID>
 <BUTTON_FRAME> STANDARD_BUTTON_FRAME </BUTTON_FRAME>
</FORM_BUTTON>
</FORM_OBJECTS>
</FORM_RESOURCE>

<STRING_RESOURCE RESOURCE_ID="1000">
 <TEXT> "This is a demonstration of forms programming for Palm OS." </TEXT>
</STRING_RESOURCE>

</PALMOS_RESOURCE_FILE>
```

Glossary

3G (Third Generation): A networking standard that uses cell phone frequencies to send Internet data to handheld devices at up to 144 Kbps. Although not as fast as Wi-Fi (802.11x), it offers broader coverage. A 3G wireless system can provide packet-switched wide-area wireless Internet access to support multimedia applications.

Adobe CodeFusion: An application server and software development framework used for the development of computer software in general, and dynamic web sites in particular.

Adobe Dreamweaver: A WYSIWYG (What You See Is What You Get) authoring software that allows web developers to generate HTML and JavaScript source code while viewing the site as they work.

Adobe Flash: An authoring environment for creating animation, advertisements, various web-page components to integrate video into web pages and to develop rich Internet applications. Flash Professional is an IDE (Integrated Development Environment), while Flash Player is a virtual machine used to run, or parse, the Flash files.

Adobe Photoshop: A software package for editing images and creating graphics.

Android: A software stack for mobile devices that includes an operating system, middleware, and key applications such as contacts. It is a project proposed by the Open Handset Alliance, a group of more than 30 technology and mobile companies including Google, Inc.

Association Rule Discovery: An association rule takes the form of "if this then that" and is used to associate events in a database. Association rule discovery can be used to find unordered correlations between items found in a set of database transactions. One example is the association between purchased items in a department.

Automatic Indexing: Describes a process that algorithmically examines information items to build a data structure that can be quickly searched.

Bluetooth: An evolving wireless networking protocol that connects various digital devices-from mobile phones to PDAs to computers. It can transmit wireless signals over a range of about 35 feet and does not require a line-of-sight connection. Bluetooth will not itself allow users to go online, but instead is a way to wirelessly connect to printers, computers, cell phones, and other devices.

BREW (Binary Runtime Environment for Wireless): An application development platform created by Qualcomm for CDMA (Code Division Multiple Access) -based mobile phones. The complete BREW solution includes:

- BREW client software and porting tools for device manufacturers;
- BREW Distribution System (BDS). This is controlled and managed by operators and enables them to easily get applications from developers to market and coordinate the billing and payment process; and
- BREW SDK (software development kit) for application developers.

CDMA (Code Division Multiple Access): A type of mobile phone network. Also known as spread spectrum, CDMA cellular systems utilize a single frequency band for all traffic, differentiating the individual transmissions by assigning them unique codes before transmission. This is used by Sprint in the USA and Telus in Canada, for example.

CGI (Common Gateway Interface): A specification providing a method of executing server-side programs from a web page. A CGI program is any program designed to accept data from the web page, process the data, and return the results, usually in an HTML format, to the web page for display.

Client-Side Handheld Computing: The use of handheld devices to perform mobile, handheld operations that do not need the power of server-side computing. Some application examples of this type of computing include (a) address books, (b) stand-alone video games, (c) note pads, and (d) to-do-lists.

CPU (Central Processing Unit): The central unit of a computer, which includes both arithmetic and control units. The CPU of a microcomputer is usually a microprocessor.

Crawler/Spider: A program that automatically scans various Web sites and collects Web documents from them. It follows the links on a site to find other relevant pages and is usually used to feed pages to search engines.

Device Independent Authoring Language (DIAL): DIAL provides a markup language for the filtering and presentation of web page content available across different delivery contexts. It uses a language profile based on existing W3C XML vocabularies and CSS modules and provides standard mechanisms for representing web page structure, presentation and form interaction.

Digital Certificate: A document issued by a certificate authority (a trusted third party) that contains the certificate holder's name, a serial number, expiration dates, a copy of the certificate holder's public encryption key, and the digital signature of the certificate-issuing authority so that a recipient can verify that the certificate is genuine.

Digital Signature: An electronic signature that can be used to authenticate the identity of the sender of a message or the signer of a document. The sender uses a private encryption key to encrypt their identification and (possibly) some additional information derived from the message that is being signed. The receiver uses a sender's public key to recover the identification and additional information, which is used to check the integrity of the received message.

Electronic Commerce or E-Commerce: The exchange or buying and selling of commodities, services, or information or the transfer of funds on the Internet using desktop or notebook computers.

Expansion (Card) Slot: The opening found on handheld devices where expansion cards are inserted, allowing users to add applications such as games, memory such as flash memory, and even peripherals such as keyboards to the device.

Expansion Card: A postage stamp-sized add-on memory that can be inserted into the expansion slot of a Palm device. Expansion cards can contain applications, songs, videos, pictures, and other information in a digital format. There are three types: MultiMediaCard (MMC), SD (Secure Digital) and SDIO (Secure Digital Input/Output).

Flash Memory: Non-volatile memory that can be electrically erased and reprogrammed. It can be either non-removable, such as a built-in flash drive, or removable, such as a USB flash drive for portable data. Its capacity is usually between a couple of hundreds of Kb and a few GB.

Flexible Screens: The company Polymer Vision has developed a new rollable display technology that enables a screen to be rolled up into a pen-sized case. The rollable screen is equipped with various connectivity options, including Bluetooth.

Fuel Cells: A device that turns fuel such as hydrogen into electricity via a chemical reaction. It offers a greener method of generating electricity because no fossil fuels are used, no combustion takes place, and no pollutants are emitted.

GSM/GPRS (Global System for Mobile Communications/General Packet Radio Service): A type of mobile phone network used throughout most of the world. GPRS enabled networks offer "always-on," higher capacity, Internet-based content and packet-based data services. This enables services such as color Internet browsing, email on the move, powerful visual communications, multimedia messages and location-based services. Wireless Service providers on a GSM/GPRS network include Cingular Wireless and T-Mobile in the USA and Rogers Wireless and Fido in Canada.

Handheld Computing: The use of handheld devices such as smart cellular phones and PDAs (Personal Digital Assistants) to perform wireless, mobile, handheld operations such as personal data management and making phone calls.

Hard Drives: Storage devices containing a read-write mechanism plus magnetic disks inside a sealed unit. At the time of writing (in 2007), a hard drive for handheld devices is capable of storing data up to a couple of gigabytes. This compares with the capacity of a hard drive on a desktop computer, which could be several hundreds of gigabytes.

HTML (HyperText Markup Language): HTML, based on SGML (Standard Generalized Markup Language), is used for publishing hypertext on the World Wide Web. Tags such as <p> and </p> are used to structure and stylize text. Refer to W3C's HyperText Markup Language (HTML) home page at http://www.w3.org/MarkUp/ for more details.

Hyperlinks: A selectable connection from one word, phrase, picture, or information object to another. By clicking on a hyperlink, a Web user can move easily from one Web page to another page. Hyperlinks are most commonly indicated by a highlighted word, phrase, or picture.

i-mode: i-mode (http://www.nttdocomo.com/corebiz/imode/index.html) is the full-color, always-on, packet-switched Internet service for cellular phone users offered by NTT DoCoMo. With i-mode, cellular phone users are able to access tens of thousands of Internet sites, as well as specialized services such as e-mail, online shopping and banking, ticket reservations, and restaurant advice. Users are charged based on the volume of data transmitted, rather than the amount of time spent connected.

Infrared Port: The component on a handheld device that is used to transmit and receive data between compatible infrared equipped devices via infrared signals. On some models the infrared port can also be used to communicate with a compatible, infrared-equipped mobile phone for connecting to the Internet.

Java ME (Java Micro Edition): An environment for applications running on consumer devices, such as mobile phones, PDAs, and TV set-top boxes, as well as on a broad range of embedded devices. Like its counterparts for the enterprise (J2EE), desktop (J2SE) and smart card (Java Card) environments, J2ME includes Java virtual machines and a set of standard Java APIs defined through the Java Community Process by expert groups whose members include device manufacturers, software vendors, and service providers.

JavaScript: The *de facto* standard language used to add dynamic behavior to HTML documents. JavaScript is one of the originating technologies of ECMAScript.

JDBC (Java Database Connectivity): A standardized database interface for Java applications accessing database data. It allows a single database application to run on different platforms and interact with different SQL-compliant DBMSs.

LAN (Local Area Network): A computer network that provides data communications to users located in a limited area such as a building or city block.

Linux: A free, open-source, Unix-type operating system. Linux and other Linux-like OSs are developed based on the Linux kernel.

Lithium-Ion Batteries: Replaceable, rechargeable Lithium-Ion batteries are the batteries most commonly used by handheld devices. Although expensive when they were first introduced, their prices have since dropped rapidly.

Micro PCs: Mini versions of PCs that differ from handheld devices because they apply a different technology. For example, Windows OSes are for PCs and micro PCs but not for handheld devices, whereas Windows Mobile OSes are for handheld devices but not for PCs and micro PCs.

Micro/Macro-Payment: A mobile payment of approximately $10 or less (often for mobile content such as video downloads or gaming) is called a micro-payment, while a macro-payment refers to larger value payment.

Microbrowsers: Miniaturized versions of desktop browsers such as Netscape Navigator or Internet Explorer. Due to the limited resources of handheld devices, microbrowsers differ from traditional desktop browsers in the following ways: (i) smaller windows, (ii) smaller footprints, and (iii) fewer functions and multimedia features.

Microsoft ASP.NET: Free technology that allows programmers to create dynamic web applications. ASP.NET is part of Microsoft's .NET platform and is the successor to ASP technology.

Microsoft Expression Web: A design tool used to create sophisticated standards-based web sites. It combines both FrontPage and Visual Studio technologies in a new user interface for creating XHTML, CSS, XML, XSLT, and ASP.NET 2.0.

Microsoft SharePoint Designer: Enables information workers to develop applications and solutions on top of the SharePoint platform to enable organizational agility, business process automation, and benefit from using Microsoft Office applications on the SharePoint platform.

Microsoft Visual Studio: Microsoft's flagship software development product, Visual Studio lets programmers create standalone applications, web sites, web applications, and web services that run on any platforms supported by Microsoft's .NET Framework.

Mobile Commerce Security: The technological and managerial procedures applied to mobile commerce to provide security services for mobile commerce information and systems.

Mobile Commerce: The exchange or buying and selling of commodities, services, or information or the transfer of funds on the Internet (wired or wireless) through the use of Internet-enabled mobile handheld devices.

Mobile Handheld Devices: Small general-purpose, programmable, battery-powered computers, that are small enough to be held in one's hand. There are two major kinds of handheld devices: (i) (voice-centric) smart cellular phones, and (ii) (data-centric) PDAs (Personal Digital Assistants). They differ from desktop or notebook computers in several important ways, namely their (i) low network bandwidth, (ii) small screen/body size, and (iii) mobility.

Mobile Payment: The transfer of financial value and corresponding services or items between different participants in mobile commerce systems.

Navigator: The two large, concentric buttons in the middle of the lower part of many Palm devices. Pressing the edges moves the cursor up, down, right, or left, and the center button selects items. The navigator (sometimes referred to as the five-way navigator) works differently in different applications, but is usually an easy way to operate the device with one hand.

NetBeans: An open-source IDE (Integrated Development Environment) used to create professional cross-platform desktop, enterprise, web, and mobile applications. NetBeans is sponsored by Sun Microsystems, Inc.

OMA (Open Mobile Alliance): A large interest group of mobile operators, device and network suppliers, information technology companies, and content and service providers, it was founded by consolidating the WAP Forum, Location Interoperability Forum (LIF), SyncML Initiative, MMS-IOP (Multimedia Messaging Interoperability Process), Wireless Village, Mobile Gaming Interoperability Forum (MGIF), and the Mobile Wireless Internet Forum (MWIF) (http://www.openmobilealliance.com/). The OMA develops market driven, interoperable mobile service enabler specifications, promoting the creation of interoperable services across countries, operators and mobile terminals that will meet mobile users' needs.

Palm Operating Systems: An ARM-compliant, 32-bit operating system running on handheld devices developed by PalmSource Inc.. Currently, there are two versions of Palm OS: (i) Palm OS Garnet, an enhanced version of Palm OS 5 and (ii) Palm OS Cobalt, the next generation of Palm OS.

Palm OS Developer Suite: The official development environment and tool chain from PalmSource Inc., intended for software developers at all levels. It offers a complete IDE (Integrated Development Environment) for (i) Protein applications (all ARM®-native code) for Palm OS Cobalt and (ii) 68K applications for all shipping versions of the Palm OS.

Persistent Storage: Persistent (non-volatile) storage is a storage medium whose contents are preserved even when the power is off. Flash memory, a kind of persistent storage, is usually used for handheld devices. Hard disks are seen in some devices, but rarely.

Public Key Encryption (PKI): A technique that uses two different keys (a private key and a public key) for encryption. Messages encrypted with the private key can be decrypted with the public key, giving the owner of the private key a way to prove their identity to anyone who knows the public key. Messages encrypted with the public key can be decrypted with the private key, giving anyone who knows the public key a way of sending a confidential message to the owner of the private key.

QWERTY: The standard layout for letter keys on computer, handheld and smartphone keyboards used to type in English, modeled after the typewriter and named for the order of the first six keys on the top row.

RAM (Random Access Memory): Stores digital information temporarily and can be changed by the user. It constitutes the basic storage element in computer terminals and has replaced magnetic core memories in main frame computers.

RISC (Reduced Instruction Set Computing): Used in devices where the number of instructions a microprocessor runs for a specific application are reduced from a general purpose Complex Instruction Set Computing (CISC) device in order to create a more efficient operating system.

ROM (Read Only Memory): Stores information used repeatedly, such as tables of data, characters for electronic displays, etc. Unlike RAM, ROM cannot be altered.

Ruby On Rails (ROR): A full-stack framework for developing database-backed web applications using Model-View-Control patterns.

Server-Side Handheld Programming: The use of handheld devices to perform wireless, mobile, handheld operations that require additional input from a server. Typical applications of this type of computing include (a) instant messages, (b) mobile Web contents, (c) online video games, and (d) wireless telephony.

SET: The Secure Electronic Transaction (SET) protocol is a technical standard designed to provide security for payment transactions among cardholders, merchants, payment gateways, and certification authorities operating in the Internet environment.

Smart Card: A plastic card that uses a silicon chip as its storage mechanism, rather than the conventional magnetic strip, for increased security and functionality.

SQL (Structured Query Language): A standard interactive, programming language for accessing, manipulating, and administering a database. It is both an ANSI and an ISO standard, and most relational database products support SQL. Its commands include selection, insertion, update, deletion, finding out the location of data, and so forth.

Stylus: An input device used to write text or draw lines on a surface as input to a handheld device.

Subscriber Identity Module (SIM): A device in the mobile handset that contains the subscriber's authentication information, such as cryptographic keys, and a unique identifier called international mobile subscriber identity (IMSI).

Sun Java Studio: A development platform with features such as UML modeling, instant collaboration, and application profiling. Java Studio is used to develop, debug, tune, and deploy enterprise applications, web services, and portal components based on the Java EE platform.

Symbian: A software licensing company that develops and supplies an operating system—Symbian OS—for data-enabled mobile phones. It is an independent, for-profit company whose mission is to establish Symbian OS as the world standard for mobile digital data systems, primarily for use in cellular telecoms.

Symmetric Encryption: A technique that uses one secret code for both encryption and decryption. It is used to support confidential exchanges of messages between two parties who share knowledge of the common key.

Synchronization: Connects handheld devices to desktop computers, notebooks, and peripherals in order to transfer or synchronize data. Other than using serial cables to connect handheld devices and other computing equipment, many handheld devices use either an infrared (IR) port or Bluetooth technology to send information to other devices.

Tablet PCs: A mini version of PCs that differ from handheld devices as they utilize different technologies. For example, Windows OSs are for PCs and tablet PCs but not for handheld devices, whereas Windows Mobile OSs are for handheld devices but not for PCs and tablet PCs.

TDMA (Time Division Multiple Access): A digital transmission technology that operates in either the 800MHz or 1900MHz frequency bands. The frequency band is split into a number of channels, so that several calls or data can share a single channel without interfering with one another.

Universal Connector: A USB-enabled communications port and hardware attachment system on computers and some handheld devices that is used to connect to accessories like cables, cradles and keyboards.

URL (Uniform Resource Locator): The address of an object accessible on the Internet. The object could be an HTML document, a text file, an image file, a program such as a common gateway interface application, etc. They are mainly used in HTML documents to specify the target of a hyperlink.

USB (Universal Serial Bus): A standardized communications protocol that enables data exchange between electronic devices. It is often used to enable communications between handheld devices and computers for synchronization. USB supports data transfer rates of up to 12 megabytes per second.

User Navigation Patterns: Interesting usage patterns that are contained in Web log data. Most algorithms use a method of sequential pattern generation, while the remaining methods tend to be rather ad hoc.

W3C (World Wide Web Consortium): An international industry consortium created in October 1994 to develop open, unifying standards such as XML and semantic Web for the World Wide Web in order to avoid duplicating, competing standards (http://www.w3c.org/).

WAN (Wide Area Network): A computer network that provides data communications to more users than a local area network (LAN) can, and usually spans a greater geographical distance, such as a town or country.

WAP (Wireless Application Protocol): A suite of open, global specifications developed by the WAP Forum. It is used for developing applications that operate over wireless communication networks, and allows users with mobile handheld devices to easily access and interact with information and services instantly. The detailed specifications can be found at http://www.openmobilealliance.org/tech/affiliates/wap/wapindex.html.

WAP Forum: The official organization developing the WAP (Wireless Application Protocol) (http://www.wapforum.org/). It has now merged with the Open Mobile Alliance (OMA) (http://www.openmobilealliance.org/) and no longer exists as an independent organization.

WAP Gap: A known security weakness in Wireless Application Protocol (WAP) caused by the inclusion of the WAP gateway in a security session such that encrypted messages sent by end systems might temporarily become clear text on the WAP gateway when messages are processed.

Web Logs: Records activity information when a web user submits a request to a Web server. A log file can be located in three different places: (i) Web servers, (ii) Web proxy servers, and (iii) client browsers.

Web Proxy Servers: An intermediary that takes HTTP requests from users and passes them to a Web server; the proxy server then returns to users the results passed to them by the web server.

Web Server: An application software that uses HyperText Transfer Protocol. Its major task is to serve the requests of clients (browsers) by returning web pages.

WEP (Wired Equivalent Privacy): A data link-level protocol that provides security for the IEEE 802.11 WLAN standards. The encryption algorithm used in WEP is a stream cipher based on RC4.

Wi-Fi: Wi-Fi or 802.11x, is a family of wireless networking protocols, with 802.11b being the most common at present. It operates in an unlicensed radio frequency band at 2.4 GHz and provides data access at 11 Mbps.

Windows Mobile: A compact operating system for handheld devices based on the Microsoft Win32 API. It is powered by Windows CE 5.x and uses the .NET Compact Framework 2.0. Windows Mobile includes three major kinds of software: (i) Windows Mobile-based Pocket PCs, (ii) Windows Mobile-based Portable Media Centers, and (iii) Windows Mobile-based Smartphones.

WML (Wireless Markup Language): A markup language that formats and stylizes Web pages for being displayed on mobile handheld devices such as smart phones and PDAs. WML is part of Wireless Access Protocol (WAP) and it is based on XML (eXtensible Markup Language). Refer to *Wireless Markup Language (WML), Version 2.0* at http://www.openmobilealliance.org/tech/affiliates/wap/wap-238-wml-20010911-a.pdf for more details.

WMLScript: A procedural scripting language and an extended subset of the JavaScript scripting language. It is employed to complement WML, a markup language for mobile handheld devices. Refer to *WMLScript Language Specification, Version 1.2* at http://enrico.seven.it/mans/wml/WAP-193-WMLScript-20000324-a.pdf for more details.

XHMTL (eXtensible Hypertext Markup Language): Reproduces, subsets, and extends HTML 4.0, which is used to publish hypertext on the World Wide Web, and has been reformulated in XML 1.0. Refer to the W3C's *HyperText Markup Language (HTML) Home Page* at http://www.w3.org/MarkUp/ for more details.

XML (eXtensible Markup Language): Originally developed by the W3C, this is effectively is a pared-down version of SGML, designed especially for Web documents. It allows designers to create their own customized tags, enabling the definition, transmission, validation, and interpretation of data between applications and between organizations. Refer to Extensible Markup Language (XML) at http://www.w3.org/XML/ for more details.

Zend's Core: The production PHP 5 stack that provides the certified, enhanced capabilities with support and services that professionals need for PHP development and production.

About the Author

Wen-Chen Hu received a BE, an ME, an MS, and a PhD, all in computer science, from Tamkang University, Taiwan, the National Central University, Taiwan, the University of Iowa, Iowa City, and the University of Florida, Gainesville, in 1984, 1986, 1993, and 1998, respectively. He was an assistant professor in the Department of Computer Science and Software Engineering at Auburn University, Alabama, for years. Currently, he is an associate professor in the Department of Computer Science of the University of North Dakota, Grand Forks. Dr. Hu has taught more than 10 different computer courses and advised over 50 graduate students, and has published more than 70 articles in refereed journals, conference proceedings, books, and encyclopedias, and edited one book, entitled *Advances in Security and Payment Methods for Mobile Commerce*. His current research interests include handheld computing, electronic and mobile commerce systems, web technologies, and databases. He is a member of the IEEE Computer Society, ACM (Association for Computing Machinery), and IRMA (Information Resources Management Association).

Index

Symbols

3G   14, 15, 22, 30, 46, 55, 61, 83,
        96, 100, 101, 103, 107, 181, 222
        237, 264, 266, 278
4G 14, 15, 100

A

Adobe Flash 12
ANDROID 264
ARM processors 62
ASP.NET 12, 21, 180, 181, 226
authentication 103, 104, 108, 115, 116

B

batteries 11, 47, 48, 86, 87, 92, 123
Bluetooth 31, 49, 51, 52, 54, 55, 56,
        59, 60, 78, 82, 88, 89, 90, 91,
        92, 93, 99, 107, 111, 115, 121,
        135, 264, 265, 271, 276, 277,
        278, 289, 335, 370
BREW 57, 72, 122, 204, 263, 266,
        267, 283, 284, 331

C

CDMA 13, 14, 15, 56, 59, 96, 97, 100
        136, 263, 266, 276, 278, 283
CDMA2000 22, 100, 107, 266
CGI GET method
        187, 215, 237, 250, 252
client-side handheld computing
        57, 204, 261, 262, 283
ColdFusion 21
Common Gateway Interface 162, 181,
        190, 205, 206, 222, 236
comparing prices 9
Connected Device Configuration 268
customization 9

D

database management systems 233, 241
database servers 19
DB2 19
DIAL 141, 160, 229
Dreamweaver 12, 143, 156

W